THE
ENDURING
QUESTIONS
OF
POLITICS

THE ENDURING QUESTIONS OF POLITICS

Edited by

**Werner Feld, Alan T. Leonhard,
and Walter W. Toxey, Jr.**

Louisiana State University in New Orleans

PRENTICE-HALL, INC., ENGLEWOOD CLIFFS, N.J.

PRENTICE-HALL INTERNATIONAL, INC., *London*
PRENTICE-HALL OF AUSTRALIA, PTY. LTD., *Sydney*
PRENTICE-HALL OF CANADA, LTD., *Toronto*
PRENTICE-HALL OF INDIA PRIVATE LTD., *New Delhi*
PRENTICE-HALL OF JAPAN, INC., *Tokyo*

© 1969

PRENTICE-HALL, INC. / ENGLEWOOD CLIFFS, N.J.

Current printing (last digit):
10   9   8   7   6   5   4   3   2   1

13-277244-2

Library of Congress Catalog Card Number: 69-17481

PRINTED IN THE UNITED STATES OF AMERICA

Preface

Why another readings book for the introductory course in political science? The editors of this volume reply that it is an attempt at innovation. Several years of teaching this course to freshmen students have convinced us that there is a need for thought-provoking commentary in a book of readings, in order to give coherence to what appears too often to be a mass of unrelated bits and pieces. We feel that entering freshmen should not be overburdened with materials which they have difficulty in digesting. The consequence is often rejection of the book by the students regardless of how excellent some of the selections may be. For this reason it seemed to us better to offer fewer readings and to introduce the selections for each chapter with comments designed to evoke the student's interest in the subject matter and to place the selections in the context of discussion. Through this technique we hope to arouse the student's curiosity sufficiently to induce him to read the selections with alacrity and care. If we succeed in this objective, we will have made a significant contribution to the student's learning process.

The choice of readings was also crucial, of course, and had to take into consideration the prospective readers. In most cases the entering freshman has had only limited contact with the many-splendored, as well as much-maligned, thing called politics. In high school the student received only a passing acquaintance with politics in his civics course, which concentrated primarily on the basic processes of federal and state government. At home, he may have heard his father occasionally discuss forthcoming elections or various activities at city hall. His third source of knowledge about politics may have been the daily newspapers, provided he had the time to cast a glance or two at the more serious parts of the news.

The level of knowledge freshmen are likely to have with respect to politics is one consideration upon which we have based our choice of readings. Another consideration was the fact that the introductory political science course or perhaps a course in American Government may be the only one that a nongovernment major may take throughout his undergraduate college career. Since we believe that enlightened citizenship requires a degree of familiarity with some of the fundamental issues of politics, our selections needed to stimulate interest in and sharpen the student's judgment on current political events.

To meet these requirements, we have concentrated on what may best be called the *enduring questions of politics*. Throughout the ages certain issues of politics have been persistent subjects of writing and discussion. For example, standards of public morality and the scope of official powers were actively debated questions 2500 years ago, and this debate continues today. Generally political theorists feel that questions about freedom, equality, dictatorship, authority, government under law, as well as other topics treated in this volume, warrant continual exploration. Knowledge of the past, as Thucydides said, is essential to those who seek to know the future, and those who write the history of their own times also write of and for all times. Hence a number of selections come from the pens of writers who have lived during periods ranging from ancient Greece to the nineteenth century. It is refreshing to discover that many of these authors, highly respected now as then, wrote in a simple and clear way. The opportunity to read works by Aristotle, John Locke, J. S. Mill, James Madison, Adam Smith, and other great authors provides the beginning student with excellent vehicles for recognizing the intricate and absorbing nature of politics.

Besides the selections taken from the formal treatises and essays of political theorists, past and present, we have included a number of excerpts from the landmark decisions of the Supreme Court of the United States. The addition of examples of judicial reasoning in the practical determination of disputes and examples of the objectives of working political groups furnishes a connecting element between theory and practice.

In the choice of the readings we have given high priority to readability, clarity, and interest, but equally important were the pertinent insights which a particular selection could provide for the understanding of the subject matter. Although we have attempted to avoid the inclusion of materials already presented in other books of readings, certain classics had to have their place in our volume. We have abridged those materials which seemed to be unduly long, but we have taken care not to cut out any passages necessary to a full understanding of the author's arguments.

Having stressed issues rather than structure and functions, we hope to have contributed to the stimulation of controversy. If the entering freshman were first exposed to a labyrinth of structures and a confusing array of functions, his enthusiasm for one of the most dynamic disciplines in the social sciences might well wane quickly. Memorizing materials is likely to be deadly for the introductory course in politics. On the other hand, prodding freshmen into thinking about issues and drawing them into active dialogue in the spirit of Socrates could produce a very meaningful learning experience. This is the aim of our book.

The volume is divided into eight chapters. The first chapter examines the nature of politics and discusses briefly the variety of viewpoints which various writers have taken in defining politics. In the second chapter the sources of authority are investigated and the types and patterns of authority described. Chapter 3 examines the varying forms of dictatorships that have existed throughout the ages and probes into the essential features of this type of governmental system, whether it was used in ancient times or in contemporary China. The fourth chapter spotlights the concept of freedom and discusses the various meanings as well as the limits of freedom. Chapter 5 explores the problem of equality and the different meanings under which this term can be understood. In the sixth chapter, we try to determine the essential features of constitutionalism and its relationship to democracy. Chapter 7 examines the interrelationships between the economic and the political orders and discusses the swings of the pendulum between *laissez-faire* philosophy and government intervention in the economy. Finally, in Chapter 8 we explore the relations among nation-states, including the birth and possible slow demise of the modern state as well as movement toward international organization and eventually perhaps toward world government.

Although, as we have noted earlier, the readings in the different chapters are preceded by explanatory and transitional comments, we have not taken a doctrinaire stand on any of the issues examined in this book. This, of course, does not mean that our general commitment to democratic government may not have colored our observations. But whatever this coloration, it should not prevent any instructor from using our book as collateral reading with any text for the introductory course in political science. For example, it would be an excellent supplement to Leslie Lipson's *Great Issues of Politics*. On the other hand, we believe that this volume can also be used alone as a core work; we feel that such use may be especially appropriate in courses constructed around large lecture sections divided into weekly discussion groups.

We would like to express our deep gratitude to our colleague, Professor Lyle A. Downing, for reading the entire manuscript and for making valuable suggestions. We also owe special thanks to Mr. James Murray, political science editor of Prentice-Hall, for his assistance and constructive comments, and we would like to thank Mrs. Beverly Tipton, Mrs. Janet Davis, and Miss Linda Morgan for their superb typing services. We, of course, bear full responsibility for all errors of commission and omission.

THE EDITORS

New Orleans, Louisiana

Contents

THE
ENDURING
QUESTIONS
OF
POLITICS

The
Nature
1   # of Politics

What is politics? When we let our thoughts wander and seek to determine which actions or situations are associated with politics, many different ideas come to mind. Clearly, elections to local, state, and federal offices are in the realm of politics. The various efforts made in support of the nomination and election of a certain individual, whether carried out through the mass media or by personal contact, are accepted by us as part of politics. We also realize that at times the proverbial "smoke-filled" room in a hotel during a party convention may play a more important role in the nomination of an individual than the desires of the public at large and that the manipulation of facts can have a bearing on the outcome of an election. While in such cases we may mutter something about "dirty politics," we recognize nevertheless that these facts are part and parcel of the political game. When it comes to the making of laws and ordinances on the local, state, and federal levels, we are at times painfully aware that special interest groups exercise more influence on the content of legislation than does the average voter. And since the subjects of legislation may range far and wide, a great variety of economic groups, church bodies, veterans' organizations, and other groups in society may be involved in bringing pressure to bear on the outcome of legislative battles. Of course, all of us are members of one or another group and sometimes of several groups, and therefore we may

1

benefit indirectly from the efforts made by the leadership of some of these organizations.

The administration of laws and ordinances also produces certain actions on the part of the population which we regard as political. For example, dairy farmers may seek higher milk prices from an administrative agency authorized to regulate these prices, and toward this end they apply pressure by withholding milk from the market. A nightclub owner whose establishment the authorities threaten to close because he is presenting a risqué show may attempt to prevent this by promising financial support to the district attorney and the sheriff in future elections. While we accept, as a normal part of politics, the provision of financial support for a candidate to defray the expenses of his election campaign, there are moral and legal boundaries to such practices.

Finally, politics may even invade the judicial process. Subtle influence can be exerted on a court through the use of special publicity regarding certain features of a case before the judges. We do not suggest that the judges will necessarily succumb to the influence exerted nor that our faith in the impartiality of the judicial system is misplaced. We simply want to point out that, depending on the motives and purpose of an endeavor to influence the court, such an attempt may be labeled political.

This brief survey of activities which we customarily associate with the term "politics" is obviously far from exhaustive. But even limited as it is, it suggests that a great diversity of activities may fall under this classification. The question therefore arises regarding the distinctive features or feature that permit an activity to be called "political." This question has been pondered by political thinkers and philosophers since the time of ancient Greece, but despite these efforts no definitive agreement has been reached on the nature of politics.

The word "politics" is derived from the Greek word *polis,* a term which refers to the relatively small city-states of ancient Greece. Aristotle, the Greek philosopher who lived in the fourth century before Christ, devoted some of his fertile thoughts and writings to elucidating the term "political." He regarded the *polis* as one of the many associations found in society, all created "for the purpose of attaining some good." The *polis,* however, was distinguished by being the "most sovereign and inclusive association"; the term "sovereign" suggests that authority was an essential ingredient of the *polis,* which Aristotle also called the "political" association. Politics, therefore, was related to the exercise of authority. Since, according to Aristotle, the basic objective of the political association or the *polis* was the promotion of the common good, the proper kind of authority was that exercised in the common interest. To ensure this kind of authority, Aristotle advocated the use of state constitutions which were directed toward the pursuit of the common interest. These were the "right" constitutions regardless of whether the One, the Few, or the Many made up the ruling authority. On the other side were the "wrong" or "perverted" constitutions under which the ruling authorities would be enabled to attain primarily their selfish interests. Our first reading selection reproduces some of the pertinent sections of Aristotle's book entitled *Politics* which expand on the idea outlined above.

The exercise of authority and rule obviously carries with it the possession of power. While Aristotle emphasizes that those wielding authority must do so for the benefit of the community and within the limits of what is considered the proper sphere of the political association or the *polis,* a number of contemporary political thinkers broaden the focus of politics by using as the chief criterion simply the accumulation and exercise of power wherever it is found. For example, Harold D. Lasswell and Abraham Kaplan declare that "a *political act* is one performed in power perspectives" and consider a *"political movement"* to be "a continuing political act performed by an aggregate of persons in a power perspective. . . ." A similarly broad view of politics is taken by Robert Dahl, who defines a political system as "any persistent pattern of human relationships that involves, to a significant extent, power, rule, or authority."[1] Dahl admits that with his definition many organizations not ordinarily regarded as "political" fall under this classification: private clubs, business firms, labor unions, religious organizations, civic groups, primitive tribes, clans, and perhaps even families. Of course, some of these organizations may on occasion act "politically" also under more restrictive criteria such as those to be discussed later. However, under the Dahl definition, they are engaged in politics simply because they have an internal "government." To give the reader a greater insight into the implications of these rather broad views of politics, we have included short excerpts from the book by Lasswell and Kaplan, *Power and Society,* and an essay by C. Wright Mills, "The Structure of Power in American Society."

It would not serve a useful purpose within the scope of this book to delve into all the definitions that contemporary political scientists have elaborated to describe the nature of politics. Let us mention only a few in summary manner. Some scholars have used concern with legal government as the main criterion for determining what falls under the classification of politics, while others have focused on the notion of struggle among groups or even individuals pursuing conflicting objectives on public issues. Again others have felt that politics must involve activities but not necessarily struggles regarding a public issue, with the latter term to be interpreted in such a way that it does not only pertain to government actions, but also to those by private organizations (*i.e.,* large business corporations or labor unions) that affect the public at large. Finally, increasing attention has been paid during the last few years to a focus on the system of interactions in a society that arises out of or is concerned with the making of authoritative or binding

---

1 Robert Dahl, *Modern Political Analysis* (Englewood Cliffs, N.J.: Prentice-Hall, Inc., 1963), p. 6.

decisions. These decisions may provide benefits for the members of the society, such as social security or access to public works, or subject them to "deprivations" such as taxes or a jail sentence.[2] In the politically developed countries of the world a major source of these decisions is the branches of government—the legislatures, the executive and administrative agencies, or the courts. Elections of all kinds are also authoritative decisions for both the voters and the candidates. In a developing country in Africa such decisions may emanate from the tribal chief or the witch doctor. This approach is adaptable to political systems all over the world but lacks usefulness for international politics where, as we will see later, the sovereign nation state does not consider itself bound by any higher authority and the factor of naked power plays a predominant role.

This brief survey of the different conceptions regarding the nature of politics suggests that each conception has somewhat different implications for the object of our inquiry. Each definition brings to the surface a different set of problems and provides special insights and emphases. None appears to offer fully clear-cut conclusions as to what the actual nature of politics is, and therefore we would not consider ourselves justified in marking any of these conceptions as either right or wrong. Perhaps politics as a major area of human and social behavior is too complex and variegated to be subsumed under a brief theoretical definition.

Politics is closely related to man's other social pursuits. For example, an intimate relationship exists between politics and economics. In many instances the dividing line between the political and economic orders is blurred; sometimes the two orders overlap each other, and in most cases they affect each other in carying degrees. To return to the example mentioned at the outset of this chapter—the agency authorized to regulate the price of milk—it is obvious that a political relationship exists between the dairy farmers and the agency. But this relationship is also economic, because the production and distribution of milk is affected by the decisions of the agency. The decision of a city government to reserve an area for recreational purposes is political because it affects the distribution of recreational facilities, making them available to the community as a whole instead of only to the few that might own land in the particular area. On the other hand, the decision is also economic, because it prevents the land from being tilled to produce food or from being mined to extract the wealth that lies below it. The activities of labor unions are also economic and political. They seek to obtain the best wages possible for their members through collective bargaining with the employers, and at the same time they are interested in influencing pending legislation to their advantage. Similar considerations apply also to many other economic interest groups.

From the foregoing examples it is evident that when we discuss politics

---

2 See David Easton, *A Framework for Political Analysis* (Englewood Cliffs, N.J.: Prentice-Hall, Inc., 1965), p. 50.

and economics in a society, we may refer in many instances to the political and the economic aspect of the same action. In Chap. 7 we will return to this subject in greater detail when we examine certain relationships between the political and economic orders from the end of the Middle Ages until the present.

We have observed that answering the question about politics has challenged political thinkers from ancient Greece to our times, and we have given examples of some of the attempts to define the nature of politics. Undoubtedly, politics was part of organized society prior to the time Aristotle wrote his famous book on the subject. It has been with us through successive periods of history and will hold a central place in the future of man. It exists in democratic societies as well as in totalitarian regimes, in primitive governmental systems, present and past, as well as in the advanced industrial societies. It has pervaded the international scene throughout history. Politics has many faces: As Peter Merkl put it so aptly, "At its best, politics is a noble quest for a good order and justice; at its worst, a selfish grab for power, glory, and riches."[3] In the following chapters some of the fundamental questions bearing on both the favorable and unfavorable sides of politics will be explored.

---

3 Peter H. Merkl, *Political Continuity and Change* (New York: Harper & Row, Inc., 1967), p. 13.

Constitutions and
Their Classification

§1. Citizenship has now been defined and determined. We have next to consider the subject of constitutions. Is there a single type, or are there a number of types? If there are a number of types, what are these types; how many of them are there; and how do they differ?[1] A constitution (or polity) may be defined as "the organization of a polis, in respect of its offices generally but especially in respect of that particular office which is sovereign in all issues."[2] The civic body [the *politeuma*,[3] or body of persons established in power by the polity] is everywhere the sovereign of the state; in fact the civic body is the polity (or constitution) itself. §2. In democratic states, for example, the people [or *dēmos*] is sovereign: in oligarchies, on the other hand, the few [or *oligoi*] have that position; and this difference of the sovereign bodies is the reason why we say that the two types of constitution differ—as we may equally apply the same reasoning to other types besides these.

[It is thus evident that there are a number of types of constitution, but before we discuss their nature] we must first ascertain two things—the nature of the end for which the state exists, and the various kinds of authority to which men and their associations are subject. § 3. So far as the first of these things is concerned, it has already been stated, in our first book (where we were concerned with the management of the household and the control of slaves), that "man is an animal impelled by his nature to live in a polis." A *natural impulse* is thus one reason why men desire to live a social life even when they stand in no need of mutual succour; but they are also drawn together by a *common interest*, in proportion as

---

Reprinted from *The Politics of Aristotle,* translated with notes by Ernest Barker (New York: Oxford University Press, 1948), pp. 127–31, by permission of the publisher.

[1] In the first two sections of c. ɪ of this book Aristotle had begun by raising the question "What is a polis?" In order to answer that question, he found it first necessary to ask (following his analytic method of resolving a compound into its elements), "What is the member of a polis, or, in other words, the citizen?" The first five chapters have fully discussed that question. We might now expect him to return to the previous question, "What is a polis?" But that question has already been answered in the course of the discussion of the other question (cf. the definition of the polis in c. ɪ, § 12); and Aristotle now turns to a different question, "What is a *politeia,* or constitution?" This is a question which logically follows on the discussion of citizenship. Since citizenship is participation in office, and since partcipation in office is regulated by the constitution, a discussion of the *polites* necessarily leads to a discussion of the *politeia.*

[2] Another and similar, but fuller, definition is given in Book IV, c. ɪ, § 10.

[3] The civic body, or *politeuma,* acts as the deliberative, and as such is the supreme authority or sovereign. Aristotle, as Newman remarks in his note, "proves that the constitution is especially an ordering of the supreme authority by showing that the supreme authority is decisive of the character of the constitution, from which it follows that the main business of the constitution is to fix the supreme authority."

each attains a share in good life [through the union of all in a form of political association].[4] § 4. The good life is the chief end, both for the community as a whole and for each of us individually. But men also come together, and form and maintain political associations, merely for the sake of life;[5] for perhaps there is some element of the good even in the simple act of living, so long as the evils of existence do not preponderate too heavily. § 5. It is an evident fact that most men cling hard enough to life to be willing to endure a good deal of suffering, which implies that life has in it a sort of healthy happiness and a natural quality of pleasure.

[So far of the end for which the state exists. As regards the second question], it is easy enough to distinguish the various kinds of rule of authority of which men commonly speak; and indeed we have often had occasion to define them ourselves in works intended

for the general public.[6] § 6. The rule of a master is one kind; and here, though there is really a common interest which unites the natural master and the natural slave, the fact remains that the rule is primarily exercised with a view to the master's interest, and only incidentally with a view to that of the slave, who must be preserved in existence if the rule itself is to remain. § 7. Rule over wife and children, and over the household generally, is a second kind of rule, which we have called by the name of household management. Here the rule is either exercised in the interest of the ruled or for the attainment of some advantage common to both ruler and ruled. Essentially it is exercised in the interest of the ruled, as is also plainly the case with other arts besides that of ruling, such as medicine 1279 a and gymnastics— though an art may incidentally be exercised for the benefit of its practitioner, and there is nothing to prevent (say) a trainer from becoming occasionally a member of the class he instructs, in the same sort of way as a steersman is always one of the crew. § 8. Thus a trainer or steersman primarily considers the good of those who are subject to his authority; but when he becomes one of them personally, he incidentally shares in the benefit of that good—the steersman thus being also a member of the crew, and the trainer (though still a trainer) becoming also a member of the class which he instructs.

§ 9. This principle also applies to a third kind of rule—that exercised by the holders of political office. When the constitution of a state is constructed

---

4 Aristotle here suggests two ends for which the state, as an association, exists— (1) the end of providing satisfaction for a natural impulse, which exists and acts even apart from interest, and (2) the end of providing satisfaction for a common interest. This common interest, it should be noted, is not only or mainly economic: it is an interest in the attainment of a *good* (rather than a comfortable) life: and it requires for its satisfaction those institutions, such as a system of justice, which are necessary to such a life. It is this common interest in the attainment of a good life which is the chief end served by the state.

5 In the previous section Aristotle has distinguished "social life" and "good life." Here he introduces a third factor—the factor of "life" itself, independently of its being "social" or "good." The state or polis is connected with all three factors: it satisfies men's impulse towards a social life (which may exist apart from any need of mutual succour); it gives men a share in the good life which is their common interest; but it also helps men simply to live—and life itself is a thing of value. Compare Book I, c. II, § 8.

6 Literally "in exoteric discourses," as contrasted with the "esoteric discourses" (such as the discourses or *logoi* on politics here translated) which were intended for the students of the Lyceum.

on the principle that its members are equals and peers, the citizens think it proper that they should hold office by turns [which implies that the office of ruler is primarily intended for the benefit of the ruled and is therefore a duty to be undertaken by each in turn, though incidentally the ruler shares in the general benefit by virtue of being himself a member of the citizen body]. At any rate this is the natural system, and the system which used to be followed in the days when men believed that they ought to serve by turns, and each assumed that others would take over the duty of considering his benefit, just as he had himself, during his term of office, considered the interest of others. § 10. To-day the case is altered. Moved by the profits to be derived from office and the handling of public property, men want to hold office continuously. It is as if the holders of office were sick men, who got the benefit of permanent health [by being permanently in office]: at any rate their ardour for office is just what it would be if that were the case. § 11. The conclusion which follows is clear. Those constitutions which consider the common interest are *right* constitutions, judged by the standard of absolute justice. Those constitutions which consider only the personal interest of the rulers are all *wrong* constitutions, or

perversions of the right forms. Such perverted forms are despotic [i.e. calculated on the model of the rule of a master, or "despotēs," over slaves]; whereas the polis is an association of freemen.

Note on the basis of Aristotle's classification of constitutions:

This preliminary classification of constitutions into the two *genera* of right and wrong, or normal and perverted, is based on the principle that political rule, by virtue of its specific nature, is essentially for the benefit of the ruled. That is the principle of absolute justice in regard to the proper use of political power; and it is a principle which squares with what has been said above, in § 4, about the main end of the polis—that it is a *common* interest, which, as such, is for the benefit not of a section, but of each and all. Aristotle has thus concluded in this chapter (partly from what has been said in §§ 2–5 about the end of the polis, and partly from what has been said in §§ 5–10 about the specific nature of political rule, or rule over a political association of freemen, as contrasted with other forms of rule) that the fundamental principle to be followed in a polis, and therefore in its *politeia* or constitution, is the principle of the holding of office for the common interest of all the members, and particularly for the interest of the ruled, who are nearly the whole of the members. That principle separates the right constitutions which follow it from the wrong which contravene it.

The Political Association

ARISTOTLE

§ 1. Observation shows us, first, that every polis [or state] is a species of association, and, secondly, that all associations are instituted for the purpose of attaining some good—for all men do all their acts with a view to achieving something which is, in their view, a good. We may therefore hold [on the basis of what we actually observe] that all associations aim at some good; and we may also hold that the particular association which is the most sovereign of all, and includes all the rest, will pursue this. aim most, and will thus be directed to the most sovereign of all goods. This most sovereign and inclusive association is the polis, as it is called, or the political association.

§ 2. It is a mistake to believe[1] that the "statesman" [the *politikos,* who handles the affairs of a political association] is the same as the monarch of a kingdom, or the manager of a household, or the master of a number of slaves.[2] Those who hold this view consider that each of these persons differs

from the others not with a difference of kind, but [merely with a difference of degree, and] according to the number, or the paucity, of the persons with whom he deals. On this view a man who is concerned with few persons is a master: one who is concerned with more is the manager of a household: one who is concerned with still more is a "statesman," or a monarch. This view abolishes any real difference between a large household and a small polis; and it also reduces the difference between the "statesman" and the monarch to the one fact that the latter has an uncontrolled and sole authority, while the former exercises his authority in conformity with the rules imposed by the art of statesmanship and as one who rules and is ruled in turn. But this is a view which cannot be accepted as correct. [There is an *essential* difference between these persons, and between the associations with which they are concerned.]

§ 3. Our point will be made clear if we proceed to consider the matter according to our normal method of analysis. Just as, in all other fields, a compound[3] should be analysed until we reach its simple and uncompounded elements (or, in other words, the smallest atoms of the whole which it constitutes), so we must also consider analytically the elements of which a polis is composed. We shall then gain a better insight into the difference from

Reprinted from *The Politics of Aristotle,* translated with notes by Ernest Barker (New York: Oxford University Press, 1948), pp. 1–8, by permission of the publisher.

[1] This belief is, in Aristotle's view, that of Plato. The immediate reference is to the *Politicus* of Plato 258 E–259 D.

[2] The political association, as appears later in Book III (see e.g. c. VI, § 9), is an association of "equal and like" members; and the *Politikos* who handles its affairs will therefore be only *primus inter pares.* That is why he differs essentially from the ruler of a kingdom, or of a household, or of a body of slaves.

[3] On the sense which Aristotle attached to the technical term 'compound' see below, Book III, c. I, § 2, and note.

one another of the persons and associations just mentioned; and we shall also be in a position to discover whether it is possible to attain a systematic view of the general issues involved.[4]

Note on the nature of associations

Two passages from the *Ethics* may be cited in illustration and explanation of the first section of this chapter. They both come from the part of the *Ethics* (Books VIII–IX) which deals with the nature of friendship, or what may be called "social sympathy."

(*a*) "Every form of friendship involves association. But kinship and comradeship may be distinguished as peculiar forms [because they depend peculiarly on natural feeling and innate sympathy]. The form of friendship which unites fellow citizens—or fellow tribesmen, or fellow voyagers—is more in the nature of pure association, since it seems to rest on a sort of compact" (*Ethics*, VIII, c. xii, § 1). Association, it will be noticed, is here connected with compact and "construction": see below, c. ii, § 15, and note.

(*b*) "All associations are in the nature of parts of the political association. Men journey together with a view to some particular advantage, and by way of providing some particular thing needed for the purposes of life; and similarly the political association seems to have come together originally, and to continue in existence, for the sake of the *general* advantage which it brings" (ibid., c. ix, § 4).

§ 1. If, accordingly, we begin at the beginning, and consider things in the process of their growth, we shall best be able, in this as in other fields, to attain scientific conclusions by the method we employ.[5] § 2. First of all,

there must necessarily be a union or pairing of those who cannot exist without one another. Male and female must unite for the reproduction of the species—not from deliberate intention, but from the natural impulse, which exists in animals generally as it also exists in plants, to leave behind them something of the same nature as themselves. Next, there must necessarily be a union of the naturally ruling element with the element which is naturally ruled, for the preservation of both. The element which is able, by virtue of its intelligence, to exercise forethought is naturally a ruling and master element; the element which is able, by virtue of its bodily power, to do what the other element plans is a ruled element, which is naturally in a state of slavery; and master and slave have accordingly [as they thus complete one another] a common interest.... 1252 b § 3. The female and the slave [we may pause to note] are naturally distinguished from one another. Nature makes nothing in a spirit of stint,[6] as smiths do when they make the Delphic knife to serve a number of purposes: she makes each separate thing for a separate end; and she does so because each instrument has the finest finish when it serves a single purpose and not a variety of purposes. § 4. Among the barbarians, however [contrary to the order of nature], the female and the slave occupy the same position—the reason being that no naturally ruling element exists among them, and conjugal union thus comes to be a union of a female who is a slave with a male who is also a

---

[4] These general issues, as they emerge later, turn on the nature of authority over slaves, the nature of marital and parental authority, and the nature of household management in general.

[5] The analytic method of the previous chapter is, in effect, identical with the genetic method here suggested (the method of

"considering things in the process of their growth"), since the genetic method begins with the simple elements, and thus implies the use of analysis.

[6] i.e. the spirit which makes the female serve the purpose of a slave as well as that of a mate.

slave.[7] This is why our poets have said,

> Meet it is that barbarous peoples should be governed by the Greeks

—the assumption being that barbarian and slave are by nature one and the same. . . .

§ 5. The first result of these two elementary associations [of male and female, and of master and slave] is the household or family. Hesiod spoke truly in the verse,

> First house, and wife, and ox to draw the plough,

for oxen serve the poor in lieu of household slaves. The first form of association naturally instituted for the satisfaction of daily recurrent needs is thus the family; and the members of the family are accordingly termed by Charondas "associates of the breadchest," as they are also termed by Epimenides the Cretan "associates of the manager." The next form of association—which is also the *first* to be formed from more households than one, and for the satisfaction of something more than daily recurrent needs—is the village. § 6. The most natural form of the village appears to be that of a colony or offshoot from a family; and some have thus called the members of the village by the name of "sucklings of the same milk," or, again,

of "sons and the sons of sons"[8]. . . . This, it may be noted, is the reason why each Greek polis was originally ruled—as the peoples of the barbarian world still are —by kings. They were formed of persons who were already monarchically governed [i.e. they were formed from households and villages, and] households are always monarchically governed by the eldest of the kin, just as villages, when they are offshoots from the household, are similarly governed in virtue of the kinship between their members. § 7. This primitive kinship is what Homer describes, [in speaking of the Cyclopes]:

> Each of them ruleth
> Over his children and wives,

a passage which shows that they lived in scattered groups, as indeed men generally did in ancient times. The fact that men generally were governed by kings in ancient times, and that some still continue to be governed in that way, is the reason that leads us all to assert that the gods are also governed by a king. We make the lives of the gods in the likeness of our own—as we also make their shapes. . . .

§ 8. When we come to the final and perfect association, formed from a number of villages, we have already reached the polis—an association which may be said to have reached the height of full self-sufficiency; or rather [to speak more exactly] we may say that while it *grows* for the sake of mere life [and

---

[7] The argument is that among the barbarians the female is slave (as well as mate) for the simple reason that all alike are slaves, men as well as women, and the emergence of a true *consortium* of marriage, distinct from the nexus of slavery, is thus impossible. The cause of this uniform condition of slavery is the absence of a free class, capable of holding office and practising the art of "ruling and being ruled in turn"—the sort of class which was the essence of the Greek political association and the cause of its freedom. On the other hand, a people, such as the Greeks, which possesses such a class may naturally aspire (Aristotle incidentally reflects) to rule the general slave world of the barbarian peoples.

[8] The latter phrase comes from Plato's *Laws*. The general argument of Aristotle at this point is clearly stated by Newman in his note: "He has proved that the household is necessary and natural, and if he can prove that the village is an outgrowth of the household, and the polis of the village, then the polis will be shown to be natural." The analytic-genetic method which he is using thus ends by providing a proof of the "natural" character of the polis.

is so far, and at that stage, still short of full self-sufficiency], it *exists* [when once it is fully grown] for the sake of a good life [and is therefore fully self-sufficient].

Because it is the completion of associations existing by nature, every polis exists by nature, having itself the same quality as the earlier associations from which it grew. It is the end or consummation to which those associations move, and the "nature" of things consists in their end or consummation; for what each thing is when its growth is completed we call the nature of that thing, whether it be a man or a horse or a family.[9] 1253 a § 9. Again [and this is a second reason for regarding the state as natural] the end, or final cause, is the best. Now self-sufficiency [which it is the object of the state to bring about] is the end, and so the best; [and on this it follows that the state brings about the best, and is therefore natural, since nature always aims at bringing about the best].[10]

From these considerations it is evident that the polis belongs to the class of things that exist by nature, and that man is by nature an animal intended to live in a polis.[11] He who is

---

9 The state is natural because it develops from natural associations. But it would be wrong to think it is only natural because *they* are natural and because it grows from *them.* It is natural *in itself,* as the completion, end, or consummation of man and man's development—the essentially natural condition of anything being its final, or complete, or perfect condition. If we could imagine a state coming into existence directly and immediately, without the preceding stages of the household and the village, it would still be natural, in virtue of completing and perfecting man and his development.

10 The explanatory passage in brackets is borrowed from Newman's note.

11 "It would be a strange thing to make the happy man a solitary: no one would choose to have all the good things of the

without a polis, by reason of his own nature and not of some accident, is either a poor sort of being, or a being higher than man: he is like the man of whom Homer wrote in denunciation:

"Clanless and lawless and heartless is he."

§ 10. The man who is such by nature [i.e. unable to join in the society of a polis] at once plunges into a passion for war; he is in the position of a solitary advanced piece in a game of draughts.

The reason why man is a being meant for political association, in a higher degree than bees or other gregarious animals can ever associate, is evident. Nature, according to our theory, makes nothing in vain; and man alone of the animals is furnished with the faculty of language. § 11. The mere making of sounds serves to indicate pleasure and pain, and is thus a faculty that belongs to animals in general: their nature enables them to attain the point at which they have perceptions of pleasure and pain, and can signify those perceptions to one another. But language serves to declare what is advantageous and what is the reverse, and it therefore serves to declare what is just and what is unjust. § 12. It is the peculiarity of man, in comparison with the rest of the animal world, that he alone possesses a perception of good and evil, of the just and the unjust, and of other similar qualities; and it is association in [a common perception of] these things which makes a family and a polis.

We may now proceed to add that [though the individual and the family are prior in the order of time] the polis

---

world in solitude: man is a being meant for political association, and whose nature it is to live with others" (*Ethics,* IX, c. IX, § 3).

is prior in the order of nature to the family and the individual. § 13. The reason for this is that the whole is necessarily prior [in nature] to the part.[12] If the whole body be destroyed, there will not be a foot or a hand, except in that ambiguous sense in which one uses the same word to indicate a different thing, as when one speaks of a "hand" made of stone; for a hand, when destroyed [by the destruction of the whole body], will be no better than a stone "hand." All things derive their essential character from their function and their capacity; and it follows that if they are no longer fit to discharge their function, we ought not to say that they are still the same things, but only that, by an ambiguity, they still have the same names.

§ 14. We thus see that the polis exists by nature and that it is prior to the individual.[13] [The proof of both propositions is the fact that the polis is a whole, and that individuals are simply its parts.] Not being self-sufficient when they are isolated, all individuals are so many parts all equally depend-

ing on the whole [which alone can bring about self-sufficiency]. The man who is isolated—who is unable to share in the benefits of political association, or has no need to share because he is already self-sufficient—is no part of the polis, and must therefore be either a beast or a god. § 15. [Main is thus intended by nature to be a part of a political whole, and] there is therefore an immanent impulse in all men towards an association of this order. But the man who first *constructed* such an association was none the less the greatest of benefactors.[14] Man, when perfected, is the best of animals; but if he be isolated from law and justice he is the worst of all. § 16. Injustice is all the graver when it is armed injustice; and man is furnished from birth with arms [such as, for instance, language] which are intended to serve the purposes of moral prudence and virtue, but which may be used in preference for opposite ends. That is why, if he be without virtue, he is a most unholy and savage being, and worse than all others in the indulgence of lust and gluttony. Justice [which is his salvation] belongs to the polis; for justice, which is the determination of what is just, is an ordering of the political association.

---

12 The whole is prior to the part in the sense that the part presupposes it; the idea of the whole must first be there before the part can be understood, and the whole itself must first be there before the part can have or exercise a function.

13 These two points are interconnected. The polis exists by nature in the sense that it is the whole to which man naturally moves in order to develop his innate capacity, and in which he is thus included as a part. Because it is the whole, of which the individual is necessarily a part, it is prior to the individuals who are its parts, as wholes generally are prior to their parts.

14 Aristotle here concedes, and indeed argues, that in saying that the state is natural he does not mean that it 'grows' naturally, without human volition and action. There is art as well as nature, and art co-operates with nature: the volition and action of human agents 'construct' the state in co-operation with a natural immanent impulse.

Process

HAROLD D. LASSWELL / ABRAHAM KAPLAN

POLITICAL ACTS, MOVEMENTS, AND CYCLES

A *political act* is one performed in power perspectives; a *political movement* is a continuing political act performed by an aggregate of persons in a power perspective of elaborated identifications, demands, and expectations.

We conclude our discussion of the political process, as we began, with a consideration of the *act* as the unit of which this process—and, indeed, all interpersonal relations—are composed. Like other acts, the political act passes through phases of "impulse," "subjectivity," and "expression." Conduct is goal-directed and hence implicates values; the impulsive phase of the act is constituted by the needs of or initial striving for those values. Every actor must take account of other actors in his environment as interfering with or supporting these strivings. Thus there emerge as further values, both instrumental and intrinsic, influence and power—control over others on the basis of lesser or greater sanctions. The political act takes its origin in a situation in which the actor strives for the attainment of various values for which power is a necessary (and perhaps also sufficient) condition.

Symbols of the ego in relation to others constitute the self of the actor, and provide identifications in the name

of which the political act continues. Symbols of demand formulate the goals of the act (as well as the subsidiary goals of enlisting others in its support). Symbols of expectation present the self and environment in relation to the attainment of these goals. The phase of subjectivity is constituted by the workings of such symbols.

In these perspectives, the operations of power striving take shape as practices of various kinds, constituting the phase of expression of the act. Groups may be formed, articulated in complex structures, and performing a variety of functions transcending, transforming, or even reversing the original goals. Of course, the act may be interrupted in any of its phases, or it may terminate and give way to a new impulse without attainment of its goal.

A political movement is most simply characterized as a collective political act so conceived. It is performed by a large number of persons, exhibiting varying degrees of solidarity and organization (so that it is a wider concept than "a political act of a group"); engaged in a continuing pattern of practices (so that a single election is not a movement, though the campaign leading up to and including it may constitute one); and in a perspective which does not antecedently limit the goals, plans, and participants (so that a movement may change its direction or composition without losing its identity).[1]

Reprinted from Harold D. Lasswell and Abraham Kaplan, *Power and Society* (New Haven: Yale University Press, 1950), pp. 240–41, by permission of the publisher.

[1] Since an act is defined as political in terms of its perspectives, its characterization

As with the individual act, a political movement originates in a situation of need or tension. Insecurity and frustration (or contrariwise, highly indulgent expectations) produce a stress toward action. Initially, the experiences on which this stress is based are individual and private. Gradually, they are related to the experiences of others, and the private malaise or sense of unrealized opportunity ("if only things were different!") acquires a vaguely social formulation. Symbols of diagnosis and prescription multiply; symbols of identification emerge in relation to these, and

the number of demands and expectations current is progressively limited. (This is the phase of subjectivity—public opinion, if the expectation of violence is relatively low.) The situation then becomes well defined, alignments take shape, and the movement passes into the phase of expression, with manipulation of directed symbols, goods, and services, and possibly violence, concurrently with such political practices as voting or legislating.

The situation is then transformed; readjustment is said to take place if the movement has had considerable effect on the environment, catharsis if its environmental impact has been minimal. In the former case, different patterns emerge according to whether or not violence is (or is expected to be) employed—we speak in this connection of crisis and its resolution. In the latter case, the needs with which the movement originated may or may not recur, and the conception of cyclical patterns becomes relevant.

---

as such may vary with changing observational standpoints. Thus a movement may appear to its participants as purely religious, say, and to outsiders as definitely political. The definition selected here takes the standpoint of the actor himself, and classifies the act as political only if power enters significantly into the perspectives of the actor as end or means for the act. Other definitions might emphasize the likelihood of later occurrence of such perspectives, or power consequences independent of perspective, and so on.

The Structure of Power
in American Society

C. WRIGHT MILLS

Power has to do with whatever decisions men make about the arrangements under which they live, and about the events which make up the history of

Reprinted from *Power, Politics and People: The Collected Essays of C. Wright Mills,* ed. Irving L. Horowitz (New York: Ballantine Books, Inc., 1963), pp. 23–38, by permission of the Oxford University Press, Inc.

their times. Events that are beyond human decision do happen; social arrangements do change without benefit of explicit decision. But in so far as such decisions are made, the problem of who is involved in making them is the basic problem of power. In so far as they could be made but are not, the problem becomes who fails to make them?

We cannot today merely assume that in the last resort men must always be governed by their own consent. For among the means of power which now prevail is the power to manage and to manipulate the consent of men. That we do not know the limits of such power, and that we hope it does have limits, does not remove the fact that much power today is successfully employed without the sanction of the reason or the conscience of the obedient.

Surely nowadays we need not argue that, in the last resort, coercion is the "final" form of power. But then, we are by no means constantly at teh last resort. Authority (power that is justified by the beliefs of the voluntarily obedient) and manipulation (power that is wielded unbeknown to the powerless)—must also be considered, along with coercion. In fact, the three types must be sorted out whenever we think about power.

In the modern world, we must bear in mind, power is often not so authoritative as it seemed to be in the medieval epoch: ideas which justify rulers no longer seem so necessary to their exercise of power. At least for many of the great decisions of our time—especially those of an international sort—mass "persuasion" has not been "necessary," the fact is simply accomplished. Furthermore, such ideas as are available to the powerful are often neither taken up nor used by them. Such ideologies usually arise as a response to an effective debunking of power; in the United States such opposition has not been effective enough recently to create the felt need for new ideologies of rule.

There has, in fact, come about a situation in which many who have lost faith in prevailing loyalties have not acquired new ones, and so pay no attention to politics of any kind. They are not radical, not liberal, not conservative, not reactionary. They are inactionary. They are out of it. If we accept the Greek's definition of the idiot as an altogether private man, then we must conclude that many American citizens are now idiots. And I should not be surprised, although I do not know, if there were not some such idiots even in Germany. This—and I use the word with care—this spiritual condition seems to me the key to many modern troubles of political intellectuals, as well as the key to much political bewilderment in modern society. Intellectual "conviction" and moral "belief" are not necessary, in either the rulers or the ruled, for a ruling power to persist and even to flourish. So far as the role of ideologies is concerned, their frequent absences and the prevalence of mass indifference are surely two of the major political facts about the western societies today.

How large a role any explicit decisions do play in the making of history is itself an historical problem. For how large that role may be depends very much upon the means of power that are available at any given time in any given society. In some societies, the innumerable actions of innumerable men modify their milieux, and so gradually modify the structure itself. These modifications—the course of history—go on behind the backs of men. History is drift, although in total "men make it." Thus, innumerable entrepreneurs and innumerable consumers by ten-thousand decisions per minute may shape and re-shape the free-market economy. Perhaps this was the chief kind of limitation Marx had in mind when he wrote, in *The 18th Brumaire:* that "Men make their own history, but they do not make it just as they please; they do not make it under circumstances chosen by themselves. . . ."

But in other societies—certainly in the United States and in the Soviet Union today—a few men may be so placed within the structure that by their decisions they modify the milieux of many other men, and in fact nowadays the structural conditions under which most men live. Such elites of power also make history under circumstances not chosen altogether by themselves, yet compared with other men, and compared with other periods of world history, these circumstances do indeed seem less limiting.

I should contend that "men are free to make history," but that some men are indeed much freer than others. For such freedom requires access to the means of decision and of power by which history can now be made. It has not always been so made; but in the later phases of the modern epoch it is. It is with reference to this epoch that I am contending that if men do not make history, they tend increasingly to become the utensils of history-makers as well as the mere objects of history.

The history of modern society may readily be understood as the story of the enlargement and the centralization of the means of power—in economic, in political, and in military institutions. The rise of industrial society has involved these developments in the means of economic production. The rise of the nation-state has involved similar developments in the means of violence and in those of political administration.

In the western societies, such transformations have generally occurred gradually, and many cultural traditions have restrained and shaped them. In most of the Soviet societies, they are happening very rapidly indeed and

without the great discourse of western civilization, without the Renaissance and without the Reformation, which so greatly strengthened and gave political focus to the idea of freedom. In those societies, the enlargement and the coordination of all the means of power has occurred more brutally, and from the beginning under tightly centralized authority. But in both types, the means of power have now become international in scope and similar in form. To be sure, each of them has its own ups and downs; neither is as yet absolute; how they are run differs quite sharply.

Yet so great is the reach of the means of violence, and so great the economy required to produce and support them, that we have in the immediate past witnessed the consolidation of these two world centers, either of which dwarfs the power of Ancient Rome. As we pay attention to the awesome means of power now available to quite small groups of men we come to realize that Caesar could do less with Rome than Napoleon with France; Napoleon less with France than Lenin with Russia. But what was Caesar's power at its height compared with the power of the changing inner circles of Soviet Russia and the temporary administrations of the United States? We come to realize —indeed they continually remind us— how a few men have access to the means by which in a few days continents can be turned into thermonuclear wastelands. That the facilities of power are so enormously enlarged and so decisively centralized surely means that the powers of quite small groups of men, which we may call elites, are now of literally inhuman consequence.

My concern here is not with the international scene but with the United

States in the middle of the twentieth century. I must emphasize "in the middle of the twentieth century" because in our attempt to understand any society we come upon images which have been drawn from its past and which often confuse our attempt to confront its present reality. That is one minor reason why history is the shank of any social science: we must study it if only to rid ourselves of it. In the United States, there are indeed many such images and usually they have to do with the first half of the nineteenth century. At that time the economic facilities of the United States were very widely dispersed and subject to little or to no central authority.

The state watched in the night but was without decisive voice in the day.

One man meant one rifle and the militia were without centralized orders.

Any American, as old-fashioned as I, can only agree with R. H. Tawney that "Whatever the future may contain, the past has shown no more excellent social order than that in which the mass of the people were the masters of the holdings which they ploughed and the tools with which they worked, and could boast . . . 'It is a quietness to a man's mind to live upon his own and to know his heir certain.' "

But then we must immediately add: all that is of the past and of little relevance to our understanding of the United States today. Within this society three broad levels of power may now be distinguished. I shall begin at the top and move downward.

The power to make decisions of national and international consequence is now so clearly seated in political, military, and economic institutions that other areas of society seem off to the side and, on occasion, readily subordinated to these. The scattered institutions of religion, education and family are increasingly shaped by the big three, in which history-making decisions now regularly occur. Behind this fact there is all the push and drive of a fabulous technology; for these three institutional orders have incorporated this technology and now guide it, even as it shapes and paces their development.

As each has assumed its modern shape, its effects upon the other two have become greater, and the traffic between the three has increased. There is no longer, on the one hand, an economy, and, on the other, a political order, containing a military establishment unimportant to politics and to money-making. There is a political economy numerously linked with military order and decision. This triangle of power is now a structural fact, and it is the key to any understanding of the higher circles in America today. For as each of these domains has coincided with the others, as decisions in each have become broader, the leading men of each—the high military, the corporation executives, the political directorate —have tended to come together to form the power elite of America.

The political order, once composed of several dozen states with a weak federal-center, has become an executive apparatus which has taken up into itself many powers previously scattered, legislative as well as administrative, and which now reaches into all parts of the social structure. The long-time tendency of business and government to become more closely connected has since World War II reached a new point of explicitness. Neither can now be seen clearly as a distinct world. The growth of executive government does not mean merely the "enlargement of government" as some kind of autonomous bureaucracy: under American conditions, it has meant the ascendency of the corporation man into political eminence. Already during the New Deal, such men had joined the political directorate; as of World War II they came to dominate it. Long involved with government, now they have moved into quite full direction of the economy of the war effort and of the post-war era.

The economy, once a great scatter of small productive units in somewhat automatic balance, has become internally dominated by a few hundred corporations, administratively and politically interrelated, which together hold the keys to economic decision. This economy is at once a permanent-war economy and a private-corporation economy. The most important relations of the corporation to the state now rest on the coincidence between military and corporate interests, as defined by the military and the corporate rich, and accepted by politicians and public. Within the elite as a whole, this coincidence of military domain and corporate realm strengthens both of them and further subordinates the merely political man. Not the party politician, but the corporation executive, is now more likely to sit with the military to answer the question: what is to be done?

The military order, once a slim establishment in a context of civilian distrust, has become the largest and most expensive feature of government; behind smiling public relations, it has all the grim and clumsy efficiency of a great and sprawling bureaucracy. The high military have gained decisive political and economic relevance. The seemingly permanent military threat places a premium upon them and virtually all political and economic actions are now judged in terms of military definitions of reality: the higher military have ascended to a firm position within the power elite of our time.

In part at least this is a result of an historical fact, pivotal for the years since 1939: the attention of the elite has shifted from domestic problems—centered in the 'thirties around slump—to international problems—centered in the 'forties and 'fifties around war. By long historical usage, the government of the United States has been shaped by domestic clash and balance; it does not have suitable agencies and traditions for the democratic handling of international affairs. In considerable part, it is in this vacuum that the power elite has grown.

(i) To understand the unity of this power elite, we must pay attention to the psychology of its several members in their respective milieux. In so far as the power elite is composed of men of similar origin and education, of similar career and style of life, their unity may be said to rest upon the fact that they are of similar social type, and to lead to the fact of their easy intermingling. This kind of unity reaches its frothier apex in the sharing of that prestige which is to be had in the world of the celebrity. It achieves a more solid culmination in the fact of the interchangeability of positions between the three dominant institutional orders. It is revealed by considerable traffic of personnel within and between these three, as well as by the rise of specialized go-betweens as in the new style high-level lobbying.

(ii) Behind such psychological and social unity are the structure and the mechanics of those institutional hierarchies over which the political directorate, the corporate rich, and the high military now preside. How each of these hierarchies is shaped and what relations it has with the others determine in large part the relations of their rulers. Were these hierarchies scattered and disjointed, then their respective elites might tend to be scattered and disjointed; but if they have many interconnections and points of coinciding interest, then their elites tend to form a coherent kind of grouping. The unity of the elite is not a simple reflection of the unity of institutions, but men and institutions are always related; that is why we must understand the elite today in connection with such institutional trends as the development of a permanent-war establishment, alongside a privately incorporated economy, inside a virtual political vacuum. For the men at the top have been selected and formed by such institutional trends.

(iii) Their unity, however, does not rest solely upon psychological similarity and social intermingling, nor entirely upon the structural blending of commanding positions and common interests. At times it is the unity of a more explicit co-ordination.

To say that these higher circles are increasingly co-ordinated, that this is *one* basis of their unity, and that at times—as during open war—such co-ordination is quite wilful, is not to say that the co-ordination is total or continuous, or even that it is very sure-footed. Much less is it to say that the power elite has emerged as the realization of a plot. Its rise cannot be adequately explained in any psychological terms.

Yet we must remember that institutional trends may be defined as opportunities by those who occupy the command posts. Once such opportunities are recognized, men may avail themselves of them. Certain types of men from each of these three areas, more far-sighted than others, have actively promoted the liaison even before it took its truly modern shape. Now more

have come to see that their several interests can more easily be realized if they work together, in informal as well as in formal ways, and accordingly they have done so.

The idea of the power elite is of course an interpretation. It rests upon and it enables us to make sense of major institutional trends, the social similarities and psychological affinities of the men at the top. But the idea is also based upon what has been happening on the middle and lower levels of power, to which I now turn.

There are of course other interpretations of the American system of power. The most usual is that it is a moving balance of many competing interests. The image of balance, at least in America, is derived from the idea of the economic market: in the nineteenth century, the balance was thought to occur between a great scatter of individuals and enterprises; in the twentieth century, it is thought to occur between great interest blocs. In both views, the politician is the key man of power because he is the broker of many conflicting powers.

I believe that the balance and the compromise in American society—the "countervailing powers" and the "veto groups," of parties and associations, of strata and unions—must now be seen as having mainly to do with the middle levels of power. It is these middle levels that the political journalist and the scholar of politics are most likely to understand and to write about—if only because, being mainly middle class themselves, they are closer to them. Moreover these levels provide the noisy content of most "political" news and gossip; the images of these levels are more or less in accord with the folklore of how democracy works; and, if the master-image of balance is accepted, many intellectuals, especially in their current patrioteering, are readily able to satisfy such political optimism as they wish to feel. Accordingly, liberal interpretations of what is happening in the United States are now virtually the only interpretations that are widely distributed.

But to believe that the power system reflects a balancing society is, I think, to confuse the present era with earlier times, and to confuse its top and bottom with its middle levels.

By the top levels, as distinguished from the middle, I intend to refer, first of all, to the scope of the decisions that are made. At the top today, these decisions have to do with all the issues of war and peace. They have also to do with slump and poverty which are now so very much problems of international scope. I intend also to refer to whether or not the groups that struggle politically have a chance to gain the positions from which such top decisions are made, and indeed whether their members do usually hope for such top national command. Most of the competing interests which make up the clang and clash of American politics are strictly concerned with their slice of the existing pie. Labor unions, for example, certainly have no policies of an international sort other than those which given unions adopt for the strict economic protection of their members. Neither do farm organizations. The actions of such middle-level powers may indeed have consequence for top-level policy; certainly at times they hamper these policies. But they are not truly concerned with them, which means of course that their influence tends to be quite irresponsible.

The facts of the middle levels may in part be understood in terms of the rise of the power elite. The expanded and centralized and interlocked hierarchies over which the power elite preside have encroached upon the old balance and relegated it to the middle level. But there are also independent developments of the middle levels. These, it seems to me, are better understood as an affair of entrenched and provincial demands than as a center of national decision. As such, the middle level often seems much more of a stalemate than a moving balance.

(i) The middle level of politics is not a forum in which there are debated the big decisions of national and international life. Such debate is not carried on by nationally responsible parties representing and clarifying alternative policies. There are no such parties in the United States. More and more, fundamental issues never come to any point or decision before the Congress, much less before the electorate in party campaigns. In the case of Formosa, in the spring of 1955 the Congress abdicated all debate concerning events and decisions which surely bordered on war. The same is largely true of the 1957 crisis in the Middle East. Such decisions now regularly by-pass the Congress, and are never clearly focused issues for public decision.

The American political campaign distracts attention from national and international issues, but that is not to say that there are no issues in these campaigns. In each district and state, issues are set up and watched by organized interests of sovereign local importance. The professional politician is of course a party politician, and the two parties are semifeudal organizations: they trade patronage and other favors for votes and for protection. The differences between them, so far as national issues are concerned, are very narrow and very mixed up. Often each seems to be fifty parties, one to each state; and accordingly, the politician as campaigner and as Congressman is not concerned with national party lines, if any are discernible. Often he is not subject to any effective national party discipline. He speaks for the interests of his own constituency, and he is concerned with national issues only in so far as they affect the interests effectively organized there, and hence his chances of re-election. That is why, when he does speak of national matters, the result is so often such an empty rhetoric. Seated in his sovereign locality, the politician is not at the national summit. He is on and of the middle levels of power.

(ii) Politics is not an arena in which free and independent organizations truly connect the lower and middle levels of society with the top levels of decision. Such organizations are not an effective and major part of American life today. As more people are drawn into the political arena, their associations become mass in scale, and the power of the individual becomes dependent upon them; to the extent that they are effective, they have become larger, and to that extent they have become less accessible to the influence of the individual. This is a central fact about associations in any mass society: it is of most consequence for political parties and for trade unions.

In the 'thirties, it often seemed that labor would become an insurgent power independent of corporation and state. Organized labor was then emerging for the first time on an American scale, and the only political sense of direction it needed was the slogan, "organize the unorganized." Now without the mandate of the slump, labor remains without political direction. Instead of economic and political struggles it has become deeply entangled in administrative routines with both corporation

and state. One of its major functions, as a vested interest of the new society, is the regulation of such irregular tendencies as may occur among the rank and file.

There is nothing, it seems to me, in the make-up of the current labor leadership to allow us to expect that it can or that it will lead, rather than merely react. In so far as it fights at all it fights over a share of the goods of a single way of life and not over that way of life itself. The typical labor leader in the U.S.A. today is better understood as an adaptive creature of the main business drift than as an independent actor in a truly national context.

(iii) The idea that this society is a balance of powers requires us to assume that the units in balance are of more or less equal power and that they are truly independent of one another. These assumptions have rested, it seems clear, upon the historical importance of a large and independent middle class. In the latter nineteenth century and during the Progressive Era, such a class of farmers and small businessmen fought politically—and lost—their last struggle for a paramount role in national decision. Even then, their aspirations seemed bound to their own imagined past.

This old, independent middle class has of course declined. On the most generous count, it is now 40 per cent of the total middle class (at most 20 per cent of the total labor force). Moreover, it has become politically as well as economically dependent upon the state, most notably in the case of the subsidized farmer.

The *new* middle class of white-collar employees is certainly not the political pivot of any balancing society. It is in no way politically unified. Its unions, such as they are, often serve merely to incorporate it as hanger-on of the labor interest. For a considerable period, the old middle class *was* an independent base of power; the new middle class cannot be. Political freedom and economic security *were* anchored in small and independent properties; they are not anchored in the worlds of the white-collar job. Scattered property holders were economically united by more or less free markets; the jobs of the new middle class are integrated by corporate authority. Economically, the white-collar classes are in the same condition as wage workers; politically, they are in a worse condition, for they are not organized. They are no vanguard of historic change; they are at best a rearguard of the welfare state.

The agrarian revolt of the 'nineties, the small-business revolt that has been more or less continuous since the 'eighties, the labor revolt of the 'thirties— each of these has failed as an independent movement which could countervail against the powers that be; they have failed as politically autonomous third parties. But they have succeeded, in varying degree, as interests vested in the expanded corporation and state; they have succeeded as parochial interests seated in particular districts, in local divisions of the two parties, and in the Congress. What they would become, in short, are well-established features of the *middle* levels of balancing power, on which we may now observe all those strata and interests which in the course of American history have been defeated in their bids for top power or which have never made such bids.

Fifty years ago many observers thought of the American state as a mask behind which an invisible government operated. But nowadays, much of what was called the old lobby, visible or invisible, is part of the quite visible government. The "governmentalization of the lobby" has proceeded in both the legislative and the executive domain, as well as between them. The executive bureaucracy becomes not only the center of decision but also the arena within which major conflicts of power are resolved or denied resolution. "Administration" replaces electoral politics; the maneuvering of cliques (which include leading Senators as well as civil servants) replaces the open clash of parties.

The shift of corporation men into the political directorate has accelerated the decline of the politicians in the Congress to the middle levels of power, the formation of the power elite rests in part upon this relegation. It rests also upon the semiorganized stalemate of the interests of sovereign localities, into which the legislative function has so largely fallen; upon the virtually complete absence of a civil service that is a politically neutral but politically relevant, depository of brain-power and executive skill; and it rests upon the increased official secrecy behind which great decisions are made without benefit of public or even of Congressional debate.

There is one last belief upon which liberal observers everywhere base their interpretations and rest their hopes. That is the idea of the public and the associated idea of public opinion. Conservative thinkers, since the French Revolution, have of course Viewed With Alarm the rise of the public, which they have usually called the masses, or something to that effect. "The populace is sovereign," wrote Gustave LeBon, "and the tide of barbarism mounts." But surely those who have supposed the masses to be well on their way to triumph are mistaken. In our time, the influence of publics or of masses within political life is in fact decreasing, and such influence as on occasion they do have tends, to an unknown but increasing degree, to be guided by the means of mass communication.

In a society of publics, discussion is the ascendant means of communication, and the mass media, if they exist, simply enlarge and animate this discussion, linking one face-to-face public with the discussions of another. In a mass society, the dominant type of communication is the formal media, and publics become mere markets for these media: the "public" of a radio program consists of all those exposed to it. When we try to look upon the United States today as a society of publics, we realize that it has moved a considerable distance along the road to the mass society.

In official circles, the very term, "the public," has come to have a phantom meaning, which dramatically reveals its eclipse. The deciding elite can identify some of those who clamor publicly as "Labor," others as "Business," still others as "Farmer." But these are not the public. "The public" consists of the unidentified and the nonpartisan in a world of defined and partisan interests. In this faint echo of the classic notion, the public is composed of these remnants of the old and new middle classes whose interests are not explicitly defined, organized, or clamorous. In a curious adaptation, "the public" often becomes, in administrative fact, "the disengaged expert," who, although never so well informed, has never taken a clear-cut and public stand on controversial issues. He is the "public" member of the board, the commission, the committee. What "the public" stands for, accordingly, is often a vagueness of policy (called "open-mindedness"), a lack of involvement in public affairs (known as "reasonableness"), and a professional disinterest (known as "tolerance").

All this is indeed far removed from the eighteenth-century idea of the public of public opinion. The idea parallels the economic idea of the magical market. Here is the market composed for freely competing entrepreneurs; there is the public composed of circles of people in discussion. As price is the result of anonymous, equally weighted, bargaining individuals, so public opinion is the result of each man's having thought things out for himself and then contributing his voice to the great chorus. To be sure, some may have more influence on the state of opinion than others, but no one group monopolizes the discussion, or by itself determines the opinions that prevail.

In this classic image, the people are presented with problems. They discuss them. They formulate viewpoints. These viewpoints are organized, and they compete. One viewpoint "wins out." Then the people act on this view, or their representatives are instructed to act it out, and this they promptly do.

Such are the images of democracy which are still used as working justifications of power in America. We must now recognize this description as more a fairy tale than a useful approximation. The issues that now shape man's fate are neither raised nor decided by any public at large. The idea of a society that is at bottom composed of publics is not a matter of fact; it is the proclamation of an ideal, and as well the assertion of a legitimation masquerading as fact.

I cannot here describe the several great forces within American society as well as elsewhere which have been at work in the debilitation of the public. I want only to remind you that publics, like free associations, can be deliberately and suddenly smashed, or they can more slowly wither away. But whether smashed in a week or withered in a generation, the demise of the public must be seen in connection with the rise of centralized organizations, with all their new means of power, including those of the mass media of distraction. These, we now know, often seem to expropriate the rationality and the will of the terrorized or—as the case may be—the voluntarily indifferent society of masses. In the more democratic process of indifference the remnants of such publics as remain may only occasionally be intimidated by fanatics in search of "disloyalty." But regardless of that, they lose their will for decision because they do not possess the instruments for decision; they lose their sense of political belonging because they do not belong; they lose their political will because they see no way to realize it.

The political structure of a modern democratic state requires that such a public as is projected by democratic theorists not only exist but that it be the very forum within which a politics of real issues is enacted.

It requires a civil service that is firmly linked with the world of knowledge and sensibility, and which is composed of skilled men who, in their careers and in their aspirations, are truly independent of any private, which is to say, corporation, interests.

It requires nationally responsible parties which debate openly and clearly the issues which the nation, and indeed the world, now so rigidly confronts.

It requires an intelligentsia, inside as well as outside the universities, who carry on the big discourse of the western world, and whose work is relevant to and influential among parties and movements and publics.

And it certainly requires, as a fact of power, that there be free association standing between familities and smaller communities and publics, on the one hand, and the state, the military, the corporation, on the other. For unless these do exist, there are no vehicles for reasoned opinion, no instruments for the rational exertion of public will.

Such democratic formations are not now ascendant in the power structure of the United States, and accordingly the men of decision are not men selected and formed by careers within such associations and by their performance before such publics. The top of modern American society is increasingly unified, and often seems wilfully coordinated: at the top there has emerged an elite whose power probably exceeds that of any small group of men in world history. The middle levels are often a drifting set of stalmated forces: the middle does not link the bottom with the top. The bottom of this society is politically fragmented, and as a passive fact, increasingly powerless: at the bottom there is emerging a mass soicety.

These developments, I believe, can be correctly understood neither in terms of the liberal nor the Marxian interpretation of politics and history. Both these ways of thought arose as guidelines to reflection about a type of society which does not now exist in the United States. We confront there a new kind of social structure, which embodies elements and tendencies of all modern society, but in which they have assumed a more naked and flamboyant prominence.

That does not mean that we must give up the ideals of these classic political expectations. I believe that both have been concerned with the problem of rationality and of freedom: liberalism, with freedom and rationality as supreme facts about the individual; Marxism, as supreme facts about man's role in the political making of history.

What I have said here, I suppose, may be taken as an attempt to make evident why the ideas of freedom and of rationality now so often seem so ambiguous in the new society of the United States of America.

2 Authority

One of the enduring questions of politics concerns the problem of authority. We observed in the preceding chapter that the exercise of authority suggests the possession of power. *The Encyclopedia of the Social Sciences* states that authority "is a manifestation of power and implies obedience on the part of those subject to it." In modern states, authority generally means legal power. "Legality" here infers the population's willing support of governmental power.

The complexity of the idea of "authority" may also be seen in the multitude of terms employed in attempts to explain it. A representative list of recurrent words in these writings might include "support," "obedience," "coercion," "legitimacy," and "effectiveness." What is phenomenal about the subject of authority is the fact that it has been discussed at length from the time of the ancient Greeks until the present without the slightest indication that it is an exhausted topic in the study of politics. Political theorists have written volumes on the essence of authority in different kinds of political systems, whether totalitarian or democratic, stable or unstable, developed or underdeveloped, and so forth.

Max Weber, a German sociologist who lived around the turn of the century, constructed a framework of analysis from which one could get many insights into the sources of authority. Weber distinguished three types of authority: traditional, institutionalized, and charismatic. The source of traditional authority is custom or belief in an elite of elders or the divine right of kings. The traditions of the society dictate who shall rule. Traditional authority is typical of pre-industrial, preliterate, or primitive societies.

In contrast, institutionalized authority is peculiar to modern industrialized societies and develops when the population gains confidence in the governmental structure. A large and efficient civil service strengthens the governmental and political structure in that such a bureaucracy reinforces the channels of power. Government becomes a routine. For example, when President Kennedy was assassinated, the expectations of the American people were in full accord with the smooth transition of power within the political structure. Some observers outside the United States erroneously predicted a *coup* or major plot.

Weber's third source of authority, which he discusses in our first selection here, is "charisma," defined as the power of a leader bordering on the mystical, which enables him to elicit active support from the people. A charismatic leader may be found most often in a political system undergoing change. Authority founded upon charismatic leadership alone is difficult to maintain for an extended period. We will encounter again the three categories of authority elaborated by Max Weber as we briefly discuss the situations in the United States, the Soviet Union, and politically unstable nations.

AUTHORITY IN THE UNITED STATES

In a stable political system like that of the United States, it is difficult to trace the precise roots of authority. The Constitution, traditions, institutions, and the consensus are but a few of the diverse elements to which theorists attribute authority. Ascertaining the bases of authority in the United States becomes such a problem that some writers speak of authority mainly in terms of "effectiveness." In our second reading, Seymour M. Lipset states: "Effectiveness means actual performance, the extent to which the system satisfies the basic functions of government as most of the population" sees those functions. When the Depression struck during a Republican Administration, the majority of voters saw that party as ineffective in handling the crisis. With a mandate from the people, the Franklin D. Roosevelt Administration exercised unprecedented powers in the search for solutions to economic dislocation. Action, or performance, was uppermost in the public mood during that period.

Another theme of authority, which is more fundamental than Lipset's functional view, is the dedication to legalism. The legacy of English Common Law, reinforced by a long history of respect for the Constitution and for law in general, makes authority and law in the United States almost indistinguishable.

The minds of Americans love to dwell on the accomplishments of the nation, achieved somehow by an unwavering attachment to the Constitution. Inherent in the devotion to that document is the idea of the living or growing Constitution. This area of authority is examined by Jerome Hall in our third reading.

AUTHORITY IN THE SOVIET UNION

The formal governmental structure in the Soviet Union is a subject of much controversy among observers in the West. Why do the Soviet leaders give lip-service to the Constitution of 1936? Why are elections held? Central to the understanding of authority in the Soviet Union is the recognition of the role of the legal façade in that country.

Power in the Soviet Union belongs to the Communist Party. However, the institutions of government, which are parallel at every level with an agency of the Party, serve many functions. The people in the Soviet Union are allowed to participate in the governmental process through such devices as elections, legislative chambers, and people's courts. Admittedly, whatever power these agencies may possess is counteracted by the Party. Nonetheless, there is established an atmosphere of mass participation as a means to win support of the regime from the people. This ostensible inclusion of the people in the political process has a substantial impact upon a population which has never experienced anything but despotism. In these circumstances, the governmental institutions may serve to fulfill Lenin's scheme of having a "transmission belt" by means of which the Party elite keeps in constant communication with the people.

Another source of authority is Marxist-Leninist theory. Soviet leaders look upon this theory as a scientific formula for molding the perfect society. While the masses of the people may not comprehend the full implications of the ideology, they are impressed by scientific advances made by Russia since the Revolution. The fourth reading, by Bauer, Inkeles, and Kluckhohn, points out that progress through science may well be one of the chief props for popular acceptance of the regime. More and more, the Soviet Union has evolved into a society in which technology is the mainstay of the government.

AUTHORITY AND POLITICAL INSTABILITY

Respect for the law is noticeably absent in politically unstable societies. The pattern for political change in such societies involves the instrument of force. In the United States, political leaders may earnestly seek to uphold the pronouncement that this is a society ruled by law, but in many countries there is no such tradition of law. Lipset explains, for example, that the Latin American republics "never developed the symbols and aura of legitimacy." Simon Bolivar, the leader of the Latin American wars for independence, once complained, "Constitutions are but scraps of paper." Recent upheavals in Cuba and the Dominican Republic illustrate the interaction of instability and the nature of power.

Toward the end of 1958, the Batista regime in Cuba collapsed, leaving a power vacuum soon to be filled by Fidel Castro's charismatic leadership. One apparent facet of this political change was the emerging support from the population for a movement striving to become the legitimate authority of Cuba. This rise to power was accompanied by the decline of the existing government's effective control over the population. On the other hand, in the Dominican Republic during April 1965, a civil war resulted in a stalemate between two diverse factions with neither group strong enough to seize power.

In comparing the Cuban and Dominican situations, we need to inquire into the sources of authority available in each country at the time when the established governments aborted. In Cuba, apart from the activities of various revolutionary groups, the major source of authority arose from the enormous charismatic qualities of Fidel Castro. In the Latin American political style of the *caudillo,* or strong leader, Castro was able to speak as the legitimate ruler of Cuba. Moreover, at least until January 1959, Castro had the enthusiastic support of the majority of the Cuban people.

There was no strong leadership in the Dominican Republic when the Reid Cabral government fell. Forces of the left and right battled to a standstill without much prospect that either faction would be capable of assuming power. An apathetic peasantry did not throw its weight to the side of either conflicting group in the capital city of Santo Domingo. Even in the wake of intervention from the United States, politics in the Dominican Republic remain badly fragmented.

The represssive measures of the dictators Batista and Trujillo, the former strong man of the Dominican Republic, inspired reactions from politically active elements of the population, especially young people and intellectuals, to challenge the authority of those regimes. In each case, the loss of control in an unstable society reveals the the fabric of authority and illustrates how dictatorship relies upon the maximum application of power while expecting acquiescence rather than support from the majority of the people.

The Sociology of Charismatic Authority

MAX WEBER

THE GENERAL CHARACTER OF CHARISMA

Bureaucratic and patriarchal structures are antagonistic in many ways, yet they have in common a most important peculiarity: permanence. In this respect they are both institutions of daily routine. Patriarchal power especially is rooted in the provisioning of recurrent and normal needs of the workaday life. Patriarchal authority thus has its original locus in the economy, that is, in those branches of the economy that can be satisfied by means of normal routine. The patriarch is the "natural leader" of the daily routine. And in this respect, the bureaucratic structure is only the counter-image of patriarchalism transposed into rationality. As a permanent structure with a system of rational rules, bureaucracy is fashioned to meet calculable and recurrent needs by means of a normal routine.

The provisioning of all demands that go beyond those of everyday routine has had, in principle, an entirely heterogeneous, namely, a *charismatic,* foundation; the further back we look in history, the more we find this to be the case. This means that the "natural" leaders—in times of psychic, physical, economic, ethical, religious, political distress—have been neither office-

From Max Weber: Essays in Sociology edited and translated by H. H. Gerth and C. Wright Mills. Copyright 1946 by Oxford University Press, Inc. Reprinted by permission.

holders nor incumbents of an "occupation" in the present sense of the word, that is, men who have acquired expert knowledge and who serve for remuneration. The natural leaders in distress have been holders of specific gifts of the body and spirit; and these gifts have been believed to be supernatural, not accessible to everybody. The concept of "charisma" is here used in a completely "value-neutral" sense.

The capacity of the Irish culture hero, Cuchulain, or of the Homeric Achilles for heroic frenzy is a manic seizure, just as is that of the Arabian berserk who bites his shield like a mad dog—biting around until he darts off in raving bloodthirstiness. For a long time it has been maintained that the seizure of the berserk is artificially produced through acute poisoning. In Byzantium, a number of "blond beasts," disposed to such seizures, were kept about, just as war elephants were formerly kept. Shamanist ecstasy is linked to constitutional epilepsy, the possession and the testing of which represents a charismatic qualification. Hence neither is "edifying" to our minds. . . . All of them have practiced their arts and ruled by virtue of this gift (charisma) and, where the idea of God has already been clearly conceived, by virtue of the divine mission lying therein. This holds for doctors and prophets, just as for judges and military leaders, or for leaders of big hunting expeditions.

It is to his credit that Rudolf Sohm brought out the sociological peculiarity of this category of domination-structure for a historically important special case, namely, the historical development of the authority of the early Christian church. Sohm performed this task with logical consistency, and hence, by necessity, he was one-sided from a purely historical point of view. In principle, however, the very same state of affairs recurs universally, although often it is most clearly developed in the field of religion.

In contrast to any kind of bureaucratic organization of offices, the charismatic structure knows nothing of a form or of an ordered procedure of appointment or dismissal. It knows no regulated "career," "advancement," "salary," or regulated and expert training of the holder of charisma or of his aides. It knows no agency of control or appeal, no local bailiwicks or exclusive functional jurisdictions; nor does it embrace permanent institutions like our bureaucratic "departments," which are independent of persons and of purely personal charisma.

Charisma knows only inner determination and inner restraint. The holder of charisma seizes the task that is adequate for him and demands obedience and a following by virtue of his mission. His success determines whether he finds them. His charismatic claim breaks down if his mission is not recognized by those to whom he feels he has been sent. If they recognize him, he is their master—so long as he knows how to maintain recognition through "proving" himself. But he does not derive his "right" from their will, in the manner of an election. Rather, the reverse holds: it is the *duty* of those to whom he addresses his mission to recognize him as their charismatically qualified leader.

In Chinese theory, the emperor's prerogatives are made dependent upon the recognition of the people. But this does not mean recognition of the sovereignty of the people any more than did the prophet's necessity of getting recognition from the believers in the early Christian community. The Chinese theory, rather, characterizes the charismatic nature of the *monarch's position*, which adheres to his *personal* qualification and to his *proved* worth.

Charisma can be, and of course regularly is, qualitatively particularized. This is an internal rather than an external affair, and results in the qualitative barrier of the charisma holder's mission and power. In meaning and in content the mission may be addressed to a group of men who are delimited locally, ethnically, socially, politically, occupationally, or in some other way. If the mission is thus addressed to a limited group of men, as is the rule, it finds its limits within their circle.

In its economic substructure, as in everything else, charismatic domination is the very opposite of bureaucratic domination. If bureaucratic domination depends upon regular income, and hence at least *a potiori* on a money economy and money taxes, charisma lives in, though not off, this world. This has to be properly understood. Frequently charisma quite deliberately shuns the possession of money and of pecuniary income *per se*, as did Saint Francis and many of his like; but this is of course not the rule. Even a pirate genius may exercise a "charismatic" domination, in the value-neutral sense intended here. Charismatic political heroes seek booty and, above all, gold. But charisma, and this is decisive, always rejects as undignified any pecuniary gain that is methodical and rational. In general, charisma rejects all rational economic conduct.

The sharp contrast between charisma and any "patriarchal" structure that rests upon the ordered base of the "household" lies in this rejection of rational economic conduct. In its "pure" form, charisma is never a source of private gain for its holders in the sense of economic exploitation by making of a deal. Nor is it a source of income in the form of pecuniary compensation, and just as little does it involve an orderly taxation for the material requirements of its mission. If the mission is one of peace, individual patrons provide the necessary means for charismatic structures; or those to whom the charisma is addressed provide honorific gifts, donations, or other voluntary contributions. In the case of charismatic warrior heroes, booty represents one of the ends as well as the material means of the mission. "Pure" charisma is contrary to all patriarchal domination (in the sense of the term used here). It is the opposite of all ordered economy. It is the very force that disregards economy. This also holds, indeed precisely, where the charismatic leader is after the acquisition of goods, as is the case with the charismatic warrior hero. Charisma can do this because by its very nature it is not an "institutional" and permanent structure, but rather, where its "pure" type is at work, it is the very opposite of the institutionally permanent.

In order to do justice to their mission, the holders of charisma, the master as well as his disciples and followers, must stand outside the ties of this world, outside of routine occupations, as well as outside the routine obligations of family life. The statutes of the Jesuit order preclude the acceptance of church offices; the members of orders are forbidden to own property or, according to the original rule of St. Francis, the order as such is forbidden to do so. The priest and the knight of an order have to live in celibacy, and

numerous holders of a prophetic or artistic charisma are actually single. All this is indicative of the unavoidable separation from this world of those who partake of charisma. In these respects, the economic conditions of participation in charisma may have an (apparently) antagonistic appearance, depending upon the type of charisma—artistic or religious, for instance—and the way of life flowing from its meaning. Modern charismatic movements of artistic origin represent "independents without gainful employment" (in everyday language, rentiers). Normally such persons are the best qualified to follow a charismatic leader. This is just as logically consistent as was the medieval friar's vow of poverty, which demanded the very opposite.

FOUNDATIONS AND INSTABILITY OF CHARISMATIC AUTHORITY

By its very nature, the existence of charismatic authority is specifically unstable. The holder may forego his charisma; he may feel "forsaken by his God," as Jesus did on the cross; he may prove to his followers that "virtue is gone out of him." It is then that his mission is extinguished, and hope waits and searches for a new holder of charisma. The charismatic holder is deserted by his following, however, (only) because pure charisma does not know any "legitimacy" other than that flowing from personal strength, that is, one which is constantly being proved. The charismatic hero does not deduce his authority from codes and statutes, as is the case with the jurisdiction of office; nor does he deduce his authority from traditional custom or feudal vows of faith, as is the case with patrimonial power.

The charismatic leader gains and

maintains authority solely by proving his strength in life. If he wants to be a prophet, he must perform miracles; if he wants to be a war lord, he must perform heroic deeds. Above all, however, his divine mission must "prove" itself in that those who faithfully surrender to him must fare well. If they do not fare well, he is obviously not the master sent by the gods.

This very serious meaning of genuine charisma evidently stands in radical contrast to the convenient pretensions of present rulers to a "divine right of kings," with its reference to the "inscrutable" will of the Lord "to whom alone the monarch is responsible." The genuinely charismatic ruler is responsible precisely to those whom he rules. He is responsible for but one thing, that he personally and actually be the God-willed master.

During these last decades we have witnessed how the Chinese monarch impeaches himself before all the people because of his sins and insufficiencies if his administration does not succeed in warding off some distress from the governed, whether it is inundations or unsuccessful wars. Thus does a ruler whose power, even in vestiges and theoretically, is genuinely charismatic deport himself. And if even this penitence does not reconcile the deities, the charismatic emperor faces dispossession and death, which often enough is consummated as a propitiatory sacrifice.

Meng-tse's (Mencius') thesis that the people's voice is "God's voice" (according to him the *only* way in which God speaks!) has a very specific meaning: if the people cease to recognize the ruler, it is expressly stated that he simply becomes a private citizen; and if he then wishes to be more, he becomes a usurper deserving of punishment. The state of affairs that corresponds to these phrases, which sound highly revolu-

tionary, recurs under primitive conditions without any such pathos. The charismatic character adheres to almost all primitive authorities with the exception of domestic power in the narrowest sense, and the chieftain is often enough simply deserted if success does not remain faithful to him.

The subjects may extend a more active or passive "recognition" to the personal mission of the charismatic master. His power rests upon this purely factual recognition and springs from faithful devotion. It is devotion to the extraordinary and unheard-of, to what is strange to all rule and tradition and which therefore is viewed as divine. It is a devotion born of distress and enthusiasm.

Genuine charismatic domination therefore knows of no abstract legal codes and statutes and of no "formal" way of adjudication. Its "objective" law emanates concretely from the highly personal experience of heavenly grace and from the god-like strength of the hero. Charismatic domination means a rejection of all ties to any external order in favor of the exclusive glorification of the genuine mentality of the prophet and hero. Hence, its attitude is revolutionary and transvalues everything; it makes a sovereign break with all traditional or rational norms: "It is written, but I say unto you."

The specifically charismatic form of settling disputes is by way of the prophet's revelation, by way of the oracle, or by way of "Solomonic" arbitration by a charismatically qualified sage. This arbitration is determined by means of strictly concrete and individual evaluations, which, however, claim absolute validity. Here lies the proper locus of "Kadi-justice" in the proverbial—not the historical—sense of the phrase. In its actual historical appearance the jurisdiction of the Islamic Kadi, is, of course, bound to sacred tradition and is often a highly formalistic interpretation.

Only where these intellectual tools fail does jurisdiction rise to an unfettered individual act valuing the particular case; but then it does indeed. Genuinely charismatic justice always acts in this manner. In its pure form it is the polar opposite of formal and traditional bonds, and it is just as free in the face of the sanctity of tradition as it is in the face of any rationalist deductions from abstract concepts.

This is not the place to discuss how the reference to the *aegum et bonum* in the Roman administration of justice and the original meaning of English "equity" are related to charismatic justice in general and to the theocratic Kadi-justice of Islamism in particular. Both the *aegum et bonum* and "equity" are partly the products of a strongly rationalized administration of justice and partly the product of abstract conceptions of natural law. In any case the *ex bona fide* contains a reference to the "mores" of business life and thus retains just as little of a genuine irrational justice as does, for instance, the German judge's "free discretion."

Any kind of ordeal as a means of evidence is, of course, a derivative of charismatic justice. But the ordeal displaces the personal authority of the holder of charisma by a mechanism of rules for formally ascertaining the divine will. This falls in the sphere of the "routinization" of charisma, with which we shall deal below.

CHARISMATIC KINGSHIP

In the evolution of political charisma, kingship represents a particularly important case in the historical development of the charismatic legitimization of institutions. The king is everywhere primarily a war lord, and kingship evolves from charismatic heroism.

In the form it displays in the history of civilized peoples, kingship is not the oldest evolutionary form of "political" domination. By "political" domination is meant a power that reaches beyond and which is, in principle, distinct from domestic authority. It is distinct because, in the first place, it is not devoted to leading the peaceful struggle of man with nature; it is, rather, devoted to leading in the violent conflict of one human community with another.

The predecessors of kingship were the holders of all those charismatic powers that guaranteed to remedy extraordinary external and internal distress, or guaranteed the success of extraordinary ventures. The chieftain of early history, the predecessor of kingship, is still a dual figure. On the one hand, he is the patriarchal head of the family or sib, and on the other, he is the charismatic leader of the hunt and war, the sorcerer, and the rainmaker, the medicine man—and thus the priest and the doctor—and finally, the arbiter. Often, yet not always, such charismatic functions are split into as many special holders of charisma. Rather frequently the chieftain of the hunt and of war stands beside the chieftain of peace, who has essentially economic functions. In contrast to the latter, the chieftain of war acquires his charisma by proving his heroism to a voluntary following in successful raids leading to victory and booty. Even the royal Assyrian inscriptions enumerate booties of the hunt and cedars from Lebanon—dragged along for building purposes—alongside figures on the slain enemies and the size of the walls of conquered cities, which are covered with skins peeled off the enemies.

The charismatic position (among

primitives) is thus acquired without regard to position in the sibs or domestic communities and without any rules whatsoever. This dualism of charisma and everyday routine is very frequently found among the American Indians, for instance, among the Confederacy of the Iroquois, as well as in Africa and elsewhere.

Where war and the big game hunt are absent, the charismatic chieftain— the "war lord" as we wish to call him, in contrast to the chieftain of peace— is absent as well. In peacetime, especially if elemental calamaties, particularly drought and diseases, are frequent, a charismatic sorcerer may have an essentially similar power in his hands. He is a priestly lord. The charisma of the war lord may or may not be unstable in nature, according to whether or not he proves himself and whether or not there is any need for a war lord. He becomes a permanent figure when warfare becomes a chronic state of affairs. It is a mere terminological question whether one wishes to let kingship, and with it the state, begin only when strangers are affiliated with and integrated into the community as sub-

jects. For our purposes it will be expedient to continue delimiting the term "state" far more narrowly.

The existence of the war lord as a regular figure certainly does not depend upon a tribal rule over subjects of other tribes or upon individual slaves. His existence depends solely upon a chronic state of war and upon a comprehensive organization set for warfare. On the other hand, the development of kingship into a regular royal administration does emerge only at the stage when a following of royal professional warriors rules over the working or paying masses; at least, that is often the case. The forceful subjection of strange tribes, however, is not an absolutely indispensable link in this development. Internal class stratification may bring about the very same social differentiation: the charismatic following of warriors develops into a ruling caste. But in every case, princely power and those groups having interests vested in it—that is, the war lord's following— strive for legitimacy as soon as the rule has become stable. They crave for a characteristic which would define the charismatically qualified ruler.

Legitimacy and Effectiveness

SEYMOUR MARTIN LIPSET

The stability of any given democracy depends not only on economic development but also upon the effectiveness

From *Political Man* by Seymour Martin Lipset. Copyright © 1960 by Seymour Martin Lipset. Reprinted by permission of the author and Doubleday & Company, Inc.

and the legitimacy of its political system. Effectiveness means actual performance, the extent to which the system satisfies the basic functions of government as most of the population and such powerful groups within it as big business or the armed forces see them.

Legitimacy involves the capacity of the system to engender and maintain the belief that the existing political institutions are the most appropriate ones for the society. The extent to which contemporary democratic political systems are legitimate depends in large measure upon the ways in which the key issues which have historically divided the society have been resolved.

While effectiveness is primarily instrumental, legitimacy is evaluative. Groups regard a political system as legitimate or illegitimate according to the way in which its values fit with theirs. Important segments of the German Army, civil service, and aristocratic classes rejected the Weimar Republic, not because it was ineffective, but because its symbolism and basic values negated their own. Legitimacy, in and of itself, may be associated with many forms of political organization, including oppressive ones. Feudal societies, before the advent of industrialism, undoubtedly enjoyed the basic loyalty of most of their members. Crises of legitimacy are primarily a recent historical phenomenon, following the rise of sharp cleavages among groups which are able, because of mass communication, to organize around different values than those previously considered to be the only acceptable ones.

A crisis of legitimacy is a crisis of change. Therefore, its roots must be sought in the character of change in modern society. Crises of legitimacy occur during a transition to a new social structure, if (1) the *status* of major conservative institutions is threatened during the period of structural change; (2) all the major groups in the society do not have access to the political system in the transitional period, or at least as soon as they develop political demands. After a new social structure is established, if the new

system is unable to sustain the expectations of major groups (on the grounds of "effectiveness") for a long enough period to develop legitimacy upon the new basis, a new crisis may develop.

Tocqueville gives a graphic description of the first general type of loss of legitimacy, referring mainly to countries which moved from aristocratic monarchies to democratic republics: "...epochs sometimes occur in the life of a nation when the old customs of a people are changed, public morality is destroyed, religious belief shaken, and the spell of tradition broken..." The citizens then have "neither the instinctive patriotism of a monarchy nor the reflecting patriotism of a republic;... they have stopped between the two in the midst of confusion and distress."[1]

If, however, the status of major conservative groups and symbols is not threatened during this transitional period, even though they lose most of their power, democracy seems to be much more secure. And thus we have the absurd fact that ten out of the twelve stable European and English-speaking democracies are monarchies. Great Britain, Sweden, Norway, Denmark, the Netherlands, Belgium, Luxembourg, Australia, Canada, and New Zealand are kingdoms, or dominions of a monarch, while the only republics which meet the conditions of stable democratic procedures are the United States and Switzerland, plus Uruguay in Latin America.

The preservation of the monarchy has apparently retained for these nations the loyalty of the aristocratic, traditionalist, and clerical sectors of the population which resented increased democratization and equali-

---

[1] Alexis de Tocqueville, *Democracy in America* (New York: Alfred A. Knopf, Vintage ed., 1945), I, 251–52.

tarianism. And by accepting the lower strata and not resisting to the point where revolution might be necessary, the conservative orders won or retained the loyalty of the new "citizens." In countries where monarchy was overthrown by revolution, and orderly succession was broken, forces aligned with the throne have sometimes continued to refuse legitimacy to republican successors down to the fifth generation or more.

The one constitutional monarchy which became a fascist dictatorship, Italy, was, like the French Republic, considered illegitimate by major groups in the society. The House of Savoy alienated the Catholics by destroying the temporal power of the Popes, and was also not a legitimate successor in the old Kingdom of the Two Sicilies. Catholics were, in fact, forbidden by the church to participate in Italian politics until almost World War I, and the church finally rescinded its position only because of its fear of the Socialists. French Catholics took a similar attitude to the Third Republic during the same period. Both the Italian and French democracies have had to operate for much of their histories without loyal support from important groups in their societies, on both the left and the right. Thus one main source of legitimacy lies in the continuity of important traditional integrative institutions during a transitional period in which new institutions are emerging.

The second general type of loss of legitimacy is related to the ways in which different societies handle the "entry into politics" crisis—the decision as to when new social groups shall obtain access to the political process. In the nineteenth century these new groups were primarily industrial workers; in the twentieth, colonial elites and peasant peoples. Whenever new

groups become politically active (*e.g.*, when the workers first seek access to economic and political power through economic organization and the suffrage, when the *bourgeoisie* demand access to and participation in government, when colonial elites insist on control over their own system), easy access to the *legitimate* political institutions tends to win the loyalty of the new groups to the system, and they in turn can permit the old dominating strata to maintain their own status. In nations like Germany where access was denied for prolonged periods, first to the *bourgeoisie* and later to the workers, and where force was used to restrict access, the lower strata were alienated from the system and adopted extremist ideologies which, in turn, kept the more established groups from accepting the workers' political movement as a legitimate alternative.

Political systems which deny new strata access to power except by revolution also inhibit the growth of legitimacy by introducing millennial hopes into the political arena. Groups which have to push their way into the body politic by force are apt to overexaggerate the possibilities which political participation affords. Consequently, democratic regimes born under such stress not only face the difficulty of being regarded as illegitimate by groups loyal to the *ancien régime* but may also be rejected by those whose millennial hopes are not fulfilled by the change. France, where right-wing clericalists have viewed the Republic as illegitimate and sections of the lower strata have found their expectations far from satisfied, is an example. And today many of the newly independent nations of Asia and Africa face the thorny problem of winning the loyalties of the masses to democratic states which can do little to meet the utopian objectives set by nationalist movements during the period of colonialism and the transitional struggle to independence.

In general, even when the political system is reasonably effective, if at any time the status of major conservative groups is threatened, or if access to politics is denied to emerging groups at crucial periods, the system's legitimacy will remain in question. On the other hand, a breakdown of effectiveness, repeatedly or for a long period, will endanger even a legitimate system's stability.

A major test of legitimacy is the extent to which given nations have developed a common "secular political culture," mainly national rituals and holidays. The United States has developed a common homogeneous culture in the veneration accorded the Founding Fathers, Abraham Lincoln, Theodore Roosevelt, and their principles. These common elements, to which all American politicians appeal, are not present in all democratic societies. In some European countries, the left and the right have a different set of symbols and different historical heroes. France offers the clearest example of such a nation. Here battles involving the use of different symbols which started in 1789 are, as Herbert Luethy points out, "still in progress, and the issue is still open; every one of these dates [of major political controversy] still divides left and right, clerical and anti-clerical, progressive and reactionary, in all their historically determined constellations."[2]

. . .

The political experiences of different countries in the early 1930s illustrate

the effect of other combinations. In the late 1920s, neither the German nor the Austrian republic was held legitimate by large and powerful segments of its population. Nevertheless, both remained reasonably effective. . . . When the effectiveness of various governments broke down in the 1930s, those societies which were high on the scale of legitimacy remained democratic, while such countries as Germany, Austria, and Spain lost their freedom, and France narrowly escaped a similar fate. . . . The military defeat of 1940 underlined French democracy's low position on the scale of legitimacy. It was the sole defeated democracy which furnished large-scale support for a Quisling regime.

. . . From a short-range point of view, a highly effective but illegitimate system, such as a well-governed colony, is more unstable than regimes which are relatively low in effectiveness and high in legitimacy. The social stability of a nation like Thailand, despite its periodic *coups d'état,* stands out in sharp contrast to the situation in neighboring former colonial nations. On the other hand, prolonged effectiveness over a number of generations may give legitimacy to a political system. In the modern world, such effectiveness means primarily constant economic development. Those nations which have adapted most successfully to the requirements of an industrial system have the fewest internal political strains, and have either preserved their traditional legitimacy or developed strong new symbols.

The social and economic structure which Latin America inherited from the Iberian peninsula prevented it from following the lead of the former English colonies, and its republics never developed the symbols and aura of legitimacy. In large measure, the sur-

---

2 Herbert Luethy, *The State of France* (London: Secker and Warburg, 1955), p. 29.

vival of the new political democracies of Asia and Africa will depend on their ability to meet the needs of their populations over a prolonged period, which will probably mean their ability to cope with industrialization.

Authority in Its American Phase: Its Originality, and Some Speculations

JEROME HALL

When Americans first learned through their studies of history and philosophy how real the limitation of authority is in every case, they conceived the further idea of setting up in a written constitution a system of limited powers that would make quite sure of the new authority for their union as a free people. The division of the powers of government would be the Americans' own special guarantee of personal liberty. Besides choosing their own government from time to time in elections, besides fostering a good education in principles, they hoped, by their deliberate artifice of distributing powers, to make some advance upon the melancholy history of human authority and hold forth a fresh hope to mankind with their great experiment in "free government."

But there is far more merit in the early American experiment than this mere device of government. A more careful examination of the Americans' own thinking about authority reveals a richer and more balanced view of it than has long been traditional in the subsequent American ethos. They actually started a theory of authority which may be more useful to us now than has yet been realized.

We should recall some well-known phrases of the debates in the Convention and the *Federalist*. "All authority is derived from the people." *From* the people, but where is it lodged? First, with honor and respect, in the Constitution itself, the fundamental law organizing the government. Then in the government: "The express authority of the people alone could give due validity of the government."[1] Through the Constitution the authority of the United States is distributed to the several parts of the federal government. Furthermore, in cases of conflicts of authority, a recourse to the people, the source of authority, was anticipated: "As the people are the only legitimate foundation of power, and it is from them that the Constitutional character is derived ...to recur to the same original authority...wherever any one of the departments may commit encroachments on the chartered authorities of the others..."[2] Thus constitutional amendments needed to be ratified by

Reprinted from Jerome Hall in *Authority*, ed. Carl J. Friedrich for the American Society of Political and Legal Philosophy (New York: Atherton Press, 1958), pp. 20–27, by permission of the author.

[1] James Madison, *The Federalist*, XLIII.
[2] *The Federalist*, XLIX.

the people through their states or through special conventions. The obvious features of the early American experiment are, then, that all authority is derived from the people and that it is delegated and distributed in accordance with the law which they have previously authorized in the manner prescribed.

The design of the Constitution of the United States was being drawn up in the light of experience with the previously established constitutions of the states. John Adams had been, for instance, the "principal engineer" of the Constitution of Massachusetts which had been adopted in June 1780 while he was absent in France.

Adams felt obliged in 1786 to devote some time to criticisms by political thinkers of France—Turgot, the Duc de La Rochefoucauld, Condorcet, and others. Turgot had written an open letter to Price in London, who was favorable to the American type of constitution, and he deplored the "imitation of the Constitution of Great Britain."[3] To this Adams replied in his book, *A Defence of the Constitutions of Government of the United States of America...*, published in 1787 at the time of the drafting of the federal Constitution.

Why copy the English system of division of powers, the critics asked, when America was a distinct nation with an individual life of its own conditioned by the many different factors which Montesquieu had taught men to take account of in their political arrangements and lawmaking? The American nation was not one in which the traditional class system of kings and lords and commoners was repeated. It was

---

[3] Quoted from the introductory statement by George A. Peek, Jr., in *The Political Writings of John Adams*, pp. 105–6.

one nation, and why not conceive of it with power indivisible instead of divided powers which were only necessary where there were already established and traditional parties of interest? Why could it not be sovereign people functioning as a democracy? Why not unified central government without the oft-demonstrated fatal weakness of the federal form?

Adams and his fellow statesmen were taking a distinctively American "line" and were more or less conscious of it. They knew that they had an alternative between the British and the French conceptions of government. But their alternative theory had to be worked out through laborious argument and debate which on that occasion furnished as good an example of practical philosophy as there ever had been in western history.

The spirit rather than the letter of the British constitution persisted in the American plan of government. That spirit had sounded forth in the triumphant words of John Wildman in the Putney Army Debates of 1647: "Authority hath been broken into pieces." The Puritans and others meant to keep it so, and the British-Americans were like-minded. The detested memory of the government of a single divine-right authority lived long in their traditions, and their lawyers were well schooled in the history of the English revolution and the formation of its constitutional order. The study of that constitution made by Montesquieu in Book XI of the *Spirit of the Laws* was an interpretation of morale and spirit and not simply an account of an artifice of politics to deal with class divisions. The Americans were particularly in sympathy with the English tradition, that while authority derives from God ultimately, it passes not to a king but through the people whence it is delegated to serve them in performing certain appointed functions, legislative, executive, and judicial.

The objection which troubled Adams most in the criticisms of the American Constitution was one which derived from a conjunction of the traditional connotation of sovereignty with the national idea. Turgot, as Adams understood, was for collecting all authority "into one centre, the nation." But what can this mean "when the centre is to be the nation?" All it says is, "the nation will be the authority, and the authority the nation." But why should Adams cavil at that truism...are not the people "sovereign"? Yes, Adams concedes, "our people are undoubtedly sovereign," the meaning of which in the context might be more plainly seen if the order were "undoubtedly our people are sovereign," that is, if one insists on talking about sovereignty.[4] But Adams found it "difficult to comprehend" such a proposition as Turgot's that simply identified "the authority" with "the nation." He went on to make his own point that any "collection" of authority (no matter where it be placed, in a center or distributed) must come from the voluntary agreement of individuals "to form themselves into a nation, people, community, or body politic, and to be governed."[5] Thus the authority must be conceived to be a constituted thing, set up for specific purposes of government. It· is a resultant of a nation's will—the substantive result, to put it differently, of an action: "We the people authorise..."

Adams was trying to avoid a simple identification of the authority of the people with the sovereignty of the people. One can declare that all authority derives from the people and still not be committed to the alien doctrine that the people themselves act as a sovereign, exercising authority as one body with undivided power, performing all the functions of government. The reason for saying "alien" is that the smell of absoluteness clung to the notion of sovereignty which had been defined by Bodin, Grotius, and many others in that line, as the power to make laws "without the consent of those governed," independently of anybody on earth, either within or without the state, that is, in reality, unlimited power. To substitute the nation for a personal sovereign is not to change the meaning of such sovereign authority. Moreover, if the authority of the people is thought of as always inherent in the whole body politic, then the very significance of the original act of constituting an authority and delegating it is lost. All authority must be determinate and vested in a particular body of officers who are to perform certain duties of government and who are responsible to the nation whence they derive their power and authority. It is possible to think of such responsible government with limited powers without having recourse to the concept of sovereignty which has quite different connotations and implications.

In the days of constitution-making a distinction between authority and sovereignty was scarcely made. During the Constitutional Convention various men versed in politics and philosophy insisted on talking about sovereignty, which seems often to have confused the discussion rather than advanced matters. The resurrection of the sovereignty idea was inevitable when those who were jealous of the powers of the separate states sought to bolster their

---

4 *The Political Writings of John Adams,* pp. 123–24.

5 *The Political Writings of John Adams,* p. 124.

position with the claim to the independent sovereignty of the states. The skill with which Madison and others firmly but diplomatically worked around these diversions to the formation of a genuine union of the people of the United States while retaining a proper authority for the states is one of the exciting pieces not only of political history but of philosophical dialogue in actual affairs. But, in not confronting at that time the difference between authority as they were working with it and sovereignty, the founding fathers left it for the crisis of civil war, and even then no decision was made as to whether Americans thinking about government should develop and apply the concept of authority with which they had begun or should continue to cling to the notion of sovereignty whose "historic conception" was in a Europe of an earlier absolutist phase before freedom and democracy had much meaning.

Nevertheless it is my opinion that there was a silent philosophical "declaration of independence" behind the discussions of the formation of the union of the American states, in the form of a break with the European tradition of sovereignty. Furthermore, guided by their notion of authority, these early statesmen accomplished something which they would have been hopelessly prevented from doing if they had thought only in terms of sovereignty with its special historic connotation. "It is obviously impracticable," wrote Washington as President of the Federal Convention transmitting the new Constitution to the Congress of the United States, "in the federal government of these states, to secure all rights of independent sovereignty to each, and to provide for the safety of all." It was obviously impracticable, too, in the mid-nineteenth century, to survive and endure as a nation if the

states were to resume the old claim to independent sovereignty. It will be obviously impracticable in the twentieth century, if the statesmen or delegates of the United States continue to think in archaic terms of the sovereignty of the United States coexisting with similar sovereignty of every other member of the United Nations. It seems that whatever constructive advance has been made in freedom and civilization within the past two centuries has come about through avoiding the notion of sovereignty, not by challenging it, but by quietly operating with the more useful concept of authority.

It is the proper business of philosophy, however, to challenge, not to be politic, to expose the issues, and to propose a theory of the working principles of the system honored in practice.

The people, according to the early American formula, are the "source of authority." Do they themselves not have as a people that which they can delegate to certain specific bodies of the government? Yes and no. Of course the authority is theirs that issues from them to the agents who are to exercise it according to the law. But only when it is actually issued and effective is it authority; what it is before that actual "emanation" is not properly called "authority." The nation or the people are the "source." The metaphor is significant: a source is like a spring running down a hillside, taking its courses according to the lay of the land. There is power in it, but the power is delivered only through the particular sluices into which it is channeled for purposes of doing work. Authority should thus always be thought of as power vested in a *determinate* agency, either in the law or in the various bodies that perform the functions of government. The people or nation are the great indeterminate reservoir of all the power that is so put to work.

Another image can be used which may wean the philosophic mind from its habit of thinking along the lines of the older notion of sovereignty. The pre-Socratic philosopher Anaximander followed upon Thales who had proposed that the one Being which manifests itself in all the variety of forms of observable reality was water, which was, to speak later language, the substance of things. Anaximander offered another idea—Being is the Boundless, the Interdeterminate, and it is actually observable only in the strife of opposition of the particular, determinate beings whose doings make up the scene of the world. There is a tendency for one part of determinate Being to push the others out of existence, but nature never quite allows any such extreme and, drawing upon the boundless, maintains a balance. That norm of equilibrium among the particulars is justice. Hence our analogy is as follows: the people from whom all power is derived are a boundless and indeterminate source of it, the bodies that actually have and use certain powers are possessed of a determinate and limited authority, and each of these bodies is held in restraint essentially by the fact that the people always have powers in reserve to bestow on whatever other determinate body can serve best the cause of justice and preserve the social order.

The cautious wisdom of the Tenth Amendment should be remembered here: "The powers not delegated to the United States by the Constitution, nor prohibited by it to the states, are reserved to the states respectively, or to the people." On one hand, this is a restraint upon unwarranted federal expansion of powers exercised beyond those delegated. On the other hand,

"to the people" opens a vision of resources in the people still indeterminate —not specified in any manner in the Constitution, uncommitted, and able to be called into play in the future as the occasion warrants.

Acts to determine authority are required throughout the life and history of the nation. The Constitution provides for a redetermination of the fundamental law through the procedure of amendment, which involves a reference to the people and a requirement of substantial majority ratifying it. Within the activities of government there is redetermination, at frequent and stated intervals, of those especially who shall exercise executive and legislative power. The determinate authority, whether of the law or of the offices of government, is thus only relatively so—one can never be sure in important vital issues which one or whether any of our institutions "has authority." A redetermination of where the authority of the people lies and who is properly acting or speaking in their name is always likely to become a problem of the day. What this means is that "the people" is not merely a substitution for the "sovereign" of the older European tradition, and further that sovereignty in a democratic society is a legendary survival. The sovereignty of the states is an ancient myth resurrected for other than either legal or peace-making reasons. The doctrine "all authority derives from the people" carries with it the consequence, then, that the original authority is indeterminate, not absolutely fixed on anything, and that it is necessary in every generation, or whenever serious issues arise, to redetermine and redefine what the relevant authority is and in which body it is vested. Authority never settles anything really important, because when matters are very important, we have to settle the authority itself which is to function in the case.

Authority in its American phase, so viewed, abolishes not only divinely authorized royal lineage and perpetual rule but also any absolutely fixed rights and powers of the government. Constitutional, democratic authority requires that the working of such a flexible system of government with shifting of the order of authority within the system shall be carried on by due process of law and not arbitrarily or recklessly. Such a system calls for an incalculable amount of labor on the part of those engaged in the work of the statesman, and others in the work of the education of the nation. For in the end, whatever form authority may take depends upon the kind of knowledge that is the fruit of free discussion and upon the patience and good will that are necessary both to the holding of public discussions, in meetings or in the press or in conventions, and to seeing the decisions through. The nation is always in the making, and so is liberty, so is authority.

The Soviet System

RAYMOND A. BAUER / ALEX INKELES /
CLYDE KLUCKHOHN

1. Ideology plays a distinctive role in Soviet society. As an instrument of policy, it is carefully manipulated by the leaders to implement their program both at home and abroad. At the same time, it importantly influences the thinking and behavior of the leaders. This ideology cannot, of course, be simply read out of a book. Rather, it is an amalgam of formal and openly expressed principles, informal and covertly held ideas which are nevertheless consciously shared by the elite, principles of action which are merely implicit and often not consciously formulated by the leadership, and lessons learned from experience in the hard school of Soviet politics. Correct interpretation of Soviet behavior, adequate assessment of their intentions, or accurate prediction of their probable behavior cannot be made without weighing the role of ideological factors together with "objective conditions" as an influence on the actions of the leaders.

2. The long-range goals of Soviet policy are importantly influenced by ideological considerations, and appear to be generally directed toward maintaining and substantially strengthening the present structure of Soviet society and toward creating a world predominantly, if not wholly, Communist under Soviet leadership or hegemony. Current policy is, of course, always considerably influenced or determined by the actions of the United States and other nations involved in the total international scene and by practical considerations arising from the resultant balance of forces. In addition, the regime's long-range policy

Reprinted by permission of the publishers from Raymond A. Bauer, Alex Inkeles, Clyde Kluckhohn, *How the Soviet System Works*, Cambridge, Mass.: Harvard University Press, Copyright, 1956, by the President and Fellows of Harvard College.

appears subject to the important reservation that every precaution should be taken to avoid immediate and major risks to the security of the home base. Thus, ultimately, the domestic requirements of the system set an absolute limit on the degree of risk undertaken in foreign affairs. Nevertheless, many of the difficulties on the domestic front stem from the regime's ambitious foreign policy goals and the consequent commitments to offensive and defensive preparedness, which strain the resources of the system to the utmost.

3. While the long-range goals of the leadership are highly stable, there have been, from a shorter-term point of view, enough sudden alternations in both domestic and foreign policy, both between rigidity and flexibility and between two drastically contrasting courses of policy and action, to justify naming 'cyclical behavior" one of the most distinctive operating characteristics of the Soviet system. This adds an important element of insecurity to the life situations of both the elite and the rank and file, which the regime may exploit to its advantage, but which also make it more difficult for the Soviet citizen to regard the system with equanimity.

4. In large measure, the internal problems of the regime stem from the leaders' persistent tendency to overcommit the system's resources. The system involves, in effect, permanent rationing and perpetual mobilization. Goals are invariably set too close to the theoretical capacity of the available resources in the effort to stimulate each unit to maximum output. Furthermore, effective expenditures of energy are usually characterized by mass assault on a single objective or a relatively narrow range of objectives, while other considerations are ignored until their sheer neglect causes sufficient problems

so that they, in turn, rise to a high position on the scale of priorities and become the focus of mass assault. As a result, despite the extensive machinery of allocation, there are always localized scarcities of resources, resulting in hoarding and inevitable costs in the form of malcoördination of effort. Overcontrol and overcentralization are therefore chronic features of the system.

5. Both because of their addition to rational planning and because of their conviction that "everyone who is not completely for us is against us," the ruling elite have made tremendous efforts to stamp out growing centers of independent power and communication. Their success, however, is not complete, particularly with regard to the military, who retain continuing capabilities for independent action and are possessed of notably increased relative power and prestige.

6. The needs of the citizen are relatively low in the priority scheme of the leaders. Nevertheless, the individual is recognized as the most flexible resource in the system. The regime is therefore necessarily concerned with the morale of the population—not as an objective in itself but as an unavoidable prerequisite to effective economic production and military preparedness. The regime's objective is to extract from the citizen a maximum of effort with a minimum of reward. The purge and the terror are the standard instruments for insuring unhesitating obedience to central command. But to maximize incentive the regime also relies heavily on sharply differentiated material and social rewards. Further, it may periodically relax the pressure and make a show of concern for popular welfare when the results of increased pressure appear to have passed the point of diminishing returns.

7. Certain features of Soviet society

win strong, widespread support and approval. These are notably the welfare-state aspects of the system, such as the health services, government support of the arts, and public educational facilities. In addition, the regime is credited with major achievements in the technological development of the country, in which Soviet citizens take obvious pride. The armed might and international prominence of the regime are recognized and held somewhat in awe. The depth of loyalty to "the motherland" is an outstanding sentiment in all classes of the population, irrespective of religion, political attitudes, and personality structure. This is coupled with a genuine fear of foreign aggression. These sentiments are strongest in the heartland of Great Russia, but they prevail generally.

8. Our data show that ignorance and distorted views of the outside world are deeper and more widespread—even among the intelligentsia—than heretofore had been realized by most students of the USSR. It is almost impossible to exaggerate the ignorance of the outside world prevalent among Soviet citizens. And, while feelings toward the American people and toward certain American achievements have distinctly positive elements, there is a general distrust of American intentions and a fear of "capitalist aggression." Most attitudes toward the West change after emigration, but not in a uniformly favorable direction.

9. The general features of Soviet life and the Soviet system that are most intensely resented are the low standard of living, the excessive pace of everyday life, the invasion of personal privacy, and the "terror," i.e., the threat of arbitrary political repression. We found little concern with "civil liberties" per se, and little pressure toward a democratic form of government. The specific institution most resented was the collective farm, which all groups, virtually without distinction and nearly unanimously, want eliminated. There was strikingly little complaint about the factory system other than dislike of harsh labor-discipline laws, which now are no longer being stringently enforced.

10. Hostility is directed mainly toward the regime—the actual people in power—rather than toward the idea of a welfare state with high concentration of economic and social as well as political power in the hands of a few men. There is a strong tendency for the rank-and-file citizen to establish a "we-they" dichotomy, in which "they" are the people, regardless of rank, who are closely identified with the regime. In general, but not exclusively, this distinction tends to correspond to that between Party and non-Party personnel, although some members of the Party are accepted in the "we" category. In any event, wherever the line is drawn, "we" see "them" as having no regard for "our" feelings, depriving "us" of just rewards, terrorizing "us" without cause, and generally failing to show proper trust and respect for the citizenry. All classes appear to channel much of their hostility and aggression in this way. Indeed, many of the routine daily frustrations of life are charged to the regime because the immediate source of those frustrations is defined as a representative of "them."

11. The conflict over straightforward matters of policy, which creates a gulf between the leaders and the rank and file, is agravated by the important psychological differences which separate the elite and the masses. The masses remain rather close to the traditional picture of Russian character. They are warm-hearted, impulsive, given to mood swings, and contradictory in be-

havior. The goal of the elite is the rather puritanical "new Soviet man": disciplined, working steadily and consistently, subordinating personal conduct and motivation to the requirements of Party discipline. It appears that the Soviet leaders have succeeded to a certain degree in devevloping among the elite a considerable proportion of people of an externally disciplined and driving character, and their patterns of behavior add to the sense of alienation felt by many of the rank and file toward the leaders.

12. Despite the high level of dissatisfaction and discontent, there seems to be only a relatively small amount of disaffection and disloyalty. The life histories of our respondents left little doubt of the extent to which most of them were unhappy about many aspects of their life situations. But these same life histories indicated that most of the citizens of the USSR feel helpless in the face of the power of the state and desire only to live peacefully. There is scant evidence for the view that more than a very tiny part of the population would, except under conditions of extreme crisis, take appreciable risks to sabotage the regime or to aid Western democracy.

13. Certain traumatic experiences, such as being arrested, had less effect than we had anticipated. Being arrested has virtually no impact on a person's general social and political attitudes and values. The individual does not generalize his experience to the point of revising his judgment concerning the kind of society in which he lives, or would want to live. Arrest, however, does increase the *intensity* of his hostility *to the regime.* Furthermore, arrest—whether his own, or that of a family member—makes him anxious about his own future, and thereby increases the probability of his leaving the Soviet

Union voluntarily if the opportunity arises.

14. Degree of dissatisfaction with, or even disaffection from, the system does not necessarily detract from the energy with which a person does the job assigned to him by "the system." The disaffected person often does his job well and may work with a little extra energy, either because he feels he has to prove himself or because he finds comfort in his work. Thus, the fact that the Soviet system tends to produce dissatisfaction in its citizens does not in itself mean that it gets less effective work from them. This applies, however, mainly in the professional and white-collar classes. In the working class and the peasantry there appears to be a fairly direct relation between the individual's level of satisfaction and the quality and quantity of his work.

15. The Soviet elite, a markedly privileged social class, inevitably has a vested interest in maintaining and perpetuating the system. This tendency, however, varies with different individuals and under various combinations of circumstances and is partly counterbalanced by one or more of the following factors: (*a*) the conviction that the ruling clique is acting contrary to the interests of the nation-state; (*b*) the conviction that the regime has betrayed the humane goals of Marxism; and (*c*) personal insecurity. On the other hand, even when these factors are operative, the conflicted members of the elite often fall into line of their own choice because of deep-rooted attitudes, such as suspicion of foreigners and their motives; belief that, after all, national patriotism and loyalty to the regime are inextricably linked; acceptance of Communist ideology; a conspiratorial mentality; and the habit of disciplined obedience.

16. A Soviet citizen's social class and

his occupation largely determine both his opportunities for advancement and his attitudes toward the Soviet system, as well as his general social and political values. The individual's social position is more important than such factors as nationality or arrest history in affecting his hostility toward, passive acceptance of, or positive identification with the regime. Members of the intelligentsia, being the more favored beneficiaries of the system, understandably show substantial satisfaction with the conditions of daily life and with opportunities for development and advancement. They are generally the persons most accepting of the broad outlines of Soviet society, with the exception of its political patterns which hit them especially hard owing to the greater surveillance to which the regime subjects them and their work. At the other pole, the peasant emerges as the "angry man" of the system, strongly rejecting most of its features, convinced of his exploitation, resentful of his deprivation of goods and opportunities, and outraged by the loss of his autonomy. The workers shared many attitudes and life experiences with the peasants, thus forming a broad manual group which can regularly be distinguished from the nonmanual. The workers are, on the whole, less intense and resentful than the peasants and generally accept the sociopolitical structure of the Soviet factory as natural and proper.

17. It has been asserted that the Soviet youth, although showing a strong early allegiance to the regime, have a high probability of becoming disaffected as they mature and experience the full dimensions of the regime. Our materials indicate that there is a period of crisis in the relation of youth to the regime as the individual reaches maturity, but that only a small minority actually turn against the system because of disillusionment. In most instances, they are able to reconcile their conflicts. Furthermore, the younger generation is coming to accept as natural many aspects of Soviet life and the Soviet system against which the older generation rebelled. The youth is relatively unlikely to turn against the regime, in spite of experiences that Americans would think would lead to disaffection.

18. The individual's nationality appears to play a lesser role in determining his attitudes toward the regime than has often been supposed. Indeed, people in the same occupation or social group hold essentially the same attitudes and values regardless of nationality, and those in the national minorities feel the same resentments toward the regime and experience the same dissatisfactions with the system as do all other citizens of the USSR. Generally, therefore, nationality is only a secondary, contributing cause for disaffection. There is a distinctive nationality feeling in sections of many national groups, however, and this national identification is supported by a sense of oppression and resentment of Great Russians.

19. Certain scholars had advanced the plausible and provocative thesis that political domination within the Soviet system was threatened by a "managerial revolution." Our data, however, indicate that technical and managerial personnel, having a stake in the existing system, have developed an interest in maintaining it in predominantly its present form. They are concerned mainly with reducing interference and extreme pressure from the center and in improving the system and making it work more smoothly. They feel that they can obtain the rewards they deserve without the risks involved in ownership.

20. The Project findings yield strong evidence as to the importance of infor-

mal mechanisms in the operation of a society that, on the surface, appears and pretends to be highly centralized, controlled, and rationalized. The rank-and-file citizen learns to apply complicated techniques of accommodation and evasion in order to carry on his day-to-day affairs and to maintain himself in reasonably successful, or at least untroubled, adaptation to the regime. In this he is often aided by others—doctors, for example—who serve as buffers between him and the pressures of the system. In addition, "localism" or "familism," the tendency for local loyalties and informal mutual protective associations to develop on the local level as defense against the pressures of the center, plays a major role. In fact, Soviet society works as well as it does only because of the existence of a series of informal, extralegal practices which are tolerated, up to a point, by the regime, even though officially disapproved. Nevertheless, these informal adjustive mechanisms create problems for the leadership as well as facilitating the functioning of the society in significant respects.

21. The life histories of our respondents indicate that the stability of the Soviet system involves a nice balance between the powers of coercion and the adjustive habits of the Soviet citizenry. The stability of the system and of the citizen's loyalty depend to a high degree on the citizen's own belief in the stability of that system and on his having no alternative but to adjust to the system. For the average citizen, political loyalty to the regime is a strange compound of apathy, passive acceptance, and cynicism. Among the elite groups, some individuals are conforming loyalists to the system; some, the "careerists," are really loyal only to themselves; more than a few are loyal to Communist "ideals." Our pessimistic finding is that the new regime can gain much more solid popular support if it supplies more consumer goods and better housing, eases up on the terror, makes some concessions to the peasants, and relieves somewhat the frantic pace at which all the population has been driven. Such a change of policy would not only alleviate many of the day-to-day grievances of the citizen, but also change his basic image of the regime as a harsh and depriving force. These may be precisely the lines along which the current regime is proceeding.

3   Dictatorship

In Chapter 1 we referred to Aristotle's *Politics* in which he distinguished between "right" and "perverted" constitutions. Corresponding to "perverted" constitutions are three perversions of government typical of his era: tyranny, oligarchy, and "democracy." These perverted forms of government are alike in that each serves the interest of a particular group in society and rejects the common good. Tyranny is a monarchy which pursues the selfish goals of the monarch and seeks to repress the people. Similarly, oligarchy operates to preserve the privileged position of the wealthy class without regard for the common interest. In Aristotle's observations of autocratic rule of the needy, which he calls "democracy" but equates it with mob rule, one can see many traits to be found in modern demagogic regimes. This form, according to Aristotle, has a leadership that tries to identify itself with the aspirations of the masses but overlooks the interest of the state.

Throughout history various kinds of dictatorships have appeared. Alfred Cobban, a leading author on the subject, sets forth in the reading on Caesarism the characteristics of a Roman type of autocratic rule which had certain refinements not to be found in the forms of dictatorship in ancient Greece as seen by Aristotle. It appears then that in different ages and diverse cultures unique dictatorships have arisen. This assumption will be followed in our treatment of the topic of dictatorship.

51

ROMAN DICTATORSHIPS

Militarism and imperialism are closely related to an ascending dictatorship. This is shown by Alfred Cobban to be true of Caesarism as an example of Roman autocratic rule. The strains of expanding the empire, along with emerging economic problems, demanded some kind of strong leadership. For Julius Caesar the absolute power of the Senate had to be broken for the good of the Roman Empire. His political maneuvering involved the waging of wars and the winning of the support of the soldiers as well as of the common people. The term "Caesarism" has been applied to modern dictatorships because of the way in which some leaders have achieved complete power. Although there are significant differences between Caesar and modern dictators, certain twentieth-century demagogues have resembled him in strategy. Benito Mussolini and Juan Perón, for example, won the enthusiastic endorsement of substantial numbers of the people while keeping the leadership of the army in check but gathering support from the rank and file.

Cobban tells us that Roman leaders were constantly aware of the importance of legitimacy and were able to sanction their regimes through various means. Dedication to an established body of law and appeal to religion seem to have been the most effective devices for legitimation. It is interesting to note that some dictatorial regimes in modern times have come to office legitimately. But, as in the case of Hitler, the constitution became a vehicle for the assumption of extraordinary powers of government.

SPECIAL TYPES OF DESPOTISM

In a book entitled *Oriental Despotisms,* Karl A. Wittfogel, a contemporary historian, examines in detail what he calls "hydraulic societies" in which there existed a framework of total power. In these societies the governments constructed irrigation systems to yield the maximum in agricultural production. The pace of life in such a community allowed very little freedom for the individual. The extensive control over the population exercised by the foreman class prompted Wittfogel to conclude that few political systems in history have been as oppressive as the oriental despotisms.

Again, analyzing dictatorship historically, one must note the tyrannies existing in the Italian city-states. Niccolo Machiavelli, writing in the sixteenth century, describes the statecraft of that age in Italy. He devotes most of his attention to the formulation of theories as to how a prince maintains power and builds a great state. For him, greatness of a state consists of wealth, power, and empire; while he recognizes the virtues of a republican form of government, his unceasing admiration for the shrewd dictator has led critics to condemn him as an advocate of evil.

What is the quality in a ruler most respected by Machiavelli? Above all else, a ruler should be cunning. The prince should try to appear to be religious and merciful if this will help his political image. Immoral acts of deceit or cruelty are permissible or desirable when such acts are done in the interest of the nation. The test of a good ruler is his resourcefulness even if at times he resorts to immoral practices. Machiavelli's work is viewed by some readers as the epitome of the dictum that "might makes right." Others say that Machiavelli was an astute political theorist who looked at political phenomena with objectivity.

JACOBINISM

In the late eighteenth century, French revolutionary political leaders such as Robespierre defended dictatorial rule by appealing to the national interest or to what the famed French philosopher Rousseau called the "General Will." Robespierre was a leader of the Jacobins, a political club founded in 1789 which actively supported the Reign of Terror and the radical changes demanded in the wake of the French Revolution. The Jacobins sought to control France through terror, propaganda, and spectacular ceremonies. Robespierre and other Jacobin leaders claimed to have special insights into the "General Will" and therefore justified their monopoly of power in order to govern without obstruction from other groups and parties.

Jacobinism was a new form of dictatorship in that it introduced an official ideology consisting of the idea of the "General Will" and slogans, symbols, and ceremonies which were aimed at instilling loyalty in the masses. Modern totalitarian dictatorship of the twentieth century was to refine these methods by employing such technological advances as mass communications.

TOTALITARIAN DICTATORSHIP

No dictatorship in history has approached the level of control exercised by modern totalitarian dictatorships, the best examples of which are the Soviet Union under Stalin and Nazi Germany. Under totalitarian dictatorship a society is transformed to such a degree that every aspect of the individual's life is touched by the regime. Hannah Arendt, a contemporary political theorist, refers to this atmosphere as the atomization of the population, a process which isolates individuals by means of the methodical use of terror as well as the application of other instruments of control.[1] In our second reading, Professor Arendt expands these ideas.

In 1953, Professor Carl J. Friedrich first presented a list of general characteristics of totalitarian dictatorship to a group of eminent social scientists

---

1 See Hannah Arendt, *The Origins of Totalitarianism* (New York: Harcourt, Brace and World, Inc., 1960).

who were meeting to discuss the topic of totalitarianism. Later Professors Friedrich and Zbigniew K. Brzezinski co-authored a book in which they discussed in detail these characteristics: an official ideology, a single party, the use of terror, monopoly of communications, monopoly of weapons, and central control and direction of the economy.[2] It is useful to take a closer look at these six traits of totalitarianism by discussing them in relation to twentieth-century dictatorships.

Marxist-Leninist doctrine is the best illustration of a totalitarian ideology. Soviet leaders, as official interpreters of the ideology, draw guides for action from the theories of Marx and Lenin. Every move by the regime may be explained in terms of the principles of Marxism-Leninism. The leaders see the ideology as systematic and scientific, a gospel offering answers to all problems confronting them. Since the ideology is taken to be the law of history and the path to utopia, there is no room for deviation or heresy. The Communist Party apparatus is the guardian of the ideology.

The Communist Party in the Soviet Union is a monolithic structure composed of a small percentage of the population fervently dedicated to the ideology. The Party parallels the governmental institutions at all levels and enters every part of society. By reaching into society, the Party keeps the top leaders in touch with the people. In order to maintain the infallibility of its directives to the people, the Party machine rarely admits a mistake in policy. If a major policy change occurs due to a miscalculation, there may be a shakeup or purge of party ranks with accompanying accusations—such as charges of counter-revolutionary activities and treason—against individuals. This is the nature of the monolithic party in its pursuit of fulfilling Marxist-Leninist dogma.

While the ideology of National Socialism lacked the coherence of Marxism-Leninism, it exhibited a penchant for symbols and equaled the Soviet regime in the systematic use of terror. Hannah Arendt explains "total terror" as a unique tool of modern totalitarian dictatorship which carefully isolates men and makes them feel superfluous. Total terror destroys any "living space of freedom" by pressing individuals "within its iron band."[3] The Nazi terror organizations executed their orders with bureaucratic efficiency so that even such grave evils as mass liquidation became part of routine fulfillment of the precepts of the ideology.

Monopoly of weapons usually involves the politicizing of the armed forces. The Bolsheviks set out to form Party cells within the army and to introduce a commissar system whereby the military was periodically checked by political agents. All officers were required to join the Party as a precaution against disloyalty. The Nazis instituted a similar pattern of control over the German armed forces by means of the Gestapo.

[2] Carl J. Friedrich and Zbigniew K. Brzezinski, *Totalitarian Dictatorship and Autocracy* (Cambridge: Harvard University Press, 1956).
[3] Arendt, *The Origins of Totalitarianism,* pp. 460–79.

A fifth characteristic of totalitarian dictatorship advanced by Friedrich and Brzezinski is the monopoly of communications. Here we could look at a regime which fell short of being classified as "totalitarian" but which operated effectively in the domination of communications—namely, the Perón government of Argentina. Under Perón, teachers had to devote part of their class time to instructing the children on the merits of *Perónismo*. Newspapers and magazines which in any way voiced opposition to the government's policies were closed down. The Argentine radio stations were forced to broadcast the regime's propaganda. George Blanksten, writing in 1953, said that "all media of communication of information and ideas— whether by the schools, the press, the radio, or the theatre—have been chained in the 'new Argentina' to the service of Perón."[4]

Last on the list of traits of totalitarianism is the central control and direction of the economy. The extent of control ranges from government ownership of industries, as under the Soviet government, to tight regulation of private enterprises, as under the Nazis or the Italian Fascists. Consumer preference is minimized while the whole economy is geared to the regime's specific plans.

NONIDEOLOGICAL DICTATORSHIPS

Dictatorships in Latin America have often been described by writers as growing out of a tradition of strong leadership known as *caudillismo*. The political culture of Latin America is conducive to the development of dictatorial rule. George Hallgarten, a researcher of dictatorship contends that Latin American dictatorship is a classical type. According to Hallgarten, a classical dictator is a talented individual not of the upper class who feels humiliated socially and uses the "revolutionary masses as tools for taking revenge on the upper stratum and for overpowering it."[5]

Classical dictatorships fall short of reaching the degree of control exercised by totalitarian dictatorships. Noticeably absent in the classical dictatorship is a well-developed ideology even to the point that the classical dictator may install himself as the protector of the status quo and form alliances with the upper class groups whom he attacks in demagogic speeches. Many Latin American dictators have certainly prospered by serving the interests of foreign investors and other conservative political forces.

G. M. Gilbert, a contemporary psychologist, emphasizes the psychological aspects of dictatorship and points out that the rise of dictatorships may be due in part to a cultural lag which prevents the society's acceptance of democratic institutions. Hallgarten concurs with Gilbert that strong men

---

4 George I. Blanksten, *Peron's Argentina* (Chicago: University of Chicago Press, 1953), p. 219.

5 George W. F. Hallgarten, *Why Dictators? The Causes and Forms of Tyrannical Rule Since 600 B.C.* (New York: The Macmillan Company, 1954), pp. 333–44.

or dictators are intriguing subjects for psychological study. There may be certain psycho-cultural elements motivating the individual to assume power as a dictator. The strong man needs the masses to break the power monopoly held by the upper classes in the same fashion as explained previously under "Caesarism." In most cases in Latin America the strong man will come from the military.

ULTRAREVOLUTIONARY DICTATORSHIPS

Hallgarten applies the phrase "ultra-revolutionary distatorship" to the Maoist movement in China.[6] Professional ultra-revolutionary leaders such as Mao Tse-Tung mobilize the lowest classes in order to overturn the established power structure. In the "revolution from the bottom" the leaders are determined not to revert to accommodation with the old ruling class. "People's democracy" is the label given to the dictatorships governing in the interest of the oppressed classes.

The ultra-revolutionary period in the Soviet Union ended with Lenin and Stalin, but in China the "ultra-revolution" rages on with Mao's periodic appeal to the revolutionary spirit as demonstrated by the so-called "cultural revolution" and the rampaging Red Guards. Some of the Communist ideologists refer to this process of turmoil as the "permanent revolution." Once the revolutionary fervor subsides, the movement will fail. Similarly, Mao wonders about the fate of his movement when he passes from the scene.

---

6 Hallgarten, *Ibid.*

The Rise of Caesarism

ALFRED COBBAN

Since the Greek word tyranny, though more appropriate, did not express quite the meaning modern advocates of tyrannical government wished to convey, it was from a Roman institution that the term dictatorship was borrowed. The Roman dictatorship was an honourable and universally respected constitutional device of the Republic for meeting a crisis during a war. In common with dictatorship as the word is used today it implied that supreme power was placed in the hands of one man. But the Roman dictator was constitutionally appointed, held office only for a limited term, and when he laid down his power was judged for his deeds while he had exercised it.

Signs of dictatorship in the modern sense do not appear in the Roman republic until after the end of the Punic wars, when Rome was already discovering the difficulty of combining republican government with Empire. They are associated, as earlier in the Greek cities, with the appearance of economic troubles. The freemen were declining in number because of the wars; for the same reason a large slave population had grown up, whose cheap labour was undermining the standard of life of the citizens. The yeomen farmers, overburdened with debt, were forced to sell their lands to members of the Senatorial and Equestrian orders,

who were building up...extensive estates worked by slave labour. In the city of Rome itself a large and impoverished urban population was developing. Faced with the dual task of governing extensive conquests and solving a complex economic problem the old system of government broke down.

The proposals of the Gracchi represent the first attempt to cope with these problems. Fog, in the words of the *Cambridge Ancient History,* "enshrouds the history of the Gracchan age." But evidently both Tiberius and Caius Gracchus were endeavouring to reform some of the worst abuses in the state, and were relying to some extent on the support of the populace of Rome in their struggle with the conservative Senatorial party. The measures they wished to force through seem to have been moderate and reasonable enough, but to overcome the resistance of the Senate they had to aim at making themselves permanent tribunes of the plebs; that is, they had to violate the constitution and obtain personal power. Caius Gracchus even went so far as to form a bodyguard of his supporters. But the Senators were too experienced and too well entrenched in power to yield; Tiberius and Caius Gracchus were each in turn attacked and killed by their opponents. Neither was a dictator, nor even aimed at a dictatorship, but their history indicates that a situation out of which dictatorship might arise already existed in Rome.

A long step was taken towards dicta-

Reprinted from Alfred Cobban, *Dictatorship: Its History and Theory* (London: Jonathan Cape Ltd., 1939), pp. 325–33, by permission of the publishers and the Executors of the Alfred Cobban Estate.

torship in the modern sense of the word during the next generation; it is summed up in the careers of the two great generals, Marius and Sulla, who although they led opposite factions reflect the same political tendency in the state. The political struggle which had begun in the time of the Gracchi was now becoming clarified. It was one between those who desired more efficient and less corrupt government, and who were at the same time not uninfluenced by a desire to share in the perquisites of Empire themselves, and the clique of Senatorial families, claiming a monopoly of the consulship, and an hereditary right to loot the Empire; for the biggest prizes that went with Senatorial rule were the corrupt provincial governorships. In the struggle the new men, trying to break into the Senatorial monopoly, called in the assistance of more popular elements in the state, but they must not for that reason be regarded as democrats.

However, Marius, a new man, who by his military ability had climbed into the consulship, which he held for five successive years (104–100 B.C.), reduced the property qualification for membership of the legions and enlisted large numbers of *proletarii* in them. It has plausibly been argued that this was the most decisive step in the whole history of the declining republic. The citizens who had filled the ranks of the legions in the earlier days of the republic, and who, when peace was declared, anxious to return to their farms and businesses, had insisted on demobilization, no longer served the state in war. The proletarians who now flocked behind the standards were prepared, so long as they received pay and booty, to remain permanently under arms. They became a standing army whose chief loyalty was to their general, and this was the force that henceforth could

be flung into the struggle, and that was eventually to dominate the political system of Rome.

The existence of this standing army was in itself an invitation to would-be tyrants; added to the rivalry between the Senatorial class and the new men, and the evident insufficiency of the republican system of administration, it made the tendency towards dictatorship irresistible. Not only did the party hostile to the Senate put up as a potential dictator a far more extreme politician than either of the Gracchi, in the person of Marius, but the need for strong personal leadership was felt even by the Senate, which in self-defence accepted first Sulla as its champion, and then Pompey, although neither of these was in a position to be an effective dictator. Their function was to bolster up existing institutions, not to refashion the state: a real dictator could only come from the anti-Senatorial side.

He appeared when Julius Caesar rose to power as the representative of the Marian party. By alternating politics in Rome with war in the provinces, Caesar built up an army devoted to himself in the field and a large body of political supporters in the capital. The Senate had no better recourse against him than to call on a counter-dictator, Pompey. The defeat and death of Pompey settled the issue and the Senate accepted its master, heaped offices on Caesar, made him dictator for life, gave him forty-eight lictors, a seat in the Senate between the two consuls, and the right of expressing his opinion there first—perhaps to give the Senators warning as to the opinion they themselves should express. He had made himself chief pontiff at a comparatively early stage in his career; he controlled the composition of the Senate, had in practice the gift of state contracts, exercised the judicial functions of the prætors when it served his purpose, and was even voted a statue and the title of demigod.

Caesar was truly a dictator, and not in the old Roman sense. A dictator in some sense or other Rome certainly needed: only an absolute ruler could put down the misrule of the Senatorial cliques. Moreover, Caesar was far from being a mere tyrannical general. As well as military power, political authority in Rome had been equally necessary to him, and he had built it up skillfully from the nucleus provided by the remnants of the Marian party. In early days he had acted as prosecutor against two corrupt provincial governors—not so much from a love of the old republican virtue, as because the prosecutions enabled him to put himself forward as an opponent of Senatorial corruption, while their failure would show that no remedy was to be expected from Senatorial juries. He made a reputation for himself as the "general refuge of men in trouble," and even while he was absent from the capital provided games and public holidays to please the "mongrel mob" which had taken the place of the *populus Romanus,* borrowing money on a huge scale to finance these activities.

Once in power Caesar showed himself a genuine administrative reformer and began to introduce changes on a grand scale; he planned great public works—roads through Italy and buildings in Rome; marshes were to be drained, new cities founded for the legionaries, libraries established, a new digest of the law planned, and, with all this, a degree of financial stability was restored in the republic.

On the other hand, we must not neglect the steps he took to complete the degradation of the Senate, packing it with new men, including even sons of freedmen and provincials, levelling downwards as well as upwards, and encouraging members of the upper classes to disgrace themselves. But the aristocracy had not yet lost all sense of shame, nor, in spite of their corruptions, had the memory of their ancient traditions entirely deserted them. Intellectually, and in executive ability, in the tasks of peace as well as in those of war, and even in practical political morality, Caesar stood head and shoulders above the whole Senatorial class. He represented efficient personal government against the inefficient and corrupt anarchy which was the only result of Senatorial rule. Yet in spite of all this he had made a mistake in despising his opponents, just as he had made a mistake in thinking that he could either win them over by a somewhat contemptuous patronage or else, who knows, rule the Empire without them. For the Senators still possessed the administrative tradition that was needed for the task of government, and they were still too imbued with the republican spirit to accept permanently Caesar's open dictatorship. In 49 B.C. he crossed the Rubicon, and in effect staked out his claim as dictator. After five years of civil strife he overcame all opposing forces; he triumphed in 45 B.C., in 44 became dictator for life, and in the same year fell beneath the daggers of Senatorial conspirators in the Forum at Rome.

The Empire plunged into a second, and even more violent and prolonged civil war, which ended in the triumph of Octavian, the heir to Caesar. Lacking, perhaps, the genius and the personal fascination of Julius, he was a more cautious, and in the end a more successful statesman. He claimed no dictatorial powers, but merely concentrated the normal republican offices in his own person; taking for himself the tribunician powers, he refrained from being made a tribune. Dictator, King or Emperor were not titles he envied, the most he would allow to be called was *princeps*—first citizen of the republic. The highest office he reserved for himself was that of high priest, *pontifex maximus*—not unaware that though the Roman state religion was a mockery to the smart society of Rome, it was acquiring significance in the provinces, and conscious that the old Roman *pietas* was still needed if a government was to be respected as well as obeyed. Wherever the religion of Rome spread, the name, and in the end the worship of Augustus spread with it. Not that he relied altogether on spiritual forces: by keeping the appointment of the proconsuls of the frontier provinces in his own hands, Augustus preserved his control of the armies, while the government of the peaceful inner provinces was left as a sop to the vanity and a bribe to the pockets of the Senate.

In effect Augustus was all that Caesar had been, and more, but his tyranny was a concealed one; it preserved the republican decencies; it showed that profound respect for existing forms which was part of the Roman genius for government. Where Julius had degraded the Senate, Augustus restored to it the dignity it had lost, purged it of the lowborn or barbarian elements, assisted the Senators with loans to maintain their status, and in appearance shared his power with them

fairly. The truth, of course, was that the Senators were little better than puppets in the hands of the Princeps: they were of use to him, but he was their master. And whereas Julius had died under the daggers of a score of assassins, Augustus lived to old age, revered and obeyed, the unquestioned master of the Roman world, passed on his authority peacefully to his successor, and laid down a structure of Empire that was to last with modifications for some four or five hundred years— the one dictator in the whole of our records to found a government which so far as human history goes can be called permanent.

A few generations later Seneca can hold him up to his promising young pupil, Nero, as a shining example of the virtues which distinguish a king from a tyrant. The Principate at Rome may still seem to us more like a tyranny than a monarchy: but in the Empire it had already acquired the divinity that hedges a king. Augustus had achieved what, according to Aristotle, should be the aim of every tyrant. He had so concealed the arbitrary nature of his authority, and exercised his power with such moderation, that in Rome the transition from a Republic to an Empire seemed but a natural, constitutional growth, and in the provinces the power and prestige surrounding Emperor and Imperial City alike, replaced government on a basis sanctioned by religious awe.

Ideology and Terror:
A Novel Form of Government

HANNAH ARENDT

In the preceding chapters we emphasized repeatedly that the means of total domination are not only more drastic but that totalitarianism differs essentially from other forms of political oppression known to us such as despotism, tyranny and dictatorship. Wherever it rose to power, it developed entirely new political institutions and destroyed all social, legal and political traditions of the country. No matter what the specifically national tradition or the particular spiritual source of its ideology, totalitarian government always transformed classes into masses, supplanted the party system, not by one-party dictatorships, but by a mass movement, shifted the center of power from the army to the police, and established a foreign policy openly directed toward world domination. Present totalitarian governments have developed from one-party systems; whenever these became truly totalitarian, they started to operate according to a system of values so radically different from all others, that none of our traditional legal, moral, or common sense utilitarian categories could any longer help us to come to terms with, or judge, or predict their course of action.

If it is true that the elements of totalitarianism can be found by retracing the history and analyzing the polit-

ical implications of what we usually call the crisis of our century, then the conclusion is unavoidable that this crisis is no mere threat from the outside, no mere result of some aggressive foreign policy of either Germany or Russia, and that it will no more disappear with the death of Stalin than it disappeared with the fall of Nazi Germany. It may even be that the true predicaments of our time will assume their authentic form— though not necessarily the cruelest— only when totalitarianism has become a thing of the past.

It is in the line of such reflections to raise the question whether totalitarian government, born of this crisis and at the same time its clearest and only unequivocal symptom, is merely a makeshift arrangement, which borrows its methods of intimidation, its means of organization and its instruments of violence from the well-known political arsenal of tyranny, despotism and dictatorships, and owes its existence only to the deplorable, but perhaps accidental failure of the traditional political forces—liberal or conservative, national or socialist, republican or monarchist, authoritarian or democratic. Or whether, on the contrary, there is such a thing as the *nature* of totalitarian government, whether it has its own essence and can be compared with and defined like other forms of government such as Western thought has known and recognized since the times of ancient philosophy. If this is true, then the entirely new and unprecedented

From *The Origins of Totalitarianism*, New Edition, copyright © 1951, 1958, 1966, by Hannah Arendt. Reprinted by permission of Harcourt, Brace & World, Inc., and George Allen & Unwin Ltd.

forms of totalitarian organization and course of action must rest on one of the few basic experiences which men can have whenever they live together, and are concerned with public affairs. If there is a basic experience which finds its political expression in totalitarian domination, then, in view of the novelty of the totalitarian form of government, this must be an experience which, for whatever reason, has never before served as the foundation of a body politic and whose general mood—although it may be familiar in every other respect—never before has pervaded, and directed the handling of, public affairs.

If we consider this in terms of the history of ideas, it seems extremely unlikely. For the forms of government under which men live have been very few; they were discovered early, classified by the Greeks and have proved extraordinarily long-lived. If we apply these findings, whose fundamental idea, despite many variations, did not change in the two and a half thousand years that separate Plato from Kant, we are tempted at once to interpret totalitarianism as some modern form of tyranny, that is a lawless government where power is wielded by one man. Arbitrary power, unrestricted by law, yielded in the interest of the ruler and hostile to the interests of the governed, on one hand, fear as the principle of action, namely fear of the people by the ruler and fear of the ruler by the people, on the other—these have been the hallmarks of tyranny throughout our tradition.

Instead of saying that totalitarian government is unprecedented, we could also say that it has exploded the very alternative on which all definitions of the essence of governments have been based in political philosophy, that is the alternative between lawful and lawless government, between arbitrary and legitimate power. That lawful government and legitimate power, on one side, lawlessness and arbitrary power on the other, belonged together and were inseparable has never been questioned. Yet, totalitarian rule confronts us with a totally different kind of government. It defies, it is true, all positive laws, even to the extreme of defying those which it has itself established (as in the case of the Soviet Constitution of 1936, to quote only the most outstanding example) or which it did not care to abolish (as in the case of the Weimar Constitution which the Nazi government never revoked). But it operates neither without guidance of law nor is it arbitrary, for it claims to obey strictly and unequivocally those laws of Nature or of History from which all positive laws always have been supposed to spring.

It is the monstrous, yet seemingly unanswerable claim of totalitarian rule that, far from being "lawless," it goes to the sources of authority from which positive laws received their ultimate legitimation, that far from being arbitrary it is more obedient to these suprahuman forces than any government ever was before, and that far from wielding its power in the interest of one man, it is quite prepared to sacrifice everybody's vital immediate interests to the execution of what it assumes to be the law of History or the law of Nature. Its defiance of positive laws claims to be a higher form of legitimacy which, since it is inspired by the sources themselves, can do away with petty legality. Totalitarian lawfulness pretends to have found a way to establish the rule of justice on earth—something which the legality of positive law admittedly could never attain. The discrepancy between legality and justice could never be bridged because the standards of right and wrong into which positive law translates its own source of authority—"natural law" governing the whole universe, or divine law revealed in human history, or customs and traditions expressing the law common to the sentiments of all men— are necessarily general and must be valid for a countless and unpredictable number of cases, so that each concrete individual case with its unrepeatable set of circumstances somehow escapes it.

Totalitarian lawfulness, defying legality and pretending to establish the direct reign of justice on earth, executes the law of History or of Nature without translating it into standards of right and wrong for individual behavior. It applies the law directly to mankind without bothering with the behavior of men. The law of Nature or the law of History, if properly executed, is expected to produce mankind as its end product; and this expectation lies behind the claim to global rule of all totalitarian governments. Totalitarian policy claims to transform the human species into an active unfailing carrier of a law to which human beings otherwise would only passively and reluctantly be subjected. If it is true that the link between totalitarian countries and the civilized world was broken through the monstrous crimes of totalitarian regimes, it is also true that this criminality was not due to simple aggressiveness, ruthlessness, warfare and treachery, but to a conscious break of that *consensus iuris* which, according to Cicero, constitutes a "people," and which, as international law, in modern times has constituted the civilized world insofar as it remains the foundation-stone of international relations even under the conditions of war. Both moral judgment and legal punishment presuppose this basic consent; the criminal can be judged justly only because he takes part in the *consensus iuris,* and even the revealed law of God can function among men only when they listen and consent to it.

At this point the fundamental difference between the totalitarian and all other concepts of law comes to light. Totalitarian policy does not replace one set of laws with another, does not establish its own *consensus iuris,* does not create, by one revolution, a new form of legality. Its defiance of all, even its own positive laws implies that it believes it can do without any *consensus iuris* whatever, and still not resign itself to the tyrannical state of lawlessness, arbitrariness and fear. It can do without the *consensus iuris* because it promises to release the fulfillment of law from all action and will of man; and it promises justice on earth because it claims to make mankind itself the embodiment of the law.

This identification of man and law, which seems to cancel the discrepancy between legality and justice that has plagued legal thought since ancient times, has nothing in common with the *lumen naturale* or the voice of conscience, by which Nature or Divinity as the sources of authority for the *ius naturale* or the historically revealed commands of God, are supposed to announce their authority in man himself. This never made man a walking embodiment of the law, but on the contrary remained distinct from him as the authority which demanded consent and obedience. Nature or Divinity as the source of authority for positive laws were thought of as permanent and eternal; positive laws were changing and changeable according to circumstances, but they possessed a relative permanence as compared with the much more rapidly changing actions of men; and they derived this permanence from the eternal presence of their source of authority. Positive laws, therefore, are primarily designed to function as stabilizing factors for the ever changing movements of men.

In the interpretation of totalitarianism, all laws have become laws of movement. When the Nazis talked about the law of nature or when the Bolsheviks talk about the law of history, neither nature nor history is any longer the stabilizing source of authority for the actions of mortal men; they are movements in themselves. Underlying the Nazis' belief in race laws as the expression of the law of nature in man, is Darwin's idea of man as the product of a natural development which does not necessarily stop with the present species of human beings, just as under the Bolsheviks' belief in class-struggle as the expression of the law of history lies Marx's notion of society as the product of a gigantic historical movement which races according to its own law of motion to the end of historical times when it will abolish itself.

The difference between Marx's historical and Darwin's naturalistic approach has frequently been pointed out, usually and rightly in favor of Marx. This has led us to forget the great and positive interest Marx took in Darwin's theories; Engels could not think of a greater compliment to Marx's scholarly achievements than to call him the "Darwin of history."[1] If one considers, not the actual achievement, but the

basic philosophies of both men, it turns out that ultimately the movement of history and the movement of nature are one and the same. Darwin's introduction of the concept of development into nature, his insistence that, at least in the field of biology, natural movement is not circular but unilinear, moving in an infinitely progressing direction, means in fact that nature is, as it were, being swept into history, that natural life is considered to be historical. The "natural" law of the survival of the fittest is just as much a historical law and could be used as such by racism as Marx's law of the survival of the most progressive class. Marx's class struggle, on the other hand, as the driving force of history is only the outward expression of the development of productive forces which in turn have their origin in the "labor-power" of men. Labor, according to Marx, is not a historical but a natural-biological force —released through man's "metabolism with nature" by which he conserves his individual life and reproduces the species.[2] Engels saw the affinity between the basic convictions of the two men very clearly because he understood the decisive role which the concept of development played in both theories. The tremendous intellectual change which took place in the middle of the last century consisted in the refusal to view or accept anything "as it is" and in the consistent interpretation of everything as being only a stage of some further development. Whether the driving force of this development was called nature or history is relatively secondary. In these ideologies, the term "law" itself

[1] In his funeral speech on Marx, Engels said: "Just as Darwin discovered the law of development of organic life, so Marx discovered the law of development of human history." A similar comment is found in Engels' introduction to the edition of the *Communist Manifesto* in 1890, and in his introduction to the *Ursprung der Familie*, he once more mentions "Darwin's theory of evolution" and "Marx's theory of surplus value" side by side.

[2] For Marx's labor concept as "an eternal nature-imposed necessity, without which there can be no metabolism between man and nature, and therefore no life," see *Capital*, Vol. I, Part I, ch. 1 and 5. The quoted passage is from ch. 1, section 2.

changed its meaning: from expressing the framework of stability within which human actions and motions can take place, it became the expression of the motion itself.

Totalitarian politics which proceeded to follow the recipes of ideologies has unmasked the true nature of these movements insofar as it clearly showed that there could be no end to this process. If it is the law of nature to eliminate everything that is harmful and unfit to live, it would mean the end of nature itself if new categories of the harmful and unfit-to-live could not be found; if it is the law of history that in a class struggle certain classes "wither away," it would mean the end of human history itself if rudimentary new classes did not form, so that they in turn could "wither away" under the hands of totalitarian rulers. In other words, the law of killing by which totalitarian movements seize and exercise power would remain a law of the movement even if they ever succeeded in making all of humanity subject to their rule.

By lawful government we understand a body politic in which positive laws are needed to translate and realize the immutable *ius naturale* or the eternal commandments of God into standards of right and wrong. Only in these standards, in the body of positive laws of each country, do the *ius naturale* or the Commandments of God achieve their political reality. In the body politic of totalitarian government, this place of positive laws is taken by total terror, which is designed to translate into reality the law of movement of history or nature. Just as positive laws, though they define transgressions, are independent of them—the absence of crimes in any society does not render laws superfluous but, on the contrary, signifies their most perfect rule—so

terror in totalitarian government has ceased to be a mere means for the suppression of opposition, though it is also used for such purposes. Terror becomes total when it becomes independent of all opposition; it rules supreme when nobody any longer stands in its way. If lawfulness is the essence of non-tyrannical government and lawlessness is the essence of tyranny, then terror is the essence of totalitarian domination.

Terror is the realization of the law of movement; its chief aim is to make it possible for the force of nature or of history to race freely through mankind, unhindered by any spontaneous human action. As such, terror seeks to "stabilize" men in order to liberate the forces of nature or history. It is this movement which singles out the foes of mankind against whom terror is let loose, and no free action of either opposition or sympathy can be permitted to interfere with the elimination of the "objective enemy" of History or Nature, of the class or the race. Guilt and innocence become senseless notions; "guilty" is he who stands in the way of the natural or historical process which has passed judgment over "inferior races," over individuals "unfit to live," over "dying classes and decadent peoples." Terror executes these judgments, and before its court, all concerned are subjectively innocent: the murdered because they did nothing against the system, and the murderers because they do not really murder but execute a death sentence pronounced by some higher tribunal. The rulers themselves do not claim to be just or wise, but only to execute historical or natural laws; they do not apply laws, but execute a movement in accordance with its inherent law. Terror is lawfulness, if law is the law of the movement of some suprahuman force, Nature or History.

Terror as the execution of a law of movement whose ultimate goal is not the welfare of men or the interest of one man but the fabrication of mankind, eliminates individuals for the sake of the species, sacrifices the "parts" for the sake of the "whole." The suprahuman force of Nature or History has its own beginning and its own end, so that it can be hindered only by the new beginning and the individual end which the life of each man actually is.

Positive laws in constitutional government are designed to erect boundaries and establish channels of communication between men whose community is continually endangered by the new men born into it. With each new birth, a new beginning is born into the world, a new world has potentially come into being. The stability of the laws corresponds to the constant motion of all human affairs, a motion which can never end as long as men are born and die. The laws hedge in each new beginning and at the same time assure its freedom of movement, the potentiality of something entirely new and unpredictable; the boundaries of positive laws are for the political existence of man what memory is for his historical existence: they guarantee the pre-existence of a common world, the reality of some continuity which transcends the individual life span of each generation, absorbs all new origins and is nourished by them.

Total terror is so easily mistaken for a symptom of tyrannical government because totalitarian government in its initial stages must behave like a tyranny and raze the boundaries of man-made law. But total terror leaves no arbitrary lawlessness behind it and does not rage for the sake of some arbitrary will or for the sake of despotic power of one man against all, least of all for the sake of a war of all against all. It substitutes for the boundaries and channels of communication between individual men a band of iron which holds them so tightly together that it is as though their plurality had disappeared into One Man of gigantic dimensions. To abolish the fences of laws between men —as tyranny does—means to take away man's liberties and destroy freedom as a living political reality; for the space between men as it is hedged in by laws, is the living space of freedom. Total terror uses this old instrument of tyranny but destroys at the same time also the lawless, fenceless wilderness of fear and suspicion which tyranny leaves behind. This desert, to be sure, is no longer a living space of freedom, but it still provides some room for the fear-guided movements and suspicion-ridden actions of its inhabitants.

By pressing men against each other, total terror destroys the space between them; compared to the condition within its iron band, even the desert of tyranny, insofar as it is still some kind of space, appears like a guarantee of freedom. Totalitarian government does not just curtail liberties or abolish essential freedoms; nor does it, at least to our limited knowledge, succeed in eradicating the love for freedom from the hearts of man. It destroys the one essential prerequisite of all freedom which is simply the capacity of motion which cannot exist without space.

Total terror, the essence of totalitarian government, exists neither for nor against men. It is supposed to provide the forces of nature or history with an incomparable instrument to accelerate their movement. This movement, proceeding according to its own law, cannot in the long run be hindered; eventually its force will always prove more powerful than the most powerful forces engendered by the actions and the will of men. But it can be slowed down and is slowed down almost inevitably by the freedom of man, which even totalitarian rulers cannot deny, for this freedom—irrelevant and arbitrary as they may deem it—is identical with the fact that men are being born and that therefore each of them *is* a new beginning, begins, in a sense, the world anew. From the totalitarian point of view, the fact that men are born and die can be only regarded as an annoying interference with higher forces. Terror, therefore, as the obedient servant of natural or historical movement has to eliminate from the process not only freedom in any specific sense, but the very source of freedom which is given with the fact of the birth of man and resides in his capacity to make a new beginning. In the iron band of terror, which destroys the plurality of men and makes out of many the One who unfailingly will act as though he himself were part of the course of history or nature, a device has been found not only to liberate the historical and natural forces, but to accelerate them to a speed they never would reach if left to themselves. Practically speaking, this means that terror executes on the spot the death sentences which Nature is supposed to have pronounced on races or individuals who are "unfit to live," or History on "dying classes," without waiting for the slower and less efficient processes of nature or history themselves.

In this concept, where the essence of government itself has become motion, a very old problem of political thought seems to have found a solution similar to the one already noted for the discrepancy between legality and justice. If the essence of government is defined as lawfulness, and if it is understood that laws are the stabilizing forces in the public affairs of men (as indeed it always has been since Plato invoked

Zeus, the god of the boundaries, in his *Laws*), then the problem of movement of the body politic and the actions of its citizens arises. Lawfulness sets limitations to actions, but does not inspire them; the greatness, but also the perplexity of laws in free societies is that they only tell what one should not, but never what one should do. The necessary movement of a body politic can never be found in its essence if only because this essence—again since Plato —has always been defined with a view to its permanence. Duration seemed one of the surest yardsticks for the goodness of a government. It is still for Montesquieu the supreme proof for the badness of tyranny that only tyrannies are liable to be destroyed from within, to decline by themselves, whereas all other governments are destroyed through exterior circumstances. Therefore what the definition of governments always needed was what Montesquieu called a "principle of action" which, different in each form of government, would inspire government and citizens alike in their public activity and serve as a criterion, beyond the merely negative yardstick of lawfulness, for judging all action in public affairs. Such guiding principles and criteria of action are, according to Montesquieu, honor in a monarchy, virtue in a republic and fear in a tyranny.

In a perfect totalitarian government, where all men have become One Man, where all action aims at the acceleration of the movement of nature or history, where every single act is the execution of a death sentence which Nature or History has already pronounced, that is, under conditions where terror can be completely relied upon to keep the movement in constant motion, no principle of action separate from its essence would be needed at all. Yet as long as totalitarian rule has not conquered the earth and with the iron band of terror made each single man a part of one mankind, terror in its double function as essence of government and principle, not of action, but of motion, cannot be fully realized. Just as lawfulness in constitutional government is insufficient to inspire and guide men's actions, so terror in totalitarian government is not sufficient to inspire and guide human behavior.

While under present conditions totalitarian domination still shares with other forms of government the need for a guide for the behavior of its citizens in public affairs, it does not need and could not even use a principle of action strictly speaking, since it will eliminate precisely the capacity of man to act. Under conditions of total terror not even fear can any longer serve as an advisor of how to behave, because terror chooses its victims without reference to individual actions or thoughts, exclusively in accordance with the objective necessity of the natural or historical process. Under totalitarian conditions, fear probably is more widespread than ever before; but fear has lost its practical usefulness when actions guided by it can no longer help to avoid the dangers man fears. The same is true for sympathy or support of the regime; for total terror not only selects its victims according to objective standards; it chooses its executioners with as complete a disregard as possible for the candidate's conviction and sympathies. The consistent elimination of conviction as a motive for action has become a matter of record since the great purges in Soviet Russia and the satellite countries. The aim of totalitarian education has never been to instill convictions but to destroy the capacity to form any. The introduction of purely objective criteria into the

selective system of the SS troops was Himmler's great organizational invention; he selected the candidates from photographs according to purely racial criteria. Nature itself decided, not only who was to be eliminated, but also who was to be trained as an executioner.

No guiding principle of behavior, taken itself from the realm of human action, such as virtue, honor, fear, is necessary or can be useful to set into motion a body politic which no longer uses terror as a means of intimidation, but whose essence is terror. In its stead, it has introduced an entirely new principle into public affairs that dispenses with human will to action altogether and appeals to the craving need for some insight into the law of movement according to which the terror functions and upon which, therefore, all private destinies depend.

The inhabitants of a totalitarian country are thrown into and caught in the process of nature or history for the sake of accelerating its movement; as such, they can only be executioners or victims of its inherent law. The process may decide that those who today eliminate races and individuals or the members of dying classes and decadent peoples are tomorrow those who must be sacrificed. What totalitarian rule needs to guide the behavior of its subjects is a preparation to fit each of them equally well for the role of executioner and the role of victim. This two-sided preparation, the substitute for a principle of action, is the ideology.

Ideologies—isms which to the satisfaction of their adherents can explain everything and every occurence by deducing it from a single premise—are a very recent phenomenon and, for many decades, played a negligible role in political life. Only with the wisdom of hindsight can we discover in them certain elements which have made them so disturbingly useful for totalitarian rule. Not before Hitler and Stalin were the great political potentialities of the ideologies discovered.

Ideologies are known for their scientific character: they combine the scientific approach with results of philosophical relevance and pretend to be scientific philosophy. The word "ideology" seems to imply that an idea can become the subject matter of a science just as animals are the subject matter of zoology, and that the suffix -*logy* in ideology, as in zoology, indicates nothing but the *logoi*, the scientific statements made on it. If this were true, an ideology would indeed be a pseudo-science and a pseudo-philosophy, transgressing at the same time the limitations of science and the limitations of philosophy. Deism, for example, would then be the ideology which treats the idea of God, with which philosophy is concerned, in the scientific manner of theology for which God is a revealed reality. (A theology which is not based on revelation as a given reality but treats God as an idea would be as mad as a zoology which is no longer sure of the physical, tangible existence of animals.) Yet we know that this is only part of the truth. Deism, though it denies divine revelation, does not simply make "scientific" statements on a God which is only an "idea," but uses the idea of God in order to explain the course of the world. The "ideas" of isms—race in racism, God in deism, etc.—never form the subject matter of the ideologies and the suffix -*logy* never indicates simply a body of "scientific" statements.

An ideology is quite literally what its name indicates: it is the logic of an idea. Its subject matter is history, to which the "idea" is applied; the result of this application is not a body of statements about something that *is,* but the unfolding of a process which is in constant change. The ideology treats the course of events as though it followed the same "law" as the logical exposition of its "idea." Ideologies pretend to know the mysteries of the whole historical process—the secrets of the past, the intricacies of the present, the uncertainties of the future—because of the logic inherent in their respective ideas.

Ideologies are never interested in the miracle of being. They are historical, concerned with becoming and perishing, with the rise and fall of cultures, even if they try to explain history by some "law of nature." The word "race" in racism does not signify any genuine curiosity about the human races as a field for scientific exploration, but is the "idea" by which the movement of history is explained as one consistent process.

The "idea" of an ideology is neither Plato's eternal essence grasped by the eyes of the mind nor Kant's regulative principle of reason but has become an instrument of explanation. To an ideology, history does not appear in the light of an idea (which would imply that history is seen *sub specie* of some ideal eternity which itself is beyond historical motion) but as something which can be calculated by it. What fits the "idea" into this new role is its own "logic," that is a movement which is the consequence of the "idea" itself and needs no outside factor to set it into motion. Racism is the belief that there is a motion inherent in the very idea of race, just as deism is the belief that a motion is inherent in the very notion of God.

The movement of history and the logical process of this notion are supposed to correspond to each other, so that whatever happens, happens according to the logic of one "idea." However, the only possible movement in the realm of logic is the process of deduction from a premise. Dialectical logic, with its process from thesis through antithesis to synthesis which in turn becomes the thesis of the next dialectical movement, is not different in principle, once an ideology gets hold of it; the first thesis becomes the premise and its advantage for ideological explanation is that this dialectical device can explain away factual contradictions as stages of one identical, consistent movement.

As soon as logic as a movement of thought—and not as a necessary control of thinking—is applied to an idea, this idea is transformed into a premise. Ideological world explanations performed this operation long before it became so eminently fruitful for totalitarian reasoning. The purely negative coercion of logic, the prohibition of contradictions, became "productive" so that a whole line of thought could be initiated, and forced upon the mind, by drawing conclusions in the manner of mere argumentation. This argumentative process could be interrupted neither by a new idea (which would have been another premise with a different set of consequences) nor by a new experience. Ideologies always assume that one idea is sufficient to explain everything in the development from the premise, and that no experience can teach anything because everything is comprehended in this consistent process of logical deduction. The danger in exchanging the necessary insecurity of philosophical thought for the total explanation of an ideology and its *Weltanschauung,* is not even so much the risk of falling for some usually vulgar, always uncritical assumption as of exchanging the freedom inherent in man's capacity to think for

the straightjacket of logic with which man can force himself almost as violently as he is forced by some outside power.

The *Weltanschauungen* and ideologies of the nineteenth century are not in themselves totalitarian, and although racism and communism have become the decisive ideologies of the twentieth century they were not, in principle, any "more totalitarian" than the others; it happened because the elements of experience on which they were originally based—the struggle between the races for world domination, and the struggle between the classes for political power in the respective countries—turned out to be politically more important than those of other ideologies. In this sense the ideological victory of racism and communism over all other isms was decided before the totalitarian movements took hold of precisely these ideologies. On the other hand, all ideologies contain totalitarian elements, but these are fully developed only by totalitarian movements, and this creates the deceptive impression that only racism and communism are totalitarian in character. The truth is, rather, that the real nature of all ideologies was revealed only in the role that the ideology plays in the apparatus of totalitarian domination. Seen from this aspect, there appear three specifically totalitarian elements that are peculiar to all ideological thinking.

First, in their claim to total explanation, ideologies have the tendency to explain not what is, but what becomes, what is born and passes away. They are in all cases concerned solely with the element of motion, that is, with history in the customary sense of the word. Ideologies are always oriented toward history, even when, as in the case of racism, they seemingly proceed from the premise of nature; here,

nature serves merely to explain historical matters and reduce them to
matters of nature. The claim to total
explanation promises to explain all historical happenings, the total explanation of the past, the total knowledge
of the present, and the reliable prediction of the future. Secondly, in this
capacity ideological thinking becomes
independent of all experience from
which it cannot learn anything new
even if it is a question of something
that has just come to pass. Hence ideological thinking becomes emancipated
from the reality that we perceive with
our five senses, and insists on a "truer"
reality concealed behind all perceptible
things, dominating them from this
place of concealment and requiring a
sixth sense that enables us to become
aware of it. The sixth sense is provided
by precisely the ideology, that particular ideological indoctrination which is
taught by the educational institutions,
established exclusively for this purpose, to train the "political soldiers"
in the *Ordensburgen* of the Nazis or
the schools of the Comintern and the
Cominform. The propaganda of the
totalitarian movement also serves to
emancipate thought from experience
and reality; it always strives to inject
a secret meaning into every public,
tangible event and to suspect a secret
intent behind every public political act.
Once the movements have come to
power, they proceed to change reality
in accordance with their ideological
claims. The concept of enmity is replaced by that of conspiracy, and this
produces a mentality in which reality—
real enmity or real friendship—is no
longer experienced and understood in
its own terms but is automatically assumed to signify something else.

Thirdly, since the ideologies have no
power to transform reality, they achieve
this emancipation of thought from ex-

perience through certain methods of
demonstration. Ideological thinking
orders facts into an absolutely logical
procedure which starts from an axio-
matically accepted premise, deducing
everything else from it; that is, it proceeds with a consistency that exists
nowhere in the realm of reality. The
deducing may proceed logically or dia-
lectically; in either case it involves a
consistent process of argumentation
which, because it thinks in terms of a
process, is supposed to be able to comprehend the movement of the suprahuman, natural or historical processes.
Comprehension is achieved by the
mind's imitating, either logically or dia-
lectically, the laws of "scientifically"
established movements with which
through the process of imitation it
becomes integrated. Ideological argumentation, always a kind of logical
reduction, corresponds to the two afore-
mentioned elements of the ideologies—
the element of movement and of emancipation from reality and experience
—first, because its thought movement
does not spring from experience but is
self-generated, and, secondly, because it
transforms the one and only point that
is taken and accepted from experienced
reality into an axiomatic premise, leaving from then on the subsequent argumentation process completely untouched from any further experience.
Once it has established its premise, its
point of departure, experiences no
longer interfere with ideological thinking, nor can it be taught by reality.

The device both totalitarian rulers
used to transform their respective ideologies into weapons with which each
of their subjects could force himself
into step with the terror movement
was deceptively simple and incon-
spicuous: they took them dead seriously, took pride the one in his supreme
gift for "ice cold reasoning" (Hitler)

and the other in the "mercilessness of his dialectics," and proceeded to drive ideological implications into extremes of logical consistency which, to the on-looker, looked preposterously "primi-tive" and absurd: a "dying class" con-sisted of people condemned to death; races that are "unfit to live" were to be exterminated. Whoever agreed that there are such things as "dying classes" and did not draw the consequence of killing their members, or that the right to live had something to do with race and did not draw the consequence of killing "unfit races," was plainly either stupid or a coward. This stringent logicality as a guide to action per-meates the whole structure of totali-tarian movements and governments. It is exclusively the work of Hitler and Stalin who, although they did not add a single new thought to the ideas and propaganda slogans of their move-ments, for this reason alone must be considered ideologists of the greatest importance.

What distinguished these new totali-tarian ideologists from their predeces-sors was that it was no longer primarily the "idea" of the ideology—the struggle of classes and the exploitation of the workers or the struggle of races and the care for Germanic peoples—which ap-pealed to them, but the logical process which could be developed from it. Ac-cording to Stalin, neither the idea nor the oratory but "the irresistible force of logic thoroughly overpowered [Lenin's] audience." The power, which Marx thought was born when the idea seized the masses, was discovered to reside, not in the idea itself, but in its logical process which "like a mighty tentacle seizes you on all sides as in a vise and from whose grip you are powerless to tear yourself away; you must either surrender or make up your mind to utter defeat."[3] Only when the realization of the ideological aims, the classless society or the master race, was at stake, could this force show itself. In the process of realization, the origi-nal substance upon which the ideologies based themselves as long as they had to appeal to the masses—the exploita-tion of the workers or the national aspirations of Germany—is gradually lost, devoured as it were by the process itself: in perfect accordance with "ice cold reasoning" and the "irresistible force of logic," the workers lost under Bolshevik rule even those rights they had been granted under Tsarist oppres-sion and the German people suffered a kind of warfare which did not pay the slightest regard to the minimum requirements for survival of the Ger-man nation. It is in the nature of ide-ological politics—and is not simply a betrayal committed for the sake of self-interest or lust for power—that the real content of the ideology (the working class or the Germanic peoples), which originally had brought about the "idea" (the struggle of classes as the law of history or the struggle of races as the law of nature), is devoured by the logic with which the "idea" is carried out.

The preparation of victims and exe-cutioners which totalitarianism requires in place of Montesquieu's principle of action is not the ideology itself—racism or dialectical materialism—but its in-herent logicality. The most persuasive argument in this respect, an argument of which Hitler like Stalin was very fond, is: You can't say A without say-ing B and C and so on, down to the

___

[3] Stalin's speech of January 28, 1924; quoted from Lenin, *Selected Works*, Vol. I, p. 33, Moscow, 1947. It is interesting to note that Stalin's "logic" is among the few quali-ties that Khrushchev praises in his devastat-ing speech at the Twentieth Party Congress.

end of the murderous alphabet. Here, the coercive force of logicality seems to have its source; it springs from our fear of contradicting ourselves. To the extent that the Bolshevik purge succeeds in making its victims confess to crimes they never committed, it relies chiefly on this basic fear and argues as follows: We are all agreed on the premise that history is a struggle of classes and on the role of the Party in its conduct. You know therefore that, historically speaking, the Party is always right (in the words of Trotsky: "We can only be right with and by the Party, for history has provided no other way of being in the right."). At this historical moment, that is in accordance with the law of history, certain crimes are due to be committed which the Party, knowing the law of history, must punish. For these crimes, the Party needs criminals; it may be that the Party, though knowing the crimes, does not quite know the criminals; more important than to be sure about the criminals is to punish the crimes, because without such punishment, History will not be advanced but may even be hindered in its course. You, therefore, either have committed the crimes or have been called by the Party to play the role of the criminal—in either case, you have objectively become an enemy of the Party. If you don't confess, you cease to help History through the Party, and have become a real enemy.—The coercive force of the argument is: if you refuse, you contradict yourself and, through this contradiction, render your whole life meaningless; the A which you said dominates your whole life through the consequences of B and C which it logically engenders.

Totalitarian rulers rely on the compulsion with which we can compel ourselves, for the limited mobilization of people which even they still need; this inner compulsion is the tyranny of logicality against which nothing stands but the great capacity of men to start something new. The tyranny of logicality begins with the mind's submission to logic as a never-ending process, on which man relies in order to engender his thoughts. By this submission, he surrenders his inner freedom as he surrenders his freedom of movement when he bows down to an outward tyranny. Freedom as an inner capacity of man is identical with the capacity to begin, just as freedom as a political reality is identical with a space of movement between men. Over the beginning, no logic, no cogent deduction can have any power, because its chain presupposes, in the form of a premise, the beginning. As terror is needed lest with the birth of each new human being a new beginning arise and raise its voice in the world, so the self-coercive force of logicality is mobilized lest anybody ever start thinking—which as the freest and purest of all human activities is the very opposite of the compulsory process of deduction. Totalitarian government can be safe only to the extent that it can mobilize man's own will power in order to force him into that gigantic movement of History or Nature which supposedly uses mankind as its material and knows neither birth nor death.

The compulsion of total terror on one side, which, with its iron band, presses masses of isolated men together *and* supports them in a world which has become a wilderness for them, and the self-coercive force of logical deduction on the other, which prepares each individual in his lonely isolation against all others, correspond to each other and need each other in order to set the terror-ruled movement into motion and keep it moving. Just as terror, even in its pre-total, merely tyrannical form ruins all relationships between men, so the self-compulsion of ideological thinking ruins all relationships with reality. The preparation has succeeded when people have lost contact with their fellow men as well as the reality around them; for together with these contacts, men lose the capacity of both experience and thought. The ideal subject of totalitarian rule is not the convinced Nazi or the convinced Communist, but people for whom the distinction between fact and fiction (*i.e.,* the reality of experience) and the distinction between true and false (*i.e,* the standards of thought) no longer exist.

The question we raised at the start of these considerations and to which we now return is what kind of basic experience in the living-together of men permeates a form of government whose essence is terror and whose principle of action is the logicality of ideological thinking. That such a combination was never used before in the varied forms of political domination is obvious. Still, the basic experience on which it rests must be human and known to men, insofar as even this most "original" of all political bodies has been devised by, and is somehow answering the needs of, men.

It has frequently been observed that terror can rule absolutely only over men who are isolated against each other and that, therefore, one of the primary concerns of all tyrannical government is to bring this isolation about. Isolation may be the beginning of terror; it certainly is its most fertile ground; it always is its result. This isolation is, as it were, pretotalitarian; its hallmark is impotence insofar as power always comes from men acting together, "acting in concert" (Burke); isolated men are powerless by definition.

Isolation and impotence, that is the fundamental inability to act at all, have always been characteristic of tyrannies. Political contacts between men are severed in tyrannical government and the human capacities for action and power are frustrated. But not all contacts between men are broken and not all human capacities destroyed. The whole sphere of private life with the capacities for experience, fabrication and thought are left intact. We know that the iron band of total terror leaves no space for such private life and that the self-coercion of totalitarian logic destroys man's capacity for experience and thought just as certainly as his capacity for action.

What we call isolation in the political sphere, is called loneliness in the sphere of social intercourse. Isolation and loneliness are not the same. I can be isolated—that is in a situation in which I cannot act, because there is nobody who will act with me—without being lonely; and I can be lonely—that is in a situation in which I as a person feel myself deserted by all human companionship—without being isolated. Isolation is that impasse into which men are driven when the political sphere of their lives, where they act together in the pursuit of a common concern, is destroyed. Yet isolation, though destructive of power and the capacity for action, not only leaves intact but is required for all so-called productive activities of men. Man insofar as he is *homo faber* tends to isolate himself with his work, that is to leave temporarily the realm of politics. Fabrication (*poiesis,* the making of things), as distinguished from action (*praxis*) on one hand and sheer labor on the other, is always performed in a certain isolation from common concerns, no matter whether the result is a piece of craftsmanship or of art. In isolation, man remains in contact with the world as the human artifice; only when the most elementary form of human creativity, which is the capacity to add something of one's own to the common world, is destroyed, isolation becomes altogether unbearable. This can happen in a world whose chief values are dictated by labor, that is where all human activities have been transformed into laboring. Under such conditions, only the sheer effort of labor which is the effort to keep alive is left and the relationship with the world as a human artifice is broken. Isolated man who lost his place in the political realm of action is deserted by the world of things as well, if he is no longer recognized as *homo faber* but treated as an *animal laborans* whose necessary "metabolism with nature" is of concern to no one. Isolation then becomes loneliness. Tyranny based on isolation generally leaves the productive capacities of man intact; a tyranny over "laborers," however, as for instance the rule over slaves in antiquity, would automatically be a rule over lonely, not only isolated, men and tend to be totalitarian.

While isolation concerns only the political realm of life, loneliness concerns human life as a whole. Totalitarian government, like all tyrannies, certainly could not exist without destroying the public realm of life, that is, without destroying, by isolating men, their political capacities. But totalitarian domination as a form of government is new in that it is not content with this isolation and destroys private life as well. It bases itself on loneliness, on the experience of not belonging to the world at all, which is among the most radical and desperate experiences of man.

Loneliness, the common ground for terror, the essence of totalitarian government, and for ideology or logicality, the preparation of its executioners and victims, is closely connected with uprootedness and superfluousness which have been the curse of modern masses since the beginning of the industrial revolution and have become acute with the rise of imperialism at the end of the last century and the break-down of political institutions and social traditions in our own time. To be uprooted means to have no place in the world, recognized and guaranteed by others; to be superfluous means not to belong to the world at all. Uprootedness can be the preliminary condition for superfluousness, just as isolation can (but must not) be the preliminary condition for loneliness. Taken in itself, without consideration of its recent historical causes and its new role in politics, loneliness is at the same time contrary to the basic requirements of the human condition *and* one of the fundamental experiences of every human life. Even the experience of the materially and sensually given world depends upon my being in contact with other men, upon our *common* sense which regulates and controls all other senses and without which each of us would be enclosed in his own particularity of sense data which in themselves are unreliable and treacherous. Only because we have common sense, that is only because not one man, but men in the plural inhabit the earth can we trust our immediate sensual experience. Yet, we have only to remind ourselves that one day we shall have to leave this common world which will go on as before and for whose continuity we are superfluous in order to realize loneliness, the experience of being abandoned by everything and everybody.

Loneliness is not solitude. Solitude requires being alone whereas loneliness shows itself most sharply in company with others. Apart from a few stray remarks—usually framed in a paradoxical mood like Cato's statement (reported by Cicero, *De Re Publica,* I, 17): *numquam minus solum esse quam cum solus esset,* "never was he less alone than when he was alone," or, rather, "never was he less lonely than when he was in solitude"—it seems that Epictetus, the emancipated slave philosopher of Greek origin, was the first to distinguish between loneliness and solitude. His discovery, in a way, was accidental, his chief interest being neither solitude nor loneliness, but being alone (*monos*) in the sense of absolute independence. As Epictetus sees it (*Dissertationes,* Book 3, ch. 13) the lonely man (*eremos*) finds himself surrounded by others with whom he cannot establish contact or to whose hostility he is exposed. The solitary man, on the contrary, is alone and therefore "can be together with himself" since men have the capacity of "talking with themselves." In solitude, in other words, I am "by myself," together with my self, and therefore two-in-one, whereas in loneliness I am actually one, deserted by all others. All thinking, strictly speaking, is done in solitude and is a dialogue between me and myself; but this dialogue of the two-in-one does not lose contact with the world of my fellow-men because they are represented in the self with whom I lead the dialogue of thought. The problem of solitude is that this two-in-one needs the others in order to become one again: one unchangeable individual whose identity can never be mistaken for that of any other. For the confirmation of my identity I depend entirely upon other people; and it is the great saving grace of companionship for solitary men that it makes them "whole" again, saves them from the dialogue of thought in which one remains always equivocal, restores the

identity which makes them speak with the single voice of one unexchangeable person.

Solitude can become loneliness; this happens when all by myself I am deserted by my own self. Solitary men have always been in danger of loneliness, when they can no longer find the redeeming grace of companionship to save them from duality and equivocality and doubt. Historically, it seems as though this danger became sufficiently great to be noticed by others and recorded by history only in the nineteenth century. It showed itself clearly when philosophers, for whom alone solitude is a way of life and a condition of work, were no longer content with the fact that "philosophy is only for the few" and began to insist that nobody "understands" them. Characteristic in this respect is the anecdote reported from Hegel's deathbed which hardly could have been told of any great philosopher before him: "Nobody has understood me except one; and he also misunderstood." Conversely, there is always the chance that a lonely man finds himself and starts the thinking dialogue of solitude. This seems to have happened to Nietzsche in Sils Maria when he conceived *Zarathustra.* In two poems ("Sils Maria" and "Aus hohen Bergen") he tells of the empty expectation and the yearning waiting of the lonely until suddenly *"um Mittag war's, da wurde Eins zu Zwei . ./ Nun feiern wir, vereinten Siegs gewiss,/ das Fest der Feste;/ Freund Zarathustra kam, der Gast der Gäste!"* ("Noon was, when One became Two...Certain of united victory we celebrate the feast of feasts; friend Zarathustra came, the guest of guests.")

What makes loneliness so unbearable is the loss of one's own self which can be realized in solitude, but confirmed in its identity only by the trusting and trustworthy company of my equals. In this situation, man loses trust in himself as the partner of his thoughts and that elementary confidence in the world which is necessary to make experiences at all. Self and world, capacity for thought and experience are lost at the same time.

The only capacity of the human mind which needs neither the self nor the other nor the world in order to function safely and which is as independent of experience as it is of thinking is the ability of logical reasoning whose premise is the self-evident. The elementary rules of cogent evidence, the truism that two and two equals four cannot be perverted even under the conditions of absolute loneliness. It is the only reliable "truth" human beings can fall back upon once they have lost the mutual guarantee, the common sense, men need in order to experience and live and know their way in a common world. But this "truth" is empty or rather no truth at all, because it does not reveal anything. (To define consistency as truth as some modern logicians do means to deny the existence of truth.) Under the conditions of loneliness, therefore, the self-evident is no longer just a means of the intellect and begins to be productive, to develop its own lines of "thought." That thought processes characterized by strict self-evident logicality, from which apparently there is no escape, have some connection with loneliness was once noticed by Luther (whose experiences in the phenomena of solitude and loneliness probably were second to no one's and who once dared to say that "there must be a God because man needs one being whom he can trust") in a little-known remark on the Bible text "it is not good that man should be alone": A lonely man, says Luther, "always deduces one thing from the other and thinks everything to the worst." The famous extremism of totalitarian movements, far from having anything to do with true radicalism, consists indeed in this "thinking everything to the worst," in this deducing process which always arrives at the worst possible conclusions.

What prepares men for totalitarian domination in the non-totalitarian world is the fact that loneliness, once a borderline experience usually suffered in certain marginal social conditions like old age, has become an everyday experience of the evergrowing masses of our century. The merciless process into which totalitarianism drives and organizes the masses looks like a suicidal escape from this reality. The "ice-cold reasoning" and the "mighty tentacle" of dialectics which "seizes you as in a vise" appears like a last support in a world where nobody is reliable and nothing can be relied upon. It is the inner coercion whose only content is the strict avoidance of contradictions that seems to confirm a man's identity outside all relationships with others. It fits him into the iron band of terror even when he is alone, and totalitarian domination tries never to leave him alone except in the extreme situation of solitary confinement. By destroying all space between men and pressing men against each other, even the productive potentialities of isolation are annihilated; by teaching and glorifying the logical reasoning of loneliness where man knows that he will be utterly lost if ever he lets go of the first premise from which the whole process is being started, even the slim chances that loneliness may be transformed into solitude and logic into thought are obliterated. If this practice is compared with that of tyranny, it seems as if a way had been found to set the desert itself in motion, to let loose a sand storm that could cover all parts of the inhabited earth.

The conditions under which we exist today in the field of politics are indeed threatened by these devastating sand storms. Their danger is not that they might establish a permanent world. Totalitarian domination, like tyranny, bears the germs of its own destruction. Just as fear and the impotence from which fear springs are antipolitical principles and throw men into a situation contrary to political action, so loneliness and the logical-ideological deducing the worst that comes from it represent an antisocial situation and harbor a principle destructive for all human living-together. Nevertheless, organized loneliness is considerably more dangerous than the unorganized impotence of all those who are ruled by the tyrannical and arbitrary will of a single man. Its danger is that it threatens to ravage the world as we know it—a world which everywhere seems to have come to an end—before a new beginning rising from this end has had time to assert itself.

Apart from such considerations— which as predictions are of little avail and less consolation—there remains the fact that the crisis of our time and its central experience have brought forth an entirely new form of government which as a potentiality and an ever-present danger is only too likely to stay with us from now on, just as other forms of government which came about at different historical moments and rested on different fundamental experiences have stayed with mankind regardless of temporary defeats—monarchies, and republics, tyrannies, dictatorships and despotism.

But there remains also the truth that every end in history necessarily contains a new beginning; this beginning is the promise, the only "message" which the end can ever produce. Beginning, before it becomes a historical event, is the supreme capacity of man; politically, it is identical with man's freedom. *Initium ut esset homo creatus est* —"that a beginning be made man was created" said Augustine. This beginning is guaranteed by each new birth; it is indeed every man.

The Emergent Pattern of Dictatorship— A Psychocultural View

G. M. GILBERT

Since wars begin in the minds of men, it is in the minds of men that the defenses of peace must be constructed.

—*Constitution, UNESCO*

From a psychological viewpoint, history may be regarded as the developmental record of man's adaptive social behavior in the struggle for survival and security. It is within that framework that one may understand the development of social institutions like government, progress in science and industry, cooperative and competitive behavior in various cultures, and even such historical crises as wars and revolutions.

In modern history, man's quest for collective security through self-government has been characterized by an increasing revolt against submission to the autocratic rule of royal dynasties. These revolutionary reactions to royal despotism have taken two significant and opposite directions in Western civilization: representative democracy and ideological totalitarianism. World War II has generally been regarded as a climax in the continuing struggle between these two incompatible systems in the government of men. In a larger sense, it was an acute phase of the conflict between constructive and destructive potentialities in man's behavior—a

Reprinted from G. M. Gilbert, *The Psychology of Dictatorship—Based on an Examination of the Leaders of Nazi Germany*. Copyright 1950, The Ronald Press Company, New York.

conflict in which no nation or system of government may be presumed to have a monopoly on the good or the evil. Nevertheless, the extremes to which a fanatic dictatorship can go in organized aggression was demonstrated by Nazi Germany as perhaps never before in human history.

The question may well be raised whether the psychological examination of leading personalities in that dictatorship can provide any significant insights into social conflicts of such magnitude and deep historical roots. It would admittedly be unrealistic to overestimate the importance of the psychodynamics of leading personalities in producing these major social upheavals, as against the socioeconomic, political, and historical forces at work. Nevertheless, we must recognize that such forces do not exist as pure abstractions, but become manifest only through the behavior of human beings; that throughout history social movements of far-reaching consequences have been decisively influenced by leaders, and that the behavior of such leaders is necessarily motivated to some extent by psychological tensions rooted in their individual character development. We must furthermore recognize the fact that the personalities of political leaders, like all human beings, are largely the products of their cultural mores and social tensions, and that they become leaders only if they effectively express the aspirations (or frustrations) of significant segments of their contemporary society. The study of political leadership thus provides a fertile field for interrelating psychodynamics with the broader social processes involved in these historic conflicts.

. . .

THE AUTHORITARIAN CULTURAL LAG

The Western revolt against royal despotism first came to a head at the end of the eighteenth century. This social upheaval was marked by the outbreak of major republican revolutions in Europe and the New World, and the revolutionary dictatorships which followed in their wake. The link between dictatorship and democracy has been generally overlooked in the assumed incompatibility of these two systems of government. Yet that link does exist from a psychocultural viewpoint, and is of the utmost significance for our study.

The Napoleonic rule which followed within a decade after the French Revolution is generally conceded to be the prototype of modern dictatorships. It was the forerunner not only historically, but psychologically as well, for it demonstrated a principal function of dictatorship as a psychocultural emergent: *a reversion to authoritarian rule after a too drastic attempt to impose democracy on an authoritarian culture.* Napoleon's assumption of the role of dictator and then emperor, with the wholehearted support of significant segments of postrevolutionary French society, illustrates a fact that has been true of virtually every dictatorship since then: the inability of an authoritarian

culture to absorb too much self-government too suddenly without reverting, at least temporarily, to some form of paternalistic-authoritarian rule. From the first French Republic to the German Weimar Republic, it has been proved again and again that, while the outward forms of democracy may be achieved overnight by revolution, the psychological changes necessary to sustain it cannot.

On the contrary, there is invariably a cultural lag (in which we emphasize the psychocultural aspect, rather than the technological) that leaves both the masses and the leaders of entrenched institutions psychologically predisposed to support any reversion to their accustomed way of life. This involves not merely the obvious material motivation of the "vested interests," which have been abundantly treated elsewhere, but the socioeconomic and psychological insecurity of the common people that follows in the wake of any drastic social change. It is a psychological truism that man abhors the insecurity of lost meanings as much as nature abhors a vacuum. In the confusion of revolutionary social change, the security of familiar patterns of behavior and a reliable frame of reference for social meanings and values are not readily abandoned, unless the social change immediately provides its own adequate rewards and substitutes. Since social upheaval invariably accentuates psychological and socioeconomic insecurity, and the acculturation process in personality development is not readily reversed, there is apt to be a persistence of the older patterns of behavior for at least a generation or two after the revolution.

Great statesmen have had insight into this cultural lag long before social psychology developed its sophisticated terminology. Thomas Jefferson, evaluating the prospects for the ultimate success of democracy in his generation of republican revolutions, wrote to Adams in 1823:

The generation which commences a revolution rarely completes it. Habituated from infancy to passive submission of body and mind to their kings and priests, they are not qualified when called on to think for themselves; and in their inexperience, their ignorance and bigotry make them instruments often, in the hands of the Bonapartes and Iturbides, to defeat their own rights and purposes. This is the present situation in Europe and Spanish America. But it is not desperate. . . . As a younger and more instructed [generation] comes on, the sentiment becomes more intuitive. . . some subsequent one of the ever renewed attempts will ultimately succeed.

Jefferson's insight and faith were vindicated by the ultimate triumph of democracy in France and in some of the other European and Latin American countries. But it was not surprising that the France and Latin America of Jefferson's time should have reverted to authoritarian rule after going through revolutions to throw off the yoke of royal tyranny. The masses could not be educated overnight to understand democracy and to adopt it as a way of life, nor could truly democratic leadership suddenly spring from their midst after centuries of autocratic rule had firmly established an authoritarian frame of reference for their thinking and behavior.

It is our thesis that authoritarian leadership, like any other, reflects the nature of the culture in which it emerges. This is expressed, first of all, in the social values developed among the potential leaders of the given culture. Case histories of Napoleon and other dictators (whose biographies provide us with some clues) would necessarily reveal the authoritarian influences in their upbringing and the cul-

tural channeling of their aggressions. The cultural lag is also expressed in the nature of the support available for any revolutionary or counterrevolutionary movement. Not even a power-driven dictator can seize and hold supreme power in the modern state by sheer personal dominance, as if it were a boy's gang or a seal's harem. His success depends principally on the support he is able to muster from other powerful and influential leaders and the institutions they represent. Historians have pointed out that even Napoleon could not have seized and maintained his power except for the support of other powerful militarists, certain politicians, financiers, etc. The emergence of a dictatorship requires an expression of the cultural lag in terms of the support of influential leaders whose purposes are thought to be served by reversion to autocratic rule.

It must not be assumed, however, that the dictator is merely the passive tool of cultural forces. On the contrary, we must recognize that social interaction implies a two-way process, in which cultural mores help to determine the nature of political leadership, and the latter in turn influences the development of the cultral pattern. It would be fruitless, in the absence of first-hand observations, to speculate on the psychodynamics of Napoleon's drive for power and the way in which it affected the course of European history. But there would presumably be ample room for the investigation of personality differences and individually motivated aggressions among dictators and their supporters. Certainly there has been as much variation in the personalities of dictators as there has been in the personalities of kings—from benevolent despots to destructive maniacs; and the history of their reigns has varied accordingly.

Yet it was precisely to eliminate that element of caprice from government that men were beginning to rebel against rule by the "divine right of kings." In the case of the successful republican revolutions, the purpose was achieved. But even where the rebellion resulted in dictatorship, the original purpose must not be lost sight of. Napoleon came to power, not merely as a reversion to the despotic-paternalistic emperor-figure, but as a strong symbol of peace and security, sanctioned by the will of the people. This may appear ironic, if not slightly incredible in retrospect, but there too Napoleon was the prototype of the modern dictator. For Napoleon, as historians point out, was supported by men of power and influence and was welcomed by the people, not so much to tyrannize them or to wage aggressive wars as to put an end to the chaos and insecurity of life in the postrevolutionary republic.

The struggle for security, which is an underlying motive of all social behavior, was necessarily a predominant motive for all these revolutionary changes. With the expansion of the ethnic identification group from the primitive tribe to the modern state, the socially identified security of the individual has been correspondingly extended. The aggressive nationalism that has characterized many dictatorships must be regarded as an enlarged manifestation of that continuing quest for security through group solidarity. As we have already intimated, dictatorship provided an easy solution in cultures that had always conceived of personal and group security in an ethnocentric-authoritarian frame of reference. But there was a conflict of value judgments in this revolutionary period following the Enlightenment. On the one hand, men realized that there was greater

security for the group and freedom for the individual if they asserted their right to self-government. On the other hand, the man on horseback was, and continued to be, the recognized symbol of law and order, strength and security for the nation. The heroic myth persisted even after men had rebelled against the mailed fist of royal despotism. To reconcile the apparently incompatible, Napoleon and his supporters had merely to resort to a device that dictators have repeatedly resorted to since—the "free plebiscite" with formal deference to constitutional government. Even a constitution presented no serious obstacle to dictatorship, since many of its provisions could be suspended in a "national emergency" where the security of the nation was threatened; and such emergencies, as Napoleon knew only too well, could always be provided by propaganda. Nevertheless, the people were enabled through these devices to maintain the illusion of government by popular mandate, while merely substituting a new form of despotism for the accustomed one.

Dictatorship thus emerged in an era of democratic revolution as a retrogressive phenomenon in man's quest for security through self-government, representing a compromise between his revolt against old symbols of suppressive authority and his inability to structure his purposes without them.

What was true of the Napoleonic era applied to the revolutionary period following World War I. The war had brought to a head the growing revolt against the remaining symbols of suppressive authority in Continental Europe, while the cultural lag perpetuated the quest for new authority. But now this quest took a new form: the political ideology. It was not any longer the "man on horseback" but the man with the ideological panacea who now represented authority for security Heroic mythology was beginning to give way to political demagoguery in the modern version of dictatorship.

This was essentially a modern development. The early barbarian war lords had been able to dominate their hordes and lead them to conquest or defeat without the benefit of fanciful ideologies. Ethnic cohesion and authoritarianism were too deeply imbedded in the cultures of early civilization to require justification. Even Napoleon required little more than lip service to the idea of self-government to secure allegiance to his autocratic rule and conquest. But the gradual enlightenment of the people and their growing revolt against autocratic rule in modern times placed a high premium on plausible ideologies to justify aggressive leadership and totalitarianism. There was a greater spread of social awareness among the people and their potential leaders, brought about by more widespread education and intercommunication, by the widely communicated gospels of social and scientific thinkers, and by the now well-established examples of self-government in the Western democracies. All this served to intensify the revolt against political and economic privilege, but on a slightly more sophisticated plane and broader base of popular comprehension than had been possible in Napoleon's time.

The revolutionary movements that came into being at the turn of the century expressed and appealed to the need for security by offering a variety of politico-economic ideologies. Essentially, this was a perverted recognition of the growth of social science since the nineteenth century. Unfortunately, in view of the cultural lag, it was still a case of a little insight being a dangerous thing. The discovery of human

evolution, translated into theories of ethnic struggles for survival by men like Spencer and Nietzsche, provided one pseudoscientific rationalization for the aggressive ideologies of modern dictators. The discovery of economic laws, translated into doctrines of implacable class warfare for the fruits of production by Marx and others, provided another. There was more than a grain of truth in these philosophies to begin with. It was their perversion into aggressive ideological dictatorship that was of crucial significance from the psychocultural viewpoint. For these ideologies represented formidable sources of confusion and digression in man's quest for security through self-government.

The clash of ideologies came to a head in the period of social disorganization at the end of World War I. War, defeat, and social chaos had created new demands for social and political reform. Ethnic tensions had been strained by war-born hostilities and postwar "settlements." The breakdown of old institutions and the economic chaos were creating increasing mass frustration. The meaning and justification of old values, authorities, and institutions were being questioned by many and stoutly defended by others. The literature and arts of dissent were flourishing as a symptom of social unrest. Revolutionary movements gathered momentum while political parties multiplied.

To the authoritarian mind the propaganda of idealists and demagogues alike took on an aura of ideological panaceas amid these social tensions. To many the socioeconomic ideology became a faith to fill the gap left by religion in the material realities of the modern world; to others religion became the focal point of the political ideology. The demand for representative government vied with the demand for strong leadership and ethnic solidarity; socialist revolution grappled with the demand for stable economy; nationalism with internationalism; democracy with dictatorship. In most European monarchies, the people were sure of only one thing: their desire to abolish the old ruling dynasties that had subjugated them and plunged them into war for centuries. As in the French Revolution, social unrest demanded the abolition of old authority, but just how to establish order and security without it was not so clear. That appeared to be an interplay of the cultural lag with numerous other factors, including the existing constellation of leadership and group interests in each country—the ideology they preached and the skill with which they pursued their goals, the nature of the underlying socioeconomic conditions that caused the social unrest, and the critical historical incidents that influenced the outcome of the conflict at each state of its development.

In several countries the struggle started with attempts to establish representative government and liberal social reform as antidotes to suppression and politico-economic privilege. The war was scarcely over when the Communist revolutionists under Lenin overthrew the Czarist regime in Russia and established a socialist republic. Revolts shattered the remains of the Hohenzollern dynasty in Germany, and the Weimar Republic came into being under Allied auspices. A fascist movement under Mussolini with a pseudo-radical reform program established a constitutional "corporate state" in Italy. Some years later a liberal republic was established in Spain. But in every one of these countries (and several others that need not concern us here), it was dictatorship, rather than free representative

government or truly liberal social reform that eventually emerged.

Of the numerous factors that may have contributed to this reversion to totalitarian government in these countries, the authoritarian cultural lag would appear to be at least one fundamental common denominator. As in postrevolutionary France, more than a century earlier, the attempts to impose the forms of representative government were defeated in part by the inability of these cultures to absorb too much self-government too suddenly, especially in the social chaos and insecurity that followed the overthrow of the old institutions. The long tradition of submission to despotism which had prevailed for centuries in Germany, Russia, Spain, and Italy had left too strong a trace of authoritarian thinking and ego-involvement among the people and their potential leaders to be readily abandoned in favor of the democratic-socialistic millennium.

Certainly that was the case in Germany. After centuries of subservience to the Junker aristocracy, church authority, and the military caste, neither the common people nor the leading members of the various social identification groups were prepared for democracy. Political freedom and equality were but awkwardly imposed on a social structure that still bore the heritage of class privilege, race consciousness, militant nationalism, and a deeply ingrained psychology of dominance-submissiveness in hierarchies of power and authority. Even in electing a president of the newly created Weimar Republic, they inevitably turned to the very embodiment of ancient symbols of authority—the aged Junker Field Marshal von Hindenburg. The potentiality of democratic leadership was not lacking, and it might conceivably have prevailed, given time and a more favorable combination of leadership and circumstances. But the growing insecurity of the people in the postwar chaos was running against the democratic tide. The people were clamoring for strong leadership and an authoritative formula to put an end to the politico-economic chaos, in accordance with the well-born pattern of authoritarian regressiveness. At this juncture, Adolf Hitler was already making his violent bid for power, offering an ideological panacea concocted of aggressive nationalism, social reform, and racial solidarity. Like Napoleon and other dictators, he soon won crucial support from other leaders when his interests appeared to coincide with theirs. With their support, a popular following, and a favorable series of crucial events, he was able to force his way into power on "a mandate from the people" and to consolidate that power into a formidable dictatorship.

Thus the emergence of successful dictatorship would seem to be determined in large part by the interaction of (a) *social unrest* carried over from the revolt against royal despotism; (b) an *authoritarian cultural lag,* with its persistent quest for security through strong leadership and political demagoguery; (c) a *favorable constellation of leadership* and the group interests they represent, providing the authoritative formula and its material implementation; (d) *crucial events,* sometimes of minor intrinsic significance, which favor the establishment and continuance of the dictator in power.

4   Freedom

Having discussed the different forms of dictatorships, we now turn to various aspects of freedom. We propose to explore freedom as seen from four perspectives: (1) freedom of expression, as argued by John Milton and John Stuart Mill; (2) freedom from tyrannical majorities, as presented by James Madison in the Federalist Papers, the great argument in favor of adopting our national Constitution; (3) protection of individual freedom from government infringement as stated by F. A. Hayek; and (4) freedom from fear as set forth by Harold J. Laski.

FREEDOM OF EXPRESSION

Freedom of expression goes beyond the mere right to express one's personal viewpoint and includes the important right to criticize generally accepted ideas and objectives of society. Those who criticize the existing social structure and suggest different ideas and objectives often find themselves in difficulty with the government and leaders of society in general. To permit such opposition to the status quo—meaning the established political and economic patterns of society—is one of the most severe tests for a political order that claims to be a democracy. As we pointed out in Chapter 3, one of the characteristics of dictatorship is to control all means of communication.

One of the first actions taken by dictatorial regimes when they achieve political power is to stifle all opposition viewpoints.

An outstanding champion of freedom of expression was John Milton, who published his monumental work, the *Areopagitica*, in 1644 in opposition to a new law of Parliament that required all books to be licensed by an official censor before publication. The objective of this act was to silence political opposition and to bring about religious uniformity. Milton and other men of independent outlook saw in the act a revival of the tyranny of the Stuart kings. For several years prior to the act, printing had been practically free of government control, and numerous pamphlets had been published representing every shade of political and religious opinion. Milton saw this diversity of writing as a wholesome sign of the free exchange of ideas stimulating intellectual creativity and progress. He argued that it was necessary to read books of every sort to attain knowledge in a world where good and evil grew up together and interconnected. He also pointed out that it was impossible to make men virtuous by imposing external prohibitions. Because degrading influences were to be found everywhere, the attempt to "purify" published writings was seen by Milton as an exercise in futility. The only way to combat corrupting factors was to encourage man's internal discipline and his intellect.

In our quoted excerpt, which is reproduced in the original seventeenth-century English, Milton attacks the law as a deterrent to intellectual activity and the pursuit of truth. He also points out that books are like powerful drugs out of which strong medicines may be compounded and from which children and fools should be protected. However, according to Milton, general censorship was not the answer. A modern parallel to this premise is the United States Supreme Court's reasoning that literature and motion pictures should not be prohibited on the grounds that they are not suitable for children. Finally, Milton points out the improbability of obtaining truly learned and judicious minds to serve as censors under the act. The result would be, he asserted, licensers who are ignorant—a most unhappy prospect for an enlightened society.

Our second reading relating to freedom of expression is taken from John Stuart Mill's famous essay *On Liberty*, written in 1859. In this enduring argument for what is frequently called the basic democratic right, Mill gives the reasons for providing equal opportunities to advocates of all shades of opinion. His thesis holds that people in general and students in particular should hear viewpoints contrary to those accepted by the majority in any given society. But it was not enough, according to Mill, to hear these "arguments of adversaries from [one's] own teachers, presented as they state them, and accompanied by what they offer as refutations." To do justice to these dissenting views requires presentation by advocates who actually believe them.

Freedom of expression is found in two of our fundamental freedoms as stated in the Bill of Rights: freedom of speech and freedom of the press. These freedoms are cornerstones of the American constitutional edifice and were the first rights to be called by the Supreme Court "principles of justice so rooted in the traditions and conscience of our people as to be ranked as fundamental...[and] that a fair and enlightened system of justice would be impossible without them."

FREEDOM FROM
TYRANNICAL MAJORITIES

In the modern age of democracy from the time of the French Revolution to the present, many political writers have warned against oppression by tyrannical majorities. These writings resemble those of Greek and Roman political thinkers who saw the dangers to freedom presented by demagogues bent on inflaming the masses. A year before the Philadelphia Convention was convoked, Daniel Shays led a group of discontented debtors against the district courts of Massachusetts in order to block hearings on mortgage foreclosures. Shays' Rebellion personified the instability present in the young nation, and no doubt Elbridge Gerry, a delegate from Massachusetts, had this incident in mind when, in one of his opening speeches before the Convention, he said: "The evils we experience flow from the excess of democracy. The people do not want virtue, but are dupes of pretended patriots."[1]

In *The Federalist,* Number 10, James Madison drew a distinction between a republic and a democracy. His fear of tyranny of the majority led him to suggest a system of dispersed power. The solution adopted by the anti-majoritarians in the United States was the concept of the "republic" into which were built precautions against political domination by a group or coalition destroying the freedom of minorities. This concept included the principle of federalism, according to which representation would reflect states as well as people, with smaller states protected from the power of the larger states. In our third reading, Madison discusses some of these ideas.

The anti-majoritarian beliefs were shaken by recent Supreme Court rulings on reapportionment. However, while the "one man, one vote" fomula, if followed closely, would appear to reduce the safeguards against majoritarian tyranny, the rulings have left intact, on the national level, the protective features existing in the federal system as the result of the equality of the states in the Senate. Today, Americans must cope with the fact that two-thirds of the total population lives in urban areas. In light of this rapid

---

[1] *The Formation of the United States: Documents Illustrative of the Formation of the Union of American States* (Washington: Government Printing Office, 1927), p. 125.

and dramatic growth of cities, reapportionment was a necessary step toward protecting the extensive urban majority from the rural minority's domination of state government.

FREEDOM FROM
ARBITRARY GOVERNMENT

At the Philadelphia Convention, Thomas Jefferson was preoccupied with the protection of the freedom of the individual from arbitrary government and withdrew his opposition to the Constitution only when assurances were given to him by the delegates that a bill of rights would be attached to the document as one of the first acts of the Federal Congress. The Bill of Rights—the first ten amendments—was approved in 1791. Since then, the Bill of Rights has provided the greatest source of legal restrictions upon government for the protection of individual rights. This section of the Constitution contains provisions for freedom of religion, speech, press, assembly, and the right of petition. Other guarantees in the Bill of Rights include protections against unreasonable search and seizure, excessive bail, cruel punishment, and self-incrimination. These limitations upon government will be examined more closely in Chapter 6, "Constitutionalism."

In modern times, as the political authority touches more and more people, questions arise over the extent of government inquiry into private affairs. The freedom of privacy is challenged by unprecedented intrusions, such as those made by technologically advanced listening devices. The use of "bugging" devices by individuals is alarming enough, but their unrestricted use by government would be even more frightening. Such practice would conjure up the image of "Big Brother" watching every move of the individual citizen and turning whatever freedom he may possess into a travesty. Our fourth selection, by F. A. Hayek, is a thoughtful commentary on the potential of modern technology with regard to "protected freedoms."

FREEDOM FROM FEAR OR WANT

Paradoxically, while some proponents of freedom call for curtailing government involvement in the economic and social spheres, others consider it a moral obligation of government to take positive action for assuring the well-being of the citizen. To Harold Laski, professor at the London School of Economics until his death in 1950, freedom is not merely the negative concept of absence of government restraints, but a positive notion of creating an atmosphere for individual self-fulfillment. According to his line of reasoning, to call a resident of a ghetto in a city in the United States "a free man" is deceitful. If the individual lacks an education, is poor and in bad health, and sees no hope for a change in his situation, does he enjoy freedom? This view of freedom is often termed "freedom from want or fear." In our fifth reading, Laski discusses some of his views on freedom. In Chapter 7 we will return to this subject when we examine the tenets of the welfare state.

While freedom of expression, freedom from the tyrannies of majorities or arbitrary governments, and freedom from fear or want all assume importance in contemporary debate over the meaning of freedom, we might conclude with a reference to another analysis of freedom: the flight from freedom in modern times. Erich Fromm, in *Escape From Freedom,* points out that while freedom has given modern man independence for developing himself to the fullest, it "has made him isolated and, thereby, anxious and powerless."[2] The rise of National Socialism in Germany showed how man might reject freedom for some form of authoritarian rule.

---

[2] Erich Fromm, *Escape From Freedom* (New York: Avon Books, 1965), p. viii.

Areopagitica

JOHN MILTON

I deny not, but that it is of greatest concernment in the Church and Commonwealth, to have a vigilant eye how Bookes demeane themselves, as well as men; and thereafter to confine, imprison, and do sharpest justice on them as malefactors: For Books are not absolutely dead things, but doe contain a potencie of life in them to be as active as that soule was whose progeny they are; nay they do preserve as in a violl the purest efficacie and extraction of that living intellect that bred them. I know they are as lively, and as vigorously productive, as those fabulous Dragons teeth; and being sown up and down, may chance to spring up armed men. And yet on the other hand unlesse warinesse be us'd, as good almost kill a Man as kill a good Book; who kills a Man kills a reasonable creature, Gods Image; but hee who destroyes a good Booke, kills reason it selfe, kills the Image of God, as it were in the eye. Many a man lives a burden to the Earth; but a good Booke is the pretious life-blood of a master spirit, imbalm'd and treasur'd up on purpose to a life beyond life. 'Tis true, no age can restore a life, whereof perhaps there is no great losse; and revolutions of ages doe not oft recover the losse of a rejected truth, for the want of which whole Nations fare the worse. We should be wary therefore what persecu-

tion we raise against the living labours of publick men, how we spill that season'd life of man preserv'd and stor'd up in Books; since we see a kinde of homicide may be thus committed, sometimes a martyrdome, and if it extend to the whole impression, a kinde of massacre, whereof the execution ends not in the slaying of an elementall life, but strikes at that ethereall and fift essence, the breath of reason it selfe, slaies an immortality rather then a life. But lest I should be condemn'd of introducing licence, while I oppose Licencing, I refuse not the pains to be so much Historicall, as will serve to shew what hath been done by ancient and famous Commonwealths, against this disorder, till the very time that this project of licencing crept out of the *Inquisition,* was catcht up by our Prelates, and hath caught some of our Presbyters.

. . .

...Seeing therefore that those books, & those in great abundance which are likeliest to taint both life and doctrine, cannot be supprest without the fall of learning, and of all ability in disputation, and that these books of either sort are most and soonest catching to the learned, from whom to the common people what ever is hereticall or dissolute may quickly be convey'd, and that evill manners are as perfectly learnt without books a thousand other ways which cannot be stopt, and evill doctrine not with books can propagate, except a teacher guide, which he might also doe without writing, and so beyond

Reprinted from *Complete Prose Works of John Milton,* Vol. II, 1643–48, ed. Ernest Sirluck (New Haven: Yale University Press, 1959), pp. 492–93, 520–21, 530–31, by permission of the publisher.

prohibiting, I am not able to unfold, how this cautelous enterprise of licencing can be exempted from the number of vain and impossible attempts. And he who were pleasantly dispos'd, could not well avoid to lik'n it to the exploit of that gallant man who thought to pound up the crows by shutting his Parkgate. Besides another inconvenience, if learned men be the first receivers out of books, & dispredders both of vice and error, how shall the lincencers themselves be confided in, unlesse we can conferr upon them, or they assume to themselves above all others in the Land, the grace of infallibility, and uncorruptednesse? And again if it be true, that a wise man like a good refiner can gather gold out of the drossiest volume, and that a fool will be a fool with the best book, yea or without book, there is no reason that we should deprive a wise man of any advantage to his wisdome, while we seek to restrain from a fool, that which being restrain'd will be no hindrance to his folly. For if there should be so much exactnesse always us'd to keep that from him which is unfit for his reading, we should in the judgement of *Aristotle*[1] not only, but of *Salomon*,[2] and of our Saviour,[3] not voutsafe him good precepts, and by consequence not willingly admit him to good books; as being certain that a wise man will make better use of an idle pamphlet, then a fool will do of sacred Scripture. 'Tis next alleg'd we must not expose our selves to tempta-

tions without necessity, and next to that, not imploy our time in vain things. To both these objections one answer will serve, out of the grounds already laid, that to all men such books are not temptations, nor vanities; but usefull drugs and materialls wherewith to temper and compose effective and strong med'cins, which mans life cannot want.[4] The rest, as children and childish men, who have not the art to qualifie and prepare these working mineralls, well may be exhorted to forbear, but hinder'd forcibly they cannot be by all the licencing that Sainted Inquisition could ever yet contrive; which is what I promis'd to deliver next, That this order of licencing conduces nothing to the end for which it was fram'd; and hath almost prevented me by being clear already while thus much hath bin explaining. See the ingenuity of Truth, who when she gets a free and willing hand, opens her self faster, then the pace of method and discours can overtake her.

. . .

Another reason, whereby to make it plain that this order will misse the end it seeks, consider by the quality which ought to be in every licencer. It cannot be deny'd but that he who is made judge to sit upon the birth, or death of books whether they may be wafted into this world, or not, had need to be a man above the common measure, both studious, learned, and judicious; there may be else no mean mistakes in the censure of what is passable or not; which is also no mean injury. If he be of such worth as behoovs him, there cannot be a more tedious and unpleasing journey-work, a greater losse of time levied upon his head, then to be made the perpetuall reader of unchosen books and pamphlets, oftimes huge volumes. There is no book that is

---

1 *Ethics,* I, iii; 1095ª (tr. W. D. Ross, in *Introduction to Aristotle,* ed. Richard McKeon, New York; Modern Library, 1947, p. 310): "Since he tends to follow his passions, his study will be vain and unprofitable."

2 Proverbs 23:9: "Speak not in the ears of a fool: for he will despise the wisdom of thy words."

3 Matthew 7:6: "Give not that which is holy unto the dogs, neither cast ye your pearls before swine."

4 *I.e.,* with which men cannot dispense.

acceptable unlesse at certain seasons; but to be enjoyn'd the reading of that at all times, and in a hand scars legible, whereof three pages would not down at any time in the fairest Print, is an imposition which I cannot beleeve how he that values time, and his own studies, or is but of a sensible nostrill should be able to endure. In this one thing I crave leave of the present licencers to be pardon'd for so thinking: who doubtlesse took this office up, looking on it through their obedience to the Parlament, whose command perhaps made all things seem easie and unlaborious to them; but that this short triall hath wearied them out already, their own expressions and excuses to them who make so many journeys to sollicit their licence, are testimony anough. Seeing therefore those who now possesse the imployment, by all evident signs wish themselves well ridd of it, and that no man of worth, none that is not a plain unthrift of his own hours is ever likely to succeed them, except he mean to put himself to the salary of a Presse-corrector, we may easily foresee what kind of licencers we are to expect hereafter, either ignorant, imperious, and remisse, or basely pecuniary. This is what I had to shew wherein this order cannot conduce to that end, whereof it bears the intention.

I lastly proceed from the no good it can do, to the manifest hurt it causes, in being first the greatest discouragement and affront, that can be offer'd to learning and to learned men.... If therefore ye be loath to dishearten utterly and discontent, not the mercenary crew of false pretenders to learning, but the free and ingenuous sort of such as evidently were born to study, and love lerning for it self, not for lucre, or any other end, but the service of God and of truth, and perhaps that lasting fame and perpetuity of praise which God and good men have consented shall be the reward of those whose publisht labours advance the good of mankind, then know, that so far to distrust the judgement & the honesty of one who hath but a common repute in learning, and never yet offended, as not to count him fit to print his mind without a tutor and examiner, lest he should drop a scism, or something of corruption, is the greatest displeasure and indignity to a free and knowing spirit that can be put upon him....

. . .

On Liberty

JOHN STUART MILL

...The peculiarity of the evidence of mathematical truths is, that all the argument is on one side. There are no objections, and no answers to objections. But on every subject on which difference of opinion is possible, the truth depends on a balance to be struck between two sets of conflicting reasons. Even in natural philosophy, there is always some other explanation possible of the same facts; some geocentric

Reprinted from John Stuart Mill, *On Liberty and Other Essays,* with an Introduction by Emery E. Neff (New York: The Macmillan Company, 1926), pp. 43–44, 56–57, by permission of the publisher.

theory instead of heliocentric, some phlogiston instead of oxygen; and it has to be shown why that other theory cannot be the true one: and until this is shown, and until we known how it is shown, we do not understand the grounds of our opinion. But when we turn to subjects infinitely more complicated, to morals, religion, politics, social relations, and the business of life, three-fourths of the arguments for every disputed opinion consist in dispelling the appearances which favour some opinion different from it. The greatest orator, save one, of antiquity, has left it on record that he always studied his adversary's case with as great, if not still greater, intensity than even his own. What Cicero practised as the means of forensic success, requires to be imitated by all who study any subject in order to arrive at the truth. He who knows only his own side of the case, knows little of that. His reasons may be good, and no one may have been able to refute them. But if he is equally unable to refute the reasons on the opposite side; if he does not so much as know what they are, he has no ground for preferring either opinion. The rational position for him would be suspension of judgment, and unless he contents himself with that, he is either led by authority, or adopts, like the generality of the world, the side to which he feels most inclination. Nor is it enough that he should hear the arguments of adversaries from his own teachers, presented as they state them, and accompanied by what they offer as refutations. That is not the way to do justice to the arguments, or bring them into real contact with his own mind. He must be able to hear them from persons who actually believe them; who defend them in earnest, and do their very utmost for them. He must know them in their most plausible and persuasive form; he must feel the whole force of the difficulty which the true view of the subject has to encounter and dispose of; else he will never really possess himself of the portion of truth which meets and removes that difficulty. Ninety-nine in a hundred of what are called educated men are in this condition; even of those who can argue fluently for their opinions. Their conclusion may be true, but it might be false for anything they know: they have thrown themselves into the mental position of those who think differently from them, and considered what such persons may have to say; and consequently they do not, in any proper sense of the word, know the doctrine which they themselves profess. They do not know those parts of it which explain and justify the remainder; the considerations which show that a fact which seemingly conflicts with another is reconcilable with it, or that, of two apparently strong reasons, one and not the other ought to be preferred. All that part of the truth which turns the scale, and decides the judgment of a completely informed mind, they are strangers to; nor is it ever really known, but to those who have attended equally and impartially to both sides, and endeavoured to see the reasons of both in the strongest light. So essential is this discipline to a real understanding of moral and human subjects, that if opponents of all important truths do not exist, it is indispensable to imagine them, and supply them with the strongest arguments which the most skilful devil's advocate can conjure up.

.   .   .

...In politics, again, it is almost a commonplace, that a party of order or stability, and a party of progress or reform, are both necessary elements of a healthy state of political life; until the one or the other shall have so enlarged its mental grasp as to be a party equally of order and of progress, knowing and distinguishing what is fit to be preserved from what ought to be swept away. Each of these modes of thinking derives its utility from the deficiencies of the other; but it is in a great measure the opposition of the other that keeps each within the limits of reason and sanity. Unless opinions favourable to democracy and to aristocracy, to property and to equality, to co-operation and to competition, to luxury and to abstinence, to sociality and individuality, to liberty and discipline, and all the other standing antagonisms of practical life, are expressed with equal freedom, and enforced and defended with equal talent and energy, there is no chance of both elements obtaining their due; one scale is sure to go up, and the other down. Truth, in the great practical concerns of life, is so much a question of the reconciling and combining of opposites, that very few have minds sufficiently capacious and impartial to make the adjustment with an approach to correctness, and it has to be made by the rough process of a struggle between combatants fighting under hostile banners. On any of the great open questions just enumerated, if either of the two opinions has a better claim than the other, not merely to be tolerated, but to be encouraged and countenanced, it is the one which happens at the particular time and place to be in a minority. That is the opinion which, for the time being, represents the neglected interests, the side of human well-being which is in danger of obtaining less than its share. I am aware that there is not, in this country, any intolerance of differences of opinion on most of these topics. They are adduced to show, by admitted and multiplied examples, the universality of the fact, that only through diversity of opinion is there, in the existing state of human intellect, a chance of fair play to all sides of the truth. When there are persons to be found, who form an exception to the apparent unanimity of the world on any subject, even if the world is in the right, it is always probable that dissentients have something worth hearing to say for themselves, and that truth would lose something by their silence. . . .

The Federalist No. 10

JAMES MADISON

To the People of the State of New York:

Among the numerous advantages promised by a well-constructed Union, none

Reprinted from Alexander Hamilton, John Jay, and James Madison, *The Federalist* (New York: Random House, Inc., 1937), pp. 53–62.

deserves to be more accurately developed than its tendency to break and control the violence of action. The friend of popular governments never finds himself so much alarmed for their character and fate, as when he contemplates their propensity to this dangerous vice. He will not fail, therefore, to set a due value on any plan which, without violating the principles to which he is attached, provides a proper cure for it. The instability, injustice, and confusion introduced into the public councils, have, in truth, been the mortal diseases under which popular governments have everywhere perished; as they continue to be the favorite and fruitful topics from which the adversaries to liberty derive their most specious declamations. The valuable improvements made by the American constitutions on the popular models, both ancient and modern, cannot certainly be too much admired; but it would be an unwarrantable partiality, to contend that they have as effectually obviated the danger on this side, as was wished and expected. Complaints are everywhere heard from our most considerate and virtuous citizens, equally the friends of public and private faith, and of public and personal liberty, that our governments are too unstable, that the public good is disregarded in the conflicts of rival parties, and that measures are too often decided, not according to the rules of justice and the rights of the minor party, but by the superior force of an interested and overbearing majority. However anxiously we may wish that these complaints had no foundation, the evidence of known facts will not permit us to deny that they are in some degree true. It will be found, indeed, on a candid review of our situation, that some of the distresses under which we labor have been erroneously charged on the operation of our governments; but it will be found, at the same time, that other causes will not alone account for many of our heaviest misfortunes; and, particularly, for that prevailing and increasing distrust of public engagements, and alarm for private rights, which are echoed from one end of the continent to the other. These must be chiefly, if not

wholly, effects of the unsteadiness and injustice with which a factious spirit has tainted our public administrations.

By a faction, I understand a number of citizens, whether amounting to a majority or minority of the whole, who are united and actuated by some common impulse of passion, or of interest, adverse to the rights of other citizens, or to the permanent and aggregate interests of the community.

There are two methods of curing the mischiefs of faction: the one, by removing its causes; the other, by controlling its effects.

There are again two methods of removing the causes of faction: the one, by destroying the liberty which is essential to its existence; the other, by giving to every citizen the same opinions, the same passions, and the same interests.

It could never be more truly said than of the first remedy, that it was worse than the disease. Liberty is to faction what air is to fire, an aliment without which it instantly expires. But it could not be less folly to abolish liberty, which is essential to political life, because it nourishes faction, than it would be to wish the annihilation of air, which is essential to animal life, because it imparts to fire its destructive agency.

The second expedient is as impracticable as the first would be unwise. As long as the reason of man continues fallible, and he is at liberty to exercise it, different opininons will be formed. As long as the connection subsists between his reason and his self-love, his opinions and his passions will have a reciprocal influence on each other; and the former will be objects to which the latter will attach themselves. The diversity in the faculties of men, from which the rights of property originate, is not less an insuperable obstacle to a uniformity of interests. The protection of these faculties is the first object of government. From the protection of different and unequal faculties of acquiring property, the possession of different degrees and kinds of property immediately results; and from the influence of these on the sentiments and views of the respective proprietors, ensues a division of the society into different interests and parties.

The latent causes of faction are thus sown in the nature of man; and we see them everywhere brought into different degrees of activity, according to the different circumstances of civil society. A zeal for different opinions concerning religion, concerning government, and many other points, as well of speculation as of practice; an attachment to different leaders ambitiously contending for pre-eminence and power; or to persons of other descriptions whose fortunes have been interesting to the human passions, have, in turn, divided mankind into parties, inflamed them with mutual animosity, and rendered them much more disposed to vex and oppress each other than to co-operate for their common good. So strong is this propensity of mankind to fall into mutual animosities, that where no substantial occasion presents itself, the most frivolous and fanciful distinctions have been sufficient to kindle their unfriendly passions and excite their most violent conflicts. But the most common and durable source of factions has been the various and unequal distribution of property. Those who hold and those who are without property have ever formed distinct interests in society. Those who are creditors, and those who are debtors, fall under a like. discrimination. A landed interest, a manufacturing interest, a mercantile interest, a moneyed interest, with many lesser interests, grow up of necessity in civilized nations, and divide them into different classes, actuated by different sentiments and views. The regulation of these various and interfering interests forms the principal task of modern legislation, and involves the spirit of party and faction in the necessary and ordinary operations of the government.

No man is allowed to be a judge in his own cause, because his interest would certainly bias his judgment, and, not improbably, corrupt his integrity. With equal, nay with greater reason, a body of men are unfit to be both judged and parties at the same time; yet what are many of the most important acts of legislation, but so many judicial determinations, not indeed concerning the rights of single persons, but concerning the rights of large bodies of citizens? And what are the different classes of legislators but advocates and parties to the causes which they determine? Is a law proposed concerning private debts? It is a question to which the creditors are parties on one side and the debtors on the other. Justice ought to hold the balance between them. Yet the parties are, and must be, themselves the judges; and the most numerous party, or, in other words, the most powerful faction must be expected to prevail. Shall domestic manufactures be encouraged, and in what degree, by restrictions on foreign manufactures? are questions which would be differently decided by the landed and the manufacturing classes, and probably by neither with a sole regard to justice and the public good. The apportionment of taxes on the various descriptions of property is an act which seems to require the most exact impartiality; yet there is, perhaps, no legislative act in which greater opportunity and temptation are given to a predominant party to trample on the rules of justice. Every shilling with which they overburden the inferior number, is a shilling saved to their own pockets.

It is in vain to say that enlightened statesmen will be able to adjust these clashing interests, and render them all subservient to the public good. Enlightened statesmen will not always be at the helm. Nor, in many cases, can such an adjustment be made at all without taking into view indirect and remote considerations, which will rarely prevail over the immediate interest which one party may find in disregarding the rights of another or the good of the whole.

The inference to which we are brought is, that the *causes* of faction cannot be removed, and that relief is only to be sought in the means of controlling its *effects*.

If a faction consists of less than a majority, relief is supplied by the republican principle, which enables the majority to defeat its sinister views by regular vote. It may clog the administration, it may convulse the society; but it will be unable to execute and mask its violence under the forms of the Constitution. When a majority is included in a faction, the form of popular government, on the other hand, enables it to sacrifice to its ruling passion or interest both the public good and the rights of other citizens. To secure the public good and private rights against the danger of such a faction, and at the same time to preserve the spirit and the form of popular government, is then the great object to which our inquiries are directed. Let me add that it is the great desideratum by which this form of government can be rescued from the opprobrium under which it has so long labored, and be recommended to the esteem and adoption of mankind.

By what means is this object attainable? Evidently by one of two only. Either the existence of the same passion or interest in a majority at the same time must be prevented, or the majority, having such coexistent passion or interest, must be rendered, by their number and local situation, unable to concert and carry into effect schemes of oppression. If the impulse and the opportunity be suffered to coincide, we well know that neither moral nor religious motives can be relied on as an adequate control. They are not found to be such on the injustice and violence of individuals, and lose their efficacy in proportion to the number combined together, that is, in proportion as their efficacy becomes needful.

From this view of the subject it may be concluded that a pure democracy, by which I mean a society consisting of a small number of citizens, who assemble and administer the government in person, can admit of no cure for the mischiefs of action. A common passion or interest will, in almost every case, be felt by a majority of the whole; a communication and concert result from the form of government itself; and there is nothing to check the inducements to sacrifice the weaker party or an obnoxious individual. Hence it is that such democracies have ever been spectacles of turbulence and contention; have ever been found incompatible with personal security or the rights of property; and have in general been as short in their lives as they have been violent in their deaths. Theoretic politicians, who have patronized this species of government, have erroneously supposed that by reducing mankind to a perfect equality in their political rights, they would, at the same time, be perfectly equalized and assimilated in their possessions, their opinions, and their passions.

A republic, by which I mean a government in which the scheme of representation takes place, opens a different prospect, and promises the cure for which we are seeking. Let us examine the points in which it varies from pure democracy, and we shall comprehend both the nature of the cure and the efficacy which it must derive from the Union.

The two great points of difference between a democracy and a republic are: first, the delegation of the government, in the latter, to a small number of citizens elected by the rest; secondly, the greater number of citizens, and greater sphere of country, over which the latter may be extended.

The effect of the first difference is, on the one hand, to refine and enlarge the public views, by passing them through the medium of a chosen body of citizens, whose wisdom may best discern the true interest of their country, and whose patriotism and love of justice will be least likely to sacrifice it to temporary or partial considerations. Under such a regulation, it may well happen that the public voice, pronounced by the representatives of the people, will be more consonant to the public good than if pronounced by the people themselves, convened for the purpose. On the other hand, the effect may be inverted. Men of factious tempers, of local prejudices, or of sinister designs, may, by intrigue, by corruption, or by other means, first obtain the suffrages, and then betray the interests, of the people. The question resulting is, whether small or extensive republics are more favorable to the election of proper guardians of the public weal; and it is clearly decided in favor of the latter by two obvious considerations:

In the first place, it is to be remarked that, however small the republic may be, the representatives must be raised to a certain number, in order to guard against the cabals of a few; and that, however large it may be, they must be limited to a certain number, in order to guard against the confusion of a multitude. Hence, the number of representatives in the two cases not being in proportion to that of the two constituents, and being proportionally greater in the small republic, it follows that, if the proportion of fit characters be not less in the large than in the small republic, the former will present a greater option, and consequently a greater probability of a fit choice.

In the next place, as each representative will be chosen by a greater number of citizens in the large than in the small republic, it will be more difficult for unworthy candidates to practise with success the vicious arts by which elections are too often carried; and the suffrages of the people being more free, will be more likely to centre in men who possess the most attractive merit and the most diffusive and established characters.

It must be confessed that in this, as in most other cases, there is a mean, on both sides of which inconveniences will be found to lie. By enlarging too much the number of electors, you render the representative too little acquainted with all their local circumstances and lesser interests; and by reducing it too much, you render him unduly attached to these, and too little fit to comprehend and pursue great and national objects. The federal Constitution forms a happy combination in this respect; the great and aggregate interests being referred to the national, the local and particular to the State legislatures.

The other point of difference is, the greater number of citizens and extent of territory which may be brought within the compass of republican than of democratic government; and it is this circumstance principally which renders factious combinations less to be dreaded in the former than in the latter. The smaller the society, the fewer probably will be the distinct parties and interests composing it; the fewer the distinct parties and interests, the more frequently will a majority be found of the same party; and the smaller the number of individuals composing a majority, and the smaller the compass within which they are placed, the more easily will they concert and execute their plans of oppression. Extend the sphere and you take in a greater variety of parties and interests; you make it less probable that a majority of the whole will have a common motive to invade the rights of other citizens; or if such a common motive exists, it will be more difficult for all who feel it to discover their own strength, and to act in unison with each other. Besides other impediments, it may be remarked that, where there is a consciousness of unjust or dishonorable purposes, communication is always checked by distrust in proportion to the number whose concurrence is necessary.

Hence, it clearly appears, that the same advantage which a republic has over a democracy, in controlling the effects of faction, is enjoyed by a large over a small republic—is enjoyed by the Union over the States composing it. Does the advantage consist in the substitution of representatives whose enlightened views and virtuous sentiments render them superior to local prejudices and to schemes of injustice? It will not be denied that the representation of the Union will be most likely to possess these requisite endowments. Does it consist in the greater security afforded by a greater variety of parties, against the event of any one party being able to outnumber and oppress the rest? In an equal degree does the increased variety of parties comprised within the Union, increase this security. Does it, in fine, consist in the greater obstacles opposed to the concert and accomplishment of the secret wishes of an unjust and interested majority? Here, again, the extent of the Union gives it the most palpable advantage.

The influence of factious leaders may kindle a flame within their particular States, but will be unable to spread a general conflagration through the other States. A religious sect may degenerate into a political faction in a part of the Confederacy; but the variety of sects dispersed over the entire face of it must secure the national councils against any danger from that source. A rage for paper money, for an abolition of debts, for an equal division of property, or for any other improper or wicked project, will be less apt to pervade the whole body of the Union than a particular member of it; in the same proportion as such a malady is more likely to taint a particular county or district, than an entire State.

In the extent and proper structure of the Union, therefore, we behold a republican remedy for the diseases most incident to republican government. And according to the degree of pleasure and pride we feel in being republicans, ought to be our zeal in cherishing the spirit and supporting the character of Federalists.

PUBLIUS

The Constitution of Liberty

F. A. HAYEK

A source of confusion is the fact that within law itself the expression "public policy" is commonly used to describe certain pervading general principles which are often not laid down as written rules but are understood to qualify the validity of more specific rules. When it is said that it is the policy of the law to protect good faith, to preserve public order, or not to recognize contracts for immoral purposes, this refers to rules, but rules which are stated in terms of some permanent end of government rather than in terms of rules of conduct. It means that, within the limits of the powers given to it, the government must so act that that end will be achieved. The reason why the term "policy" is used in such instances appears to be that it is felt that to specify the end to be achieved is in conflict with the conception of law as an abstract rule. Though such reasoning may explain the practice, it is clèarly one which is not without danger.

Policy is rightly contrasted with legislation when it means the pursuit by government of the concrete, ever changing aims of the day. It is with the execution of policy in this sense that administration proper is largely concerned. Its task is the direction and allocation of resources put at the disposal of government in the service of the constantly changing needs of the

community. All the services which the government provides for the citizen, from national defense to upkeep of roads, from sanitary safeguards to the policing of the streets, are necessarily of this kind. For these tasks it is allowed definite means and its own paid servants, and it will constantly have to decide on the next urgent task and the means to be used. The tendency of the professional administrators concerned with these tasks is inevitably to draw everything they can into the service of the public aims they are pursuing. It is largely as a protection of the private citizen against this tendency of an ever growing administrative machinery to engulf the private sphere that the rule of law is so important today. It means in the last resort that the agencies intrusted with such special tasks cannot wield for their purpose any sovereign powers (no *Hoheitsrechte,* as the Germans call it) but must confine themselves to the means specially granted to them.

Under a reign of freedom the free sphere of the individual includes all action not explicitly restricted by a general law. We have seen that it was found especially necessary to protect against infringement by authority some of the more important private rights, and also how apprehension was felt that such an explicit enumeration of some might be interpreted to mean that only they enjoyed the special protection of the constitution. These fears have proved to be only too well founded.

Reprinted from *The Constitution of Liberty* by F. A. Hayek by permission of The University of Chicago Press. Copyright © 1960 by The University of Chicago Press.

On the whole, however, experience seems to confirm the argument that, in spite of the inevitable incompleteness of any bill of rights, such a bill affords an important protection for certain rights known to be easily endangered. Today we must be particularly aware that, as a result of technological change, which constantly creates new potential threats to individual liberty, no list of protected rights can be regarded as exhaustive. In an age of radio and television, the problem of free access to information is no longer a problem of the freedom of the press. In an age when drugs or psychological techniques can be used to control a person's actions, the problem of free control over one's body is no longer a matter of protection against physical restraint. The problem of the freedom of movement takes on a new significance when foreign travel has become impossible for those to whom the authorities of their own country are not willing to issue a passport.

The problem assumes the greatest importance when we consider that we are probably only at the threshold of an age in which the technological possibilities of mind control are likely to grow rapidly and what may appear at first as innocuous or beneficial powers over the personality of the individual will be at the disposal of government. The greatest threats to human freedom probably still lie in the future. The day may not be far off when authority, by adding appropriate drugs to our water supply or by some other similar device, will be able to elate or depress, stimulate or paralyze, the minds of whole populations for its own purposes. If bills of rights are to remain in any way meaningful, it must be recognized early that their intention was certainly to protect the individual against all vital infringements of his liberty and that

therefore they must be presumed to contain a general clause protecting against government's interference those immunities which individuals in fact have enjoyed in the past.

In the last resort these legal guaranties of certain fundamental rights are no more than part of the safeguards of individual liberty which constitutionalism provides, and they cannot give greater security against legislative infringements of liberty than the constitutions themselves. As we have seen, they can do no more than give protection against hasty and improvident action of current legislation and cannot prevent any suppression of rights by the deliberate action of the ultimate legislator. The only safeguard against this is clear awareness of the dangers on the part of public opinion. Such provisions are important mainly because they impress upon the public mind the value of these individual rights and make them part of a political creed which the people will defend even when they do not fully understand its significance.

We have up to this point represented those guaranties of individual freedom as if they were absolute rights which could never be infringed. In actual fact they cannot mean more than that the normal running of society is based on them and that any departure from them requires special justification. Even the most fundamental principles of a free society, however, may have to be temporarily sacrificed when, but only when, it is a question of preserving liberty in the long run, as in the case of war. Concerning the need of such emergency powers of government in such instances (and of safeguards against their abuse) there exists widespread agreement.

It is not the occasional necessity of

withdrawing some of the civil liberties by a suspension of habeas corpus or the proclamation of a state of siege that we need to consider further, but the conditions under which the particular rights of individual or groups may occasionally be infringed in the public interest. That even such fundamental rights as freedom of speech may have to be curtailed in situations of "clear and present danger," or that the government may have to exercise the right of eminent domain for the compulsory purchase of land, can hardly be disputed. But if the rule of law is to be preserved, it is necessary that such actions be confined to exceptional cases defined by rule, so that their justification does not rest on the arbitrary decision of any authority but can be reviewed by an independent court; and, second, it is necessary that the individuals affected be not harmed by the disappointment of their legitimate expectations but be fully indemnified for any damage they suffer as a result of such action.

The principle of "no expropriation without just compensation" has always been recognized wherever the rule of law has prevailed. It is, however, not always recognized that this is an integral and indispensable element of the principle of the supremacy of the law. Justice requires it; but what is more important is that it is our chief assurance that those necessary infringements of the private sphere will be allowed only in instances where the public gain is clearly greater than the harm done by the disappointment of normal individual expectations. The chief purpose of the requirement of full compensation is indeed to act as a curb on such infringements of the private sphere and to provide a means of ascertaining whether the particular purpose is important enough to justify an exception to the principle on which the normal working of society rests. In view of the difficulty of estimating the often intangible advantages of public action and of the notorious tendency of the expert administrator to overestimate the importance of the particular goal of the moment, it would even seem desirable that the private owner should always have the benefit of the doubt and that compensation should be fixed as high as possible without opening the door to outright abuse. This means, after all, no more than that the public gain must clearly and substantially exceed the loss if an exception to the normal rule is to be allowed.

We have now concluded the enumeration of the essential factors which together make up the rule of law, without considering those procedural safeguards such as habeas corpus, trial by jury, and so on, which, in the Anglo-Saxon countries, appear to most people as the chief foundations of their liberty. English and American readers will probably feel that I have put the cart before the horse and concentrated on minor features while leaving out what is fundamental. This has been quite deliberate.

I do not wish in any way to disparage the importance of these procedural safeguards. Their value for the preservation of liberty can hardly be overstated. But while their importance is generally recognized, it is not understood that they presuppose for their effectiveness the acceptance of the rule of law as here defined and that, without it, all procedural safeguards would be valueless. True, it is probably the reverence for these procedural safeguards that has enabled the English-speaking world to preserve the medieval conception of the rule of law over men. Yet this is no proof that liberty will be preserved if the basic belief in the existence of abstract rules of law which bind all authority in their action is shaken. Judicial forms are intended to insure that decisions will be made according to rules and not according to the relative desirability of particular ends or values. All the rules of judicial procedure, all the principles intended to protect the individual and to secure impartiality of justice, presuppose that every dispute between individuals or between individuals and the state can be decided by the application of general law. They are designed to make the law prevail, but they are powerless to protect justice where the law deliberately leaves the decision to the discretion of authority. It is only where the law decides—and this means only where independent courts have the last word—that the procedural safeguards are safeguards of liberty.

I have here concentrated on the fundamental conception of law which the traditional institutions presuppose because the belief that adherence to the external forms of judicial procedure will preserve the rule of law seems to me the greatest threat to its preservation. I do not question, but rather wish to emphasize, that the belief in the rule of law and the reverence for the forms of justice belong together and that neither will be effective without the other. But it is the first which is chiefly threatened today; and it is the illusion that it will be preserved by scrupulous observation of the forms of justice that is one of the chief causes of this threat. "Society is not going to be saved by importing the forms and rules of judicial procedure into places where they do not naturally belong." To use the trappings of judicial form where the essential conditions for a judicial decision are absent, or to give judges power to decide issues which cannot be decided by the application of rules, can have no effect but to destroy the respect for them even where they deserve it.

Liberty and Equality

HAROLD J. LASKI

By liberty I mean the eager maintenance of that atmosphere in which men have the opportunity to be their best selves. Liberty, therefore, is a product of rights. A State built upon the conditions essential to the full development of our faculties will confer freedom upon its citizens. It will release their individuality. It will enable them

Reprinted from Harold J. Laski, *Grammar of Politics* (London: George Allen and Unwin Ltd., 1937), pp. 142–49, by permission of the publisher.

to contribute their peculiar and intimate experience to the common stock. It will offer security that the decisions of the government are built upon the widest knowledge open to its members. It will prevent that frustration of creative impulse which destroys the special character of men. Without rights there cannot be liberty, because, without rights, men are the subjects of law unrelated to the needs of personality.

Liberty, therefore, is a positive thing. It does not merely mean absence of restraint. Regulation, obviously enough, is the consequence of gregariousness; for we cannot live together without common rules. What is important is that the rules made should embody an experience I can follow and, in general, accept. I shall not feel that my liberty is endangered when I am refused permission to commit murder. My creative impulses do not suffer frustration when I am bidden to drive on a given side of the road. I am not even deprived of freedom when the law ordains that I must educate my children. Historic experience has evolved for us rules of convenience which promote right living. To compel obedience to them is not to make a man unfree. Wherever there are avenues of conduct which must be prohibited in the common interest, their removal from the sphere of unrestrained action need not constitute an invasion of liberty.

That is not, of course, to argue that every such prohibition is justified merely because it is made by an authority legally competent to issue it. Governments may in fact invade liberty even while they claim to be acting in the common interest. The exclusion of Nonconformists from full political privilege was an invasion of liberty. The restriction of the franchise to the owners of property was an invasion of liberty. The Combination Acts of 1799–1800 destroyed the liberty of working men. They could not realise their best selves because they could not unite in the effort to translate their experience into terms of statute. It is, in other words, essential to freedom that the prohibitions issued should be built upon the wills of those whom they affect. I must be able to feel that my will has access to avenues through which it can impress itself upon the holders of power. If I have the sense that the orders issued

are beyond my scrutiny or criticism, I shall be, in a vital sense, unfree.

Liberty, therefore, is not merely obedience to a rule. My self is too distinct from other selves to accept a given order as good unless I feel that my will is embodied in its substance. I shall, of course, be compelled to endure irksome restraints. I must fill up income-tax returns; I must light the lamps upon my own motor-car at a set time. But no normal person will regard restrictions of this kind as so unrelated to his will as to constitute coercion of it. Where restraint becomes an invasion of liberty is where the given prohibition acts so as to destroy that harmony of impulses which comes when a man knows that he is doing something it is worth while to do. Restraint is felt as evil when it frustrates the life of spiritual enrichment. What each of us desires in life is room for our personal initiative in the things that add to our moral stature. What is destructive of our freedom is a system of prohibitions which limits the initiative there implied. And it is important that the initiative be a continuous one. The minds of citizens must be active minds. They must be given the habit of thought. They must be given the avenues through which thought can act. They must be accustomed to the exercise of will and conscience if they are to be alert to the duties implied in their function as citizens. Liberty consists in nothing so much as the encouragement of the will based on the instructed conscience of humble men.

In such a background, we cannot accept Mill's famous attempt to define the limits of State interference. All conduct is social conduct in the sense that whatever I do has results upon me as a member of society. There are certain freedoms I must have in order to be more than an inert recipient of orders;

there is an atmosphere about those freedoms of quick vigilance without which they cannot be maintained. Liberty thus involves in its nature restraints, because the separate freedoms I use are not freedoms to destroy the freedoms of those with whom I live. My freedoms are avenues of choice through which I may, as I deem fit, construct for myself my own course of conduct. And the freedoms I must possess to enjoy a general liberty are those which, in their sum, will constitute the path through which, my best self is capable of attainment. That is not to say it will be attained. It is to say only that I alone can make that best self, and that without those freedoms I have not the means of manufacture at my disposal.

Freedoms are therefore opportunities which history has shown to be essential to the development of personality. And freedoms are inseparable from rights because, otherwise, their realisation is hedged about with an uncertainty which destroys their quality. If, for example, my utterance of opinion is followed by persecution, I shall, in general, cease to express my mind. I shall cease, in fact, to be a citizen; and the state for me ceases to have meaning. For if I cannot embody my experience in its will, it ceases, sooner or later, to assume that I have a will at all. Nothing, therefore, is so likely to maintain a condition of liberty as the knowledge that the invasion of rights will result in protest, and, if need be, resistance. Liberty is nothing if it is not the organised and conscious power to resist in the last resort. The implied threat of contingent anarchy is a safeguard against the abuse of government.

I have set liberty here in the context of opportunity, and, in its turn, opportunity in the context of the State. That is the only atmosphere in which it admits of organisation. We can create channels; we cannot force men to take advantage of those channels. We can, further, create channels only in limited number. A man may feel that all that he cares for in life depends upon success in love; we can remove the barriers of caste or race or religion which, in the past, have barred his access to that love. But we cannot guarantee to him that his plea will be successful. The avenues which organisation can create are always limited by the fact that the most intimate realisation of oneself is personal and built upon isolations which evade social control.

Yet the social control is important. If in the last resort, the State cannot make me happy, certainly it can, if it so will, compel unhappiness. It can invade my private life in wanton fashion. It can degrade me as a political unit in a fashion which distinguishes me from other citizens. It can protect an economic order which "implicates," in William James' phrase, unfreedom. None of these things is, of course, a genuinely separate category; at most the distinction is one of convenience. For liberty is a definite whole, because the life I lead is a totality in which I strive to realise a whole personality as harmonious. Yet each of these aspects is sufficiently clear to warrant a separate word.

But it must first be urged that in this context State-action is action by government. It means the maintenance of rules which affect my liberty. Those rules will be issued by persons, and, normally, those persons will be the government. Theories which seek to differentiate between State and government almost always ignore the substance of the administrative act. Rights withheld mean rights which the holders of power withhold. To say that in a democratic theory the mass of citizens are the holders of power is to miss the vital fact that the people, in the pressure of daily affairs, cannot exercise that power in detail in States of the modern size. They may have influence and opinion; but these are not the power of government. It is the cumulative force of administrative acts which are the heart of the modern State. The principles behind these acts are, of course, of prime importance. But principles may be invalidated by the method of their application; and it is governments which have the actual administration of them.

Liberty, therefore, is never real unless the government can be called to account; and it should always be called to account when it invades rights. It will always invade them unless its organisation prevents it from being weighted in some special interest. The three aspects of liberty I have noted are always relative to this situation. By private liberty, for example, I mean the opportunity to exercise freedom of choice in those areas of life where the results of my effort mainly affect me in that isolation by which, at least ultimately, I am always surrounded. Religion is a good instance of this aspect. I am not truly free to decide without hindrance upon my creed unless there is not merely no penalty on any form of religious faith, but, also, no advantage of a political kind attached to one form rather than another. When the government of England denied public employment to Dissenters it invaded private liberty. It did not directly punish; but, at least, it offered special benefit to an alternative faith. When France repealed the Edict of Nantes it invaded private liberty; for the honourable profession of

religious conviction involved political outlawry.

These are simple instances. In the complex modern State invasions of private liberty may be more subtle. Private liberty may be denied when the poor citizen is unable to secure adequate legal protection in the Courts of Justice. A divorce law, for example, which gives the rich access to its facilities but, broadly, makes them difficult, if not impossible, for the poor, invades their private freedom. So does the demand for excessive bail; so, too, when the poor prisoner, with inadequate counsel, confronts the legal ability at the command of government. Private liberty is thus that aspect of which the substance is mainly personal to a man's self. It is the opportunity to be fully himself in the private relations of life. It is the chance practically to avail himself of the safeguards evolved for the maintenance of those relations.

Political liberty means the power to be active in affairs of State. It means that I can let my mind play freely about the substance of public business. I must be able without hindrance to add my special experience to the general sum of experience. I must find no barriers that are not general barriers in the way of access to positions of authority. I must be able to announce my opinion and to concert with others in the announcement of opinion. For political liberty to be real, two conditions are essential. I must be educated to the point where I can express what I want in a way that is intelligible to others. Anyone who has seen the dumb inarticulateness of the poor will realise the urgency of education in this regard. Nothing is more striking than the way in which our educational systems train the children of rich or well-born men to habits of authority while the children of the poor are trained to habits of deference. Such a division of attitude can never produce political freedom, because a class trained to govern will exert its power because it is conscious of it, while a class trained to deference will not fulfil its wants because it does not know how to formulate its demands. Combination in the period of experience will, of course, as with trade unions, do something to restore the balance; but it will never fully compensate for the defect of early training. For the inculcation of deferential habits will never produce a free people. It is only when men have learned that they themselves make and work institutions that they can learn to adjust them to their needs.

The second condition of political liberty is the provision of an honest and straightforward supply of news. Those who are to decide must have truthful material upon which to decide. Their judgment must not be thwarted by the presentation of a biased case. We have learned, especially of late years, that this is no easy matter. A statesman cannot seldom be made what the press chooses to make him. A policy may be represented as entirely good or bad by the skilful omission of relevant facts. Our civilisation has stimulated the creation of agencies which live deliberately on the falsification of news. It would, indeed, not be very wide of the mark to argue that much of what had been achieved by the art of education in the nineteenth century had been frustrated by the art of propaganda in the twentieth. The problem is made more complex than in the past by the area over which our judgment must pass. We have no leisure to survey that area with comprehensive accuracy. We must, very largely, take our facts on trust. But if the facts are deliberately perverted, our judgment will be unrelated to the truth. A people without reliable news is, sooner or later, a people without the basis of freedom. For to exercise one's judgment in a miasma of distortion is, ultimately, to go disastrously astray.

By economic liberty I mean security and the opportunity to find reasonable significance in the earning of one's daily bread. I must, that is, be free from the constant fear of unemployment and insufficiency which, perhaps more than any other inadequacies, sap the whole strength of personality. I must be safeguarded against the wants of to-morrow. I must know that I can build a home, and make that home a means of self-expression. I must be able to make my personality flow through my effort as a producer of services, and find in that effort the capacity of enrichment. For, otherwise, I become a stunted and shrunken being in that aspect of myself which lends colour and texture to all that I am. Either I must, in this sense, be free, or I become one of those half-souls who are found in the slums and prisons as the casualties of civilisation. Nor is this all. I must be more than the recipient of orders which I must obey unthinkingly because my labour is only a commodity bought and sold in the market, like coal and boots and chairs. Without these freedoms, or, at least, an access to them, men are hardly less truly slaves than when they were exposed for purchase and sale.

Economic liberty, therefore, implies democracy in industry. That means two things. It means that industrial government is subject to the system of rights which obtain for men as citizens, and it means that industrial direction must be of a character that makes it the rule of laws made by co-operation and not by compulsion. Obviously, the character of those laws must depend upon the needs of production. Those needs leave less room for spontaneity than is true either of private or of political liberty. A man is entitled to be original about his politics or his religion; he is not entitled to be original when he is working with others, say, in a nitro-glycerine factory. But he is entitled to co-operate in the setting of the standards by which he is judged industrially and in the application of those standards. Otherwise, he lives at the behest of other men. His initiative becomes not the free expression of his own individuality, but a routine made from without and enforced upon him by fear of starvation. A system built upon fear is always fatal to the release of the creative faculties, and it is therefore incompatible with liberty.

Constitutionalism and
5 Democracy

In Chapter 3 we examined dictatorship, which is characterized by arbitrary action of government. Now we turn to a discussion of government limited by law. The dictionary defines "constitution" as the fundamental principles of government of a nation or other organized body of men embodied in written documents or implied in customs. In this sense there is a constitution in every state that has an organized ruling establishment, whether it be a democratic republic or an absolute dictatorship. On the other hand, "constitutionalism" means more than a state possessing a constitution. It is intertwined with the concept of limitations on the government that the British call the "rule of law."

Constitutionalism is the theory that officials should not be permitted to do anything they please, but instead must conduct themselves according to fair and well-established ways of doing things. American government experience has expanded this theory into what is called due process of law, several basic ingredients of which will be explored in this chapter. In the final analysis, of course, it is men who must define and carry out the rule of law; it is still valid, however, to make a distinction between systems with government by law and those with government by men. All working democracies, like those found in Western Europe and North America, recognize certain limitations upon official action; dictatorships, whether under a Hitler or a Stalin, provide no restraints upon the ruler. It follows, therefore, that constitutionalism is generally related to democratic principles and that it suggests the opposite of a government of absolute and uncontrollable powers.

THE SOCIAL CONTRACT

One of the earliest explanations of, as well as justifications for, the theory of constitutionalism is the concept of the social contract. Under this doctrine all history is regarded as being divided into two periods, the state of nature and the period of civil society. Life in the state of nature had become increasingly dangerous, and men felt a natural inclination to join into an organized society. The social order itself, however, is based on conventions or contractual agreements. John Locke, an English political philosopher of the late seventeenth century, was one of the first to consider government as flowing from a contract between the sovereign and the people. Using this explanation for the establishment of government, he logically postulated the limits of government. Our first selection reproduces Locke's pertinent section of the *Two Treatises of Government*.

Another version of the social contract theory was expounded by a famous French philosopher, Jean Jacques Rousseau, in 1762. Rousseau's ideas, part of which are found in our second reading, were to have a considerable impact upon the leaders of the French Revolution a generation later. The theory of a contract between the government and the people was used as a support for popular liberties, a device for upholding individual rights against the government. According to Rousseau, popular consent to a government required a constitutional means of expression if it was to be more than just lip-service. He indicated that active agreement, periodically reasserted, was the proper means of expression. Thus, public participation in lawmaking was a necessary ingredient of popular consent. Rousseau's theory was designed for a city-state much like his native Geneva. He was unable to believe that large-scale, representative democracy as practiced in the United States Congress could operate effectively.

The social contract theory grew into the concept of a written constitution guaranteeing certain individual rights against the government. The national leaders who met at Philadelphia to write our Constitution in 1787 believed in democratic government as embodied in the social contract doctrine, especially as presented by Locke. Today our vastly increased knowledge in the areas of history, anthropology, and archeology does not support the concept of men in a state of nature entering into a formal contract to establish civil government. Nevertheless, the theory that government is obligated to perform within certain bounds and the whole setting of constitutional conventions have a considerable flavor of contractual arrangements.

SEPARATION OF POWERS

Another ingredient of constitutionalism, especially in its American development, is the doctrine of separation of powers. The political thinker who
developed this doctrine as a necessary part of constitution-making in the
eighteenth century was Charles Secondat, Baron de Montesquieu. The third
reading of this chapter is from Montesquieu's *The Spirit of the Laws,*
published in 1748; the extent of his influence may be seen in the American
(both state and national) and French constitutions written in the last
quarter of the eighteenth century.

Montesquieu made separation of powers a system of legal checks and
balances by particular branches of the government: legislative, executive,
and judicial. A rather unusual aspect of his system was that he announced
it as the basis of the English constitution, which by 1688 had largely
abandoned legal separation and substituted parliamentary supremacy, or
a fusion of powers. He firmly believed that the liberty found in England,
as contrasted with the injustice found in France, was based upon such a
separation. In his theory liberty is considered most likely to exist in a moderate government, one in which the three powers are held by different and
competing hands. While this may not have been the actual situation in
eighteenth-century England, the constitutional principle of separation of
powers was a logical one to encourage the existence of moderate government. Certainly it was accepted by the framers of the American Constitution of 1787 and is a cardinal principle of our constitutionalism.

FEDERALISM

Another fundamental principle found in several working democracies is
federalism. In a sense it is a geographical application of the principle of
separation of powers, its objective being in part to prevent the concentration
of power in one place. Although several important modern countries—the
Federal Republic of Germany, Canada, Switzerland, and Australia—have
various forms of federalism in their governments, it is the United States that
is regarded as the prime example of the federal arrangement. Briefly,
federalism means that a country has two levels of government, a central or
national level and a regional or state level. Both levels operate directly upon
the people, as in tax and judicial matters, and there is a formal division of
power between the two governments. While both governments may operate
some of the same activities, certain areas belong exclusively to one or the
other. When either level of government is operating within its exclusive
area, it is independent of the other level. The consequence of this rather
complex arrangement is that every citizen in a federal system is subject to
two governments.

The division of powers between state and national levels is stipulated in several parts of the Constitution, but in many cases the language used is general and is subject to differences in interpretation. A unique aspect of American constitutionalism is that we give to the courts, and ultimately to the United States Supreme Court, the power to settle differences in interpretation. Article VI of the Constitution, the "supreme law of the land" clause, is our fourth selection; it provides that, when state and national laws deal differently with the same subject, the national law stands and the state law falls. The Tenth Amendment to the Constitution is included, to show the language used in separating the listed national powers from the retained state powers.

The fifth reading in this chapter, an excerpt from the famous Supreme Court case of *Gibbons v. Ogden,* is an example of the reasoning of Chief Justice John Marshall with regard to federalism. The background of this controversy was that both the New York Legislature and the United States Congress had passed laws dealing with shipping rights of ship owners operating between New York and New Jersey. As an example of court interpretation of constitutional language, the opinion here interpreted "commerce among the several states" to include navigation, which thus became a national power. For this reason the New York law was struck down. Had the activity been wholly within New York state and not affecting another state, the New York law would have been valid. This is a classical example of how a forceful chief justice contributed to the strengthening of the national power.

THE CONCEPT OF DUE PROCESS

The last aspect of constitutionalism to be dealt with in this chapter is due process of law, probably the most fundamental and far-reaching element in the Anglo-American tradition of personal liberty. In accordance with the belief in limits placed on government, the Magna Charta signed by King John in 1215 provided that he would not take any action against his subjects except by "the law of the land." Our founding fathers put this theory into more familiar language in the Fifth Amendment in 1791, later copied in the Fourteenth Amendment in 1868, to the effect that life, liberty, or property shall not be taken from a person by the national or state governments without due process of law. The generally accepted purpose of due process is procedural, which means that the way or method used by officials in governing must be fair and familiar.[1] For example, the reading

---

[1] In the late nineteenth and early twentieth centuries, the Supreme Court of the United States embarked on a course of striking down laws, especially state laws, because of disapproval of the substance of or object of these laws rather than the procedure used. This is frequently referred to as substantive due process, a notion largely abandoned by the Court since 1937.

selection of *Tumey v. Ohio* deals with a state law against bootlegging. The Ohio law was struck down not because the state lacked the power to punish bootleggers, but because the procedure used gave the judge a financial interest in convicting persons so charged. In the Joint Anti-Fascist Refugee Committee case, also included as a reading, Justice Felix Frankfurter made the following very expressive point:

..."due process," unlike some legal rules, is not a technical conception with a fixed content unrelated to time, place and circumstances. Expressing as it does in its ultimate analysis respect enforced by law for that feeling of just treatment which has been evolved through centuries of Anglo-American constitutional history and civilization, "due process" cannot be imprisoned within the treacherous limits of any formula. Representing a profound attitude of fairness between man and man, more particularly between the individual and government, "due process" is compounded of history, reason, the past course of decisions, and stout confidence in the strength of the democratic faith which we profess.

Just as the rules of equity developed in England to supplement the Common Law and were designed to ensure fair dealings between individual citizens, due process has become a similar set of rules used in judicial review of actions by all branches of the government. Executive, administrative, legislative and judicial policies which arbitrarily restrict individual rights may be struck down in this manner.

ADMINISTRATIVE APPLICATION

One of the most rapidly growing areas of this general subject is administrative due process. Public administrators are assigned increasingly broad areas of activity and discretion, involving administrative treatment in national security or antisubversive activities matters. The Joint Anti-Fascist Refugee Committee case referred to above is included as our sixth reading. The Supreme Court examined the problem of the fair hearing and found that the Attorney General and the Department of Justice had not provided necessary procedural safeguards to the associations labeled as subversive. The court majority set aside the administrative action as being invalid because it was made "without notice, without disclosure of any reason justifying it, without opportunity to meet the undisclosed evidence or suspicion on which designation may have been based, and without opportunity to establish affirmatively that the aims and acts of the organization are innocent."

In a Supreme Court case decided within the past decade the concept of administrative due process was summed up in the following language: "Certain principles have remained relatively immutable in our jurisprudence. One of these is that where governmental action seriously injures an individual, and the reasonableness of the action depends on fact findings, the evidence used to prove the Government's case must be disclosed to the individual so that he has an opportunity to show that it is untrue."[2]

In several countries there are special agencies established to provide just treatment to the citizen in dealings with administrative officials. The French and Germans have a separate system of administrative courts which are very inexpensive and zealous in safeguarding the private citizen from arbitrary governmental action. Many common law countries (and several American states) have adopted the Scandinavian office of *Ombudsman*, who is something of a public defender in administrative matters. The *Ombudsman*, on request or on his own initiative, inquires into allegations of administrative unfairness. He may publicize his findings and bring public opinion into operation if the administrator at fault does not correct the improper action.

LEGISLATIVE APPLICATION

A second aspect of due process as a limit on government is concerned with the legislative branch. As in the case of administrative action just examined, legislative due process applies to the methods that legislatures use in establishing the law of the land. Over a century ago the Supreme Court gave a definition of legislative due process as follows:

The constitution contains no description of those processes which it was intended to allow or forbid. It does not even declare what principles are to be applied to ascertain whether it be due process. It is manifest that it was not left to the legislative power to enact any process which might be devised. The article (Fifth Amendment) is a restraint on the legislative as well as the executive and judicial powers of the government, and cannot be so construed as to leave Congress free to make any process "due process of law" by its mere will.[3]

In the *Anderson National Bank v. Luckett,* our seventh reading, the court reiterated that the fundamental requirement of due process is the opportunity to be heard in a fair hearing. A bank contested a Kentucky state law which provided notice to be given by the sheriff's posting a paper on the court house door. The state law was upheld in part on the ground that this posting procedure was so old as to have become customary and well established in the community.

JUDICIAL APPLICATION

The last aspect of constitutionalism taken up in this chapter is judicial due process. The average citizen is probably better acquainted with the judicial variety than with the others because it occurs in the most dramatic

2 *Green v. McElroy,* 360 U.S. 474 (1959).
3 *Murray's Lesee v. Hoboken Land and Improvement Co.,* 18 How. 272 (1856).

and newsworthy activity of government: the criminal trial. A fair trial requires many items to be present: proper notice to the accused, opportunity to prepare an adequate defense, rights to remain silent and to cross-examine witnesses. In the last two reading selections included here the requirement of an impartial court is demonstrated. The Tumey case points out that officers acting in a judicial capacity are disqualified if they have an interest in the controversy to be decided. The conviction was invalid because the judge received a fee that he would not have received if the defendant had been acquitted. A different version of impartiality was involved in the Murchison case. There the trial judge had also been the investigating agency (similar to a grand jury) that decided whether or not a trial should be held. While continental European countries (Civil or Roman law systems) do permit the judge in a lawsuit to have been involved in the case at another time in a different capacity, Anglo-American tradition does not. This reasoning also forbids the same persons from being grand jurors and trial jurors in the same case. Judicial due process is designed to ensure that all the evidence used to convict a person be introduced in the presence of that person and his attorney in order that it can be denied or explained if possible.

Of the Extent of the Legislative Power

JOHN LOCKE

The great end of men's entering into society being the enjoyment of their properties in peace and safety, and the great instrument and means of that being the laws established in that society, the first and fundamental positive law of all commonwealths is the establishing of the legislative power; as the first and fundamental natural law which is to govern even the legislative itself is the preservation of the society and, as far as will consist with the public good, of every person in it. This legislative is not only the supreme power of the commonwealth, but sacred and unalterable in the hands where the community have once placed it; nor can any edict of anybody else, in what form soever conceived or by what power soever backed, have the force and obligation of a law which has not its sanction from that legislative which the public has chosen and appointed; for without this the law could not have that which is absolutely necessary to its being a law: the consent of the society over whom nobody can have a power to make laws, but by their own consent and by authority received from them.[1] And therefore all the

obedience, which by the most solemn ties any one can be obliged to pay, ultimately terminates in this supreme power and is directed by those laws which it enacts; nor can any oaths to any foreign power whatsoever, or any domestic subordinate power, discharge any member of the society from his obedience to the legislative acting pursuant to their trust, nor oblige him to any obedience contrary to the laws so enacted, or farther than they do allow; it being ridiculous to imagine one can be tied ultimately to obey any power in the society which is not supreme.

Though the legislative, whether placed in one or more, whether it be always in being, or only by intervals, though it be the supreme power in every commonwealth; yet:

First, It is not, nor can possibly be, absolutely arbitrary over the lives and

Reprinted from John Locke, *Two Treatises of Government*, ed. Thomas I. Cook (New York: Hafner Publishing Co., Inc., 1947), pp. 188–94, by permission of the publisher.

[1] "The lawful power of making laws to command whole politic societies of men, belonging so properly unto the same entire societies, that for any prince or protentate of what kind soever upon earth to exercise the same of himself, and not by express commission immediately and personally received from God, or else by authority derived at the first from their consent, upon whose persons they impose laws, it is no better than mere tyranny. Laws they are not, therefore, which public approbation hath not made so."—Hooker's *Eccl. Pol.,* lib. i. sect. 10. "Of this point, therefore, we are to note, that such men naturally have no full and perfect power to command whole politic multitudes of men, therefore utterly without our consent we could in such sort be at no man's commandment living. And to be commanded we do consent, when that society whereof we be a part hath at any time before consented, without revoking the same by the like universal agreement. Laws therefore human, of what kind soever, are available by consent."—*Ibid.*

fortunes of the people; for it being but the joint power of every member of the society given up to that person or assembly which is legislator, it can be no more than those persons had in a state of nature before they entered into society and gave up to the community; for nobody can transfer to another more power than he has in himself, and nobody has an absolute arbitrary power over himself, or over any other, to destroy his own life, or take away the life or property of another. A man, as has been proved, cannot subject himself to the arbitrary power of another; and having in the state of nature no arbitrary power over the life, liberty, or possession of another, but only so much as the law of nature gave him for the preservation of himself and the rest of mankind, this is all he doth or can give up to the commonwealth, and by it to the legislative power, so that the legislative can have no more than this. Their power, in the utmost bounds of it, is limited to the public good of the society. It is a power that hath no other end but preservation, and therefore can never have a right to destroy, enslave, or designedly to impoverish the subjects.[2] The obligations

of the law of nature cease not in society but only in many cases are drawn closer and have by human laws known penalties annexed to them to enforce their observation. Thus the law of nature stands as an eternal rule to all men, legislators as well as others. The rules that they make for other men's actions must, as well as their own and other men's actions, be conformable to the law of nature—i.e., to the will of God, of which that is a declaration—and the fundamental law of nature being the preservation of mankind, no human sanction can be good or valid against it.

Secondly, The legislative or supreme authority cannot assume to itself a power to rule by extemporary, arbitrary decrees, but is bound to dispense justice and to decide the rights of the subject by promulgated, standing laws, and known authorized judges.[3] For the law of nature being unwritten, and so nowhere to be found but in the minds of men, they who through passion or interest shall miscite or misapply it, cannot so easily be convinced of their mistake where there is no established judge; and so it serves not, as it ought, to determine the rights and fence the properties of those that live under it, especially where every one is judge,

---

[2] "Two foundations there are which bear up public societies; the one a natural inclination whereby all men desire sociable life and fellowship; the other an order, expressly or secretly agreed upon, touching the manner of their union in living together. The latter is that which we call the law of a commonweal, the very soul of a politic body, the parts whereof are by law animated, held together, and set on work in such actions as the common good requireth. Laws politic, ordained for external order and regiment amongst men, are never framed as they should be, unless presuming the will of man to be inwardly obstinate, rebellious, and averse from all obedience to the sacred laws of his nature; in a word, unless presuming man to be, in regard of his depraved mind, little better than a wild beast, they do accordingly pro-

vide, notwithstanding, so to frame his outward actions that they be no hindrance unto the common good, for which societies are instituted. Unless they do this, they are not perfect."—Hooker's *Eccl. Pol.,* lib i. sect. 10.

[3] "Human laws are measures in respect of men whose actions they must direct, howbeit such measures they are as have also their higher rules to be measured by, which rules are two, law of God, and the law of nature; so that laws human must be made according to the general laws of nature, and without contradiction to any positive law of Scripture, otherwise they are ill-made."—Hooker's *Eccl. Pol.* lib. iii. sect. 9.

"To constain men to anything inconvenient doth seem unreasonable."—*Ibid.* lib. i. sect. 10.

interpreter, and executioner of it, too, and that in his own case; and he that has right on his side, having ordinarily but his own single strength, hath not force enough to defend himself from injuries, or to punish delinquents. To avoid these inconveniences which disorder men's properties in the state of nature, men unite into societies that they may have the united strength of the whole society to secure and defend their properties, and may have standing rules to bound it by which every one may know what is his. To this end it is that men give up all their natural power to the society which they enter into, and the community put the legislative power into such hands as they think fit with this trust, that they shall be governed by declared laws, or else their peace, quiet, and property will still be at the same uncertainty as it was in the state of nature.

Absolute arbitrary power, or governing without settled standing laws, can neither of them consist with the ends of society and government which men would not quit the freedom of the state of nature for, and tie themselves up under, were it not to preserve their lives, liberties, and fortunes, and by stated rules of right and property to secure their peace and quiet. It cannot be supposed that they should intend, had they a power so to do, to give to any one or more an absolute arbitrary power over their persons and estates and put a force into the magistrate's hand to execute his unlimited will arbitrarily upon them. This were to put themselves into a worse condition than the state of nature wherein they had a liberty to defend their right against the injuries of others and were upon equal terms of force to maintain it, whether invaded by a single man or many in combination. Whereas, by

supposing they have given up themselves to the absolute arbitrary power and will of a legislator, they have disarmed themselves and armed him to make a prey of them when he pleases, he being in a much worse condition who is exposed to the arbitrary power of one man who has the command of 100,000, than he that is exposed to the arbitrary power of 100,000 single men, nobody being secure that his will, who has such a command, is better than that of other men, though his force be 100,000 times stronger. And, therefore, whatever form the commonwealth is under, the ruling power ought to govern by declared and received laws and not by extemporary dictates and undetermined resolutions; for then mankind will be in a far worse condition than in the state of nature if they shall have armed one or a few men with the joint power of a multitude, to force them to obey at pleasure the exorbitant and unlimited decrees of their sudden thoughts or unrestrained and, till that moment, unknown wills, without having any measures set down which may guide and justify their actions. For all the power the government has, being only for the good of the society, as it ought not to be arbitrary and at pleasure, so it ought to be exercised by established and promulgated laws; that both the people may know their duty and be safe and secure within the limits of the law; and the rulers too kept within their bounds, and not be tempted by the power they have in their hands to employ it to such purposes and by such measures as they would not have known, and own not willingly.

Thirdly, The supreme power cannot take from any man part of his property without his own consent; for the preservation of property being the end of government and that for which men enter into society, it necessarily supposes and requires that the people should have property, without which they must be supposed to lose that, by entering into society, which was the end for which they entered into it— too gross an absurdity for any man to own. Men, therefore, in society having property, they have such right to the goods which by the law of the community are theirs, that nobody hath a right to take their substance or any part of it from them without their own consent; without this, they have no property at all, for I have truly no property in that which another can by right take from me when he pleases, against my consent. Hence it is a mistake to think that the supreme or legislative power of any commonwealth can do what it will, and dispose of the estates of the subject arbitrarily, or take any part of them at pleasure. This is not much to be feared in governments where the legislative consists, wholly or in part, in assemblies which are variable, whose members, upon the dissolution of the assembly, are subjects under the common laws of their country, equally with the rest. But in governments where the legislative is in one lasting assembly, always in being, or in one man, as in absolute monarchies, there is danger still that they will think themselves to have a distinct interest from the rest of the community, and so will be apt to increase their own riches and power by taking what they think fit from the people; for a man's property is not at all secure, though there be good and equitable laws to set the bounds of it between him and his fellow subjects, if he who commands those subjects have power to take from any private man what part he pleases of his property and use and dispose of it as he thinks good.

But government, into whatsoever hands it is put, being, as I have before shown, entrusted with this condition, and for this end, that men might have and secure their properties, the prince, or senate, however it may have power to make laws for the regulating of property between the subjects one amongst another, yet can never have a power to take to themselves the whole or any part of the subject's property without their own consent; for this would be in effect to leave them no property at all. And to let us see that even absolute power, where it is necessary, is not arbitrary by being absolute, but is still limited by that reason and confined to those ends which required it in some cases to be absolute, we need look no farther than the common practice of martial discipline; for the preservation of the army, and in it of the whole commonwealth, requires an absolute obedience to the command of every superior officer, and it is justly death to disobey or dispute the most dangerous or unreasonable of them; but yet we see that neither the sergeant, that could command a soldier to march up to the mouth of a cannon or stand in a breach where he is almost sure to perish, can command that soldier to give him one penny of his money; nor the general, that can condemn him to death for deserting his post, or for not obeying the most desperate orders, can yet, with all his absolute power of life and death, dispose of one farthing of that soldier's estate or seize one jot of his goods, whom yet he can command anything, and hand for the least disobedience. Because such a blind obedience is necessary to that end for which the commander has his power, viz., the preservation of the rest; but the disposing of his goods has nothing to do with it.

It is true, governments cannot be supported without great charge, and it is fit every one who enjoys his share of the protection should pay out of his estate his proportion for the maintenance of it. But still it must be with his own consent—*i.e.*, the consent of the majority, giving it either by themselves or their representatives chosen by them. For if any one shall claim a power to lay and levy taxes on the people, by his own authority and without such consent of the people, he thereby invades the fundamental law of property and subverts the end of government; for what property have I in that which another may by right take, when he pleases, to himself?

Fourthly, The legislative cannot transfer the power of making laws to any other hands; for it being but a delegated power from the people, they who have it cannot pass it over to others. The people alone can appoint the form of the commonwealth, which is by constituting the legislative and appointing in whose hands that shall be. And when the people have said, we will submit to rules and be governed by laws made by such men, and in such forms, nobody else can say other men shall make laws for them; nor can the people be bound by any laws but such as are enacted by those whom they have chosen and authorized to make laws for them. The power of the legislative, being derived from the people by a positive voluntary grant and institution, can be no other than what that positive grant conveyed, which being only to make laws, and not to make legislators, the legislative can have no power to transfer their authority of making laws and place it in other hands.

These are the bounds which the trust that is put in them by the society and the law of God and nature have set to the legislative power of every commonwealth, in all forms of government:

First, They are to govern by promulgated established laws, not to be varied in particular cases, but to have one rule for rich and poor, for the favourite at court and the countryman at plough.

Secondly, These laws also ought to be designed for no other end ultimately but the good of the people.

Thirdly, They must not raise taxes on the property of the people without the consent of the people, given by themselves or their deputies. And this properly concerns only such governments where the legislative is always in being, or at least where the people have not reserved any part of the legislative to deputies to be from time to time chosen by themselves.

Fourthly, The legislative neither must nor can transfer the power of making laws to anybody else, or place it anywhere but where the people have.

The Social Contract

JEAN JACQUES ROUSSEAU

...Man is born free; and everywhere he is in chains. One thinks himself the master of others, and still remains a greater slave than they. How did this change come about? I do not know. What can make it legitimate? That question I think I can answer.

If I took into account only force, and the effects derived from it, I should say: "As long as a people is compelled to obey, and obeys, it does well; as soon as it can shake off the yoke, and shakes it off, it does still better; for, regaining its liberty by the same right as took it away, either it is justified in resuming it, or there was no justification for those who took it away." But the social order is a sacred right which is the basis of all rights. Nevertheless, this right does not come from nature, and must therefore be founded on conventions. Before coming to that, I have to prove what I have just asserted.

The most ancient of all societies, and the only one that is natural, is the family: and even so the children remain attached to the father only so long as they need him for their preservation. As soon as this need ceases, the natural bond is dissolved. The children, released from the obedience they owed to the father, and the father, released from the care he owed his children, return equally to independence. If they remain united, they continue so no

longer naturally, but voluntarily; and the family itself is then maintained only by convention.

This common liberty results from the nature of man. His first law is to provide for his own preservation, his first cares are those which he owes to himself; and, as soon as he reaches years of discretion, he is the sole judge of the proper means of preserving himself, and consequently becomes his own master.

The family then may be called the first model of political societies: the ruler corresponds to the father, and the people to the children; and all, being born free and equal, alienate their liberty only for their own advantage. The whole difference is that, in the family, the love of the father for his children repays him for the care he takes of them, while, in the State, the pleasure of commanding takes the place of the love which the chief cannot have for the peoples under him....

. . .

The strongest is never strong enough to be always the master, unless he transforms strength into right, and obedience into duty. Hence the right of the strongest, which, though to all seeming meant ironically, is really laid down as a fundamental principle. But are we never to have an explanation of this phrase? Force is a physical power, and I fail to see what moral effect it can have. To yield to force is an act of necessity, not of will—at the most, an act of prudence. In what sense can it be a duty?

From the book *The Social Contract and Discourses* by Jean Jacques Rousseau. Translated by G. D. H. Cole. Everyman's Library Edition. Reprinted by permission of E. P. Dutton & Co., Inc.

Suppose for a moment that this so-called "right" exists. I maintain that the sole result is a mass of inexplicable nonsense. For, if force creates right, the effect changes with the cause: every force that is greater than the first succeeds to its right. As soon as it is possible to disobey with impunity, disobedience is legitimate; and, the strongest being always in the right, the only thing that matters is to act so as to become the strongest. But what kind of right is that which perishes when force fails? If we must obey perforce, there is no need to obey because we ought; and if we are not forced to obey, we are under no obligation to do so. Clearly, the word "right" adds nothing to force: in this connection, it means absolutely nothing.

Obey the powers that be. If this means yield to force, it is a good precept, but superfluous: I can answer for its never being violated. All power comes from God, I admit; but so does all sickness: does that mean that we are forbidden to call in the doctor? A brigand surprises me at the edge of a wood: must I not merely surrender my purse on compulsion; but, even if I could withhold it, am I in conscience bound to give it up? For certainly the pistol he holds is also a power.

Let us then admit that force does not create right, and that we are obliged to obey only legitimate powers. In that case, my original question recurs.

Since no man has a natural authority over his fellow, and force creates no right, we must conclude that conventions form the basis of all legitimate authority among men. . . .

. . .

"The problem is to find a form of association which will defend and protect with the whole common force the person and goods of each associate, and in which each, while uniting himself with all, may still obey himself alone, and remain as free as before." This is the fundamental problem of which the *Social Contract* provides the solution.

The clauses of this contract are so determined by the nature of the act that the slightest modification would make them vain and ineffective; so that although they have perhaps never been formally set forth, they are everywhere the same and everywhere tacitly admitted and recognized, until, on the violation of the social compact, each regains his original rights and resumes his natural liberty, while losing the conventional liberty in favor of which he renounced it.

These clauses, properly understood, may be reduced to one—the total alienation of each associate, together with all his rights, to the whole community; for, in the first place, as each gives himself absolutely, the conditions are the same for all; and, this being so, no one has any interest in making them burdensome to others.

Moreover, the alienation being without reserve, the union is as perfect as it can be, and no associate has anything more to demand: for, if the individuals retained certain rights, as there would be no common superior to decide between them and the public, each, being on one point his own judge, would ask to be so on all; the state of nature would thus continue, and the association would necessarily become inoperative or tyrannical.

Finally, each man, in giving himself to all, gives himself to nobody; and as there is no associate over which he does not acquire the same right as he yields others over himself, he gains an equivalent for everything he loses, and an increase of force for the preservation of what he has.

If then we discard from the social compact what is not of its essence, we shall find that it reduces itself to the following terms:

"Each of us puts his person and all his power in common under the supreme direction of the general will, and, in our corporate capacity, we receive each member as an indivisible part of the whole."

At once, in place of the individual personality of each contracting party, this act of association creates a moral and collective body, composed of as many members as the assembly contains voters, and receiving from this act its unity, its common identity, its life, and its will. This public person, so formed by the union of all other persons, formerly took the name of *city,* and now takes that of *Republic* or *body politic;* it is called by its members *State* when passive, *Sovereign* when active, and *Power* when compared with others like itself. Those who are associated in it take collectively the name of *people* and severally are called *citizens,* as sharing in the sovereign power, and *subjects,* as being under the laws of the State....

The passage from the state of nature to the civil state produces a very remarkable change in man, by substituting justice for instinct in his conduct, and giving his actions the morality they had formerly lacked. Then only, when the voice of duty takes the place of physical impulses and right of appetite, does man, who so far had considered only himself, find that he is forced to act on different principles, and to consult his reason before listening to his inclinations. Although, in this state, he deprives himself of some advantages which he got from nature, he gains in return others so great, his faculties are so stimulated and developed, his ideas so extended, his feelings so ennobled, and his whole soul so uplifted, that, did not the abuses of this new condition often degrade him below that which he left, he would be bound to bless continually the happy moment which took him from it for ever, and, instead of a stupid and unimaginative animal, made him an intelligent being and a man.

Let us draw up the whole account in terms easily commensurable. What man loses by the social contract is his natural liberty and an unlimited right to everything he tries to get and succeeds in getting; what he gains is civil liberty and the proprietorship of all he possesses. If we are to avoid mistake in weighing one against the other, we must clearly distinguish natural liberty, which is bounded only by the strength of the individual, from civil liberty, which is limited by the general will; and possession, which is merely the effect of force or the right of the first occupier, from property, which can be founded only on a positive title....

.   .   .

It is not enough for the assembled people to have once fixed the constitution of the State by giving its sanction to a body of law; it is not enough for it to have set up a perpetual government, or provided once for all for the election of magistrates. Besides the extraordinary assemblies unforeseen circumstances may demand, there must be fixed periodical assemblies which cannot be abrogated or prorogued so that on the proper day the people is legitimately called together by law, without need of any formal summoning....

The Spirit of The Laws

MONTESQUIEU

Democratic and aristocratic states are not in their own nature free. Political liberty is to be found only in moderate governments; and even in these it is not always found. It is there only when there is no abuse of power. But constant experience shows us that every man invested with power is apt to abuse it, and to carry his authority as far as it will go. Is it not strange, though true, to say that virtue itself has need of limits?

To prevent this abuse, it is necessary from the very nature of things that power should be a check to power. A government may be so constituted, as no man shall be compelled to do things to which the law does not oblige him, nor forced to abstain from things which the law permits.

Though all governments have the same general end, which is that of preservation, yet each has another particular object. Increase of dominion was the object of Rome; war, that of Sparta; religion, that of the Jewish laws; commerce, that of Marseilles; public tranquillity, that of the laws of China; navigation, that of the laws of Rhodes; natural liberty, that of the policy of the Savages; in general, the pleasures of the prince, that of despotic states; that of monarchies, the prince's and the kingdom's glory; the independence of individuals is the end aimed

Reprinted from Baron de Montesquieu, *The Spirit of the Laws,* trans. Thomas Nugent (New York: Hafner Publishing Co., Inc., 1962), pp. 150–55, 160–61, by permission of the publisher.

at by the laws of Poland, thence results the oppression of the whole.

One nation there is also in the world that has for the direct end of its constitution political liberty. We shall presently examine the principles on which this liberty is founded; if they are sound, liberty will appear in its highest perfection.

To discover political liberty in a constitution, no great labor is requisite. If we are capable of seeing it where it exists, it is soon found, and we need not go far in search of it.

In every government there are three sorts of power: the legislative; the executive in respect to things dependent on the law of nations; and the executive in regard to matters that depend on the civil law.

By virtue of the first, the prince or magistrate enacts temporary or perpetual laws, and amends or abrogates those that have been already enacted. By the second, he makes peace or war, sends or receives embassies, establishes the public security, and provides against invasions. By the third, he punishes criminals, or determines the disputes that arise between individuals. The latter we shall call the judiciary power, and the other simply the executive power of the state.

The political liberty of the subject is a tranquillity of mind arising from the opinion each person has of his safety. In order to have this liberty, it is requisite the government be so constituted as one man need not be afraid of another.

When the legislative and executive powers are united in the same person, or in the same body of magistrates, there can be no liberty; because apprehensions may arise, lest the same monarch or senate should enact tyrannical laws, to execute them in a tyrannical manner.

Again, there is no liberty, if the judiciary power be not separated from the legislative and executive. Were it joined with the legislative, the life and liberty of the subject would be exposed to arbitrary control; for the judge would be then the legislator. Were it joined to the executive power, the judge might behave with violence and oppression.

There would be an end of everything, were the same man or the same body, whether of the nobles or of the people, to exercise those three powers, that of enacting laws, that of executing the public resolutions, and of trying the causes of individuals.

Most kingdoms in Europe enjoy a moderate government because the prince who is invested with the two first powers leaves the third to his subjects. In Turkey, where these three powers are united in the Sultan's person, the subjects groan under the most dreadful oppression.

In the republics of Italy, where these three powers are united, there is less liberty than in our monarchies. Hence their government is obliged to have recourse to as violent methods for its support as even that of the Turks; witness the state inquisitors, and the lion's mouth into which every informer may at all hours throw his written accusations.

In what a situation must the poor subject be in those republics! The same body of magistrates are possessed, as executors of the laws, of the whole power they have given themselves in quality of legislators. They may plunder the state by their general determinations; and as they have likewise the judiciary power in their hands, every private citizen may be ruined by their particular decisions.

The whole power is here united in one body; and though there is no external pomp that indicates a despotic sway, yet the people feel the effects of it every moment.

Hence it is that many of the princes of Europe, whose aim has been leveled at arbitrary power, have constantly set out with uniting in their own persons all the branches of magistracy, and all the great offices of state.

I allow indeed that the mere hereditary aristocracy of the Italian republics does not exactly answer to the despotic power of the Eastern princes. The number of magistrates sometimes moderate the power of the magistracy; the whole body of the nobles do not always concur in the same design; and different tribunals are erected, that temper each other. Thus at Venice the legislative power is in the council, the executive in the *pregadi,* and the judiciary in the *quarantia.* But the mischief is, that these different tribunals are composed of magistrates all belonging to the same body; which constitutes almost one and the same power.

The judiciary power ought not to be given to a standing senate; it should be exercised by persons taken from the body of the people at certain times of the year, and consistently with a form and manner prescribed by law, in order to erect a tribunal that should last only as necessity requires.

By this method the judicial power, so terrible to mankind, not being annexed to any particular state or profession, becomes, as it were, invisible. People have not then the judges continually present to their view; they fear the office, but not the magistrate.

In accusations of a deep and criminal nature, it is proper the person accused should have the privilege of choosing, in some measure, his judges, in concurrence with the law; or at least he should have a right to except against so great a number that the remaining part may be deemed his own choice.

The other two powers may be given rather to magistrates or permanent bodies, because they are not exercised on any private subject; one being no more than the general will of the state, and the other execution of that general will.

But though the tribunals ought not to be fixed, the judgments ought; and to such a degree as to be ever conformable to the letter of the law. Were they to be the private opinion of the judge, people would then live in society, without exactly knowing the nature of their obligations.

The judges ought likewise to be of the same rank as the accused, or, in other words, his peers; to the end that he may not imagine he is fallen into the hands of persons inclined to treat him with rigor.

If the legislature leaves the executive power in possession of a right to imprison those subjects who can give security for their good behavior, there is an end of liberty; unless they are taken up, in order to answer without delay to a capital crime, in which case they are really free, being subject only to the power of the law.

But should the legislature think itself in danger by some secret conspiracy against the state, or by a correspondence with a foreign enemy, it might authorize the executive power, for a short and limited time, to imprison suspected persons, who in that case would lose their liberty only for a while, to preserve it forever.

And this is the only reasonable method that can be substituted to the tyrannical magistracy of the Ephori, and to the state inquisitors of Venice, who are also despotic.

As in a country of liberty, every man who is supposed a free agent ought to be his own governor; the legislative power should reside in the whole body of the people. But since this is impossible in large states, and in small ones is subject to many inconveniences, it is fit the people should transact by their representatives what they cannot transact by themselves.

The inhabitants of a particular town are much better acquainted with its wants and interests than with those of other places; and are better judges of the capacity of their neighbors than of that of the rest of their countrymen. The members, therefore, of the legislature should not be chosen from the general body of the nation; but it is proper that in every considerable place a representative should be elected by the inhabitants.

The great advantage of representatives is their capacity of discussing public affairs. For this the people collectively are extremely unfit, which is one of the chief inconveniences of a democracy.

It is not at all necessary that the representatives who have received a general instruction from their constituents should wait to be directed on each particular affair, as is practised in the diets of Germany. True it is that by this way of proceeding the speeches of the deputies might with greater propriety be called the voice of the nation; but, on the other hand, this would occasion infinite delays; would give each deputy a power of controlling the assembly; and, on the most urgent and pressing occasions, the wheels of government might be stopped by the caprice of a single person.

When the deputies. . . represent a body of people, as in Holland, they ought to be accountable to their constituents; but it is a different thing in England, where they are deputed by boroughs.

All the inhabitants of the several districts ought to have a right of voting at the election of a representative, except such as are in so mean a situation as to be deemed to have no will of their own.

One great fault there was in most of the ancient republics, that the people had a right to active resolutions, such as require some execution, a thing of which they are absolutely incapable. They ought to have no share in the government but for the choosing of representatives, which is within their reach. For though few can tell the exact degree of men's capacities, yet there are none but are capable of knowing in general whether the person they choose is better qualified than most of his neighbors.

Neither ought the representative body to be chosen for the executive part of government, for which it is not so fit; but for the enacting of laws, or to see whether the laws in being are duly executed, a thing suited to their abilities, and which none indeed but themselves can properly perform. . . .

. . .

Here, then, is the fundamental constitution of the government we are treating of. The legislative body being composed of two parts, they check one another by the mutual privilege of rejecting. They are both restrained by the executive power, as the executive is by the legislative.

These three powers should naturally form a state of repose or inaction. But as there is a necessity for movement in the course of human affairs, they are forced to move, but still in concert.

As the executive power has no other part in the legislative than the privilege of rejecting, it can have no share in the public debates. It is not even necessary that it should propose, because as it may always disapprove of the resolutions that shall be taken, it may likewise reject the decisions on those proporsals which were made against its will.

In some ancient commonwealths, where public debates were carried on by the people in a body, it was natural for the executive power to propose and debate in conjunction with the people, otherwise their resolutions must have been attended with a strange confusion.

Were the executive power to determine the raising of public money, otherwise than by giving its consent, liberty would be at an end; because it would become legislative in the most important point of legislation.

If the legislative power was to settle the subsidies, not from year to year, but forever, it would run the risk of losing its liberty, because the executive power would be no longer dependent; and when once it was possessed of such a perpetual right, it would be a matter of indifference whether it held it of itself or of another. The same may be said if it should come to a resolution of intrusting, not an annual, but a perpetual command of the fleets and armies to the executive power.

To prevent the executive power from being able to oppress, it is requisite that the armies with which it is instrusted should consist of the people, and have the same spirit as the people, as was the case at Rome till the time of Marius. . . .

The Constitution
of the United States

ARTICLE VI [THE SUPREME LAW OF THE LAND CLAUSE]

...This Constitution, and the Laws of the United States which shall be made in Pursuance thereof; and all Treaties made, or which shall be made, under the Authority of the United States shall be the supreme Law of the Land; and the Judges in every State shall be bound thereby, any Thing in the Constitution or Laws of any State to the Contrary notwithstanding....

AMENDMENT X

The powers not delegated to the United States by the Constitution, nor prohibited by it to the States, are reserved to the States respectively, or to the people.

Gibbons *v.* Ogden

UNITED STATES SUPREME COURT

. . .

As preliminary to the very able discussions of the Constitution, which we have heard from the bar, and as having some influence on its construction, reference has been made to the political situation of these states, anterior to its formation. It has been said that they were sovereign, were completely independent, and were connected with each other only by a league. This is true. But, when these allied sovereigns converted their league into a government, when they converted their congress of ambassadors, deputed to deliberate on their common concerns, and

to recommend measures of general utility, into a legislature, empowered to enact laws on the most interesting subjects, the whole character in which the states appear underwent a change, the extent of which must be determined by a fair consideration of the instrument by which that change was effected.

This instrument contains an enumeration of powers expressly granted by the people to their government. It has been said that these powers ought to be construed strictly. But why ought they to be so construed? Is there one sentence in the Constitution which gives countenance to this rule? In the last of the enumerated powers, that which grants, expressly, the means for carrying all others into execution, Congress is authorized "to make all laws which

9 Wheaton 1 (1824) [*Reports of Cases, The Supreme Court of the United States* (New York: R. Donaldson, 1824), pp. 187–95.]

shall be necessary and proper" for the purpose. But this limitation on the means which may be used is not extended to the powers which are conferred; nor is there one sentence in the Constitution, which has been pointed out by the gentlemen of the bar, or which we have been able to discern, that prescribes this rule. We do not, therefore, think ourselves justified in adopting it. What do gentlemen mean by a strict construction? If they contend only against that enlarged construction, which would extend words beyond their natural and obvious import, we might question the application of the term, but should not controvert the principle. If they contend for that narrow construction which, in support of some theory not to be found in the Constitution, would deny to the government those powers which the words of the grant, as usually understood, import, and which are consistent with the general views and objects of the instrument; for that narrow construction, which would cripple the government, and render it unequal to the objects for which it is declared to be instituted, and to which the powers given, as fairly understood, render it competent; then we cannot perceive the propriety of this strict construction, nor adopt it as the rule by which the Constitution is to be expounded. As men whose intentions require no concealment generally employ the words which most directly and aptly express the ideas they intend to convey, the enlightened patriots who framed our Constitution, and the people who adopted it, must be understood to have employed words in their natural sense, and to have intended what they have said. If, from the imperfection of human language, there should be serious doubts respecting the extent of any given power, it is a well-settled rule that the objects for which it was

given, especially when those objects are expressed in the instrument itself, should have great influence in the construction. We know of no reason for excluding this rule from the present case. The grant does not convey power which might be beneficial to the grantor, if retained by himself, or which can enure solely to the benefit of the grantee; but is an investment of power for the general advantage, in the hands of agents selected for that purpose; which power can never be exercised by the people themselves, but must be placed in the hands of agents, or lie dormant. We know of no rule for construing the extent of such powers, other than is given by the language of the instrument which confers them, taken in connexion with the purposes for which they were conferred.

The words are: "Congress shall have Power to regulate Commerce with foreign Nations, and among the several States, and with the Indian Tribes."

The subject to be regulated is commerce; and our Constitution being, as was aptly said at the bar, one of enumeration, and not of definition, to ascertain the extent of the power, it becomes necessary to settle the meaning of the word. The counsel for the appellee would limit it to traffic, to buying and selling, or the interchange of commodities, and do not admit that it comprehends navigation. This would restrict a general term, applicable to many objects, to one of its significations. Commerce, undoubtedly, is traffic, but it is something more: it is intercourse. It describes the commercial intercourse between nations, and parts of nations, in all its branches, and is regulated by prescribing rules for carrying on that intercourse. The mind can scarcely conceive a system for regulating commerce between nations which shall exclude all laws concerning navigation, which shall be silent on the admission of the vessels of the one nation into the ports of the other, and be confined to prescribing rules for the conduct of individuals, in the actual employment of buying and selling, or of barter.

If commerce does not include navigation, the government of the Union has no direct power over that subject, and can make no law prescribing what shall constitute American vessels, or requiring that they shall be navigated by American seamen. Yet this power has been exercised from the commencement of the government, has been exercised with the consent of all, and has been understood by all to be a commercial regulation. All America understands, and has uniformly understood, the word "commerce" to comprehend navigation. It was so understood, and must have been so understood, when the Constitution was framed. The power over commerce, including navigation, was one of the primary objects for which the people of America adopted their government, and must have been contemplated in forming it. The Convention must have used the word in that sense, because all have understood it in that sense; and the attempt to restrict it comes too late. . . .

The word used in the Constitution, then, comprehends, and has been always understood to comprehend, navigation within its meaning; and a power to regulate navigation is as expressly granted as if that term had been added to the word "commerce."

To what commerce does this power extend? The Constitution informs us, to commerce "with foreign Nations, and among the several States, and with the Indian Tribes."

It has, we believe, been universally admitted that these words comprehend every species of commercial intercourse between the United States and foreign nations. No sort of trade can be carried on between this country and any other, to which this power does not extend. It has been truly said that commerce, as the word is used in the Constitution, is a unit, every part of which is indicated by the term.

If this be the admitted meaning of the word, in its application to foreign nations, it must carry the same meaning throughout the sentence, and remain a unit, unless there be some plain intelligible cause which alters it.

The subject to which the power is next applied is to commerce "among the several States." The word "among" means intermingled with. A thing which is among others is intermingled with them. Commerce among the states cannot stop at the external boundary line of each state, but may be introduced into the interior.

It is not intended to say that these words comprehend that commerce which is completely internal, which is carried on between man and man in a state, or between different parts of the same state, and which does not extend to or affect other states. Such a power would be inconvenient and is certainly unnecessary.

Comprehensive as the word "among" is, it may very properly be restricted to that commerce which concerns more states than one. . . . The completely internal commerce of a state, then, may be considered as reserved for the state itself.

Joint Anti-Fascist Refugee Committee Case

Actions for declaratory and injunctive relief by the Joint Anti-Fascist Refugee Committee, and by the National Council of American-Soviet Friendship, Inc., and others, and by the International Workers Order, Inc., and another, against Tom C. Clark, Attorney General of the United States, and others, J. Howard McGrath was substituted as the Attorney General. . . .

In each of these cases the same issue is raised. . . . That issue is whether, in the face of the facts alleged in the complaint and therefore admitted by the motion to dismiss, the Attorney General of the United States has authority to include the complaining organization in a list of organizations designated by him as Communist and furnished by him to the Loyalty Review Board of the United States Civil Service Commission. He claims to derive authority to do this from the following provisions of Executive Order No. 9835 issued by the President, March 21, 1947.

The Loyalty Review Board shall currently be furnished by the Department of Justice the name of each foreign or domestic organization, association,

movement, group or combination of persons which the Attorney General, after appropriate investigation and determination, designates as totalitarian, fascist, communist or subversive. . . .

The respective complaints describe the complaining organizations as engaged in charitable or civic activities or in the business of fraternal insurance. . . .

For the reasons hereinafter stated, we conclude that, *if the allegations of the complaints are taken as true* (as they must be on the motions to dismiss), the Executive Order does not authorize the Attorney General to furnish the Loyalty Review Board with a list containing such a designation as he gave to each of these organizations without other justification. . . .

. . .

No. 8.—The Refugee Committee Case.

The complainant is the Joint Anti-Fascist Refugee Committee, an unincorporated association in the City and State of New York. It is the petitioner here. The defendants in the original action were the Attorney General, Tom C. Clark, and the members of the Loyalty Review Board. J. Howard McGrath has been substituted as the Attorney General and he and the members of that Board are the respondents here.

The following statement, based on the allegations of the complaint, sum-

Joint Anti-Facist Refugee Committee *v.* McGrath, Atty. Gen. of the United States, et al., National Council of American-Soviet Friendship, Inc., et al. *v.* McGrath, Atty. Gen. of the United States, et al., International Workers Order, Inc., et al. *v.* McGrath, Atty. Gen. of the United States, et al., 341 U.S. 123, 71 S. Ct. 624 (1951), Nos. 8, 7, 71. Argued Oct. 11, 1950. Decided April 30, 1951.

marizes the situation before us: The complainant is "a charitable organization engaged in relief work" which carried on its relief activities from 1942 to 1946 under a license from the President's War Relief Control Board. Thereafter, it voluntarily submitted its program, budgets and audits for inspection by the Advisory Committee on Voluntary Foreign Aid of the United States Government. Since its inception, it has, through voluntary contributions, raised and disbursed funds for the benefit of anti-Fascist refugees who assisted the Government of Spain against its overthrow by force and violence. . . .

It has disbursed $1,011,448 in cash, and $217,903 in kind, for the relief of anti-Fascist refugees and their families. This relief has included money, food, shelter, educational facilities, medical treatment and supplies, and clothing to recipients in 11 countries including the United States. The acts of the Attorney General and the Loyalty Review Board, purporting to be taken by them under authority of the Executive Order, have seriously and irreparably impaired, and will continue to so impair, the reputation of the organization and the moral support and good will of the American people necessary for the continuance of its charitable activities. Upon information and belief, these acts have caused many contributors, especially present and prospective civil servants, to reduce or discontinue their contributions to the organization; members and participants in its activities have been "vilified and subjected to public shame, disgrace, ridicule and obloquy. . ." thereby inflicting upon it economic injury and discouraging participation in its activities; it has been hampered in securing meeting places; and many people have refused to take part in its fund-raising activities.

. . .

Nothing we have said purports to adjudicate the truth of petitioners' allegations that they are not in fact communistic. We have assumed that the designations made by the Attorney General are arbitrary because we are compelled to make that assumption by his motions to dismiss the complaints. Whether the complaining organizations are in fact communistic or whether the Attorney General possesses information from which he could reasonably find them to be so must await determination by the District Court upon remand.

Reversed and remanded.

Mr. Justice BLACK, concurring.

Without notice or hearing and under color of the President's Executive Order No. 9835, the Attorney General found petitioners guilty of harboring treasonable opinions and designs, officially branded them as Communists, and promulgated his findings and conclusions for particular use as evidence against government employees suspected of disloyalty. In the present climate of public opinion it appears certain that the Attorney General's much publicized findings, regardless of their truth or falsity, are the practical equivalents of confiscation and death sentences for any blacklisted organization not possessing extraordinary financial, political or religious prestige and influence. The Government not only defends the power of the Attorney General to pronounce such deadly edicts but also argues that individuals or groups so condemned have no standing to seek redress in the courts, even though a fair judicial hearing might conclusively demonstrate their loyalty. My basic reasons for rejecting these and other contentions of the Government are in summary the following: I agree with Mr. Justice BURTON that petitioners have standing to sue for the reason among others that they have a right to conduct their admittedly legitimate political, charitable and business operations free from unjustified governmental defamation. Otherwise, executive officers could act lawlessly with impunity. . . .

Anderson National Bank
v. Luckett

UNITED STATES SUPREME COURT

Appeal from the Court of Appeals of the State of Kentucky.

Suit by the Anderson National Bank . . . against J. E. Luckett, individually and as Commissioner of Revenue of the State of Kentucky . . . (and) others to enjoin defendants from enforcing Kentucky statute providing for transfer of abandoned bank deposits to State Department of Revenue.

Mr. Chief Justice STONE delivered the opinion of the court.

Under Kentucky Revised Statutes of 1942, . . . every bank or trust company in the state is required to turn over to the state, deposits which have remained inactive and unclaimed for specified periods. The questions for decision are: (1) whether the statute under which the state purports to acquire the right to demand custody of the deposits, affords due process of law, even though the depositors may not receive personal notice of the pending transfer and there may be no prior judicial proceedings, and (2) whether the statute, as applied to deposits in a national bank, conflicts with the national banking laws or is an unconstitutional interference by the state with appellant's operations as a banking instrumentality of the United States.

---

321 U.S. 233, 64 S. Ct. 599 (1944).

So far as here relevant, the provisions of the statute may be summarily stated as follows. Demand deposits held by a bank, with accrued interest, are presumed abandoned unless the owner has, within ten years preceding the date for making the report required, . . . negotiated in writing with the bank, or been credited with interest on his passbook at his request, or had a transaction noted upon the books of the bank, or increased or decreased the amount of his deposit. . . . Non-demand deposits, with accrued interest, are likewise presumed abandoned, unless the owner, within the twenty-five years preceding the report, has taken one or more of such enumerated actions. . . .

The holder of property presumed abandoned, including any national bank, is required to file with the state Department of Revenue, annually before September 1, a report in duplicate of such property as of the preceding July 1; the copy is sent to the sheriff of the county in which the property is located, and he is under the statutory duty of posting the copy on the court house door or bulletin board, before the following October 1. . . .

A person refusing to turn over property under this statute is subject to a penalty of 10% of its amount, but not to exceed $500; he is subject to no penalty, however, if he posts a compliance bond. . . .

The statute thus sets up a comprehensive scheme for the administration of abandoned bank deposits. Upon a report by the bank and notice to the depositors and with an opportunity to be heard, if either wish it, the state takes into its protective custody bank accounts which, having been inactive for at least ten years if demand accounts, or at least twenty-five years if non-demand, the statute declares to be presumptively abandoned. The bank is relieved of its liability to the depositors, who receive instead a claim against the state, enforcible at any time until the deposits are judicially found to be abandoned in fact and for five years thereafter. . . .

. . . The Kentucky Court of Appeals sustained the Act in its entirety, holding that it affords due process, and that it neither infringes the national banking laws nor is a prohibited interference with a banking instrumentality of the United States. . . .

Appellant contends here: (1) that the statute, in requiring payment of the deposit accounts to the state on the prescribed notice, without recourse to judicial proceedings or any court order or judgment, deprives the depositors and appellant of property without due process of law, and (2) that such withdrawal of accounts from a national bank infringes the national banking laws. . . .

Appellant argues that. . . the procedure by which the state acquires its asserted right to demand payment of the accounts is so lacking in notice to depositors and in an opportunity for them to be heard as to deny the state the right to assert the depositors' claims and afford to the bank no protection if it responds to the state's demand for payment of the accounts. . . .

Apart from questions which may arise under the national banking laws in the case of national banks, it is no longer open to doubt that a state, by a procedure satisfying constitutional requirements, may compel surrender to it of deposit balances, when there is substantial ground for belief that they have been abandoned or forgotten. . . .

The deposits are debtor obligations of the bank, incurred and to be performed in the state where the bank is located, and hence are subject to the state's dominion. . . . And it is within the constitutional power of the state to protect the interests of depositors from the risks which attend long neglected accounts, by taking them into custody when they have been inactive so long as to be presumptively abandoned. . . just as it may provide for the administration of the property of a missing person. . . .

. . . Hence our inquiry must be directed to the question whether the procedure by which the state undertakes to acquiry the depositors' right to demand payment of the deposits was upon adequate notice of them and opportunity for them to be heard.

As we have said, the statute provides for notice to the depositors by requiring the sheriff to post on the court house door or bulletin board a copy of the bank's report of deposits presumed abandoned. We think that this, in conjunction with the notice provided by the statute itself and by the taking of possession of the bank balances by the state, is sufficient notice to the depositors to satisfy all requirements of due process.

The statute itself is notice to all depositors of banks within the state, of the conditions on which the balances of inactive accounts will be deemed presumptively abandoned, and their surrender to the state compelled. All persons having property located within a state and subject to its dominion must take note of its statutes affecting the control or disposition of such property and of the procedure which they set up for those purposes....

The report of the bank required to be posted on the court house door or bulletin board, lists the abandoned accounts as defined by the statute and thus gives notice to the owners of all those accounts which, because of their inactivity for the periods and in the ways specified by the statute, are deemed abandoned and required to be paid to the state....

Posting on the court house door, as a method of giving notice of proceedings affecting property within the county, is an ancient one and is time-honored in Kentucky.... This means of giving notice was employed in the escheat statutes of Kentucky at least as early as 1852.... The fact that a procedure is so old as to have become customary and well known in the community is of great weight in determining whether it conforms to due process, for "Not lightly vacated is the verdict of quiescent years"....

We cannot say that the posting of a notice on the door of the court house in a Kentucky county is a less efficacious method of giving notice to depositors in banks of the county than publication in a local newspaper or that in the circumstances of this case it is an inadequate means of giving notice of the summary taking into custody of the designated bank accounts by the state....

...This is not confiscation or even an attempted deprivation of property. Escheat or forfeiture to the state may follow, but only on proof of abandonment in fact. We cannot say that the protective custody of long inactive bank accounts, for which the Kentucky statute provides, and which in many circumstances may operate for the benefit and security of depositors,... will deter from placing their funds in national banks in that state....

In all this we can perceive no denial of constitutional right and no unlawful encroachment on the rights and privileges of national banks.

Since Kentucky may enforce its statute requiring the surrender to it of presumptively abandoned accounts in national as well as state banks, it may, as an appropriate incident to this exercise of authority, require the banks to file reports of inactive accounts, as the statute directs....

Tumey *v.* State of Ohio

UNITED STATES SUPREME COURT

Mr. Chief Justice TAFT delivered the opinion of the Court.

The question in this case is whether certain statutes of Ohio, in providing

273 U.S. 510, 47 S. Ct. (1926).

for the trial by the mayor of a village of one accused of violating the Prohibition Act of the state deprive the accused of due process of law and violate the Fourteenth Amendment to the Federal Constitution, because of the pecuniary and other interest which those statutes give the mayor in the result of the trial.

Tumey, the plaintiff in error hereafter to be called the defendant, was arrested and brought before Mayor Pugh, of the village of North College Hill, charged with unlawfully possessing intoxicating liquor. He moved for his dismissal because of the disqualification of the mayor to try him under the Fourteenth Amendment. The mayor denied the motion, proceeded to the trial, convicted the defendant of unlawfully possessing intoxicating liquor within Hamilton county as charged, fined him $100, and ordered that he be imprisoned until the fine and costs were paid.

In determining what due process of law is under the Fifth and Fourteenth Amendments, the court must look to those settled usages and modes of proceeding existing in the common and statute law of England before migration of our ancestors.

Mr. Justice Cooley, in his work on Constitutional Limitations points out that the real ground of the ruling in these cases (dealing with judges who are personally interested in cases being tried before them) is that:

Interest is so remote, trifling, and insignificant that it may fairly be supposed to be incapable of affecting the judgment of or of influencing the conduct of an individual. And where penalties are imposed, to be recovered only in a municipal court, the judge or jurors in which would be interested as corporators in the recovery must be regarded as precluding the objection of interest.

But the learned judge then proceeds:

But, except in cases resting upon such reason, we do not see how the Legislature can have any power to abolish a maxim which is among the fundamentals of judicial authority.

From this review we conclude that a system by which an inferior judge is paid for his service only when he convicts the defendant has not become so embedded by custom in the general practice, either at common law or in this country, that it can be regarded as due process of law, unless the costs usually imposed are so small that they may be properly ignored as within the maxim "de minimis non curat lex."

The mayor received for his fees and costs in the present case $12, and from costs under the Prohibition Act for seven months he made about $100 a month, in addition to his salary. We cannot regard the prospect of receipt or loss of such an emolument in each case as a minute, remote, trifling, or insignificant interest. It is certainly not fair to each defendant brought before the mayor for the careful and judicial consideration of his guilt or innocence that the prospect of such a prospective loss by the mayor should weigh against his acquittal.

These are not cases in which the penalties and the costs are negligible. The field of jurisdiction is not that of a small community, engaged in enforcing its own local regulations. The court is a state agency, imposing substantial punishment, and the cases to be considered are gathered from the whole county by the energy of the village marshals and detective regularly employed by the village for the purpose. It is not to be treated as a mere village tribunal for village peccadilloes. There are doubtless mayors who would not allow such a consideration as $12 costs in each case to affect their judgment in it, but the requirement of due process of law in judicial procedure is not satisfied by the argument that men of the highest honor and the greatest self-sacrifice could carry it on without danger of injustice. Every procedure which would offer a possible temptation to the average man as a judge to forget the burden of proof required to convict the defendant, or which might lead him not to hold the balance nice, clear, and true between the state and the accused denies the latter due process of law.

But the pecuniary interest of the mayor in the result of his judgment is not the only reason for holding that due process of law is denied to the defendant here. The statutes were drawn to stimulate small municipalities, in the country part of counties in which there are large cities, to organize and maintain courts to try persons accused of violations of the Prohibition Act everywhere in the country. The inducement is offered of dividing between the state and the village the large fines provided by the law for its violations. The trial is to be had before a mayor without a jury, without opportunity for retrial, and with a review confined to questions of law presented by a bill of exceptions, with no opportunity by the reviewing court to set aside the judgment on the weighing of evidence, unless it should appear to be so manifestly against the evidence as to indicate mistake, bias, or willful disregard of duty by the trial court. It specifically authorizes the village to employ detectives, deputy marshals and other assistants to detect crime of this kind all over the county, and to bring offenders before the mayor's court, and it offers to the village council and its officers a means of substantially adding to the income of the village to relieve it from further taxation. The mayor is the chief executive of the village. He supervises all the other executive officers. He is charged with the business of looking after the finances of the village. It appears from the evidence in this case, and would be plain if the

evidence did not show it, that the law is calculated to awaken the interest of all those in the village charged with the responsibility of raising the public money and expending it, in the pecuniarily successful conduct of such a court. The mayor represents the village and cannot escape his representative capacity. On the other hand, he is given the judicial duty, first, of determining whether the defendant is guilty at all; and, second, having found his guilt, to measure his punishment between $100 as a minimum and $1,000 as a maximum for first offenses, and $300 as a minimum and $2,000 as a maximum for second offenses. With his interest as mayor in the financial condition of the village and his responsibility therefore, might not a defendant with reason say that he feared he could not get a fair trial or a fair sentence from one who would have so strong a motive to help his village by conviction and a heavy fine? The old English cases cited above in the days of Coke and Holt and Mansfield are not nearly so strong. A situation in which an official perforce occupies two practically and seriously inconsistent positions, one partisan and the other judicial, necessarily involves a lack of due process of law in the trial of defendants charged with crimes before him. . . . It is, of course, so common to vest the mayor of villages with inferior judicial functions that the mere union of the executive power and the judicial power in him cannot be said to violate due process of law. The minor penalties usually attaching to the ordinances of a village council, or to the misdemeanors in which the mayor may pronounce final judgment without a jury, do not involve any such addition to the revenue of the village as to justify the fear that the mayor would be influenced in his judicial judgment by that fact.

The difference between such a case and the plan and operation of the statutes before us is so plain as not to call for further elaboration.

Counsel for the state argue that it has been decided by this court that the Legislature of a state may provide such system of courts as it chooses, that there is nothing in the Fourteenth Amendment that requires a jury trial for any offender, that it may give such territorial jurisdiction to its courts as it sees fit, and therefore that there is nothing sinister or constitutionally invalid in giving to a village mayor the jurisdiction of a justice of the peace to try misdemeanors committed anywhere in the county, even though the mayor presides over a village of 1,100 people and exercises jurisdiction over offenses committed in a county of 500,000. This is true and is established by the decisions of this court.... It is also correctly pointed out that it is completely within the power of the Legislature to dispose of the fines collected in criminal cases as it will, and it may therefore divide the fines as it does here, one-half to the state and one-half to the village by whose mayor they are imposed and collected. It is further said with truth that the Legislature of a state may and often ought to stimulate prosecutions for crime by offering to those who shall initiate and carry on such prosecutions rewards for thus acting in the interest of the state and the people. The Legislature may offer rewards or a percentage of the recovery to informers.... It may authorize the employment of detectives. But these principles do not all direct the question whether the state, by the operation of the statutes we have considered, has not vested the judicial power in one who by reason of his interest, both as an individual and as chief executive of the village, is disqualified to exercise it in the trial of the defendant.

It is finally argued that the evidence shows clearly that the defendant was guilty and that he was only fined $100 which was the minimum amount, and therefore that he cannot complain of a lack of due process, either in his conviction or in the amount of the judgment. The plea was not guilty and he was convicted. No matter what the evidence was against him, he had the right to have an impartial judge. He seasonably raised the objection, and was entitled to half the trial because of the disqualification of the judge, which existed both because of his direct pecuniary interest in the outcome, and because of his official motive to convict and to graduate the fine to help the financial needs of the village. There were thus presented at the outset both features of the disqualification.

The judgment of the Supreme Court of Ohio must be reversed, and the cause remanded for further proceedings not inconsistent with this opinion.

Judgment reversed.

In re Murchison

Certiorari to the Supreme Court of Michigan.

Mr. Justice BLACK delivered the opinion of the Court.

Michigan law authorizes any judge of its courts of record to act as a so-called "one-man grand jury." He can compel witnesses to appear before him in secret to testify about suspected crimes. We have previously held that such a Michigan "judge-grand jury" cannot consistently with the Due Process Clause of the Fourteenth Amendment summarily convict a witness of contempt for conduct in the secret hearings. *In re Oliver,* 333 U.S. 257. We held that before such a conviction could stand, due process requires as a minimum that an accused be given a public trial after reasonable notice of the charges, have a right to examine witnesses against him, call witnesses on his own behalf, and be represented by counsel. The question now before us is whether a contempt proceeding conducted in accordance with these standards complies with the due process requirement of an impartial tribunal where the same judge presiding at the contempt hearing had also served as the "one-man grand jury" out of which the contempt charges arose. This does not involve, of course, the long-exercised power of courts summarily to punish certain conduct occurring in open court.

The petitioners, Murchison and White, were called as witnesses before

a "one-man judge-grand jury." Murchison, a Detroit policeman, was interrogated at length in the judge's secret hearings where questions were asked him about suspected gambling in Detroit and bribery of policemen. His answers left the judge persuaded that he had committed perjury, particularly in view of other evidence before the "judge-grand jury." The judge then charged Murchison with perjury and ordered him to appear and show cause why he should not be punished for criminal contempt. White, the other petitioner, was also summoned to appear as a witness in the same "one-man grand jury" hearing. Asked numerous questions about gambling and bribery, he refused to answer on the ground that he was entitled under Michigan Law to have counsel present with him. The "judge-grand jury" charged White with contempt and ordered him to appear and show cause. The judge who had been the "grand jury" then tried both petitioners in open court, convicted and sentenced them for contempt. Petitioners objected to being tried for contempt by this particular judge for a number of reasons including: (1) Michigan law expressly provides that a judge conducting a "oneman grand jury" inquiry will be disqualified from hearing or trying any case arising from his inquiry or from hearing any motion to dismiss or quash any complaint or indictment growing out of it, or from hearing any charge of contempt "except alleged contempt for neglect or refusal to appear in

349 U.S. 133, 75 S. Ct. 623, 99 L. Ed. 942 (1955).

response to a summons or subpoena"; (2) trial before the judge who was at the same time the complainant, indicter and prosecutor, constituted a denial of the fair and impartial trial required by the Due Process Clause of the Fourteenth Amendment to the Constitution of the United States. The trial judge answered the first challenge by holding that the state statute barring him from trying the contempt cases violated the Michigan Constitution on the ground that it would deprive a judge of inherent power to punish contempt. This interpretation of the Michigan Constitution is binding here. As to the second challenge the trial judge held that due process did not forbid him to try the contempt charges. . . . The State Supreme Court sustained all the trial judge's holdings and affirmed. Importance of the federal constitutional questions raised caused us to grant certiorari. . . .

A fair trial in a fair tribunal is a basic requirement of due process. Fairness of course requires an absence of actual bias in the trial of cases. But our system of law has always endeavored to prevent even the probability of unfairness. To this end no man can be a judge in his own case and no man is permitted to try cases where he has an interest in the outcome. That interest cannot be defined with precision. Circumstances and relationships must be considered. This Court has said, however, that "every procedure which would offer a possible temptation to the average man as a judge. . .not to hold the balance nice, clear and true between the State and the accused, denies the latter due process of law." *Tumey v. Ohio*, 273 U.S. 510, 532. Such a stringent rule may sometimes bar trial by judges who have no actual bias and who would do their very best to weigh the scales of justice equally between

contending parties. But to perform its high function in the best way "justice must satisfy the appearance of justice." . . .

It would be very strange if our system of law permitted a judge to act as a grand jury and then try the very persons accused as a result of his investigations. Perhaps no State has ever forced a defendant to accept grand jurors as proper trial jurors to pass on charges growing out of their hearings. A single "judge-grand jury" is even more a part of the accusatory process than an ordinary lay grand juror. Having been a part of that process a judge cannot be, in the very nature of things, wholly disinterested in the conviction or acquittal of those accused. While he would not likely have all the zeal of a prosecutor, it can certainly not be said that he would have none of that zeal. Fair trials are too important a part of our free society to let prosecuting judges be trial judges of the charges they prefer. It is true that contempt committed in a trial court room can under some circumstances be punished summarily by the trial judge. . . . But adjudication by a trial judge of a contempt committed in his immediate presence in open court cannot be likened to the proceedings here. . . .

As a practical matter it is difficult if not impossible for a judge to free himself from the influence of what took place in his "grand-jury" secret session. His recollection of that is likely to weigh far more heavily with him than any testimony given in the open hearings. That it sometimes does is illustrated by an incident which occurred in White's case. In finding White guilty of contempt the trial judge said, "There is one thing the record does not show, and that was Mr. White's attitude, and I must say that his attitude was almost insolent in the manner in which he answered questions and his attitude upon the witness stand. . . . Not only was the personal attitude insolent, but it was defiant, and I want to put that on the record.". . . Thus the judge whom due process requires to be impartial in weighing the evidence presented before him, called on his own personal knowledge and impression of what had occurred in the grand jury room and his judgment was based in part on this impression, the accuracy of which could not be tested by adequate cross-examination.

This incident also shows that the judge was doubtless more familiar with the facts and circumstances in which the charges were rooted than was any other witness. There were no public witnesses upon whom petitioners could call to give disinterested testimony concerning what took place in the secret chambers of the judge. If there had been they might have been able to refute the judge's statement about White's insolence. Moreover, as shown by the judge's statement here, a "judge-grand jury" might himself many times be a very material witness in a later trial for contempt. If the charge should be heard before that judge, the result would be either that the defendant must be deprived of examining or cross-examining him or else there would be the spectacle of the trial judge presenting testimony upon which he must finally pass in determining the guilt or innocence of the defendant. In either event the State would have the benefit of the judge's personal knowledge while the accused would be denied an opportunity to cross-examine. The right of a defendant to examine and cross-examine witnesses is too essential to a fair trial to have that right jeopardized in such way.

We hold that it was a violation of due process for the "judge-grand jury" to try these petitioners, and it was therefore error for the Supreme Court of Michigan to uphold the convictions. The judgments are reversed and the causes are remanded for proceedings not inconsistent with this opinion.

6   Equality

It may come as a shock to some people to be told that, in a sense, freedom and equality are incompatible. Strict enforcement of equality is a restriction on freedom, particularly since in the nature of things some individuals have greater capabilities for advancement—economically, educationally, and politically—than others. But looking at the relationship between freedom and equality from another perspective, we can see in the principle of equality a limitation on privilege based on birth, social position, or economic class. In this sense, then, equality provides the vehicle by which a gifted person, though he may be poverty striken and without social position, can develop his talents and fulfill his potentialities.

CLASSICAL VIEWPOINTS

In dealing with the theory of the fundamental equality of mankind, Western history contains two principal periods of development, the classical Greek and Roman era and the modern period going back some three hundred years.

In Chapter 12 of *Politics*, our first selection, Aristotle illustrates the argument that the high-born or wealthy should not have greater political rights than others not so fortunate, simply on the basis of birth or wealth or some other quality irrelevant to political affairs. He stresses that in matters political, just as in matters belonging to other arts and sciences, there is no good reason for basing a claim to the exercise of a greater right on any and every kind of superiority. One person may be a fast runner and another may be crippled, but this is no reason why the one should have more political rights than the other. "It is in athletic contests that the superiority of the swift receives its reward." Personal appearance or social status have nothing to do with claims to political leadership.

In Chapter 11 of his *Politics,* Aristotle addresses himself to the question of the most practicable type of constitution for a state. He emphasizes that "a state which is based on the middle class is bound to be the best constituted. . . ." Aristotle's conclusions have been borne out over and over in history, including the modern examples of the Latin American and the new Afro-Asian nations; the most stable kind of state is one possessing a large middle class. True community requires a nation of peers or equals.

Another early development was the Stoic idea that on earth all men, and *only* men, have the ability to reason. The ability to reason was seen as part of deity, and therefore all men share something of a divine nature. The great exponent of Stoic thought during the Roman period was the orator Cicero, who is the source of our next selection. In his treatises on laws and the nature of the gods, written a hundred years before the Christian era, he refers to a "natural inclination" of men to love mankind and declares this to be the true basis of justice. Justice, in turn, implies giving each his due and thereby becomes the foundation of equality. Another basis for equality is derived by Cicero from the Latin word *humanitas,* which he uses to denote men's awareness of a common humanity and the recognition of the dignity of man as man.

The Roman law that evolved to govern the far-flung empire, the *jus gentium,* also emphasized a unity of mankind in the common legal principles developed by the different peoples within the empire and the equitable nature of justice. This is illustrated by a brief excerpt from the works of the Emperor Justinian, our fifth reading. In sum, then, two ingredients— the classical Stoic philosophy of a unity of all men in the ability to reason and a set of rules common to many different peoples—were important influences in the third century A.D., granting Roman citizenship to all free inhabitants of the empire. The Christian religion began midway in this period and contributed to a conception of unity and equality in that all men are considered children of God.

MODERN DEVELOPMENTS

The modern development of the concept of equality can be traced to events leading to the English, American, and French revolutions. Human equality was both a rallying cry for the protestors against their government and a justification for victory. In describing the "nature" of man, the revolutionary

writers of the seventeenth and eighteenth centuries used a convenient hypothetical situation, the "state of nature." John Locke, whose views on the
social contract were examined in Chapter 5, set forth a description of
absolute equality in the state of nature and also the necessity for forming
an organized government in Chapters 2, 4, and 9 of *The Second Treatise
of Civil Government,* the sixth, seventh, and eighth readings of this section.
Locke's book first appeared anonymously in London in 1690. Its immediate
objectives were the general defense of the Glorious Revolution of 1688 and,
specifically, the justification of the ouster of King James II. It has particular
interest for Americans in that the same justifications were used less than
a century later by Thomas Jefferson against King George III. In fact, the
Declaration of Independence of 1776 borrowed heavily from Locke.

Our ninth reading is an excerpt from Alexis de Tocqueville, a French
statesman who traveled in and wrote about America in the early nineteenth
century. His descriptions of conditions in the new republic, including
equality, are considered to be among the finest written on this subject.

The basis for much of our present law on the subject of equality, Section
I of the Fourteenth Amendment to the United States Constitution, proposed
by Congress in 1868, is the tenth reading. The "equal protection of the
laws" clause has been the foundation for the bulk of civil rights cases of
recent decades. The Supreme Court case of *Brown v. Topeka Board of
Education* (1954) is quoted as the eleventh reading. This landmark decision
is an example of the official reasoning of our national government with
regard to the meaning of equality before the law in contemporary America.
In 1896, the Supreme Court decision of *Plessy v. Ferguson* had established
the "separate but equal" doctrine. This meant that equal protection of
the laws was given by governmental authorities if equal facilities, such as
schools, public waiting rooms, seats on public conveyances, and public
recreation facilities, were provided for Negroes even though these facilities
were separated from those provided for white people. This decision legalized
racial segregation, commonly called "Jim Crow" laws, in a number of
states from 1896 to 1954. The *Brown v. Topeka Board of Education* decision
overruled the Plessy case by stating that separate facilities are "inherently
unequal."

The twelfth selection of the chapter is from the Supreme Court decision
of *Miranda v. Arizona* (1966) and is an example of judicial interpretation
of several other parts of our Bill of Rights. The decision makes it clear
that there is an underlying right to a fair trial included in the gurantees
found in the Fifth and Fourteenth Amendments. The Fifth Amendment
also includes the right to remain silent (the right not to be compelled to
be a witness against oneself). Finally, the Sixth Amendment guarantees the
right to have the assistance of counsel in all criminal prosecutions. The Court
is attempting to make a reality of the American motto "Equal justice under
the law." A defense attorney is considered a necessity rather than a luxury

in the reasoning of this case. The judicial language concludes with these words: "Were we to limit these constitutional rights to those who can retain an attorney, our decision today would be of little significance."

So far we have focused our discussion on equality before the law. However, the principle that equality can be achieved through a limitation on privilege can also be applied in a positive sense by a government which promotes equality of opportunity. In recent years a number of laws have been enacted to ensure that equality of opportunity is not infringed upon.

Our final selections in this chapter consist of excerpts from two recent statutes, one from Ohio and the other an act of Congress. These current laws demonstrate government's concern with keeping channels of opportunity open. The state statute used here illustrates the trend toward outlawing in real estate transactions all discriminations based on race, color, religion, ancestry, or national origin. The national law quoted is part of the Civil Rights Act of 1966. With regard to the discriminations referred to above, the act of Congress makes it a criminal act to treat people unequally in employment practices. Equality in our democracy is an expanding concept. Although some people may argue that this expanding concept of equality may in fact impinge on the exercise of freedom, others hold that the exercise of freedom is subject to respect for the rights of others.

The Principles of Oligarchy and Democracy, and the Nature of Distributive Justice

ARISTOTLE

...In all arts and sciences the end in view is some good. In the most sovereign of all the arts and sciences—and this is the art and science of politics—the end in view is the greatest good and the good which is most pursued. The good in the sphere of politics is justice; and justice consists in what tends to promote the common interest. General opinion makes it consist in some sort of equality. Up to a point this general opinion agrees with the philosophical inquiries which contain our conclusions on ethics. In other words, it holds that justice involves two factors—things, and the persons to whom things are assigned—and it considers that persons who are equal should have assigned to them equal things. But here there arises a question which must not be overlooked. Equals and unequals—yes; but equals and unequals *in what?* This is a question which raises difficulties, and involves us in philosophical speculation on politics. It is possible to argue that offices and honours ought to be distributed unequally [i.e. that superior amounts should be assigned to superior persons] on the basis of superiority *in any respect whatsoever*—even though there were similarity, and no shadow of any difference, in every other respect; and it may be urged, in favour of this

From *The Politics of Aristotle*, translated with notes by Ernest Barker (London: Oxford University Press, 1950), pp. 150–53, by permission of the publisher.

argument, that where people differ from one another there must be difference in what is just and proportionate to their merits. If this argument were accepted, the mere fact of a better complexion, or greater height, or any other such advantage would establish a claim for a greater share of political rights to be given to its possessor. But is not the argument obviously wrong? To be clear that it is, we have only to study the analogy of the other arts and sciences. If you were dealing with a number of flute-players who were equal in their art, you would not assign them flutes on the principle that the better born should have a greater amount. Nobody will play the better for being better born; and it is to those who are better at the job that the better supply of tools should be given. If our point is not yet plain, it can be made so if we push it still further. Let us suppose a man who is superior to others in flute-playing, but far inferior in birth and beauty. Birth and beauty may be greater goods than ability to play the flute, and those who possess them may, upon balance, surpass the flute-player more in these qualities than he surpasses them in his flute-playing; but the fact remains that *he* is the man who ought to get the better supply of flutes. [If it is to be recognized in connexion with a given function], superiority in a quality such as birth—or for that matter wealth—ought to contribute something to the performance of that function; and here these qualities contribute nothing to such performance.

There is a further objection. If we accept this argument [that offices and honours should be assigned on the basis of excellence in *any* respect], every quality will have to be commensurable with every other. You will begin by reckoning a given degree of (say) height as superior to a given degree of some other quality, and you will thus be driven to pit height in general against (say) wealth and birth in general. But on this basis—*i.e.* that, *in a given case,* A is counted as excelling in height to a greater degree than B does in goodness, and that, *in general,* height is counted as excelling to a greater degree than goodness does—qualities are made commensurable. [We are involved in mere arithmetic]; for if amount X

of some quality is "better" than amount Y of some other, some amount which is other than X must clearly be equal to it [*i.e.* must be *equally* good]. This is impossible [because things that differ in quality cannot be treated in terms of quantity, or regarded as commensurable]. It is therefore clear that in matters political [just as in matters belonging to other arts and sciences] there is no good reason for basing a claim to the exercise of authority on any and every kind of superiority. Some may be swift and others slow; but this is no reason why the one should have more [political rights], and the other less. It is in athletic contests that the superiority of the swift receives its reward. Claims to political rights must be based on the ground of contribution to the elements which constitute the being of the state....

The Type of Constitution Which Is Most Generally Practicable

ARISTOTLE

...We have now to consider what is the best constitution and the best way of life for the *majority* of states and men. In doing so we shall not employ, [for the purpose of measuring "the best"], a standard of excellence above the reach of ordinary men, or a standard of education requiring exceptional endowments and equipment, or the standard of a constitution which attains an ideal height. We shall only be concerned with the sort of life which most men are able to share and the sort of constitution which it is possible for most states to enjoy. The "aristocracies," so called, of which we have just been treating, [will not serve us for this purpose: they] either lie, at one extreme, beyond the reach of most states, or they approach, at the other, so closely to the constitution called "polity" that they need not be considered separately and must be treated as identical with it. The issues we have just raised can all be decided in the light of one body of fundamental principles. If we adopt

From *The Politics of Aristotle,* translated with notes by Ernest Barker (London: Oxford University Press, 1950), pp. 213–15, by permission of the publisher.

as true the statements made in the *Ethics*—(1) that a truly happy life is a life of goodness lived in freedom from impediments, and (2) that goodness consists in a mean—it follows that the best way of life [for the *majority* of men] is one which consists in a mean, and a mean of the kind attainable by every individual. Further, the same criteria which determine whether the citizen-body [*i.e.*, all its members, considered as *individuals*] have a good or bad way of life must also apply to the constitution; for a constitution is the way of life of a citizen-body. In all states there may be distinguished three parts, or classes, of the citizen-body—the very rich; the very poor; and the middle class which forms the mean. Now it is admitted, as a general principle, that moderation and the mean are always best. We may therefore conclude that in the ownership of all gifts of fortune a middle condition will be the best. Men who are in this condition are the most ready to listen to reason. Those who belong to either extreme—the over-handsome, the over-strong, the over-noble, the over-wealthy; or at the opposite end the over-poor, the over-weak, the utterly ignoble—find it hard to follow the lead of reason. Men in the first class tend more to violence and serious crime: men in the second tend too much to roguery and petty offences; and most wrongdoing arises either from violence or roguery. It is a further merit of the middle class that its members suffer least from ambition, which both in the military and the civil sphere is dangerous to states. It must also be added that those who enjoy too many advantages—strength,

wealth, connexions, and so forth—are both unwilling to obey and ignorant how to obey. This is a defect which appears in them from the first, during childhood and in home-life: nurtured in luxury, they never acquire a habit of discipline, even in the matter of lessons. But there are also defects in those who suffer from the opposite extreme of a lack of advantages: they are far too mean and poor-spirited. We have thus, on the one hand, people who are ignorant how to rule and only know how to obey, as if they were so many slaves, and, on the other hand, people who are ignorant how to obey any sort of authority and only know how to rule as if they were masters of slaves. The result is a state, not of freemen, but only of slaves and masters: a state of envy on the one side and on the other contempt. Nothing could be farther removed from the spirit of friendship or the temper of a political community. Community depends on friendship; and when there is enmity instead of friendship, men will not even share the same path. A state aims at being, as far as it can be, a society composed of equals and peers [who, as such, can be friends and associates]; and the middle class, more than any other, has this sort of composition. It follows that a state which is based on the middle class is bound to be the best constituted in respect of the elements [*i.e.*, equals and peers] of which, on our view, a state is naturally composed. The middle classes [besides contributing, in this way, to the security of the state] enjoy a greater security themselves than any other class....

Treatise on the Nature of the Gods

MARCUS TULLIUS CICERO

XIV. But man himself was born to contemplate and imitate the world; being in nowise perfect, but, if I may so express myself, a particle of perfection. . . .

LXI. But what shall I say of human reason? Has it not even entered the heavens? Man alone of all animals has observed the courses of the stars, their risings and settings. By man the day, the month, the year is determined. He foresees the eclipses of the sun and moon, and foretells them to futurity, marking their greatness, duration, and precise time. From the contemplation of these things, the mind extracts the knowledge of the Gods,—a knowledge that produces piety, with which is connected justice, and all the other virtues. . . .

LXII. I am now to prove, by way of conclusion, that everything in this world, of use to us, was made designedly for us.

First of all, the universe was made for the Gods and men, and all things therein were prepared and provided for our service. For the world is the common habitation or city of the Gods and men; for they are the only reasonable beings: they alone live by justice and law. . . .

Reprinted from *The Treatises of M. T. Cicero*, ed. C. D. Young (London: George Bell and Sons, 1887), pp. 46–82.

Treatise on the Laws

MARCUS TULLIUS CICERO

For what becomes of generosity, patriotism, or friendship? Where will the desire of benefitting our neighbours, or the gratitude that acknowledges kindness, be able to exist at all? For all these virtues proceed from our natural inclination to love mankind. And this is the true basis of justice, and without this not only the mutual charities of men, but the religious services of the Gods, would be at an end; for these are preserved, as I imagine, rather by the natural sympathy which subsists between divine and human beings, than by mere fear and timidity. . . .

Reprinted from *The Treatises of M. T. Cicero*, p. 187.

Institutionum Flavius Justinianus
(The Institutions of Justinian)

TITLE I. OF JUSTICE AND LAW

Justice is the constant and perpetual desire of giving to every man that which is due to him. Jurisprudence is the knowledge of things divine and human, and the exact discernment of what is just and unjust.

The precepts of the law are these: to live honestly, not to hurt any man, and to give to every one that which is his due. The law is divided into public and private. Public law regards the state of the commonwealth; but private law, of which we shall here treat, concerns the interest of individuals, and is tripartite, being collected from natural precepts, from the law of nations, and from the civil law of any particular city or state.

The law of nature is not a law to man only, but likewise to all other animals. Thus in the matters of matrimony and the bringing up of children, not only man but also the rest of the animal creation are regarded as having a knowledge of this law, by which they are actuated.

The laws of nature, which are observed by all nations, inasmuch as they are the appointment of divine Providence, remain constantly fixed and immutable. But those laws, which every city has enacted for the government of itself, suffer frequent changes, either by tacit consent, or by some subsequent law repealing a former.

Civil law is distinguished from the law of nations, because every community uses partly its own particular laws, and partly the general laws, which are common to all mankind. That law which a people enacts for the government of itself is called the civil law of that people; but that law which natural reason appoints for all mankind is called the law of nations (*jus gentium*), because all nations make use of it.

The law of nations is common to all men, and all nations have framed laws through human necessity. Wars arose and consequences were captivity and slavery, both of which are contrary to the laws of nature, for by that law all men are free. But almost all contracts were at first introduced by the law of nations, as for instance buying, selling, renting, demand deposits, and others without number.

The Roman law is divided, like the Greek, into written and unwritten. The written comprehends plebiscites, acts of the senate, and decrees of princes. A plebiscite is what the citizens enact when requested by a plebeian magistrate, as by a tribune.

An act of the senate (*senatus-consultum*) is what the senate commands and appoints; for, when the people of Rome were increased to a degree which made it difficult for them to assemble for the enacting of laws, it seemed but right that the senate should be consulted instead of the whole body of the people.

The decrees of the prince also have the force of law, because the people, by a law called *lex regia,* make a concession to him of their power. Therefore, whatever the emperor ordains by rescript, decree, or edict is a law.

Trans. George Harris (London: W. H. Lunn, J. Butterworth, and Clarke and Sons, 1811), pp. 5–11.

Of the State of Nature

JOHN LOCKE

To understand political power right, and derive it from its original, we must consider what state all men are naturally in, and that is a state of perfect freedom to order their actions and dispose of their possessions and persons as they think fit, within the bounds of the law of nature, without asking leavev or depending upon the will of any other man.

A state also of equality, wherein all the power and jurisdiction is reciprocal, no one having more than another; there being nothing more evident than that creatures of the same species and rank, promiscuously born to all the same advantages of nature and the use of the same faculties, should also be equal one amongst another without subordination or subjection; unless the lord and master of them all should, by any manifest declaration of his will, set one above another, and confer on him by evident and clear appointment an undoubted right to dominion and sovereignty.

Reprinted from John Locke, *Two Treatises of Government*, ed. Thomas I. Cook (New York: Hafner Publishing Co., Inc., 1947), p. 122, by permission of the publisher.

Of Slavery

JOHN LOCKE

The natural liberty of man is to be free from any superior power on earth, and not to be under the will or legislative authority of man, but to have only the law of nature for his rule. The liberty of man in society is to be under no other legislative power but that established by consent in the commonwealth; nor under the dominion of any will or restraint of any law, but what that legislative shall enact according to the trust put in it. Freedom then is not what Sir Robert Filmer tells us, "a liberty for every one to do what he lists, to live as he pleases, and not to be tied by any laws"; but freedom of men under government is to have a standing rule to live by, common to everyone of that society and made by the legislative power erected in it, a liberty to follow my own will in all things where the rule prescribes not, and not to be subject to the inconstant, uncertain, unknown, arbitrary will of another man; as freedom of nature is to be under no other restraint but the law of nature.

Reprinted from Locke, *Two Treatises of Government*, p. 132, by permission of the publisher.

This freedom from absolute, arbitrary power is so necessary to and closely joined with a man's preservation that he cannot part with it but by what forfeits his preservation and life together. . . .

Of the Ends of Political Society and Government

JOHN LOCKE

If man in the state of nature be so free, as has been said, if he be absolute lord of his own person and possessions, equal to the greatest, and subject to nobody, why will he part with his freedom, why will he give up his empire and subject himself to the dominion and control of any other power? To which it is obvious to answer that though in the state of nature he hath such a right, yet the enjoyment of it is very uncertain and constantly exposed to the invasion of others; for all being kings as much as he, every man his equal, and the greater part no strict observers of equity and justice, the enjoyment of the property he has in this state is very unsafe, very unsecure. This makes him willing to quit a condition which, however free, is full of fears and continual dangers; and it is not without reason that he seeks out and is willing to join in society with others who are already united, or have a mind to unite, for the mutual preservation of their lives, liberties, and estates, which I call by the general name "property."

The great and chief end, therefore, of men's uniting into commonwealths and putting themselves under government is the preservation of their property. To which in the state of nature there are many things wanting:

First, There wants an established, settled, known law, received and allowed by common consent to be the standard of right and wrong and the common measure to decide all controversies between them; for though the law of nature be plain and intelligible to all rational creatures, yet men, being biased by their interest as well as ignorant for want of studying it, are not apt to allow of it as a law binding to them in the application of it to their particular cases.

Secondly, In the state of nature there wants a known and indifferent judge with authority to determine all differences according to the established law; for every one in that state being both judge and executioner of law of nature, men being partial to themselves, passion and revenge is very apt to carry them too far and with too much heat in their own cases, as well as negligence and unconcernedness to make them too remiss in other men's.

Thirdly, In the state of nature, there often wants power to back and support the sentence when right, and to give it due execution. They who by any injustice offend will seldom fail, where they are able, by force, to make good

Reprinted from Locke, *Two Treatises of Government,* pp. 184–85, by permission of the publisher.

their injustice; such resistance many times makes the punishment dangerous and frequently destructive to those who attempt it.

Thus mankind, notwithstanding all the privileges of the state of nature, being but in an ill condition while they remain in it, are quickly driven into society. Hence it comes to pass that we seldom find any number of men live any time together in this state. The inconveniences that they are therein exposed to by the irregular and uncertain exercise of the power every man has of punishing the transgressions of others make them take sanctuary under the established laws of government and therein seek the preservation of their property. It is this makes them so willingly give up every one his single power of punishing, to be exercised by such alone as shall be appointed to it amongst them; and by such rules as the community, or those authorized by them to that purpose, shall agree on. And in this we have the original right of both the legislative and executive power, as well as of the governments and societies themselves.

Democracy in America

ALEXIS DE TOCQUEVILLE

THE PRINCIPLE OF EQUALITY SUGGESTS TO THE AMERICANS THE IDEA OF THE INDEFINITE PERFECTIBILITY OF MAN

Equality suggests to the human mind several ideas which would not have originated from any other source, and it modifies almost all those previously entertained. I take as an example the idea of human perfectibility, because it is one of the principal notions that the intellect can conceive, and because it constitutes of itself a great philosophical theory, which is every instant to be traced by its consequences in the practice of human affairs. Although man has many points of resemblance with the brute creation, one characteristic is peculiar to himself—he im-

Reprinted from Alexis de Tocqueville, *Democracy in America*, Vol. II, trans. Henry Reeve, rev. ed. (London: The Colonial Press, 1900), pp. 34–35, 172–76.

proves: they are incapable of improvement. Mankind could not fail to discover this difference from its earliest period. The idea of perfectibility is therefore as old as the world; equality did not give birth to it, although it has imparted to it a novel character.

When the citizens of a community are classed according to their rank, their profession, or their birth, and when all men are constrained to follow the career which happens to open before them, everyone thinks that the utmost limits of human power are to be discerned in proximity to himself, and none seeks any longer to resist the inevitable law of his destiny. Not indeed that an aristocratic people absolutely contests man's faculty of self-improvement, but they do not hold it to be indefinite; amelioration they conceive, but not change: they imagine that the future condition of society may be better, but not essentially different;

and whilst they admit that mankind has made vast strides in improvement, and may still have some to make, they assign to it beforehand certain impassable limits. Thus they do not presume that they have arrived at the supreme good or at absolute truth (what people or what man was ever wild enough to imagine it?) but they cherish a persuasion that they have pretty nearly reached that degree of greatness and knowledge which our imperfect nature admits of; and as nothing moves about them they are willing to fancy that everything is in its fit place. Then it is that the legislator affects to lay down eternal laws; that kings and nations will raise none but imperishable monuments; and that the present generation undertakes to spare generations to come the care of regulating their destinies.

In proportion as castes disappear and the classes of society approximate—as manners, customs, and laws vary, from the tumultuous intercourse of men—as new facts arise—as new truths are brought to light—as ancient opinions are dissipated and others take their place—the image of an ideal perfection, forever on the wing, presents itself to the human mind. Continual changes are then every instant occurring under the observation of every man: the position of some is rendered worse; and he learns but too well, that no people and no individual, how enlightened soever they may be, can lay claim to infallibility;—the condition of others is improved; whence he infers that man is endowed with an indefinite faculty of improvement. His reverses teach him that none may hope to have discovered absolute good—his success stimulates him to the never-ending pursuit of it. Thus, forever seeking—forever falling, to rise again—often disappointed, but not discouraged—he tends unceasingly towards that unmea-

sured greatness so indistinctly visible at the end of the long track which humanity has yet to tread. It can hardly be believed how many facts naturally flow from the philosophical theory of the indefinite perfectibility of man, or how strong an influence it exercises even on men who, living entirely for the purposes of action and not of thought, seem to conform their actions to it, without knowing anything about it. I accost an American sailor, and I inquire why the ships of his country are built so as to last but for a short time; he answers without hesitation that the art of navigation is every day making such rapid progress that the finest vessel would become almost useless if it lasted beyond a certain number of years. In these words, which fell accidentally and on a particular subject from a man of rude attainments, I recognize the general and systematic idea upon which a great people directs all its concerns.

Aristocratic nations are naturally too apt to narrow the scope of human perfectibility; democratic nations to expand it beyond compass.

· · ·

THAT MANNERS ARE SOFTENED AS SOCIAL CONDITIONS BECOME MORE EQUAL

We perceive that for several ages social conditions have tended to equality, and we discover that in the course of the same period the manners of society have been softened. Are these two things merely contemporaneous, or does any secret link exist between them, so that the one cannot go on without making the other advance? Several causes may concur to render the manners of a people less rude; but, of all these causes, the most powerful appears to me to be the equality of conditions. Equality of conditions and growing civility in manners are, then, in my eyes, not only contemporaneous occurrences, but correlative facts. When the fabulists seek to interest us in the actions of beasts, they invest them with human notions and passions; the poets who sing of spirits and angels do the same; there is no wretchedness so deep, nor any happiness so pure, as to fill the human mind and touch the heart, unless we are ourselves held up to our own eyes under other features.

This is strictly applicable to the subject upon which we are at present engaged. When all men are irrevocably marshalled in an aristocratic community, according to their professions, their property, and their birth, the members of each class, considering themselves as children of the same family, cherish a constant and lively sympathy towards each other, which can never be felt in an equal degree by the citizens of a democracy. But the same feeling does not exist between the several classes towards each other. Amongst an aristocratic people each caste has its own opinions, feelings, rights, manners, and modes of living. Thus the men of whom each caste is composed do not resemble the mass of their fellow-citizens; they do not think or feel in the same manner, and they scarcely believe that they belong to the same human race. They cannot, therefore, thoroughly understand what others feel, nor judge of others by themselves. Yet they are sometimes eager to lend each other mutual aid; but this is not contrary to my previous observation. These aristocratic institutions, which made the beings of one and the same race so different, nevertheless bound them to each other by close political ties. Although the serf had no natural interest in the fate of nobles, he did not the less think himself obliged to devote his person to the service of that noble who happened to be his lord; and although the noble held himself to be of a different nature from that of his serfs, he nevertheless held that his duty and his honor constrained him to defend, at the risk of his own life, those who dwelt upon his domains.

It is evident that these mutual obligations did not originate in the law of nature, but in the law of society; and that the claim of social duty was more stringent than that of mere humanity. These services were not supposed to be due from man to man, but to the vassal or to the lord. Feudal institutions awakened a lively sympathy for the sufferings of certain men, but none at all for the miseries of mankind. They infused generosity rather than mildness into the manners of the time, and although they prompted men to great acts of self-devotion, they engendered no real sympathies; for real sympathies can only exist between those who are alike; and in aristocratic ages men acknowledge none but the members of their own caste to be like themselves.

When the chroniclers of the Middle Ages, who all belonged to the aristocracy by birth or education, relate the tragical end of a noble, their grief flows apace; whereas they tell you at a breath, and without wincing, of massacres and tortures inflicted on the common sort of people. Not that these writers felt habitual hatred or systematic disdain for the people; war between the several classes of the community was not yet declared. They were impelled by an instinct rather than by a passion; as they had formed no clear notion of a poor man's sufferings, they cared but little for his fate. The same feelings animated the lower orders whenever the feudal tie was broken. The same ages which witnessed so many heroic acts of selfdevotion on the part of vassals for their lords, were stained with atrocious barbarities, exercised from time to time by the lower classes on the higher. It must not be supposed that this mutual insensibility arose solely from the absence of public order and education; for traces of it are to be found in the following centuries, which became tranquil and enlightened whilst they remained aristocratic. In 1675 the lower classes in Brittany revolted at the imposition of a new tax. These disturbances were put down with unexampled atrocity. Observe the language in which Madame de Sévigné, a witness of these horrors, relates them to her daughter:

'Aux Rochers, 30 Octobre, 1675. Mon Dieu, ma fille, que votre lettre d'Aix est plaisante! Au moins relisez vos lettres avant que de les envoyer; laissez-vous surpendre à leur agrément, et consolez-vous par ce plaisir de la peine que vous avez d'en tant écrire. Vous avez donc baisé toute la Provence? il n'y aurait pas satisfaction à baiser toute la Bretagne, à moins qu'on n'aimât à sentir le vin.... Voulez-vous savoir des nouvelles de Rennes? On a fait une taxe de cent mille écus sur le bourgeois; et si on ne trouve point cette somme dans vingt-quatre heures, elle sera doublée et exigible par les soldats. On a chassé et banni toute une grand rue, et défendu de les recueillir sous peine de la vie; de sorte qu'on voyait tous ces misérables, veillards, femmes accouchées, enfans, errer en pleurs au sortir de cette ville sans savoir où aller. On roua avant-hier un violon, qui avait commencé la danse et la pillerie du papier timbré; il a été écartelé après sa mort, et ses quatre quartiers exposés aux quatre coins de la ville. On a pris soixante bourgeois, et on commence demain les punitions. Cette province est un bel exemple pour les autres, et surtout de respecter les gouverneurs et les gouvernantes, et de ne point jeter de pierres dans leur jardin. Madame de Tarente était hier dans ces bois par un temps enchanté: il n'est question ni de chambre ni de collation; elle entre par la barrière et s'en retourne de même....

[My goodness your letter from Aix is amusing, my daughter! Really, though, you should read your letters over again before sending them. Their humor might surprise you and console you for all the trouble of writing so many.

So you have kissed all of Provence, have you? It would not be very satisfying to kiss all Brittany, unless one wanted to smell of wine....

Would you like to hear the latest news from Rennes? A new tax of a hundred thousand crowns has been placed on the citizens; and if it is not paid within twenty-four hours, it will be doubled and collected by the soldiers. They have emptied all the houses of one of the main streets and sent away the inhabitants. No one may assist these unfortunates, including elderly men, pregnant women, and children, on pain of death; and they may be seen wandering around miserable and not knowing where to go.

Two days ago a musician was tortured to death on the wheel for starting up a dance and for stealing some stamps. He was then quartered and his severed body exposed at the four corners of the city. Sixty local inhabitants have been imprisoned, and their punishment will begin tomorrow. All in all, this province is a fine example for the others; it teaches them especially to respect the governors and their wives and not to throw stones into their garden. (Note: This was a joking reference to the fact that the daughter here was wife of the Governor of Provence.)

Yesterday I had a delightful time with Madame de Tarente here in my hinterland. There is no problem about preparing a chamber or luncheon for her; she comes by the gate and leaves the same way....]*

In another letter she adds:

Vous me parlez bien plaisamment de nos misères; nous ne sommes plus si roués; un en huit jours, pour entretenir la justice. Il est vrai que la penderie me paraît maintenant un refraîchissement. J'ai une tout autre idée de la justice, depuis que je suis en ce pays. Vos galériens me paraissent une société d'honnêtes gens qui se sont retirés du monde pour mener une vie douce.

---

* Translation by the editors.

["You jest about our miseries here, but we really are not so jaded. Once a week we have an execution, just for the appearance of justice. It is true that hanging now appears to me rather refreshing. I have a totally new idea of justice since I have been in this area. Your galley slaves seem to me to be a society of honest men who have retired from the world to lead a good life."]*

It would be a mistake to suppose that Madame de Sévigné, who wrote these lines, was a selfish or cruel person; she was passionately attached to her children, and very ready to sympathize in the sorrows of her friends; nay, her letters show that she treated her vassals and servants with kindness and indulgence. But Madame de Sévigné had no clear notion of suffering in anyone who was not a person of quality.

In our time the harshest man writing to the most insensible person of his acquaintance would not venture wantonly to indulge in the cruel jocularity which I have quoted; and even if his own manners allowed him to do so, the manners of society at large would forbid it. Whence does this arise? Have we more sensibility than our forefathers? I know not that we have; but I am sure that our insensibility is extended to a far greater range of objects. When all the ranks of a community are nearly equal, as all men think and feel

* Translation by the editors.

in nearly the same manner, each of them may judge in a moment of the sensations of all the others; he casts a rapid glance upon himself, and that is enough. There is no wretchedness into which he cannot readily enter, and a secret instinct reveals to him its extent. It signifies not that strangers or foes be the sufferers; imagination puts him in their place; something like a personal feeling is mingled with his pity, and makes himself suffer whilst the body of his fellow-creature is in torture. In democratic ages men rarely sacrifice themselves for one another; but they display general compassion for the members of the human race. They inflict no useless ills; and they are happy to relieve the griefs of others, when they can do so without much hurting themselves; they are not disinterested, but they are humane.

Although the Americans have in a manner reduced egotism to a social and philosophical theory, they are nevertheless extremely open to compassion. In no other country is criminal justice administered with more mildness than in the United States. . . . (They) have almost expunged capital punishment from their codes. North America is, I think, the only country upon earth in which the life of no one citizen has been taken for a political offence in the course of the last fifty years. . . .

Amendment XIV (1868)

THE CONSTITUTION OF THE UNITED STATES

Section 1. All persons born or naturalized in the United States, and subject to the jurisdiction thereof, are citizens of the United States and of the State wherein they reside. No State shall make or enforce any law which shall abridge the privileges or immunities of citizens of the United States; nor shall any States deprive any person of life, liberty, or property, without due process of law; nor deny to any person within its jurisdiction the equal protection of the laws.

Brown *v.* Board of Education of Topeka

UNITED STATES SUPREME COURT

Mr. Chief Justice WARREN delivered the opinion of the Court.

These cases come to us from the States of Kansas, South Carolina, Virginia, and Delaware. They are premised on different facts and different local conditions, but a common legal question justifies their consideration together in this consolidated opinion.

In each of the cases, minors of the Negro race, through their legal representatives, seek the aid of the courts in obtaining admission to the public schools of their community on a non-segregated basis. In each instance, they had been denied admission to schools attended by white children under laws requiring or permitting segregation according to race. This segregation was alleged to deprive the plaintiffs of the equal protection of the laws under the Fourteenth Amendment. In each of the cases other than the Delaware case, a three-judge federal district court denied relief to the plaintiffs on the so-called "separate but equal" doctrine announced by this Court in *Plessy v. Ferguson,* 163 U. S. 537. Under that doctrine, equality of treatment is accorded when the races are provided substantially equal facilities, even though these facilities be separate. In the Delaware case, the Supreme Court of Delaware adhered to that doctrine, but ordered that the plaintiffs be admitted to the white schools because of their superiority to the Negro schools.

The plaintiffs contend that segregated public schools are not "equal" and cannot be made "equal," and that hence they are deprived of the equal protection of the laws. Because of the obvious importance of the question presented, the Court took jurisdiction. Argument was heard in the 1952 Term, and reargument was heard this Term on certain questions propounded by the Court.

...In the first cases in this Court construing the Fourteenth Amendment, decided shortly after its adoption, the Court interpreted it as proscribing all state-imposed discriminations against the Negro race. The doctrine of "separate but equal" did not make its appearance in this Court until 1896 in the case of *Plessy v. Ferguson,* supra, involving not education but transportation. American courts have since labored with the doctrine for over half a century.... In more recent cases, all on the graduate school level, inequality was found in that specific benefits enjoyed by white students were denied to

347 U.S. 483, 74 S. Ct. 686, 98 L. Ed. 873 (1954).

Negro students of the same educational qualifications. . . . In none of these cases was it necessary to reexamine the doctrine to grant relief to the Negro plaintiff. And in *Sweatt v. Painter,* supra, the Court expressly reserved decision on the question whether *Plessy v. Ferguson* should be held inapplicable to public education.

In the instant cases, that question is directly presented. Here, unlike *Sweatt v. Painter,* there are findings below that the Negro and white schools involved have been equalized, or are being equalized, with respect to buildings, curricula, qualifications and salaries of teachers, and other "tangible" factors. Our decision, therefore, cannot turn on merely a comparison of these tangible factors in the Negro and white schools involved in each of the cases. We must look instead to the effect of segregation itself on public education.

In approaching this problem, we cannot turn the clock back to 1868 when the Amendment was adopted, or even to 1896 when *Plessy v. Ferguson* was written. We must consider public education in the light of its full development and its present place in American life throughout the Nation. Only in this way can it be determined if segregation in public schools deprives these plaintiffs of the equal protection of the laws.

Today, education is perhaps the most important function of state and local governments. Compulsory school attendance laws and the great expenditures for education both demonstrate our recognition of the importance of education to our democratic society. It is required in the performance of our most basic public responsibilities, even service in the armed forces. It is the very foundation of good citizenship. Today it is a principal instrument in awakening the child to cultural values, in preparing him for later professional training, and in helping him to adjust normally to his environment. In these days, it is doubtful that any child may reasonably be expected to succeed in life if he is denied the opportunity of an education. Such an opportunity, where the state has undertaken to provide it, is a right which must be made available to all on equal terms.

We come then to the question presented: Does segregation of children in public schools solely on the basis of race, even though the physical facilities and other "tangible" factors may be equal, deprive the children of the minority group of equal education opportunities? We believe that it does.

In *Sweatt v. Painter,* supra, in finding that a segregated law school for Negroes could not provide them equal educational opportunities, this Court relied in large part on "those qualities which are incapable of objective measurement but which make for greatness in a law school." In *McLaurin v. Oklahoma State Regents,* supra, the Court, in requiring that a Negro admitted to a white graduate school be treated like all other students, again resorted to intangible considerations: ". . . his ability to study, to engage in discussions and exchange views with other students, and, in general, to learn his profession." Such considerations apply with added force to children in grade and high schools. To separate them from others of similar age and qualifications solely because of their race generates a feeling of inferiority as to their status in the community that may affect their hearts and minds in a way unlikely ever to be undone. The effect of this separation on their educational opportunities was well stated by a finding in the Kansas case by a court which nevertheless felt compelled to rule against the Negro plaintiffs:

Segregation of white and colored children in public schools has a detrimental effect upon the colored children. The impact is greater when it has the sanction of the law; for the policy of separating the races is usually interpreted as denoting the inferiority of the Negro group. A sense of inferiority affects the motivation of a child to learn. Segregation with the sanction of law, therefore, has a tendency to retard the educational and mental development of Negro children and to deprive them of some of the benefits they would receive in a racially integrated school system.

Whatever may have been the extent of psychological knowledge at the time of *Plessy v. Ferguson,* this finding is amply supported by modern authority.

Any language in *Plessy v. Ferguson* contrary to this finding is rejected.

We conclude that in the field of public education the doctrine of "separate but equal" has no place. Separate educational facilities are inherently unequal. Therefore, we hold that the plaintiffs and others similarly situated for whom the actions have been brought are, by reason of the segregation complained of, deprived of the equal protection of the laws guaranteed by the Fourteenth Amendment. This disposition makes unnecessary any discussion whether such segregation also violates the Due Process Clause of the Fourteenth Amendment.

Miranda v. Arizona

UNITED STATES SUPREME COURT

Mr. Chief Justice Warren delivered the opinion of the Court.

The cases before us raise questions which go to the roots of our concepts of American criminal jurisprudence: the restraints society must observe consistent with the Federal Constitution in prosecuting individuals for crime. More specifically, we deal with the admissibility of statements obtained from an individual who is subjected to custodial police interrogation and the necessity for procedures which assure that the individual is accorded his privilege under the Fifth Amendment to the Constitution not to be compelled to incriminate himself.

We dealt with certain phases of this problem recently in *Escobedo* v. *Illinois,* 378 U. S. 478 (1964). There, as in the

384 U.S. 436, 86 S. Ct. 1602, 16 L. Ed. 2d 694 (1966).

four cases before us, law enforcement officials took the defendant into custody and interrogated him in a police station for the purpose of obtaining a confession. The police did not effectively advise him of his right to remain silent or of his right to consult with his attorney. Rather, they confronted him with an alleged accomplice who accused him of having perpetrated a murder. When the defendant denied the accusation and said "I didn't shoot Manuel, you did it," they handcuffed him and took him to an interrogation room. There, while handcuffed and standing, he was questioned for four hours until he confessed. During this interrogation, the police denied his request to speak to his attorney, and they prevented his retained attorney, who had come to the police station, from consulting with him. At his trial, the

State, over his objection, introduced the confession against him. We held that the statements thus made were constitutionally inadmissible.

This case has been the subject of judicial interpretation and spirited legal debate since it was decided two years ago. Both state and federal courts, in assessing its implications, have arrived at varying conclusions. A wealth of scholarly material has been written tracing its ramifications and underpinnings. Police and prosecutor have speculated on its range and desirability.[1] We granted certiorari in these cases, 382 U. S. 924, 925, 937, in order further to explore some facets of the problems thus exposed, of applying the privilege against self-incrimination to incustody interrogation, and to give concrete constitutional guidelines for law enforcement agencies and courts to follow.

We start here, as we did in *Escobedo*, with the premise that our holding is not an innovation in our jurisprudence, but is an application of principles long recognized and applied in other settings. We have undertaken a thorough re-examination of the *Escobedo* decision and the principles it announced, and we reaffirm it. That case was but an explication of basic rights that are enshrined in our Constitution—that "No person...shall be compelled in any criminal case to be a witness against himself," and that "the accused shall...have the Assistance of Counsel" —rights which were put in jeopardy in that case through official overbearing. These precious rights were fixed in our Constitution only after centuries of persecution and struggle. And in the words of Chief Justice Marshall, they were secured "for ages to come, and... designed to approach immortality as nearly as human institutions can approach it," *Cohens* v. *Virginia,* 6 Wheat. 264, 387 (1821)....

.   .   .

Because of the nature of the problem and because of its recurrent significance in numerous cases, we have to this point discussed the relationship of the Fifth Amendment privilege to police interrogation without specific concentration on the facts of the cases before us. We turn now to these facts to con-

---

[1] For example, the Los Angeles Police Chief stated that "If the police are required ...to...establish that the defendant was apprised of his constitutional guarantees of silence and legal counsel prior to the uttering of any admission or confession, and that he intelligently waived these guarantees... a whole Pandora's box is opened as to under what circumstances...can a defendant intelligently waive these rights.... Allegations that modern criminal investigation can compensate for the lack of a confession or admission in every criminal case is totally absurd!" Parker, 40 L. A. Bar Bull. 603, 607, 642 (1965). His prosecutorial counterpart, District Attorney Younger, stated that "[I]t begins to appear that many of these seemingly restrictive decisions are going to contribute directly to a more effective, efficient and professional level of law enforcement." L. A. Times, Oct. 2, 1965, p. 1. The former Police Commissioner of New York, Michael J. Murphy, stated of *Escobedo:* "What the Court is doing is akin to requiring one boxer to fight by Marquis of Queensbury rules while permitting the other to butt, gouge and bite." N. Y. Times, May 14, 1965, p. 39. The former United States Attorney for the District of Columbia, David C. Acheson, who is presently Special Assistant to the Secretary of the Treasury (for Enforcement), and directly in charge of the Secret Service and the Bureau of Narcotics, observed that "Prosecution procedure has, at most, only the most remote causal connection with crime. Changes in court decisions and prosecution procedure would have about the same effect on the crime rate as an aspirin would have on a tumor of the brain." Quoted in Herman, *supra,* n. 2, at 500, n. 270. Other views on the subject in general are collected in Weisberg, Police Interrogation of Arrested Persons: A Skeptical View, 52 J. Crim. L., C. & P. S. 21 (1961).

sider the application to these cases of the constitutional principles discussed above. In each instance, we have concluded that statements were obtained from the defendant under circumstances that did not meet constitutional standards for protection of the privilege.

No. 759. *Miranda* v. *Arizona*

On March 13, 1963, petitioner, Ernesto Miranda, was arrested at his home and taken in custody to a Phoenix police station. He was there identified by the complaining witness. The police then took him to "Interrogation Room No. 2" of the detective bureau. There he was questioned by two police officers. The officers admitted at trial that Miranda was not advised that he had a right to have an attorney present.[2] Two hours later, the officers emerged from the interrogation room with a written confession signed by Miranda. At the top of the statement was a typed paragraph stating that the confession was made voluntarily, without threats or promises of immunity and "with full knowledge of my legal rights, understanding any

---

2 Miranda was also convicted in a separate trial on an unrelated robbery charge not presented here for review. A statement introduced at that trial was obtained from Miranda during the same interrogation which resulted in the confession involved here. At the robbery trial, one officer testified that during the interrogation he did not tell Miranda that anything he said would be held against him or that he could consult with an attorney. The other officer stated that they had both told Miranda that anything he said would be used against him and that he was not required by law to tell them anything.

statement I make may be used against me."[3]

At his trial before a jury, the written confession was admitted into evidence over the objection of defense counsel, and the officers testified to the prior oral confession made by Miranda during the interrogation. Miranda was found guilty of kidnapping and rape. He was sentenced to 20 to 30 years' imprisonment on each count, the sentences to run concurrently. On appeal, the Supreme Court of Arizona held that Miranda's constitutional rights were not violated in obtaining the confession and affirmed the conviction. 98 Ariz. 18, 401 P. 2d 721. In reaching its decision, the court emphasized heavily the fact that Miranda did not specifically request counsel.

We reverse. From the testimony of the officers and by the admission of respondent, it is clear that Miranda was not in any way apprised of his right to consult with an attorney and to have one present during the interrogation, nor was his right not to be compelled to incriminate himself effectively protected in any other manner. Without these warnings the statements were inadmissible. The mere fact that he signed a statement which contained a typed-in clause stating that he had "full knowledge" of his "legal rights" does not approach the knowing and intelligent waiver required to relinquish constitutional rights. . . .

Therefore, in accordance with the foregoing, the judgment of the Supreme Court of Arizona is reversed.

---

3 One of the officers testified that he read this paragraph to Miranda. Apparently, however, he did not do so until after Miranda had confessed orally.

The Ohio Unlawful Discriminatory Practices Law

It shall be an unlawful discriminatory practice for any person to make any inquiry, elicit any information, make or keep any record, or use any form of application containing questions or entries concerning race, color, religion, ancestry, or national original in connection with the sale or lease of any commercial housing or the loan of any money, whether or not secured by mortgage or otherwise, for the acquisition, construction, rehabilitation, repair, or maintenance of commercial housing or a personal residence.

Ohio Revised Code § 4112.02 (H) (7) [*Legislative Acts of the State of Ohio,* Vol. 131 (Columbus: Columbus Blank Book Co., 1965), p. 984.]

Civil Rights Act of 1964

Title V of the Civil Rights Act of 1966 expands 1964 Civil Rights Act in the following manner:

Section 501. Whoever, whether or not acting under color of law, by force or threat of force, injures, intimidates, or interferes with or attempts to injure, intimidate, or interfere with any person because of his race, color, religion, or national origin while he is engaging or seeking to engage in applying for or enjoying employment, or any prerequisite thereof, by any private employer or agency of the United States or any State or subdivision thereof, or of joining or using the services or advantages of any labor organization or using the services of any employment agency, shall be fined not more than $1,000.00 or imprisoned not more than ten years or both; and if bodily injury results shall be fined not more than $10,000.00 or imprisoned not more than ten years or both and if death results shall be subject to imprisonment for any term of years or for life.

78 Stat. 246; 42 USC 2006.501. [Both of these Acts, 1964 and 1966, are incorporated into Title 42 of the *United States Code.* § 20006 of Title 42 is the 1966 amendment of the basic 1964 Act.]

7 Government and the Economic Order

The degree of influence that government has been exerting over the economic order has varied greatly during the last three to four hundred years. When the feudal system of the Middle Ages faded away, the merchant welcomed the power of kings and princes over increasingly large territorial units because it provided protection for his shipments and supplies. At the same time, the creation of state-wide markets brought competition to the cities and eroded the authority of merchants' and manufacturers' guilds to control prices and the distribution of goods on the local level. The need for additional taxes and the prospects that the emerging economic system might yield the necessary revenues prompted the rulers of the states evolving at the end of the Middle Ages to turn their attention to the economic order.

The governments began to intervene actively in the economy by protecting industry and agriculture through tariffs and bounties, by building merchant fleets and navies for the opening of new markets around the world, and by stimulating the manufacture of goods for export in order to bring gold and silver into the country. State intervention of this kind, which aimed at the accumulation of wealth, has been labeled mercantilism. Our first selection, by Henri Pirenne, a Belgian professor of history, describes briefly some of the activities that characterized the evolution from the feudal system to the mercantilist order in Western Europe.

The immediate consequences of mercantilism were the growth of commercial institutions and a rise in the importance of banking and credit. As the commercial classes became more prominent and assumed greater significance for the achievement of governmental objectives, they moved closer to the sources of political power. Their representation increased in Parliament, as in England, and their influence expanded in the royal courts on the Continent. A new elite, oriented toward economic activity and progress, began to emerge, slowly taking over political power that for centuries had been based on the holding of land.

LAISSEZ-FAIRE CAPITALISM

Although there can be no doubt that mercantilism gave great impetus to the economic aspect of society, the intervention of the state in the economy came under increasing attack. In the forefront of this attack was Adam Smith, a Scottish professor of philosophy who lived from 1723 to 1790. In his book, *The Wealth of Nations,* he extolled the division of labor and the unfettered law of supply and demand as the keys to a successful, modern industrial society. If the market were left free, the economic self-interest of thousands of consumers and hundreds of producers would unconsciously direct the system toward ends that are best for the economic welfare of the whole society. The system, whose driving force was competition, would be continually expanding in such a way that capital surpluses would accumulate, which in turn would be reinvested to tap an ever-expanding market. Smith opposed any kind of monopoly because it was incompatible with competition. He also believed that every man, as long as he did not violate the law, should be left completely free to pursue his own interest in his own way. The activities of the state should be restricted to three legitimate functions: the protection of society from violence and invasion, the administration of justice, and the establishment and maintenance of public institutions such as the postal service and educational facilities.

In the second, third, and fourth selections of this chapter we have reproduced passages of *The Wealth of Nations* that expand the above ideas. Smith has become famous as the foremost advocate of laissez-faire, usually taken to mean noninterference by the government in the operation of a capitalist economy. However, Smith was not opposed to every conceivable act of government in the sphere. He recognized that the economic system had to serve society, a situation which might require minimum governmental regulations. It was another British writer, Herbert Spencer, who, a few decades later, extended the concept of laissez-faire to its extreme by linking it to the harsh doctrine of the "survival of the fittest," made famous by Charles Darwin, the proponent of the theory that man is the product of biological evolution. In economic terms this meant that the laws of supply and demand were elevated to the highest principles of society with which the government was not to interfere under any circumstances.

The operation of laissez-faire capitalism in the wake of the industrial revolution produced a number of unfortunate effects for the workers in the factories, especially in Europe. Working hours were extremely long, the working conditions in many factories unbelievably poor, and extensive use of child labor was often the order of the day. The wages were frequently so low that the workers were hardly able to eke out a mere subsistence. Many small merchants suffered in the merciless economic struggle which tended to destroy the weaker while adding to the strength of the already powerful and prosperous. As a consequence, broad movements of resentment and unrest arose against the strains and dislocations that the philosophy of laissez-faire capitalism wrought in the social and economic fabric. These movements spawned a new ecomic-political philosophy, socialism, which voiced strong protests not only against the deplorable conditions of life caused by unrestrained capitalism, but also against the lingering trappings of aristocratic society in Europe that were slow to disappear. Among the protestors none was more extreme, determined, and intellectually glittering than Karl Marx, who, in 1848, with his friend Friedrich Engels, indicted contemporary society in the Communist Manifesto.

MARXISTS AND OTHERS

We must understand that the Communist Manifesto, pertinent parts of which are our fifth selection, is a revolutionary pamphlet containing a mixture of penetrating insights into society, half-truths, and powerful propaganda. But Marx was more than an apostle of revolution. In his monumental work, *Das Kapital,* or *Capital,* and other writings, he devised economic and historical theories which, although faulty, have left their imprint on mankind and continue to be followed in the communist one-third of the world. Although the theories of Marx have been modified by Lenin, Stalin, Mao Tse-Tung, and others, and are applied in accordance with different interpretations, they are still acclaimed as infallible by the communists of the world and by many socialists.

While it would exceed the framework of this commentary to discuss in detail the theories of Marx, a few observations highlighting his concepts will assist the reader in better understanding the Manifesto. According to Marx, history was directed by changes that occurred in the forces of production, each of which required a particular set of social relations to be operative— *i.e.,* ownership or nonownership of the means of production. Feudal farming arrangements, for example, were the result of a specific set of social relations inasmuch as land was cultivated by nonowners for the owners in return for personal and economic security. Small-scale manufacturers required another set of relations, namely the individually owned factory and workers subject to the orders of a capitalist employer. The latter social relations had become the basis for the formation of classes—the "exploiting" and the "exploited"—

because under the pressure of competition the capitalist was anxious to keep the wages of workers as low as possible and their working hours at maximum length. The resulting antagonism between the capitalist class, the *bourgoisie,* as Marx often calls it, and the workers, the *proletariat,* was to culminate in a revolutionary overthrow of the capitalist system, the abolition of private property, and the establishment of a classless society. The state, which had been the instrument of the capitalist class to keep the workers under its control, would wither away because in the resulting harmony of society the state as an instrument of coercion would not be necessary any longer. However, Marx thought that a transitional period for the state might be needed during which the dictatorship of the proletariat would transfer all instruments of production and capital from the bourgoisie to the state, resulting in the end of all exploitation.

While Marx stressed the revolutionary aspects of the socialist protest movement, others in Britain, France, and Germany placed their faith in the evolutionary element of the Marxist doctrines. These individuals were frequently called "revisionists" because they were accused of revising Marx's original doctrine. Some, such as Ferdinand Lassalle in Germany, demanded universal and direct suffrage to give the workers control of the government to eliminate the oppressive conditions of European life in the nineteenth century and achieve equality and a share of the fruits of the economy. French socialists hoped to reorganize society in the form of worker-run industries. Others again emphasized trade unionism and cooperative enterprises as the means for obtaining socialist objectives. Finally, there was the approach of the Fabian Society in England which, imbued with great idealism, sought to transform Great Britain into a socialist society in a pragmatic step-by-step manner and through democratic constitutional means, combining humane concern for the worker with at times the puritan desire to improve him. The Fabian Society, founded in 1883 and still in existence today, has counted among its membership a number of intellectually and politically very prominent Britons, including George Bernard Shaw, Sidney Webb, H. G. Wells, J. Ramsey MacDonald, Harold J. Laski, and G. D. H. Cole. The basic philosophy of the Society was enunciated in 1888 in the Fabian Essays, edited by G. B. Shaw. In the Introduction to a book entitled *New Fabian Essays,* our sixth reading selection, R. H. S. Crossman, one of the contemporary intellectual leaders of Fabianism, discusses briefly the evolution from the early principles of Fabianism to some of the problems confronting the contemporary members of the society.

THE PENDULUM SWINGS BACK

Some of the nineteenth-century liberal thinkers in Great Britain, such as John Stuart Mill and Thomas Hill Green, also voiced concern about the excesses of laissez-faire capitalism. Green considered poverty as one of the greatest obstacles to the freedom of the individual, and he held it to be one of the functions of the state to remove those obstacles. His concept of freedom was not the strict nonintervention of the state in the affairs of its citizens, but rather the assistance of the state to permit the citizen to develop fully his potential for individual freedom and responsibility. He laid the groundwork for the concept of Freedom from Fear and Want to which we have referred already in Chapter 4. For this reason he favored considerable intervention and regulation by the state to overcome poverty and ignorance; his arguments laid the intellectual foundations for today's modern social welfare state. We have included in this chapter brief excerpts from Green's *Lectures on the Principles of Political Obligation,* presenting some of his pertinent thoughts.

A new wave of monopolies that emerged in America as the result of unrestrained economic power and threatened to dominate the business world also gave rise to demands by the people for governmental action. Clearly, the operation of the free market based on the forces of supply and demand was impaired by the overwhelming power of monopolies which sought to control the market and regulate the distribution of goods and services by shutting out free competition. Heeding the popular demands, Congress passed antitrust laws and set up commissions to regulate railroads and public utilities. Widespread repugnance for the frequently very poor conditions under which workers had to labor prompted other legislation designed to protect the health and safety of the workers, prevent the abuse of child labor, and regulate wages and hours for certain categories of workers.

Another factor arousing concern about the operation of laissez-faire capitalism was the tendency of the economic system to move in cycles between booms and depressions. Although this movement was viewed at first as self-correction of a free and growing economy, an increasing number of economists began to change their interpretation of this aspect of the economy during the early 1930's, the years of the Great Depression. It was John Maynard Keynes, an eminent British economist, who pointed out that the balancing and regulating mechanisms of a free market could in fact achieve equilibrium at so low a level that a large part of the labor force would be unemployed permanently. For this reason, the self-regulating market could halt an economic boom and turn the economy down into stagnation. Keynes suggested that the government step in and adjust or counteract the market regulators according to certain principles which would keep the economy at a high level of employing.

Although many economists disputed Keynes' contentions—and a few still do so—most of the modern countries of the world have now accepted many of the measures Keynes proposed. In the United States, the Keynesian notions are reflected to some degree in the public works programs of the 1930's, the social security programs including unemployment compensation, the minimum wage and maximum hour laws, the collective bargaining legislation, and the banking reserve requirements. The Council of Economic Advisors, a small group of prominent economists operating on the Presidential level, may also be seen as implementing the Keynesian conceptual framework. The Council makes frequent analyses of the American economy, and on the basis of these analyses the Federal government—by far the largest buyer, employer, borrower, and investor on the American scene—adjusts its economic activities to counter and correct the swings of the economy. Changes in taxation and interest rates also fall within the context of these activities.

The theories of John Maynard Keynes are difficult for the average layman to grasp. However, John K. Galbraith, in his book *American Capitalism,* explains the main features of Keynes' theories and their influence on American economic thinking in a lucid manner; for this reason, excerpts from his book have been selected as the ninth reading of this chapter.

It is obvious from the foregoing that governmental intervention in the economy has been increasingly exercised during this century in the United States, and similar trends have been noticed in western European countries as well. Considering that in addition to the American laws mentioned earlier, the United States has enacted price subsidies and acreage control in agriculture, Federal deposit and mortgage insurance, old age pensions and Medicare, and other programs of an economic nature, it is clear that the pendulum has indeed swung back from the period when nonintervention of the state in the economic order was the key principle of industrial society.

These programs and others designed to alleviate poverty have frequently evoked an apprehension in the United States that the country is moving toward the welfare state which would be the first step to socialism. The term "welfare state" is ambiguous. While some take it to suggest economic security from the cradle to the grave, others give it a less extensive meaning. In the opinion of the latter, it implies state functions to raise the standard of living, work toward full employment, and assure minimum sustenance, shelter, and health. Certainly this interpretation is compatible with capitalism, perhaps even a necessary corollary to a healthy capitalistic system whose basic objectives include an economy of ever increasing abundance and equality of opportunity. On the other hand, this interpretation of the welfare state does not necessarily imply an enhancement of socialism, whose major objectives are social control of economic power and substantial social equality.[1]

GOVERNMENT-DOMINATED
ECONOMIC SYSTEMS

So far we have directed our attention mainly toward the degree of government intervention in the economy exercised in capitalistic systems. Now we

---

[1] See N. S. Preston, *Politics, Economics, and Power* (New York: MacMillan Co., 1967), pp. 43 and 100.

will examine briefly some of the economic systems which are completely dominated by the state or in which the state has a controlling influence.

The concept of the corporate state was the underlying economic philosophy for Benito Mussolini's Fascist Italy and to a lesser degree also for Adolf Hitler's Nazi Germany. The corporate state was perceived as being composed of associations representing every form of economic activity such as industry, commerce, agriculture, and others. These associations had their own pyramidal structure ranging from local through regional to central organizations on the national level. At the top, the central organizations were joined into one large body, which was dominated by the state and the ruling party. This body and its subordinate associations served as devices for full governmental control of every aspect of the national economy, as was brought out in the chapter on dictatorship.

According to the doctrine of Fascism (derived from the Italian word *fascio*, literally a bundle, also meaning political groups)[2] the economy was not the only concern of the state. Rather, the state was viewed as a living organism which held a pivotal position in every social activity and was endowed with the utmost authority. The brief excerpt from Mussolini's writings—our tenth selection—enlarges on this concept and highlights the state's function in the economy. Much of what Mussolini has to say in this selection was also accepted by the ideological advocates of Nazi Germany.

Although the era of Fascism ended in Italy and Germany in 1945, modifications of its economic doctrine have found their way into other countries. In Argentina the regime of Juan Perón from 1946 to 1955 borrowed several of Fascism's authoritarian features to control the economy to some degree. In Spain and Portugal, the extreme rightist governments of Franco and Salazar often employ economic measures which in both form and substance are reminiscent of the Fascist practices.

While Fascism produced a very high degree of control of the economic order by the government, the domination of the state over the economy is considerably more comprehensive in communist countries. This can be seen from the operating principles of the communist system: state ownership of all means of industrial production and distribution, state or collective ownership of agricultural productive resources, total government planning and control of the economic order, and a system of rewards (and punishments) to maximize productive effort.[3] A prominent feature of the communist economic system until the latter part of the 1950's was the central decision-making with respect to planning and executive functions. However, a measure of decentralization has been introduced since then in order to improve the efficiency of industrial production and the quality of the goods produced, especially those for the consumer. As a consequence, plant

---

2 The term Fascism can also be related to the Latin word "fasces," meaning a bundle of sticks tied around an axe, which was the symbol of authority in ancient Rome.

3 See Preston, *Politics, Economcis, and Power*, p. 162.

managers in the Soviet Union and other East European Communist states now have some freedom of decision, but the amount of discretion allowed is still very small when measured against the standards of the capitalist systems. Moreover, the communist plant manager remains subject to checks of the efficiency and effectiveness of his plant by a full apparatus of government and party agencies.

The incentive system in the Soviet Union is tied to the achievement of planned output targets for managers and to increased productivity for workers. Since concentration upon output goals by managers has often led to the ignoring of cost factors, and since the quality of produced goods has frequently suffered, the incentive system for plant managers was reorganized in 1965. Targets were set not merely in terms of output that managers actually produce but in terms of their ability to sell the produced goods at a "profit" for the enterprise. In addition, interest charges were introduced on investment capital used by individual plants. The man largely responsible for these changes was a Russian economist by the name of Yevsei Liberman, and so the new methods used have been labeled "Libermanism" by Western students of the Soviet system. An evaluation of Libermanism is found in our last two selections of this chapter.

It would be premature to call these changes in the Soviet economic system "creeping capitalism," as has been done by some observers. Rather, the inclusion of "profits" and "interest" into the criteria for measuring the performance of plant managers should be seen primarily as an attempt on the part of the Soviet governmental apparatus to use more sophisticated methods for the creation of an efficient, modern industrial economy considered necessary to attain long-range communist goals. In Poland, Czechoslovakia, and Hungary even greater managerial discretion is allowed than under Liberman's methods in the Soviet Union, but it would be again an error to see in these developments the slow abandonment of government control over the economy and a gradual approach to a free market system.

We should note in this connection that the new schemes have been only a mixed blessing for the communist countries. Many managers, accustomed to receiving strict directives from governmental sources, have great difficulty in using properly the newly won freedom of decision, and as a consequence the operation of the economy in many instances has been suffering rather than gaining greater efficiency.

One of the East European Communist countries, Yugoslavia, has introduced radical changes into its formerly traditional communist economic system by seeking to create a "socialist market" economy during the last few years. In this system the state continues to set the general target and engages in overall planning, but the plants themselves determine through joint decisions by the managers and the workers' councils future production plans, most prices, and the use of profits for reinvestment or employee compensation. Of course, the government and the Communist party seek to retain a measure of control over the plant decisions, but in the determination of what and how much to produce the market conditions play a decidedly greater role than the announced goals of the government.

It is evident that Yugoslavia is moving economically in a different direction from that taken by the Soviet Union. Her economic order now seems to be headed toward concepts under which democratic socialism attempts to operate. The basic operating principles of the socialist system are state ownership or state control of basic industries and financial establishments, subjection of the market to government planning and controls, and conscious use of governmental policies to bring about economic and social equality.[4] Some of these principles have been put into practice in a number of countries of western Europe and the developing world. Great Britain under the Labor Party government has nationalized a number of basic industries, among them the important iron and steel enterprises. The socialist governments of Sweden, Norway, and Britain have introduced planning schemes that curtail operation of the free market economy to the extent perceived necessary to obtain certain social and economic goals. In addition, the three countries have established national health and welfare services which, in terms of comprehensiveness, exceed materially those existing in such basically capitalist countries as the United States and West Germany.

Democratic socialism does not seek to attain its goals through revolution but through the democratic process, the ballot box. While the above examples suggest some progress toward its goals, democratic socialism as practiced at present has not succeeded fully in transferring control over all basic industries from private hands to the government. Moreover—and this is confusing—some of the activities asserted to be typical of socialism are also practiced under capitalistic systems. Certain social welfare measures are now found in all capitalistic countries; in fact, national health insurance was introduced in Germany by Bismarck as early as the 1880's. Economic planning by the government is to varying degrees carried out in practically all capitalistic countries and is especially developed in France. And even various kinds of state ownership exist in many capitalistic countries, ranging from state-owned railroads and public utilities in all West European democracies to the hydroelectric plants of TVA in the United States.

There can be little doubt that today the notion of laissez faire is virtually dead and that capitalist and socialist economic systems have much in common as far as governmental intervention in the economy is concerned. Yet there remain significant differences in concept and emphasis. In the modern capitalistic system the free play of market forces remains the basic principle, but the government is given the responsibility of placing restraints on private economic despotism and of ensuring a reasonable balance of

---

4 *Ibid.*, p. 104.

power among the participants in the economic order. Government support for education, retraining programs, employment services, assistance to depressed areas of the economy, and social welfare measures are seen as ways to ensure equality of opportunity in the economic struggle rather than as social values in themselves. In the contemporary socialist economic system, the government is committed to the development of substantial economic equality requiring intervention considerably more extensive than that seen necessary under the capitalist system. In addition, the social objectives of the state have a much broader range and greater depth. Finally—and here lies perhaps the greatest difference—the state under the socialist system is committed to restructuring the bases of the economy through the nationalization of certain industries and services.

Mercantilism

HENRI PIRENNE

...The conception of the State which began to emerge as their [the kings' and princes'] power increased, led them to consider themselves as protectors of the "common good." The same fourteenth century which saw urban particularism at its height, also saw the advent of the royal power in the sphere of economic history. Hitherto it had intervened there only indirectly, or rather in pursuance of its judicial, financial and military prerogatives. Though in its capacity as guardian of the public peace it had protected merchants, laid tolls upon commerce, and in case of war placed embargoes on enemy ships and promulgated stoppages of trade, it had left the economic activities of its subjects to themselves. Only the towns made laws and regulations for them. But the competence of the towns was limited by their municipal boundaries, and their particularism caused them to be continually in opposition to each other and made it manifestly impossible for them to take measures to secure the general good, at the possible expense of their individual interests. The princes alone were capable of conceiving a territorial economy, which would comprise and control the urban economies. At the close of the Middle Ages men were, of course, still far from a decided movement, or a conscious policy, directed towards this

Reprinted from Henri Pirenne, *Economic and Social History of Medieval Europe* (New York: Harcourt, Brace and Company, 1937, and London: Routledge & Kegan Paul Ltd.), pp. 216–19, by permission of the publishers.

end. As a rule only intermittent tendencies are to be observed, but they are such as to make it evident that, wherever it had the power, the State was moving in the direction of mercantilism. Obviously the word can only be used within strict limitations, but, alien as the conception of a national economy still was to the governments of the late fourteenth and early fifteenth centuries, it is plain from their conduct that they desired to protect the industry and commerce of their subjects against foreign competition, and even, here and there, to introduce new forms of activity into their countries. In this they were inspired by the example of the towns, and their policy was really no more than the urban policy writ large. It still retained the chief characteristic of that policy, to wit, its protectionism. It was the beginning of a process which in the long run was destined to throw aside medieval internationalism, and to imbue the relations of states with each other with a particularism every whit as exclusive as that of the towns had been for centuries.

The first signs of this evolution showed themselves in England, the country which enjoyed a more powerful and united government than any other. In the first half of the fourteenth century Edward II tried to prohibit the import of foreign cloth, except such as was destined for the use of nobility. In 1331 Edward III invited Flemish weavers to settle in England. Most significant of all, an Act was passed in 1381 reserving the trade of the country for English ships, an early forerunner of Cromwell's Navigation Act, which it was of course impossible to carry out. The movement became still more active in the fifteenth century. In 1455 the import of silken goods was forbidden in order to protect the native manufacture; in 1463 foreigners were forbidden to export wool; and in 1464 the prohibition of Continental cloth foreshadowed the resolutely protectionist and mercantilist policy of Henry VII (1485–1509), the first modern King of England, which had now become a country in which industry was gaining steadily upon agriculture.

These measures naturally provoked reprisals in the Low Countries, whose most important manufacture suffered from them. Philip the Good, Duke of Burgundy (1419–67), who had united the different territories under his rule, replied by prohibiting the entry of English cloth. But he ruled over a land through which too much trade passed to allow him to content himself with a policy of pure protectionism. He set to work to promote the rising mercantile marine of Holland and to encourage it in a competition with the Teutonic Hanse, which was to be completely successful in the following century. Not only did he encourage the Dutch carrying trade and fishing industry (the latter being favoured by the invention of the herring cask in 1380), but he assisted the rise of the port of Antwerp, which henceforth ousted Bruges from its position of supremacy, and was to become, a century later, the greatest commercial entrepot in the world.

France was ruined by the Hundred Years' War, and it was not until Louis XI came to the throne that measures were taken to bring about its economic revival. The energy and ability with which he pursued his policy are well known. He ensured the pre-eminence of the fair of Lyons over that of Geneva, tried to acclimatise the silkworm in the kingdom and to introduce the mining industry in Dauphine, and even thought of organising a kind of exhibition at the French embassy in London. . . .

The political anarchy which reigned in Germany prevented it, in the absence of central government, from imitating its western neighbours. The capitalist movement which grew at this period in the South German towns, notably in Nuremberg and Augsburg, and to which the prosperity of the mines of Bohemia and the Tyrol is due, owed nothing to the influence of the State. Italy, torn between princes and republics all struggling for supremacy, continued to fall into independent economic areas, two at least of which, Venice and Genoa, were, by reason of their establishments on the Levant, great economic powers. Indeed, the supremacy of Italy in banking and luxury industries was still so marked that it was successfully maintained over the rest of Europe, in spite of her political disunion, until the discovery of new routes to the Indies turned the main current of navigation and commerce from the Mediterranean to the Atlantic.

The Price of Commodities

ADAM SMITH

...The market price of every particular commodity is regulated by the proportion between the quantity which is actually brought to market, and the demand of those who are willing to pay the natural price of the commodity, or the whole value of the rent, labour, and profit, which must be paid in order to bring it thither. Such people may be called the effectual demanders, and their demand the effectual demand; since it may be sufficient to effectuate the bringing of the commodity to market. It is different from the absolute demand. A very poor man may be said in some sense to have a demand for a coach and six; he might like to have it; but his demand is not an effectual demand, as the commodity can never be brought to market in order to satisfy it.

When the quantity of any commodity which is brought to market falls short of the effectual demand, all those who are willing to pay the whole value of the rent, wages, and profit, which must be paid in order to bring it thither, cannot be supplied with the quantity which they want. Rather than want it altogether, some of them will be willing to give more. A competition will immediately begin among them, and the market price will rise more or less above the natural price, according as either the greatness of the deficiency, or the wealth and wanton luxury of the

competitors, happen to animate more or less the eagerness of the competition. Among competitors of equal wealth and luxury the same deficiency will generally occasion a more or less eager competition, according as the acquisition of the commodity happens to be of more or less importance to them. Hence the exorbitant price of the necessaries of life during the blockade of town or in a famine.

When the quantity brought to market exceeds the effectual demand, it cannot be all sold to those who are willing to pay the whole value of the rent, wages, and profit, which must be paid in order to bring it thither. Some part must be sold to those who are willing to pay less, and the low price which they give for it must reduce the price of the whole. The market price will sink more or less below the natural price, according as the greatness of the excess increases more or less the competition of the sellers, or according as it happens to be more or less important to them to get immediately rid of the commodity. The same excess in the importation of perishable, will occasion a much greater competition than in that of durable commodities; in the importation of oranges, for example, than in that of old iron.

When the quantity brought to market is just sufficient to supply the effectual demand, and no more, the market price naturally comes to be either exactly, or as nearly as can be judged of, the same with the natural price. The whole quantity upon hand can be disposed of for this price, and cannot be

Reprinted from Adam Smith, *The Wealth of Nations,* Everyman's Library (New York: E. P. Dutton & Co., Inc., 1957, and London: J. M. Dent & Sons Ltd., 1957), I, 49–51, by permission of the publishers.

disposed of for more. The competition of the different dealers obliges them all to accept of this price, but does not oblige them to accept of less.

The quantity of every commodity brought to market naturally suits itself to the effectual demand. It is the interest of all those who employ their land, labour, or stock, in bringing any commodity to market, that the quantity never should exceed the effectual demand; and it is the interest of all other people that it never should fall short of that demand.

If at any time it exceeds the effectual demand, some of the component parts of its price must be paid below their natural rate. If it is rent, the interest of the landlords will immediately prompt them to withdraw a part of their land; and if it is wages or profit, the interest of the labourers in the one case, and of their employers in the other, will prompt them to withdraw a part of their labour or stock from this employment. The quantity brought to market will soon be no more than sufficient to supply the effectual demand. All the different parts of its price will rise to their natural rate, and the whole price to its natural price.

If, on the contrary, the quantity brought to market should at any time fall short of the effectual demand, some of the component parts of its price must rise above their natural rate. If it is rent, the interest of all other landlords will naturally prompt them to prepare more land for the raising of this commodity; if it is wages or profit, the interest of all other labourers and dealers will soon prompt them to employ more labour and stock in preparing and bringing it to market. The quantity brought thither will soon be sufficient to supply the effectual demand. All the different parts of its price will soon sink to their natural rate, and the whole price to its natural price.

The natural price, therefore, is, as it were, the central price, to which the prices of all commodities are continually gravitating. Different accidents may sometimes keep them suspended a good deal above it, and sometimes force them down even somewhat below it. But whatever may be the obstacles which hinder them from settling in this centre of repose and continuance, they are constantly tending towards it.

The whole quantity of industry annually employed in order to bring any commodity to market naturally suits itself in this manner to the effectual demand. It naturally aims at bringing always that precise quantity thither which may be sufficient to supply, and no more than supply, that demand. . . .

Principle of Division of Labour

ADAM SMITH

This division of labour, from which so many advantages are derived, is not

Reprinted from Smith, *The Wealth of Nations*, pp. 12–14, by permission of the publishers.

originally the effect of any human wisdom, which foresees and intends that general opulence to which it gives occasion. It is the necessary, though very slow and gradual consequence of a certain propensity in human nature which has in view no such extensive utility; the propensity to truck, barter, and exchange one thing for another.

Whether this propensity be one of those original principles in human nature of which no further account can be given; or whether, as seems more probable, it be the necessary consequence of the faculties of reason and speech, it belongs not to our present subject to inquire. It is common to all men, and to be found in no other race of animals, which seem to know neither this nor any other species of contracts. Two grey-hounds, in running down the same hare, have sometimes the appearance of acting in some sort of concert. Each turns her towards his companion, or endeavours to intercept her when his companion turns her towards himself. This, however, is not the effect of any contract, but of the accidental concurrence of their passions in the same object at that particular time. Nobody ever saw a dog make a fair and deliberate exchange of one bone for another with another dog. Nobody ever saw one animal by its gestures and natural cries signify to another, this is mine, that yours; I am willing to give this for that. When an animal wants to obtain something either of a man or of another animal, it has no other means of persuasion but to gain the favour of those whose service it requires. A puppy fawns upon its dam, and a spaniel endeavours by a thousand attractions to engage the attention of its master who is at dinner, when it wants to be fed by him. Man sometimes uses the same arts with his brethren, and when he has no other means of engaging them to act according to his inclinations, endeavours by every servile and fawning attention to obtain their good will. He has not time, however, to do this upon every occasion. In civilised society he stands at all times in need of the cooperation and assistance of great multitudes, while his whole life is scarce sufficient to gain the friendship of a few persons. In almost every other race of animals each individual, when it is grown up to maturity, is entirely independent, and in its natural state has occasion for the assistance of no other living creature. But man has almost constant occasion for the help of his brethren, and it is in vain for him to expect it from their benevolence only. He will be more likely to prevail if he can interest their self-love in his favour, and show them that it is for their own advantage to do for him what he requires of them. Whoever offers to another a bargain of any kind, proposes to do this. Give me that which I want, and you shall have this which you want, is the meaning of every such offer; and it is in this manner that we obtain from one another the far greater part of those good offices which we stand in need of. It is not from the benevolence of the butcher, the brewer, or the baker that we expect our dinner, but from their regard to their own interest. We address ourselves, not to their humanity but to their self-love, and never talk to them of our own necessities but of their advantages. Nobody but a beggar chooses to depend chiefly upon the benevolence of his fellow-citizens. Even a beggar does not depend upon it entirely. The charity of well-disposed people, indeed, supplies him with the whole fund of his subsistence. But though this principle ultimately provides him with all the necessaries of life which he has occasion for, it neither does nor can provide him with them as he has occasion for them. The greater part of his occasional wants are supplied in the same manner as those of other people, by treaty, by barter, and by purchase. With the money which one man gives him he purchases food. The old clothes which another bestows upon him he exchanges for other old clothes which suit him better, or for lodging, or for food, or for money, with which he can buy either food, clothes, or lodging, as he has occasion.

As it is by treaty, by barter, and by purchase that we obtain from one another the greater part of those mutual good offices which we stand in need of, so it is this same trucking disposition which originally gives occasion to the division of labour. In a tribe of hunters or shepherds a particular person makes bows and arrows, for example, with more readiness and dexterity than any other. He frequently exchanges them for cattle or for venison with his companions; and he finds at last that he can in this manner get more cattle and venison than if he himself went to the field to catch them. From a regard to his own interest, therefore, the making of bows and arrows grows to be his chief business, and he becomes a sort

of armourer. Another excels in making the frames and covers of their little huts or movable houses. He is accustomed to be of use in this way to his neighbours, who reward him in the same manner with cattle and with venison, till at last he finds it his interest to dedicate himself entirely to this employment, and to become a sort of house-carpenter. In the same manner a third becomes a smith or a brazier, a fourth a tanner or dresser of hides or skins, the principal part of the clothing of savages. And thus the certainty of being able to exchange all that surplus part of the produce of his own labour, which is over and above his own consumption, for such parts of the produce of other men's labour as he may have occasion for, encourages every man to apply himself to a particular occupation, and to cultivate and bring to perfection whatever talent or genius he may possess for that particular species of business. . . .

Of the Funds or Sources of Revenue Which May Peculiarly Belong to the Sovereign or Commonwealth

ADAM SMITH

The funds or sources of revenue which may peculiarly belong to the sovereign or commonwealth must consist either in stock or in land.

The sovereign, like any other owner of stock, may derive a revenue from it, either by employing it himself, or by

Reprinted from Smith, *The Wealth of Nations* (1957), Vol. II, 299–300, by permission of the publishers.

lending it. His revenue is in the one case profit, in the other interest.

The revenue of a Tartar or Arabian chief consists in profit. It arises principally from the milk and increase of his own herds and flocks, of which he himself superintends the management, and is the principal shepherd or herdsman of his own horde or tribe. It is, however, in this earliest and rudest state of civil government only that profit has ever made the principal part of the public revenue of a monarchical state.

Small republics have sometimes derived a considerable revenue from the profit of mercantile projects. The republic of Hamburg is said to do from the profits of a public wine cellar and apothecary's shop. The state cannot be very great of which the sovereign has leisure to carry on the trade of a wine merchant or apothecary. The profit of a public bank has been a source of revenue to more considerable states. It has been so not only to Hamburg, but to Venice and Amsterdam. A revenue of this kind has even by some people been thought not below the attention of so great an empire as that of Great Britain. Reckoning the ordinary dividend of the Bank of England at five and a half per cent, and its capital at ten millions seven hundred and eighty thousand pounds, the net annual profit, after paying the expense of management, must amount, it is said, to five hundred and ninety-two thousand nine hundred pounds. Government, it is pretended, could borrow this capital at three per cent interest, and by taking the management of the bank into its own hands, might make a clear profit of two hundred and sixty-nine thousand five hundred pounds a year. The orderly. vigilant, and parsimonious administration of such aristocracies as those of Venice and Amsterdam is extremely proper, it appears from experience, for the management of a mercantile project of this kind. But whether such a government as that of England —which, whatever may be its virtues, has never been famous for good economy; which in time of peace, has generally conducted itself with the slothful and negligent profusion that is perhaps natural to monarchies; and in time of war has constantly acted with all the thoughtless extravagance that democracies are apt to fall into—could be safely trusted with the management of such a project, must at least be a good deal more doubtful.

.   .   .

Manifesto of the Communist Party

KARL MARX / FRIEDRICH ENGELS

A spectre is haunting Europe—the spectre of Communism. All the powers of old Europe have entered into a holy alliance to exorcise this spectre; Pope and Czar, Metternich and Guizot, French Radicals and German policespies.

Where is the party in opposition that has not been decried as communistic by its opponents in power? Where the Opposition that has not hurled back the branding reproach of Communism, against the more advanced opposition parties, as well as against its reactionary adversaries?

Two things result from this fact.

Reprinted from Karl Marx and Friedrich Engels, *Manifesto of the Communist Party*, authorized English translation: edited and annotated by Friedrich Engels (Chicago: Charles H. Kerr and Company, 1874), pp. 11–15, 22–23, and 30–42.

I. Communism is already acknowledged by all European Powers to be itself a Power.

II. It is high time that Communists should openly, in the face of the whole world, publish their views, their aims, their tendencies, and meet this nursery tale of the Spectre of Communism with a Manifesto of the party itself.

To this end, Communists of various nationalities have assembled in London, and sketched the following manifesto, to be published in the English, French, German, Italian, Flemish and Danish languages.

BOURGEOIS AND PROLETARIANS

The history of all hitherto existing society is the history of class struggles.

Freeman and slave, patrician and plebeian, lord and serf, guild-master and journeyman, in a word, oppressor and oppressed, stood in constant opposition to one another, carried on an uninterrupted, now hidden, now open fight, a fight that each time ended, either in a revolutionary re-constitution of society at large, or in the common ruin of the contending classes.

In the earlier epochs of history, we find almost everywhere a complicated arrangement of society into various orders, a manifold graduation of social rank. In ancient Rome we have patricians, knights, plebeians, slaves; in the middle ages, feudal lords, vassals, guild-masters, journeymen, apprentices, serfs; in almost all of these classes, again, subordinate gradations.

The modern bourgeois society that has sprouted from the ruins of feudal society, has not done away with class antagonisms. It has but established new classes, new conditions of oppression, new forms of struggle in place of the old ones.

Our epoch, the epoch of the bourgeoisie, possesses, however, this distinctive feature; it has simplified the class antagonisms. Society as a whole is more and more splitting up into two great hostile camps, into two great classes directly facing each other: Bourgeoisie and Proletariat.

From the serfs of the middle ages sprang the chartered burghers of the earliest towns. From these burgesses the first elements of the bourgeoisie were developed.

The discovery of America, the rounding of the Cape, opened up fresh ground for the rising bourgeoisie. The East-Indian and Chinese markets, the colonization of America, trade with the colonies, the increase in the means of exchange and in commodities generally, gave to commerce, to navigation, to industry, an impulse never before known, and thereby, to the revolutionary element in the tottering feudal society, a rapid development.

The feudal system of industry, under which industrial production was monopolized by close guilds, now no longer sufficed for the growing wants of the new markets. The manufacturing system took its place. The guild-masters were pushed on one side by the manufacturing middleclass; division of labor between the different corporate guilds vanished in the face of division of labor in each single workshop.

Meantime the markets kept ever growing, the demand, ever rising. Even manufacture no longer sufficed. Thereupon, steam and machinery revolutionized industrial production. The place of manufacture was taken by the giant, Modern Industry, the place of the industrial middle-class, by industrial millionaires, the leaders of whole industrial armies, the modern bourgeois.

Modern industry has established the world-market, for which the discovery of America paved the way. This market has given an immense development to commerce, to navigation, to communication by land. This development has, in its turn, reacted on the extension of industry; and in proportion as industry, commerce, navigation, railways extended, in the same proportion the bourgeoisie developed, increased its capital, and pushed into the background every class handed down from the Middle Ages.

We see, therefore, how the modern bourgeoisie is itself the product of a long course of development, of a series of revolutions in the modes of production and of exchange.

Each step in the development of the bourgeoisie was accompanied by a corresponding political advance of that class. An oppressed class under the sway of the feudal nobility, an armed and selfgoverning association in the mediaeval commune, here independent urban republic (as in Italy and Germany), there taxable "third estate" of the monarchy (as in France), afterwards, in the period of manufacture proper, serving either the semi-feudal or the absolute monarchy as a counterpoise against the nobility, and, in fact, corner stone of the great monarchies in general, the bourgeoisie has at last, since the establishment of Modern Industry and of the world-market, conquered for itself, in the modern representative State, exclusive political sway. The executive of the modern State is but a committee for managing the common affairs of the whole bourgeoisie.

The bourgeoisie, historically, has played a most revolutionary part.

The bourgeoisie, wherever it has got the upper hand, has put an end to all feudal, patriarchal, idyllic relations. It has pitilessly torn asunder the motley feudal ties that bound man to his "natural superiors," and has left remaining no other nexus between man and man than naked self-interest, than callous "cash payment." It has drowned the most heavenly ecstacies of religious fervor, of chivalrous enthusiasm, of philistine sentimentalism, in the icy water of egotistical calculation. It has resolved personal worth into exchange value, and in place of the numberless indefeasible chartered freedoms, has set up that single, unconscionable freedom—Free Trade. In one word, for exploitation, veiled by religious and political illusions, it has substituted naked, shameless, direct, brutal exploitation.

. . .

Modern industry has converted the little workshop of the patriarchal master into the great factory of the industrial capitalist. Masses of laborers, crowded into the factory, are organized like soldiers. As privates of the industrial army they are placed under the command of a perfect hierarchy of officers and sergeants. Not only are they the slaves of the bourgeois class, and of the bourgeois State, they are daily and hourly enslaved by the machine, by the over-looker, and, above all, by the individual bourgeois manufacturer himself. The more openly this despotism proclaims gain to be its end and aim, the more petty, the more hateful and the more embittering it is.

The less the skill and exertion or strength implied in manual labor, in other words, the more modern industry becomes developed, the more is the labor of men superseded by that of women. Differences of age and sex have no longer any distinctive social validity for the working class. All are instruments of labor, more or less expensive to use, according to their age and sex.

No sooner is the exploitation of the

laborer by the manufacturer, so far at an end, that he receives his wages in cash, than he is set upon by the other portions of the bourgeoisie, the landlord, the shopkeeper, the pawnbroker, etc.

The lower strata of the Middle class —the small tradespeople, shopkeepers, and retired tradesmen generally, the handicraftsmen and peasants—all these sink gradually into the proletariat, partly because their diminutive capital does not suffice for the scale on which Modern Industry is carried on, and is swamped in the competition with the large capitalists, partly because their specialized skill is rendered worthless by new methods of production. Thus the proletariat is recruited from all classes of the population.

. . .

PROLETARIANS AND COMMUNISTS

In what relation do the Communists stand to the proletarians as a whole?

The Communists do not form a separate party opposed to other working-class parties.

They have no interests separate and apart from those of the proletariat as a whole.

They do not set up any sectarian principles of their own, by which to shape and mould the proletarian movement.

The Communists are distinguished from the other working class parties by this only: 1. In the national struggles of the proletarians of the different countries, they point out and bring to the front the common interests of the entire proletariat independently of all nationality. 2. In the various stages of development which the struggle of the working class against the bourgeoisie has to pass through, they always and everywhere represent the interests of the movement as a whole.

The Communists, therefore, are on the one hand, practically, the most advanced and resolute section of the working class parties of every country, that section which pushes forward all others; on the other hand, theoretically, they have over the great mass of the proletariat the advantage of clearly understanding the line of march, the conditions, and the ultimate general results of the proletarian movement.

The immediate aim of the Communists is the same as that of all the other proletarian parties; formation of the proletariat into a class, overthrow of the bourgeois supremacy, conquest of political power by the proletariat.

The theoretical conclusions of the Communists are in no way based on ideas or principles that have been invented, or discovered, by this or that would-be universal reformer.

They merely express, in general terms, actual relations springing from an existing class struggle, from a historical movement going on under our very eyes. The abolition of existing property relations is not at all a distinctive feature of Communism.

All property relations in the past have continually been subject to historical change consequent upon the change in historical conditions.

The French Revolution, for example, abolished feudal property in favor of bourgeois property.

The distinguishing feature of Communism is not the abolition of property generally, but the abolition of bourgeois property. But modern bourgeois private property is the final and most complete expression of the system of producing and appropriating products, that is based on class antagonism, on the exploitation of the many by the few.

In this sense, the theory of the Communists may be summed up in the single sentence: Abolition of private property.

We Communists have been reproached with the desire of abolishing the right of personally acquiring property as the fruit of a man's own labor, which property is alleged to be the ground work of all personal freedom, activity and independence.

Hard-won, self-acquired, self-earned property! Do you mean the property of the petty artisan and of the small peasant, a form of property that preceded the bourgeois form? There is no need to abolish that; the development of industry has to a great extent already destroyed it, and is still destroying it daily.

Or do you mean modern bourgeois private property?

But does wage-labor create any property for the laborer? Not a bit. It creates capital, i. e., that kind of property which exploits wage-labor, and which cannot increase except upon condition of getting a new supply of wage-labor for fresh exploitation. Property, in its present form, is based on the antagonism of capital and wage-labor. Let us examine both sides of this antagonism.

To be a capitalist, is to have not only a purely personal, but a social status in production. Capital is a collective product, and only by the united action of many members, nay, in the last resort, only by the united action of all members of society, can it be set in motion.

Capital is therefore not a personal, it is a social power.

When, therefore, capital is converted into common property, into the property of all members of society, personal property is not thereby transformed into social property. It is only the social character of the property that is changed. It loses its class-character.

Let us now take wage-labor.

The average price of wage-labor is the minimum wage, i. e., that quantum of the means of subsistence, which is absolutely requisite to keep the laborer in bare existence as a laborer. What, therefore, the wage-laborer appropriates by means of his labor, merely suffices to prolong and reproduce a bare existence. We by no means intend to abolish this personal appropriation of the products of labor, an appropriation that is made for the maintenance and reproduction of human life, and that leaves no surplus wherewith to command the labor of others. All that we want to do away with is the miserable character of this appropriation, under which the laborer lives merely to increase capital, and is allowed to live only in so far as the interest of the ruling class requires it.

In bourgeois society, living labor is but a means to increase accumulated labor. In Communist society, accumulated labor is but a means to widen, to enrich, to promote the existence of the laborer.

In bourgeois society, therefore, the past dominates the present; in communist society, the present dominates the past. In bourgeois society capital is independent and has individuality, while the living person is dependent and has no individuality.

And the abolition of this state of things is called by the bourgeois, abolition of individuality and freedom! And rightly so. The abolition of bourgeois individuality, bourgeois independence, and bourgeois freedom is undoubtedly aimed at.

By freedom is meant, under the present bourgeois conditions of production, free trade, free selling and buying.

But if selling and buying disappears,

free selling and buying disappears also. This talk about free selling and buying, and all the other "brave words" of our bourgeoisie about freedom in general, have a meaning, if any, only in contrast with restricted selling and buying, with the fettered traders of the Middle Ages, but have no meaning when opposed to the Communistic abolition of buying and selling, of the bourgeois conditions of production, and of the bourgeoisie itself.

You are horrified at our intending to do away with private property. But in your existing society, private property is already done away with for nine-tenths of the population; its existence for the few is solely due to its non-existence in the hands of those nine-tenths. You reproach us, therefore, with intending to do away with a form of property, the necessary condition for whose existence is, the non-existence of any property for the immense majority of society.

In one word, you reproach us with intending to do away with your property. Precisely so; that is just what we intend.

From the moment when labor can no longer be converted into capital, money, or rent, into a social power capable of being monopolized, i. e., from the moment when individual property can no longer be transformed into bourgeois property, into capital, from that moment, you say, individuality vanishes.

You must, therefore, confess that by "individual" you mean no other person than the bourgeois, than the middle-class owner of property. This person must, indeed, be swept out of the way, and made impossible.

Communism deprives no man of the power to appropriate the products of society: all that it does it to deprive him of the power to subjugate the labor of others by means of such appropriation.

It has been objected, that upon the abolition of private property all work will cease, and universal laziness will overtake us.

According to this, bourgeois society ought long ago to have gone to the dogs through sheer idleness; for those of its members who work, acquire nothing, and those who acquire anything, do not work. The whole of this objection is but another expression of the tautology: that there can no longer be any wage-labor when there is no longer any capital.

All objections urged against the Communistic mode of producing and appropriating material products, have, in the same way, been urged against the Communistic modes of producing and appropriating intellectual products. Just as, to the bourgeois, the disappearance of class property is the disappearance of production itself, so the disappearance of class culture is to him identical with the disappearance of all culture.

That culture, the loss of which he laments, is, for the enormous majority, a mere training to act as a machine.

But don't wrangle with us so long as you apply, to our intended abolition of bourgeois property, the standard of your bourgeois notions of freedom, culture, law, etc. Your very ideas are but the outgrowth of the conditions of your bourgeois production and bourgeois property, just as your jurisprudence is but the will of your class made into a law for all, a will, whose essential character and direction are determined by the economic conditions of existence of your class.

The selfish misconception that induces you to transform into eternal laws of nature and of reason, the social forms springing from your present mode of production and form of property—historical relations that rise and disappear in the progress of production—this misconception you share with every ruling class that has preceded you. What you see clearly in the case of ancient property, what you admit in the case of feudal property, you are of course forbidden to admit in the case of your own bourgeois form of property.

Abolition of the family! Even the most radical flare up at this infamous proposal of the Communists.

On what foundation is the present family, the bourgeois family, based? On capital, on private gain. In its completely developed form this family exists only among the bourgeoisie. But this state of things finds its complement in the practical absence of the family among the proletarians, and in public prostitution.

The bourgeois family will vanish as a matter of course when its complement vanishes, and both will vanish with the vanishing of capital.

Do you charge us with wanting to stop the exploitation of children by their parents? To this crime we plead guilty.

But, you will say, we destroy the most hallowed of relations, when we replace home education by social.

And your education! Is not that also social, and determined by the social conditions under which you educate, by the intervention, direct or indirect, of society by means of schools, etc.? The Communists have not invented the intervention of society in education; they do but seek to alter the character of that intervention, and to rescue education from the influence of the ruling class.

The bourgeois clap-trap about the family and education, about the hallowed co-relation of parent and child, becomes all the more disgusting, the more, by the action of Modern Industry, all family ties among the proletarians are torn asunder, and their children transformed into simple articles of commerce and instruments of labor.

But you Communists would introduce community of women, screams the whole bourgeoisie in chorus.

The bourgeois sees in his wife a mere instrument of production. He hears that the instruments of production are to be exploited in common, and, naturally, can come to no other conclusion, than that the lot of being common to all will likewise fall to the women.

He has not even a suspicion that the real point aimed at is to do away with the status of women as mere instruments of production.

For the rest, nothing is more ridiculous than the virtuous indignation of our bourgeois at the community of women which, they pretend, is to be openly and officially established by the Communists. The Communists have no need to introduce community of women; it has existed almost from time immemorial.

Our bourgeois, not content with having the wives and daughters of their proletarians at their disposal, not to speak of common prostitutes, take the greatest pleasure in seducing each others' wives.

Bourgeois marriage is in reality a system of wives in common and thus, at the most, what the Communists might possibly be reproached with, is that they desire to introduce, in substitution for a hypocritically concealed, an openly legalized community of women. For the rest, it is self-evident, that the abolition of the present system of production must bring with it the abolition of the community of women springing from that system, i. e., of prostitution both public and private.

The Communists are further reproached with desiring to abolish countries and nationalities.

The working men have no country. We cannot take from them what they have not got. Since the proletariat must first of all acquire political supremacy, must rise to be the leading class of the nation, must constitute itself the nation, it is, so far, itself national, though not in the bourgeois sense of the word.

National differences, and antagonisms between peoples, are daily more and more vanishing, owing to the development of the bourgeoisie, to freedom of commerce, to the world-market, to uniformity in the mode of production and in the conditions of life corresponding thereto.

The supremacy of the proletariat will cause them to vanish still faster. United action, of the leading civilized countries at least, is one of the first conditions for the emancipation of the proletariat.

In proportion as the exploitation of one individual by another is put an end to, the exploitation of one nation by another will also be put an end to. In proportion as the antagonism between classes within the nation vanishes, the hostility of one nation to another will come to an end.

The charges against Communism made from a religious, a philosophical, and generally, from an ideological standpoint, are not deserving of serious examination.

Does it require deep intuition to comprehend that man's ideas, views, and conceptions, in one word, man's consciousness, changes with every change in the conditions of his material existence, in his social relations and in his social life?

What else does the history of ideas prove, than that intellectual production changes in character in proportion as material production is changed? The ruling ideas of each age have ever been the ideas of its ruling class.

When people speak of ideas that revolutionize society, they do but express the fact, that within the old society, the elements of a new one have been created, and that the dissolution of the old ideas keeps even pace with the dissolution of the old conditions of existence.

When the ancient world was in its last throes, the ancient religions were overcome by Christianity. When Christian ideas succumbed in the 18th century to rationalist ideas, feudal society fought its death-battle with the then revolutionary bourgeoisie. The ideas of religious liberty and freedom of conscience, merely gave expression to the sway of free competition within the domain of knowledge.

"Undoubtedly," it will be said, "religious, moral, philosophical and juridical ideas have been modified in the course of historical development. But religion, morality, philosophy, political science, and law, constantly survived this change."

"There are, besides, eternal truths, such as Freedom, Justice, etc., that are common to all states of society. But Communism abolishes eternal truths, it abolishes all religion, and all morality, instead of constituting them on a new basis; it therefore acts in contradiction to all past historical experience."

What does this accusation reduce itself to? The history of all past society has consisted in the development of class antagonisms, antagonisms that assumed different forms at different epochs.

But whatever form they may have taken, one fact is common to all past ages, viz., the exploitation of one part of society by the other. No wonder, then, that the social consciousness of past ages, despite all the multiplicity and variety it displays, moves within certain common forms, or general ideas, which cannot completely vanish except with the total disappearance of class antagonisms.

The Communist revolution is the most radical rupture with traditional property-relations; no wonder that its development involves the most radical rupture with traditional ideas.

But let us have done with the bourgeois objections to Communism.

We have seen above, that the first step in the revolution by the working class, is to raise the proletariat to the position of ruling class, to win the battle of democracy.

The proletariat will use its political supremacy, to wrest, by degrees, all capital from the bourgeoisie, to centralize all instruments of production in the hands of the State, i. e., of the proletariat organized as the ruling class; and to increase the total of productive forces as rapidly as possible.

Of course, in the beginning, this cannot be effected except by means of despotic inroads on the rights of property, and on the conditions of bourgeois production; but means of measures, therefore, which appear economically insufficient and untenable, but which, in the course of the movement, outstrip themselves, necessitate further inroads upon the old social order, and are unavoidable as a means of entirely revolutionizing the mode of production.

These measures will of course be different in different countries.

Nevertheless in the most advanced countries the following will be pretty generally applicable:

1. Abolition of property in land and application of all rents of land to public purposes.

2. A heavy progressive or graduated income tax.

3. Abolition of all right of inheritance.

4. Confiscation of the property of all emigrants and rebels.

5. Centralization of credit in the hands of the state, by means of a national bank with State capital and an exclusive monopoly.

6. Centralization of the means of communication and transport in the hands of the State.

7. Extension of factories and instruments of production owned by the State; the bringing into cultivation of waste lands, and improvement of the soil generally in accordance with a common plan.

8. Equal liability of all to labor. Establishment of industrial armies, especially for agriculture.

9. Combination of agriculture with manufacturing industries; gradual abolition of the distinction between town and country, by a more equable distribution of population over the country.

10. Free education for all children in public schools. Abolition of children's factory labor in its present form. Combination of education with industrial production, etc., etc.

When, in the course of development, class distinctions have disappeared, and all production has been concentrated in the hands of a vast association of the whole nation, the public power will lose its political character. Political power, properly so called, is merely the organized power of one class for oppressing another. If the proletariat during its contest with the bourgeoisie is compelled, by the force of circumstances, to organize itself as a class, if, by circumstances, to organize itself as a class, if, by means of a revolution, it makes itself the ruling class, and, as such, sweeps away by force the old conditions of production, then it will, along with these conditions, have swept away the conditions for the existence of class antagonisms, and of classes generally, and will thereby have abolished its own supremacy as a class.

In place of the old bourgeois society, with its classes and class antagonisms, we shall have an association, in which the free development of each is the condition for the free development of all.

Introduction to the
New Fabian Essays

R.H.S. CROSSMAN

Early in 1889 the Executive Committee of the Fabian Society issued its printed report for the Annual Business Meeting. In this modest, four-page document occurred an announcement that the course of lectures on *The Basis and Prospects of Socialism,* delivered in the previous autumn session, was to be published in book form. Edited by Bernard Shaw, these lectures formed *Fabian Essays.* Three hundred copies were subscribed for in advance; and when the prospective publisher refused to produce the book under fair trade conditions, the Fabian Society (which then had a little over a hundred members) published it at its own expense.

The result astonished all concerned. The first edition was sold out within a month; the second scarcely less rapidly; and through sixty years the demand continued (the final edition, issued in 1948, had no fewer than four Prefaces, as well as a postcript by Shaw). The exact number of copies sold is unknown, but it must run into

hundreds of thousands; translations are too numerous to list.

This success certainly astonished the seven lecturers responsible for the Essays. When they composed them, they had no idea that they were contributing to a work of major political importance; nor did they conceive of themselves as the evangelists of a new brand of Fabian orthodoxy. Indeed the small esteem in which they held themselves, and the meaning they gave to Fabianism, can be gauged from Shaw's original Preface:

Country readers may accept the book as a sample of the propaganda carried on by volunteer lecturers in the workmen's clubs and political associations of London.

And again:

Everything that is usually implied by the authorship and editing of a book has in this case been done by the seven essayists, associated in the Executive Council of the Fabian Society, and not one of the essays could be what it is had the writer been a stranger to his six colleagues and to the Society. But there has been no sacrifice of individuality—no attempt to cut out every phrase and opinion the responsibility for which would not be accepted by every one of the seven. . . . There are at present no

---

Reprinted from *New Fabian Essays,* by R. H. S. Crossman, editor; published by Frederick A. Praeger, Inc., Publishers, New York, 1952, and J. M. Dent & Sons Ltd., London.

authoritative teachers of Socialism. The essayists make no claim to be more than communicative learners.

These sentences express the spirit of Fabianism. They describe Fabians, first, as socialists; secondly, as colleagues collaborating to discover the best answers to insistent questions; thirdly, as individual thinkers, respecting one another's individuality; and fourthly, as advisers rather than dogmatic politicians— "clerks to the Labour Movement," as Beatrice Webb put it. It is worth observing that the Fabian Society had been in existence for nearly five years— busily campaigning and pamphleteering for socialism—before it felt the necessity to formulate its ideas even in the undogmatic form of seven unconnected essays. This practical empiricism, which bases theory upon experience as well as upon group discussion, very largely accounts for the long-continued appeal of *Fabian Essays*.

But times change, and even the best empirically-based theories eventually get out of date. To the present generation of socialists, the detailed proposals and formulations of the original *Fabian Essays* can mean very little. Partly this is due to the achievements of the Labour Movement—Fabian blueprints for social welfare, redistributive taxation, nationalisation and national minima now form part of the law of the land; partly to changing social conditions (the trade unions, for instance, have altered enormously since Annie Besant wrote about them—before the first great dock strike). But partly the outdatedness of *Fabian Essays* derives from inadequacies in the original analysis. In 1952, for example, we realise that we cannot completely ignore the rest of the world, as our forbears did in 1889; nor can we accept the concept of a world automatically progressing

towards expanding wealth and wider freedoms, which was so deeply rooted in Victorian thought that the first Fabians took it for granted without serious consideration.

Ever since the revival of the Fabian Society, which occurred in 1939, projects for a new series of Fabian Essays have been under discussion. The task was not an easy one. Not only are the problems of to-day more complex and far-reaching than those of sixty years ago; the information available—the sheer facts upon which policy must be grounded—have multiplied overwhelmingly. Moreover the modern Fabian, whose business it is to study and interpret those facts, has to spend much more time and energy earning his living than his predecessor, whose leisure-time propagandist activities Shaw described in his *Early History of the Fabian Society*. For these reasons, the first attempts at new Fabian Essays came to nothing. It was not until G.D.H. Cole —then Chairman of the Society—persuaded a group of Fabians to spend a week-end at Buscot Park in July, 1949, that a real start was made. The range of this first conference was very wide, including much argument on details; but then, rather unexpectedly, agreement was reached on the nature of the main problem. For two generations, socialist thought had been largely concentrated on the techniques for carrying out the programme envisaged in the original Essays and the expedients required to adapt that programme to the emergencies which had arisen. Comparatively little attention had been given to the structural changes in society which had been taking place and the new social sciences which were emerging. As a result, the election of the Labour Government in 1945, and the rapid completion of the Fabian programme, had been followed by a dangerous hiatus both of thought and action. It was not merely new expedients which were required, or new planks in an election programme, but a new analysis of the political, economic and social scene as a basis for reformulating socialist principles.

So conference succeeded conference; and, between conferences, papers were circulated on particular problems. There were withdrawals from the group. It lost some members owing to pressure of business; and one, the Chairman—to whose energy and inspiration the whole project was due—owing to a basic disagreement on policy. But, despite these losses, the unity of the group was successfully maintained; and, by the end of 1950, it became clear that some interim term must be set to all this intellectual activity. Everyone agreed that a comprehensive study of socialism was out of the question until much more work had been done. Time had returned on its spiral, and all that could be attempted was once again a series of individual essays in socialist thought. As Bernard Shaw said in 1889, "There are at present no authoritative teachers of Socialism." So the unity sought has been a unity of approach, not of specific opinions or propositions. The essayists have criticised one another, and been criticised by other members of the group, who have not contributed to the present series. It stands to reason that these latter, even less than the eight essayists, can be held committed to every line in the book. Nevertheless, as the eight authors would be the first to admit, this book is a product of Fabian group activity.

A word about the individual essays. The eight subjects were selected, from a list of about twice that number, in order to achieve a balance between theoretical analysis and practical application. R. H. S. Crossman begins by

an attempt to redefine the nature of Progress in a world which is certainly not progressing automatically towards social democracy; and then asks what changes in socialist attitudes are required in "the century of totalitarianism." C. A. R. Crosland follows with a new approach to "post-capitalist economics," analysing what has happened —in contrast with what Marx *said* would happen—to Western capitalism. Roy Jenkins, recognising equality as the concept which differentiates socialism from both liberalism and communism, examines the extent to which the aim of economic equalisation can be further pursued. Margaret Cole writes about education, which every socialist, from Robert Owen onwards, has recognised to be part of the foundation of any socialist society, but which formed the most glaring gap in the Labour Party's programme in 1945, 1950 and 1951. Austen Albu deals with the organisation of industry, and, in particular, with methods of bringing the private sector of industry under democratic control; and Ian Mikado tackles the contentious issue of how the structure of trade unionism should be adapted to the requirements of a full-time economy. In the concluding sections, Denis Healey, faced perhaps with the most difficult task, tries to show what the methods of socialist foreign policy should be, now that it is clear that power politics cannot be "abolished" either by disarmament or international machinery; and John Strachey, who has combined socialist theory with Cabinet experience, seeks to assess the changes achieved by the Labour Government as a basis on which to construct the next stage of socialism.

New Fabian Essays contains a good deal more historical background than the original volume. In the optimistic mood of the 1880's, the first Fabians took for granted both the shape of things past and the shape of things to come. We cannot write to-day without a much soberer consciousness of history, and a much more acute scepticism about the particular interpretation that we give it. In fact, we do not claim either finality or comprehensiveness for *New Fabian Essays.* Even the three years during which they were composed have brought changes which defied our predictions and warned us against ready-made conclusions. These essays, for instance, were written under a Labour Government, and revised in proof under a Tory Government. If they ask at least some of the new, pertinent questions, their authors will be content. And, in anticipation of what it believes to be the live and continuing interest of the Labour Movement, the Fabian Society has already started the group discussions for a second volume, which will both fill in gaps and open up new inquiries.

Meanwhile the eight essayists, not one of whom was alive at the time when *Fabian Essays* appeared, can still find no better description of themselves than "communicative learners." If the problems of 1952 are different from those of 1889, we believe that the Fabian spirit is still essential to the cause of democratic socialism.

The Right of the State to Promote Morality

THOMAS HILL GREEN

...On the same principle the freedom of contract ought probably to be more restricted in certain directions than is at present the case. The freedom to do as they like on the part of one set of men may involve the ultimate disqualification of many others, or of a succeeding generation, for the exercise of rights. This applies most obviously to such kinds of contract or traffic as affect the health and housing of the people, the growth of population relatively to the means of subsistence, and the accumulation or distribution of landed property. In the hurry of removing those restraints on free dealing between man and man, which have arisen partly perhaps from some confused idea of maintaining morality, but much more from the power of class-interests, we have apt to take too narrow a view of the range of persons—not one generation merely, but succeeding generations —whose freedom ought to be taken into account, and of the conditions necessary to their freedom ("freedom" here meaning their qualification for the exercise of rights). Hence the massing of population without regard to conditions of health; unrestrained traffic in deleterious commodities; unlimited upgrowth of the class of hired labourers in particular industries which circumstances have suddenly stimulated, without any provision against the danger of

Reprinted from Thomas Hill Green, *Lectures on the Principles of Political Obligation* in *Works of Thomas Hill Green,* ed. R. L. Nettleship, Vol. II (London: Longmans, Green, and Co., 1900), pp. 515–16.

an impoverished proletariate in following generations. Meanwhile, under pretence of allowing freedom of bequest and settlement, a system has grown up which prevents the landlords of each generation from being free either in the government of their families or in the disposal of their land, and aggravates the tendency to crowd into towns, as well as the difficulties of providing healthy house-room, by keeping land in a few hands. It would be out of place here to consider in detail the remedies for these evils, or to discuss the question how far it is well to trust to the initiative of the state or of individuals in dealing with them. It is enough to point out the directions in which the state may remove obstacles to the realisation of the capacity for beneficial exercise of rights, without defeating its own object by vitiating the spontaneous character of that capacity.

The Right of the State in Regard to Property

THOMAS HILL GREEN

...It is too long a business here to attempt an account of the process by which the organisation of rights in the state has superseded that of the clan, and at the same time the restriction of the powers of appropriation implied in the latter has been removed. It is important to observe, however, that this process has by no means contributed unmixedly to the end to which, from the moral point of view, it should have contributed. That end is at once the emancipation of the individual from all restrictions upon the free moral life, and his provision with means for it. But the actual result of the development of rights of property in Europe, as part of its general political development, has so far been a state of things in which all indeed *may* have property, but great numbers in fact cannot have it in that sense in which alone it is of

Reprinted from Green, *Lectures on the Principles of Political Obligation,* pp. 525–34.

value, viz. as a permanent apparatus for carrying out a plan of life, for expressing ideas of what is beautiful, or giving effect to benevolent wishes. In the eye of the law they have rights of appropriation, but in fact they have not the chance of providing means for a free moral life, of developing and giving reality or expression to a good will, an interest in social well-being. A man who possesses nothing but his powers of labour and who has to sell these to a capitalist for bare daily maintenance, might as well, in respect of the ethical purposes which the possession of property should serve, be denied rights of property altogether. Is the existence of so many men in this position, and the apparent liability of many more to be brought to it by a general fall of wages, if increase of population goes along with decrease in the productiveness of the earth, a necessary result of the emancipation of the individual and the free play given to powers of appropriation? or is it an evil incident, which may yet be remedied, of that historical process by which the development of the rights of property has been brought about, but in which the agents have for the most part had no moral objects in view at all?

Let us first be clear about the points in which the conditions of property, as it actually exists, are at variance with property according to its idea or as it should be. The rationale of property, as we have seen, is that everyone should be secured by society in the power of getting and keeping the means of realising a will, which in possibility is a will directed to social good. Whether anyone's will is actually and positively so directed, does not affect his claim to the power. This power should be secured to the individual irrespectively of the use which he actually makes of it, so long as he does not use it in a way that interferes with the exercise of like power by another, on the ground that its uncontrolled exercise is the condition of attainment by man of that free morality which is his highest good. It is not then a valid objection to the manner in which property is possessed among us, that its holders constantly use it in a way demoralising to themselves and others, any more than such misuse of any other liberties is an objection to securing men in their possession. Only then is property held in a way inconsistent with its idea, and which should, if possible, be got rid of, when the possession of property by one man interferes with the possession of property by another; when one set of men are secured in the power of getting and keeping the means of realising their will, in such a way that others are practically denied the power. In that case it may truly be said that "property is theft." The rationale of property, in short, requires that everyone who will

conform to the positive condition of possessing it, viz. labour, and the negative condition, viz. respect for it as possessed by others, should, so far as social arrangements can make him so, be a possessor of property himself, and of such property as will at least enable him to develop a sense of responsibility, as distinct from mere property in the immediate necessaries of life.

...It is difficult to summarise the influences to which is due the fact that in all the chief seats of population in Europe the labourmarket is constantly thronged with men who are too badly reared and fed to be efficient labourers; who for this reason, and from the competition for employment with each other, have to sell their labour very cheap; who have thus seldom the means to save, and whose standard of living and social expectation is so low that, if they have the opportunity of saving, they do not use it, and keep bringing children into the world at a rate which perpetuates the evil. It is certain, however, that these influences have no necessary connection with the maintenance of the right of the individual property and consequent unlimited accumulation of capital, though they no doubt are connected with that regime of force and conquest by which existing governments have been established,— governments which do not indeed create the rights of individual property, any more than other rights, but which serve to maintain them. It must always be borne in mind that the appropriation of land by individuals has in most countries—probably in all where it approaches completeness—has been originally effected, not by the expenditure of labour or the results of labour on the land, but by force. The original landlords have been conquerors.

This has affected the condition of the industrial classes in at least two ways: (1) When the application of accumulated capital to any work in the way of mining or manufacture has created a demand for labour, the supply has been forthcoming from men whose ancestors, if not themselves, were trained in habits of serfdom; men whose life has been one of virtually forced labour, relieved by church-charities or the poor law (which in part took the place of these charities) ; who were thus in no condition to contract freely for the sale of their labour, and had nothing of that sense of family-responsibility which might have made them insist on having the chance of saving. Landless countrymen, whose ancestors were serfs, are the parents of the proletariate of great towns. (2) Rights have been allowed to landlords, incompatible with the true principle on which rights of property rest, and tending to interfere with the development of the proprietorial capacity in others. The right to freedom in unlimited acquisition of wealth, by means of labour and by means of the saving and successful application of the results of labour, does not imply the right of anyone to do as he likes with those gifts of nature, without which there would be nothing to spend labour upon. The earth is just as much an original natural material necessary to productive industry, as are air, light, and water, but while the latter from the nature of the case cannot be appropriated the earth can be and has been. The only justification for this appropriation, as for any other, is that it contributes on the whole to social well-being; that the earth as appropriated by individuals under certain conditions becomes more serviceable to society as a whole, including those who are not proprietors of the soil, than if it were held in common. The justification disappears if these conditions are not observed; and

from government having been chiefly in the hands of appropriators of the soil, they have not been duly observed. Landlords have been allowed to "do what they would with their own," as if land were merely like so much capital, admitting of indefinite extension. The capital gained by one is not taken from another, but one man cannot acquire more land without others having less; and though a growing reduction in the number of landlords is not necessarily a social evil, if it is compensated by the acquisition of other wealth on the part of those extruded from the soil, it is only not an evil if the landlord is prevented from so using his land as to make it unserviceable to the wants of men (e.g. by turning fertile land into a forest), and from taking liberties with it incompatible with the conditions of general freedom and health; e.g. by clearing out a village and leaving the people to pick up houseroom as they can elsewhere (a practice common under the old poor-law, when the distinction between close and open villages grew up), or, on the other hand, by building houses in unhealthy places or of unhealthy structure, by stopping up means of communication, or forbidding the erection of dissenting chapels. In fact the restraints which the public interest requires to be placed on the use of land if individual property in it is to be allowed at all, have been pretty much ignored, while on the other hand, that full development of its resources, which individual ownership would naturally favour, has been interfered with by laws or customs which, in securing estates to certain families, have taken away the interest, and tied the hands, of the nominal owner—the tenant for life—in making the most of his property.

Thus the whole history of the ownership of land in Europe has been of a kind to lead to the agglomeration of a proletariate, neither holding nor seeking property, wherever a sudden demand has arisen for labour in mines or manufactures. This at any rate was the case down to the epoch of the French Revolution; and this, which brought to other countries deliverance from feudalism left England, where feudalism had previously passed into unrestrained landlordism, almost untouched. And while those influences of feudalism and landlordism which tend to throw a shiftless population upon the centres of industry have been left unchecked, nothing till quite lately was done to give such a population a chance of bettering itself, when it had been brought together. Their health, housing, and schooling were unprovided for. They were left to be freely victimised by deleterious employments, foul air, and consequent craving for deleterious drinks. When we consider all this, we shall see the unfairness of laying on capitalism or the free development of individual wealth the blame which is really due to the arbitrary and violent manner in which rights over land have been acquired and exercised, and to the failure of the state to fulfil those functions which under a system of unlimited private ownership are necessary to maintain the conditions of a free life. . . .

American Capitalism

JOHN KENNETH GALBRAITH

. . . The competitive model of a capitalist economy allowed . . . for rhythmic increases and decreases in prices and production and even for occasional bouts of unemployment. It did not contemplate the possibility of a catastrophic and enduring depression. Economists, and through them politicians, businessmen and the public, were insulated from the need to think of such a tragedy by the benign theorem that the act of production provided the purchasing power for all that was produced at approximate full employment.

In 1930 a *really* serious depression was not part of the experience of the current generation of Americans. In

Reprinted from John Kenneth Galbraith, *American Capitalism* (Boston: Houghton Mifflin Company, 1956, and London: Hamish Hamilton Ltd.), pp. 63–83, by permission of the publishers.

late 1920 and early 1921 there was a sharp fall in prices and incomes, and, in somewhat lesser degree, in employment. But the recovery was prompt. Moreover, the whole episode was inextricably associated with the war and its aftermath and could be blamed on what economists are pleased to call exogenous forces. Except by farmers, who continued to feel themselves at a disadvantage, it was almost universally dismissed as the inevitable reaction to the wartime inflation in prices and profits. For an earlier slump of comparable importance it was necessary to go back to the preceding century.

One can only suppose that in 1929 the fates undertook, after great deliberation, to shake the confidence of the people of the United States in their economy. Nothing could have been more ingeniously or more elaborately designed to achieve this result. There was the shock effect—the sudden dramatic collapse in stock-market values with which the lives and fortunes of thousands of innocents, who only then became aware of their innocence, had become entwined. This was followed by the inexorable decline in output, values and employment which, in a little more than two years, cut the value of national production almost in half and left twelve million workers—ten and a half million more than in 1929—without jobs and mostly without reliable means of support. Those who still had jobs lived in the penetrating fear that their turn would be next. Meanwhile hundreds of thousands of well-to-do citizens either made a sudden and irretrievable descent into poverty or dwelt in the cold fear that they soon would. It would have added to the security of the country if businessmen and bankers had escaped the debacle. But their well-publicized plight suggested, all too plainly, that they too had no formula for contending with capitalism when the latter was on shipwreck tack. The broken banker was as commonplace a figure in the news as the unemployed worker, and a much less reassuring one. The economy was the impartial destroyer of all.

When there was nothing else to hope for, it could still be hoped that the depression would be temporary. A rhythm of good times and bad was the minimum promise of the competitive model. To this shaky standard the defenders of the system repaired in droves. Then, the most malicious act of all, the depression was made to last ten years. The very notion that depressions in the United States were self-correcting—that there were corners that would be turned—became a national jest. As if to sharpen the point, a modest recovery prior to the summer of 1937, which however had left between seven and eight million still unemployed, was followed by a slump in production that was even sharper than the one following 1929. The Great Depression of the thirties never came to an end. It merely disappeared in the great mobilization of the forties. For a whole generation it became the normal aspect of peacetime life in the United States—the thing to be both feared and expected. . . .

The depression not only contributed deeply to the insecurity with which Americans viewed their economy. It also had an important bearing on economic behavior. In the years following World War II the fear of a recurrence of depression was without question a dominant factor in the calculations of a large proportion of all businessmen. The convention, so scrupulously observed by the business community, which bans the public expression of fear of economic collapse lest to express fear be to invite the fact, concealed much of this alarm. Nonetheless, when *Fortune* magazine in 1946 asked some 15,000 leading business executives in confidence whether they expected an "extended major depression with large-scale unemployment in the next ten years"—a phrasing that was not designed to minimize the scope of the contemplated disaster—fifty-eight per cent of those replying said they did. Of the remainder only twenty-eight per cent said they did not. In these same years labor was preoccupied with measures to maintain the level of employment and farmers with support prices that would provide shelter in a slump. Even the radicals had long ceased to talk about the inequality or exploitation under capitalism or its "inherent contradictions." They stressed only the utter unreliability of its performance.

These attitudes have since changed.

With prosperity and the passage of time the fear of depression has been somewhat dulled. In 1949 and again in 1954 there were minor setbacks, which were first viewed as the beginning of a new disaster but from which there was a prompt recovery. These provided more reassurance. The convention which requires businessmen and politicians who are in office to say that all will always be well—that at any time prosperity is assured—has brought a rich yield of optimism. This too has had an effect. . . .

By the mid-thirties, the layman—whether worker, businessman, farmer or unemployed—had undoubtedly reached his own conclusions concerning American capitalism. Asked were its norm an equilibrium of stable prices and full employment, the conclusion of the competitive model, he would have recommended his interrogator to the care of a good doctor. But, as ideas to be influential need the support of experience, so experience needs interpretation by ideas. Only then does it become the basis for generalization, for a theory. The Great Depression might, conceivably, have remained the great accident if ideas had not again intervened. These, in their mature form, made depression, or its counterpart inflation, the normal behavior pattern of uninhibited and unmanaged capitalism. While this discouraging analysis carried with it a remedy—a remedy that was received with profound enthusiasm by many economists and much of the public at large—the remedy was unorthodox and disturbing. It is only partial comfort for a patient, who is being told he is chronically ill, to learn that there are violent and painful cures for his disease.

The ideas which interpreted the depression, and which warned that depression or inflation might be as much a part of the free-enterprise destiny as stable full employment, were those of John Maynard Keynes. A case could easily be made by those who make such cases, that his were the most influential social ideas of the first half of the century. A proper distribution of emphasis as between the role of ideas and the role of action might attribute more influence on modern economic history to Keynes than to Roosevelt. Certainly his final book, *The General Theory of Employment, Interest and Money,* shaped the course of events as only the books of three earlier economists—Smith's *Wealth of Nations,* Ricardo's *Principles of Political Economy* and Marx's *Capital*—have done.

This is a judgment which has the impressive support of Keynes himself. Writing to George Bernard Shaw in early 1935, he said ". . . I believe myself to be writing a book on economic theory which will largely revolutionize —not, I suppose, at once but in the course of the next ten years—the way the world thinks about economic problems." It is not a judgment which greater historical perspective has yet altered.

Keynes' *General Theory* could not normally be read, even by the intelligent layman, unless he was schooled in the language and, even more, in the abstractions of economics. As a result its influence on practical affairs was almost entirely by proxy. It was not from Keynes but from his interpreters at first, second or third remove that most men learned of his ideas. The interpreters were almost exclusively other economists. Keynes was also beyond the reach of those who do brokerage in fashionable thoughts and, in fact, his ideas gained their ascendancy without creating appreciable stir among intellectuals at large. In any case, millions came to accept Keynes' conclusions who had never read a word he had written. More interesting, thousands came to be advocates of his proposals who, if asked, would have indignantly denied they were Keynesians. While everyone knows that Keynes was important and influential, there has always been a remarkable uncertainty as to just how or why.

The major conclusion of Keynes' argument—the one of greatest general importance and the one that is relevant here—is that depression and unemployment are in no sense abnormal. (Neither, although the point is made less explicitly, is inflation.) On the contrary, the economy can find its equilibrium at any level of performance. The chance that production in the United States will be at that level where all, or nearly all, willing workers can find jobs is no greater than the chance that four, six, eight or ten million workers will be unemployed. Alternatively the demand for goods may exceed what the economy can supply even when everyone is employed. Accordingly there can be, even under peacetime conditions, a persistent upward pressure on prices, i.e., more or less serious inflation. . . .

For purpose of displaying the essentials of the Keynesian argument it is convenient to assume an increase in saving and to see what happens—or rather what does not happen. The important consequence is that investment does not necessarily increase in order to absorb the saving; instead total production and employment may be reduced sufficiently to bring reduced saving into line with investment. In practice, economists have almost uniformly stressed fluctuations in investment rather than changes in saving as the important factor affecting total production. What people will endeavor to save from any given volume of income is commonly supposed to be less subject

to change than what business concerns may seek to invest. It has become customary, therefore, to think of changes in investment as the principal cause of changes in total production and employment. Insufficient investment has become the shorthand Keynesian explanation of low production and high unemployment. The obvious remedy is more investment and, in principle, it is not important whether this be from private or public funds. But the expenditure of public funds is subject to central determination by government, as that of private funds is not, so the Keynesian remedy leads directly to public expenditure as a depression remedy.

It is apparent that public spending is only one of the remedies implicit in the Keynesian system. Abatement of taxes in order to leave private individuals more money to spend and measures to stimulate private investment or discourage saving would have a similar effect. However, it is always for his prodigality that a man is known—Henry VIII for his wives, Louis XV for his mistresses and General Douglas MacArthur for his prose. The Keynesian has become forever associated with public spending. . . .

The time has now come to consider the political consequences of Keynes for, more than any man of the century, he reformulated attitudes on the agitated question of the relation of the state to the economy.

The United States, in the thirties, was urgently in need of a new theory of the relation of government to economic life. The American political parties had long been in the habit of assuming full responsibility for economic well-being and of campaigning with promises of prosperity for all. The inconsistency of these promises, which Republicans and Democrats had made with equal fervor, with the role assigned to the state by the competitive model was untroublesome so long as there was reasonable prosperity in any event. It was bound to be troublesome to a party which was forced to contend with a serious depression. The New Deal came to power on the usual promises and with little clearer view than predecessor administrations of how the government might intervene to bring prosperity.

It was inevitable that the attention of liberals in a liberal administration would be directed toward the structure of the economy. The preconceptions of the competitive model guided their thinking in this direction. Implicit in the rise of big business was the possibility that it had created a structure that departed so far from the competitive model that it could not work. Two courses of action were open. The incentives which, under the competitive model, were presumed to guide businessmen to a socially desirable behavior could be replaced by some kind of central guidance which would get the desired results. Perhaps businessmen could be brought together under the aegis of government and be told, or made to agree, to increase employment and stabilize wages and prices. Or, alternatively, perhaps private incentives could be rehabilitated by remaking business enterprise so that it conformed more closely to the preconceptions of the model.

Both enterprises involved the most serious difficulties. The first, which was given a trial run in the NRA [National Recovery Act], suffered from a grievous unclarity of both methods and goals. The self-interest of the businessman dictated the particular low level of employment he was offering and investment he was making in 1933. This simple fact was not altered by bringing him together with other businessmen

under the supervision of a Code Authority. It seems improbable that much would have been accomplished had he been ordered directly by government to increase employment and investment outlays at his own cost and contrary to his own assessment of interest.

To remake the economy in accordance with the requirements of the competitive model was obviously a time-consuming enterprise. To take time out to break up large corporate units and re-establish the competition of the model was hardly in keeping with the temper of a country which found depression tiresome and which was not noted for its patience. To the extent that it was contemplated in the later years of the New Deal it was as a decidedly long-run reform. There remained in 1933 only the possibility of abandoning capitalism entirely. This was a project which raised the question of alternatives concerning which only a handful of Communists were in any way clear. It is hardly surprising that the early days of the New Deal were distinguished in American history for their foggy semanticism—for meaningless or incomprehensible talk about social planning, guided capitalism and industrial self-government. When stumped by a problem the American liberal rarely admits defeat. He takes the offensive with words.

It was Keynes who provided the escape from the dilemma—and the words. It would be hard, at first glance, to imagine a formula that was better designed for the American scene. The depression was overwhelmingly the important problem. The notion of an excess of savings or a deficiency of investment defined the nature of the government intervention. By public borrowing or expenditure, or the appropriate changes in taxation, the government could make up for the deficiency in private spending. By so doing it could return the economy to full employment and keep it there. To the naked eye, the scope of private business decision remained as before. General Motors still decided what cars to produce, what prices to charge, how to advertise and sell them, when to build a new assembly plant and how many workers to employ. It merely sold more cars because employees on public works projects became customers for second-hand Chevrolets, their foremen for new ones and the contractor for a Buick. . . .

Liberals almost spontaneously adopted the Keynesian formula. They were also puzzled by the reluctance of conservatives, especially businessmen, to embrace it. Here was protection from the overwhelming threat of depression, the only threat of potentially revolutionary proportions seemingly faced by capitalism. The businessman remained undisturbed in his prerogatives as an owner and manager and had the promise of better business to boot. What could he lose?

With time there has been some explicit and a great deal of implicit acceptance of the Keynesian formula by American businessmen. However, as often happens, it encountered the sharp cleavage which exists in our attitude toward technological and social change. If a man seeks to design a better mousetrap he is the soul of enterprise; if he seeks to design a better society he is a crackpot. For those who mistrust social change it was not an argument that profits might be increased, even that disaster might be avoided. They were opposed to change and they could not be bought. They were men of principle.

There were also more positive grounds for business opposition to Keynes than liberals have been inclined to suppose. The Keynesian system,

though it perhaps involved a less than revolutionary change in the relation of the government to the economy, implied, nonetheless, an important one. For a doctrine that excluded government it substituted one that made government indispensable. Keynes was sufficiently unpalatable when he made depression and inflation not adventitious or war-induced misfortunes but normal occurrences. He went on to make government the indispensable partner of business. In failing to recognize the prestige that goes with power and decision-making in American life, American liberals failed to recognize that, for some businessmen, the Keynesian remedy was at least as damaging as the depression it presumed to eliminate. Even though the businessman might profit in a narrow pecuniary sense from the new role of government there was no chance that his prestige would survive intact. Where, in economic life, people had previously looked upon business decisions as the ones that had shaped their destiny, now they would have regard for government decisions as well, or instead. Those of an Assistant Secretary of the Treasury on interest rates were now of more importance than those of any banker. Those of a regional administrator of public works on investment attained a significance greater than those of a corporation president. To share the prestige of decision-making is to lose prestige. The Keynesian remedies thus represented an assault on a valued possession. Those who were losers could hardly be expected to embrace the ideas that brought this loss. Much of their dissatisfaction was expressed in personal terms—it was directed against the Administration and against the public servants who implemented the new ideas. But a good deal was directed at Keynes. His American followers, taking at face value our conventional disavowal of any interest in power, failed to understand the discontent over its impairment.

The Keynesian system also, though unobtrusively, opened the way for a large expansion of government services and activities. This was the result of a new and very important concept of social waste which followed in its train. If the normal tendency of the economy is toward full employment, then the use of labor and other economic resources by government is at the expense of their use by the private economy. Dams and post offices are built at the cost of private consumption or investment. If there is full employment in the first place, something must be given up. But if unemployment is chronic, the dams and post offices require no sacrifice of private production or consumption. The labor, plants and materials that are used would otherwise have been unemployed. They are wasted if someone does not employ them. Again ideas had produced a topsy-turvy world. Government spending, long the mark of profligacy, was now sanctioned in the sacred name of avoiding waste. It was inevitable also that wild men would draw from this paradox, and the substantial truths on

which it is built, a sanction for any and all expenditures at any and all times. Here was further discomfort for the conservative.

The Keynesian ideas had other new, heterodox and even threatening corollaries. Thrift, an ancient and once an absolute virtue, was brought into question; it suffered from the guilt of association with redundant saving and depression. A doctrine which cast doubt on so conventional a good was bound to be suspect. We commonly bring a deep theological conviction to the defense of our chosen principles. Those who dissent are not wrong, they are evil. Nothing could better prove that a man was secretly in the service of the devil or communism than that he should raise his voice against thrift....

The disagreements arising out of Keynes' proposals should not be magnified. He was not a divisive figure; on the contrary his work was solidly in the Anglo-American tradition of compromise which seeks progress by reconciling the maximum number of conflicts of interest. But it is also easy to see how his formula, and the speed with which it was accepted, provided its own ground for uneasiness....

The Political and Social Doctrine of Fascism

BENITO MUSSOLINI

The foundation of Fascism is the conception of the State, its character, its

Reprinted from Benito Mussolini, "The Political and Social Doctrine of Fascism," *International Conciliation* (January, 1935), No. 306, pp. 13–15, by permission of *International Conciliation*.

duty, and its aim. Fascism conceives of the State as an absolute, in comparison with which all individuals or groups are relative, only to be conceived of in their relation to the State. The conception of the Liberal State is not that of a directing force, guiding the play and development, both material and spiritual, of a collective body, but merely a force limited to the function of recording results: on the other hand, the Fascist State is itself conscious, and has itself a will and a personality—thus it may be called the "ethic" State. In 1929, at the first five-yearly assembly of the Fascist régime, I said:

For us Fascists, the State is not merely a guardian, preoccupied solely with the duty of assuring the personal safety of the citizens; nor is it an organization with purely material aims, such as to guarantee a certain level of well-being and peaceful conditions of life; for a mere council of administration would be sufficient to realize such objects. Nor is it a purely political creation, divorced from all contact with the complex material reality which makes up the life of the individual and the life of the people as a whole. The State, as conceived of and as created by Fascism, is a spiritual and moral fact in itself, since its political, juridical, and economic organization of the nation is a concrete thing: and such an organization must be in its origins and development a manifestation of the spirit. The State is the guarantor of security both internal and external, but it is also the custodian and transmitter of the spirit of the people, as it has grown up through the centuries in language, in customs, and in faith. And the State is not only a living reality of the present, it is also linked with the past and above all with the future, and thus transcending the brief limits of individual life, it represents the immanent spirit of the nation. The forms in which States express themselves may change, but the necessity for such forms is eternal. It is the State which educates its citizens in civic virtue, gives them a consciousness of their mission and welds them into unity; harmonizing their various interests through justice, and transmitting to future generations the mental conquests of science, of art, of law and the solidarity of humanity. It leads men from primitive tribal life to that highest expression of human power which is Empire: it links up through the centuries the names of those of its members who have died for its existence and in obedience to its laws, it holds up the memory of the leaders who have increased its territory and the geniuses who have illumined it with glory as an example to be followed by future generations. When the conception of the State declines, and disunifying and centrifugal tendencies prevail, whether of individuals or of particular groups, the nations where such phenomena appear are in their decline.

From 1929 until today, evolution, both political and economic has everywhere gone to prove the validity of these doctrinal premises. Of such gigantic importance is the State. It is the force which alone can provide a solution to the dramatic contradictions of capitalism, and that state of affairs which we call the crisis can only be dealt with by the State, as between other States. Where is the shade of Jules Simon, who in the dawn of Liberalism proclaimed that, "The State must labor to make itself unnecessary, and prepare the way for its own dismissal"? Or of McCulloch, who, in the second half of the last century, affirmed that the State must guard against the danger of governing too much? What would the Englishman, Bentham, say today to the continual and inevitably-invoked intervention of the State in the sphere of economics, while according to his theories industry should ask no more of the State than to be left in peace? Or the German, Humboldt, according to whom the "lazy" State should be considered the best? It is true that the second wave of Liberal economists were less extreme than the first, and Adam Smith himself opened the door—if only very cautiously—which leads to State intervention in the economic field: but whoever says Liberalism implies individualism, and whoever says Fascism implies the State. Yet the Fascist State is unique, and an original creation. It is not reactionary, but revolutionary, in that it anticipates the solution of the universal political problems which elsewhere have to be settled in the political field by the rivalry of parties, the excessive power of the parliamentary régime and the irresponsibility of political assemblies; while it meets the problems of the economic field by a system of syndicalism which is continually increasing in importance, as much in the sphere of labor as of industry: and in the moral field enforces order, discipline, and obedience to that which is the determined moral code of the country. Fascism desires the State to be a strong and organic body, at the same time reposing upon broad and popular support. The Fascist State has drawn into itself even the economic activities of the nation, and, through the corporative social and educational institutions created by it, its influence reaches every aspect of the national life and includes, framed in their respective

organizations, all the political, economic and spiritual forces of the nation. A State which reposes upon the support of millions of individuals who recognize its authority, are continually conscious of its power and are ready at once to serve it, is not the old tyrannical State of the medieval lord nor has it anything in common with the absolute governments either before or after 1789. The individual in the Fascist State is not annulled but rather multiplied, just in the same way that a soldier in a regiment is not diminished but rather increased by the number of his comrades. The Fascist State organizes the nation, but leaves a sufficient margin of liberty to the individual; the latter is deprived of all useless and possibly harmful freedom, but retains what is essential; the deciding power in this question cannot be the individual, but the State alone.

The Russian Revolution—
Fifty Years After /
The Soviet Economic Reform

YEVSEI LIBERMAN

. . .

THE ROLE OF PROFIT
IN THE SOVIET UNION

The question of profit has been widely discussed in recent times in the U.S.S.R.

Reprinted by special permission from *Foreign Affairs,* October 1967 issue. Copyright © by the Council on Foreign Relations, Inc., New York.

—not because profit was previously unknown there or was being introduced for the first time, but because prior to the reform profit was not employed as the chief criterion or overall indicator of the effectiveness of an enterprise. Profit was only one of many required indicators which were set as goals. These indicators established as targets for the enterprise included gross volume of output, an excessively detailed list of the items to be produced, cost reduction, number of employees, output per employee, average wage, etc. The number of obligatory targets fettered initiative. Often the enterprises concerned themselves primarily with increasing gross volume of output, since their performance was judged above all by that and not by the amount of output sold, as is now the case. In addition, enterprises gave little heed to the utilization of production assets. Trying to find the easiest way to meet the assigned volume of output, they asked and received from the state, free of charge, a great deal of equipment and new structures which they did not always use rationally and fully.

Much of this is explained by the fact that for a long time the Soviet Union was the world's only socialist country. It was faced with the task of creating industry as fast as possible and providing for the country's defense. No thought was given at that time to the quality or attractiveness of goods, not even to production cost or profit. This was entirely justified, for the Soviet Union not only withstood the war of 1941–1945 but played a decisive role in ridding the world of fascism. This was worth any price. It was our "profit" and, if you please, the "profit" of the whole civilized world.

But, as Lenin said more than once, our virtues, if carried too far, can turn into faults. This is what happened in our country when the practices of management by administrative fiat were continued into the period after our country had entered the stage of peaceful economic competition with the developed countries of the West.

Success in this competition cannot be gained by the old methods of administrative and excessively centralized management. It was necessary to change so as to give the enterprises themselves a material stake in the bet-

ter utilization of their assets and in providing the best possible service to their consumers. To do this the enterprises obviously had to be relieved of the excessive number of planned targets and their work had to be judged, first, by how they fulfilled the contracts for deliveries of commodities and, if they did this, secondly by their profit level.

Profit sums up all the aspects of an enterprise's work, including quality of output, since the price for better goods is correspondingly higher than for outmoded or relatively inefficient items. But it is important to note that profit is neither the only nor the chief goal of production. We are interested above all in output of specific commodities to satisfy consumer and producer needs. Profit is used as the chief index of, and incentive to, efficiency of production, as a mechanism for appraising and stimulating the work of an enterprise and also as a source of accumulation and investment.

By means of bonuses drawn from profits we wish to encourage enterprises to draw up their own plans which would be good—that is, advantageous —alike for society and themselves; and not only to draw up such plans, but to carry them out, something which should be encouraged at the expense of the profits. It is not a question of weakening or discarding planning, but, on the contrary, of reinforcing and improving it by drawing the enterprises themselves into the planning process, for they always know better than anyone their own real potentialities and should study and know the needs of their clients.

The introduction of contract relations with consumers or clients (for the contractual relationship now exists in a number of light industries) does not at all signify a change to regulation by the anarchy of the market. Effective consumer demand can be predicted more easily in our country than in the West, since we know the wage fund of the urban population and the earnings of the collective farmers. Hence, we can draw up well-based balance sheets of the public's income and expenditure. The total volume of purchasing power is a figure which lends itself easily to planning. But specifically which goods are to constitute this total, what are to be the colors of the clothing, which styles are to be used and how best to organize their production—this is not the prerogative of centralized planning. It is, rather, a matter for agreement between trade outlets and producers. Thus, our market requirements, the calculation of public demand and the planning of production not only are integral, they should support and supplement each other.

What is the difference between "capitalist" and "socialist" profit, in my opinion? The difference will be best understood if we consider: (1) how the profit is formed; (2) what it indicates; and (3) how it is spent.

From the viewpoint of private enterprise, all profit belongs to the capitalists alone. To justify this, there was long ago devised a theory that three factors —capital, land and labor—create value. Joseph A. Schumpeter, in his "Theory of Economic Development," wrote that profit is the excess over production cost. But this "cost" includes "payment" for the entrepreneur's labor, land rent and interest on capital, as well as a premium for "risk." Over and above this, profit should reward the entrepreneur if, by a fresh combination of production elements, he reduces the production cost below the prevailing average level of expenditures.

The nature of this "combination of elements" can be perceived from the fact that in the private enterprise sys-tem most profit is now derived from redistribution of income in the market in the process of exchange. It is common knowledge, for instance, that big profits are most easily obtained by the advantageous purchase of raw materials, by a monopoly-controlled raising of retail prices, by unequal exchanges with underdeveloped countries, by the export of capital to countries with low wage levels, by a system of preferential duties and tariffs, by the increase in stock-market prices through capitalization above profit, and, finally, by military orders.

In our country all these sources of profit are precluded by the very nature of socialism, under which there is neither private ownership of the means of production nor holding of stock (and hence no stock market). The level at which labor is paid depends on the productivity of the labor and is regulated by law. Prices of raw materials and supplies are planned; the market cannot be taken advantage of in purchasing raw materials or hiring labor. Nor is it possible to take advantage of market conditions to raise the prices of finished goods. Exchange with other countries is conducted on a basis of equality and by long-term agreements.

In the Soviet Union, by virtue of the very nature of the mode of production and distribution, profit indicates only the level of production efficiency. Profit is the difference between production cost and the factory sale price. But since in our country the price represents, in principle, the norms of expenditure of socially necessary labor, any increase in profit is an index of relative economy in production. Higher profits in the Soviet Union are based solely on economized hours of working time, economized tons of raw materials and supplies and fuel, and economized kilowatt hours of electricity. We do not justify profits obtained from chance circumstances, such as excessively high prices, and do not regard such profits as being to the credit of the enterprise. Rather do we consider such profit the consequence of insufficiently flexible price setting. All profits of this kind go into the state budget; from such profits no bonuses are granted to the enterprises.

Now let us see what is done with profit in the U.S.S.R., that is, what it is spent on. First of all, no private individual and no enterprise as a group of private individuals may acquire profit. Profit may not be invested arbitrarily by any persons or groups for the purpose of deriving personal income.

Profit in our country belongs to those who own the means of production; that is to say, to society, to all the working people as a whole. All profit in our country goes first of all into the planned expansion or improvement of social production, and next into providing free social services to the public, such as education and science, public health services, pensions and stipends. A part is spent on the administrative apparatus and, unfortunately, quite a large part on defense requirements. We would be happy to dispense with the latter expenditures if a program of universal disarmament were adopted.

Profit used to be given insufficient importance in our country because of a certain disregard of the law of value. Some Soviet economists incorrectly interpreted this economic law as an unpleasant leftover of capitalism; they held that the sooner we got rid of it the better. Disregard of the requirements of the law of value led to the establishment of arbitrarily planned prices—prices which, moreover, remained in force for overly long periods. Prices thus became divorced from the real value of goods; profit varied greatly from enterprise to enterprise and even from article to article within the same general group of goods. In these circumstances profit did not reflect the actual achievements of the producers. Because of this, many economists and managers began to regard profit as something totally independent of the enterprise and therefore an unreliable barometer of economic management. It is this mistake that many of our economists, including the author, are now trying to eradicate. And our economic reform is aimed at this. We have no intention of reverting to private enterprise; on the contrary, we want to put into operation the economic laws of socialism. Central planning is entirely compatible with the initiative of enterprises in managing the economy profitably. This is as far from "private enterprise" as the latter is from feudalism.

The law of value is not a law of capitalism, but of any form of production for the market, including planned commodity production, which is what socialism is. The difference from capitalism is that ends and means are reversed. Under capitalism, profit is the basic aim, whereas satisfaction of the needs of the public is the means of attaining that aim and is secondary. Under socialism, on the contrary, the aim is to satisfy the needs of the public, and profit is the means toward that end. This is not a verbal distinction but the crux of the matter, since in our conditions profit does not work counter to social needs but helps to satisfy them.

THE REFORM AND THE PROBLEMS

The first stage of the economic reform has confronted us with certain difficulties in realizing its basic principles—difficulties which appear to be inherent in this period of the reform. The transfer of the first 704 enterprises to the new system was not immediately accompanied by substantial changes in their relations with the superior agencies, with other enterprises, with agencies supplying materials and equipment, etc.

Necessary changes have not been fully put into effect in the methods of planning production at the level of the ministries and industry administrations —particularly in the method of setting goals for enterprises. Due to lack of experience, sometimes the same old sharply criticized targets were simply made the new ones. For example, output has been considered as being the same as sales volume; and the assortment of items produced has not always been determined in consultation with the consumer or clients on the basis of direct contract arrangements. Instances of the inevitable deviation of practice from theory could be multiplied, but they all are due to the fact that the reform as yet covers only a limited number of enterprises. It is to be assumed that everything will gradually take proper shape.

The 1966 experience of working by the new method did show that, on the one hand, enterprises are becoming more dynamic and independent in their economic life, but, on the other hand, that the superior agencies frequently have been incapable of freeing themselves fast enough from old habits and from superfluous regimentation of the work of plants and factories. The inertia of thought, views and ideas which was so characteristic of some executive agencies over a long period has proved more persistent than had been expected.

The reform puts the old established relationships in industry to a severe test. The enlargement of the rights of enterprises is an important condition of the reform. In many cases, however, the superior agencies have proved insufficiently prepared for this development. Sometimes this has taken the form of the old bureaucratic ills— inflexibility, irresponsibility and lack of initiative, reliance upon the formality of issuing orders instead of working out economic as opposed to administrative methods of influencing production.

Perhaps one of the most significant consequences of the economic reform is the growing influence of industrial enterprises on the superior agencies. The reform is destroying and will continue to destroy many established patterns, including the distrust shown by executive agencies for production organizers and economists at the enterprises.

Unquestionably, the reform has strengthened anti-bureaucratic views and the tendency of enterprises to strive for independence. This, however, does not in the least signify that the principle of democratic centralism in the management of our economy is being abandoned. To strengthen and intensify central planning of production by combining it with the initiative and full economic accountability of enterprises is to realize the principle of democratic centralism.

The reform has not yet sufficiently permeated the administrative interrelationships between enterprises and superior agencies. This is indeed a complicated process of many steps. Complaints and mutual dissatisfactions are inevitable. First of all, the reform requires a sharp improvement in the qualifications of those engaged in the management process. If the economic and organizational level of management is low, the efficiency and profitability of the enterprise are generally low. The point of the reform is to raise production efficiency, increase labor productivity and open wide the road to rapid technical improvement. As it goes on, the reform inevitably will foster the selection and promotion of the more able, both below and at the top, to executive managerial positions. The reform will not tolerate the retention of anything that is obsolete and that has failed to justify itself in our methods of management.

A New Incentive Plan
for Soviet Managers

HARRY G. SHAFFER

On September 9, 1962, *Pravda* published a proposal by Yevsey G. Liberman, until then a little-known professor at the Kharkov Engineering and Economics Institute. The *New York Times* referred to Liberman as "a heretic... obviously influenced by capitalist experience"; Radio Free Europe tagged his plan "notably revisionist—and rational"; but in the Soviet Union his proposal called forth a stormy controversy which, for weeks on end, filled the pages of the leading Soviet newspapers and economic journals, and monopolized the agenda at numerous official and semi-official meetings and conferences. Some of those who participated in these debates saw in Liberman's proposal the greatest contribution to progressive Marxism since Lenin re-interpreted some of the basic theories of Karl Marx; others took a somewhat more skeptical view of what, at least at the surface, appeared to be a deviation from Communist ideology; yet others dubbed Liberman's plan a threat to the very survival of socialist central planning and predicted that its adoption would spell a return to capitalist

modes of production. Long before its official publication in *Pravda,* Liberman's plan had been given substantial backing by the Soviet Academy of Sciences' influential "Learned Council for Problems of Scientific Principles of Planning." But the controversy did not quiet down until Khrushchev himself, on November 19, 1962, endorsed some of Liberman's ideas, called on the planning agencies and the Economic Institute of the U.S.S.R. Academy of Sciences to examine the proposals further, and advocated that experiments along the lines proposed by Liberman be carried on. Ten days later, even the chairman of the "orthodox" East German State Planning Commission came out for the proposed plan. Yet, Liberman's recommendations, if adopted, would amount to nothing less than the end of specific, detailed planning from Moscow, the use of profits as the basic indicator of a plant's efficiency, the utilization of the profit motive as the exclusive incentive to induce Soviet managers to perform more efficiently, and greatly enhanced freedom for these managers to make decisions affecting their plants. What deficiencies in the Soviet planning mechanism, what serious inadequacies in Soviet enterprise

From *The Russian Review,* XXII, No. 4 (1963), 410–16. Reprinted with the permission of *The Russian Review.*

efficiency, would warrant such drastic measures?

Many a visitor to the Soviet Union has wondered why the nation that placed the first man in orbit, that has built up a military might second only to that of the United States, and that graduates more engineers every year than any other country on earth does not seem capable of mass producing door knobs that keep doors closed or faucets that do not leak. One of the reasons for this apparent contradiction is certainly the low priority placed on the production of consumer goods. At least part of the explanation, however, lies in a system of incentives for Soviet managers that encourages the continuation of obsolete production techniques, the output of low quality consumer goods, wastefulness, and misallocation of productive resources.

To make the interests of Soviet managers identical with those of Soviet society at large, their income is closely tied to the successful and efficient completion of the objectives assigned to them by the Plan. While managers in various industries or plants may get rewards for increasing labor productivity, decreasing unit costs, economizing on one or another scarce raw material, etc., the main achievement indicator is total output. Hence, the Soviet manager's take-home pay (and incidentally also his professional reputation and even the income of his employees) depends largely upon the extent to which he fulfills or overfulfills the "output plan."

Where "output" can be clearly specified, the performance of the enterprise can be evaluated fairly easily. In the case of a completely homogenous product, output is readily measurable (pure gold in ounces, electricity in kilowatt-hours, etc.). Again, in the case of highly technical and expensive machinery or equipment, the Soviet government has little choice but to give production specifications in minute detail. But one central planning agency obviously cannot give detailed instructions to thousands upon thousands of producing units, turning out consumer goods in a multitude of sizes, shades, patterns, styles, designs, and qualities. "Output" must be defined in more general terms—and that is where the problem starts!

Whenever orders are given in units of weight, managers find it easiest to fulfill their output plan by making goods unnecessarily heavy. Thus, writing paper or roofing materials become too thick, screws and bolts are manufactured predominantly in larger sizes. The Soviet humor magazine *Krokodil* once carried a cartoon showing a nail factory which had fulfilled its output plan by producing one single nail, the size of the plant, suspended from the ceiling. To give the orders in square meters of writing paper or in millions of nails would have the opposite, equally undesirable, effect, as paper would then be too thin or nails available in smaller sizes only. During the past year or two, the pages of the Soviet press have been full of examples of frustrating observations and experiences reported by loyal party members, despairing customers, and irate government officials: A truck pool in Moscow province whose output plan is measured in ton-kilometers is reported to be sending some of its trucks on long runs to such far away cities as Kharkov or Minsk; a customer complains that his automobile tire is inadequately repaired and is told by the shop operator that a better repair job would take more time which would prevent the shop from meeting its output quota of 13,500 tire repairs; a lady waits for hours in a beauty parlor for her permanent while other ladies who come in for a shampoo and set are taken ahead of her, because at the government-decreed price the beauty parlor finds it difficult to meet its quota expressed in rubles by giving permanents; the manager of a state retail store finds it disquieting that one of his suppliers sends him dozens upon dozens of ladies' undergarments, all in one color and in but two or three sizes—an easy way to fulfill an output plan specified in numbers of slips and panties! Since the workmanship, as a rule, cannot be measured precisely, many a quantitative output plan is fulfilled at the expense of perfection. But while complaints about the shoddy quality of consumers' goods are an everyday occurrence, harried planners also encounter the opposite situation: One children's clothing factory, for instance, met its output expressed in thousands of rubles of merchandise by putting expensive fur collars on boys' overcoats.

Under the present incentive system, Soviet managers are also under direct inducement to conceal the productive capacities of their plants and to operate their enterprises at less than full capacity. Since their bonuses (which make up a very substantial part of their total income) depend primarily upon their fulfillment or overfulfillment of the output plan, they have a financial interest in getting an easy plan. On the other hand, to greatly overfill the output quota, although momentarily profitable, would be ill advised. As each year's output plan is determined by adding a certain percentage to the output achieved by the plant during the preceding year, gross overfulfillment would inevitably result in gross readjustment of the following year's target.

By the same token, the introduction of new techniques usually represents a drain on the pocketbook of the Soviet executive and of his workers. Since innovating and retooling requires time and effort, it ordinarily involves a temporary reduction in output with obvious consequences on bonuses. Should the new machines fail to augment output, once they have been installed, nothing has been gained. Should they increase productivity, not much has been gained either, as far as the plant manager's take-home pay is concerned, because a more exacting output target is assigned to the plant at the earliest possible moment. Attempts to remedy the situation by granting special bonuses for fulfillment of an "innovation target" have not improved the situation very much. Obviously, a ten per cent increase in the *number* of inventions is no indication of their economic importance, and, in any case, significant inventions are not easily developed according to a preconceived plan. Is it any wonder that the pages of *Pravda* and *Izvestia* frequently depict the trials and tribulations of exasperated Soviet inventors in their attempts to get their inventions adopted?

With regard to the acquisition of machinery and equipment, the Soviet manager, in one way, is in an enviable position, compared with his American peer: neither he nor his company is charged for any equipment allocated to his enterprise by the planning authorities. But, on the other hand, to procure a piece of machinery, a tool, or even a spare part when needed can become a real problem. Under these circumstances, the Soviet manager, primarily interested in fulfilling or overfulfilling the output plan, is obviously under strong temptation to get hold of all the equipment he possibly can, irrespective of immediate or even anticipated needs. As a result, innumerable machines rust idly in storage rooms in a nation which places high priority on rapid industrialization. At the beginning of 1962, uninstalled equipment in the U.S.S.R. equalled approximately the total quantity of such equipment included in the production plans for the entire year.

To overcome such inadequacies as the ones described above, Yevsey G. Liberman proposed a new approach. Under his scheme the central planning authorities would still decide the types of goods to be produced, set quantitative output targets, and specify delivery dates. However, most other decisions, such as number of workers to be hired, wages to be paid, production techniques to be employed, etc. would be made by each plant manager for his own enterprise. Each enterprise would submit its own "profit plan," and profits would become the exclusive basis for managerial bonuses (although different standards would have to be set up for different branches of industry, or even for firms within one industry operating under different natural or technological conditions). Higher incentive premium would be paid for planned than for excess profits in order to give enterprise directors a financial stake in "bidding high." As a further inducement for managers to reveal their plants' true productive capacities and to introduce economically sound innovations, output targets would be kept unchanged for several years, thus removing apprehension that honesty and competent, profitable operation would be penalized by more stringent output assignments. To discourage the hoarding of machinery and equipment, the rate of profit would be computed as a percentage of total fixed and working capital, and the incentive premium scale would rise with an increase in the rate of profit. Since bonuses would not be paid for total output *per se,* and since unsaleable or rejected goods would yield no profits—and therefore no bonuses—the production of unwanted items or of poor quality goods would presumably be strongly discouraged.

Liberman readily admits that his proposal is but a tentative blueprint, subject to revisions, modifications, and improvements. Undoubtedly, many shortcomings will become apparent, many problems will be ironed out, and many alterations will be introduced, as experience is gained through experiments now being carried out in the Kharkov area where Liberman heads the economic laboratory of the regional council.

Some Western commentators see in Liberman's proposals a major step in the direction of a capitalist, free enterprise system. Such an interpretation, however, is surely unwarranted. Although the role of profits and of the profit motive might be traceable to "bourgeois" social science, nothing in the plan should be taken as an indication of an eventual return of the means of production to private ownership, or of a weakening of the foundations of socialism in the U.S.S.R. Profit, while of predominant importance as a measuring rod of efficiency at the enterprise level, is in no way meant to be the determining influence in the central planners' major economic decisions; and the envisaged purpose of the profit motive is only to induce those who administer the local producing units to carry out more efficiently their part of the over-all Plan.

Liberman's plan could probably play an important role in improving the efficiency of Soviet economic performance but Khrushchev, apparently hesitant to delegate too much authority to local enterprise directors, has called for further study and experimentation. However, as Soviet economic life increases in complexity, detailed planning from the center will necessarily become ever more difficult. It therefore seems a reasonable prediction that reforms à la Liberman are in the offing in the U.S.S.R. in the not too distant future.

Be that as it may, the greatest significance of the Liberman proposals lies perhaps neither in their bearing upon the question of the private versus the public ownership of the means of production nor in their prospective impact upon economic efficiency in the U.S.S.R. Their major significance, rather, may well lie in the fact that they arose in the course of frank criticism of long-standing government policies and planning operations, and that they led to an open and uninhibited debate over the feasibility of a revision of Soviet planning procedure, so drastic that in the days of Stalin no one would have dared to propose it.

The

International

8   Society

We now turn to the international scene, where the sovereign nation-state is the basic unit and the major actor. Although during the twentieth century international organizations such as the United Nations, the Organization of American States, NATO, the European Common Market, and many others have played and continue to play an increasingly important role in the international society, their constituent members are nation-states, and their activities are largely determined and controlled by these states.

International society as a whole lacks the institutional framework of the state. Under this framework, peaceful changes can be initiated and carried out through legislation and enforcement of laws by the state government. There is a body of rules called international law, which is to guide the behavior of states in the international arena, but no effective enforcement machinery exists. States follow these norms usually in areas of minor significance such as commercial and diplomatic intercourse because they derive mutual benefits from the orderly conduct of such relations. For fear of retaliation, other international rules—for example, those pertaining to the treatment of prisoners of war—are also adhered to in most cases. But when vital stakes of a state are involved, considerations of what is perceived as the national interest may prompt governments to disregard international law and pursue courses of action that, in their opinion, will best serve their own interests. In such cases, the legal machinery for the settlement of international disputes as provided by the United Nations is largely ignored.

The rejection by national governments of binding international laws for the resolution of essentially political and strategic problems should not be surprising, so long as the concept of sovereignty prevails. It suggests freedom from external control for as long as the sovereign state is the kingpin of international society. Sovereign states and an international law possessing effective sanctions as found in national law are logically incompatible. Either the states are truly sovereign and recognize no superior, in which case no enforcement of any norm from the outside can be accepted; or enforcement against the will of the states is recognized, and then the states are no longer sovereign.

As a consequence of this difficulty, international society has not progressed much beyond the time when the sovereign nation-state emerged in the sixteenth and seventeenth centuries. It is a competitive and in many respects anarchical society in which power is more important than justice, survival is often menaced, and the threat of violence is commonplace. Thomas Hobbes' description of the nature of man characterized by competition, diffidence, and glory is unfortunately even today applicable to the relations between the nation-states. To realize the truth of this statement one needs only to think of the many smaller and larger wars that have occurred in all parts of the globe since 1945 when World War II, the greatest of all holocausts, ended. For this reason it is instructive to recall Hobbes' vivid description of the nature of man in his *Leviathan,* a small excerpt of which is included as the first selected reading in this chapter.

NATIONALISM

One of the most powerful forces in international relations during the last two centuries has been nationalism. It has been both a destructive and a constructive factor, producing international tension and hostility and providing the prerequisites for the emergence of the newly independent states in Asia and Africa since 1945. It has been transforming the political map of the world during the last 180 years and has been gaining in importance as an element in social solidarity as other social ties such as those of the family, the church, and the local community have been weakening.

Nationalism arose as a mass movement following the French Revolution when the national feelings of the common man became an immensely important factor in the relations between states. From then on, wars were fought by common men who proudly called themselves citizens but no longer felt themselves subjects. The battle flags were deployed in the name of freedom and equality, as well as for the sacred and inalienable rights of nations. Thus, the common man was entering on his new political career both as a citizen and as a patriot. The French example of genuine mass patriotism infected the whole continent of Europe, and mass nationalism began to spread all the way from Spain to Russia. The idea that man owed his highest allegiance to his nation was taking hold among all European peoples, reinforcing political structures that had previously come into existence.

The elements of nationalism, whose nature is extremely complex, have been most ably examined and analyzed by Carlton J. H. Hayes in our second selection, entitled "What Nationalism Is." It is interesting to note that nationalism can coexist with any ideology, as the history of the nineteenth and twentieth centuries has demonstrated. It has been liberal-democratic in several Western countries such as the United States, Britain, and France, where popular attachment to democratic ideals is prevalent. It also prospered under all sorts of authoritarian and Fascist regimes, especially Hitler's Germany and Mussolini's Italy. In the Soviet Union and Communist China, nationalism has been wedded to the Marxist-Leninist ideology, which originally was truly cosmopolitan.

A frequent result of nationalism is ethnocentrism, which consists in regarding one's own country as the center of the world and as the only measure of the accomplishments and failures of foreign nations. One's own nationality is viewed as intellectually and morally superior to other nationalities, and other countries are labeled as backward, evil, or unenlightened communities. Most modern nation-states are guilty of ethnocentric bias to varying degrees, and for this reason international understanding between different countries has often suffered. In addition, the meaning of terms such as "democracy" and "liberation" varies between the Western and Communist worlds, giving rise to confusion and conflicts and thereby further accentuating the differences between the nations of the world.

Perhaps the most striking example of destructive nationalism in recent times has been the Germany of Adolf Hitler. Nationalism was shaped by Hitler into a force bent on aggression, territorial expansion, and the subjugation of other nationalities. The German nation was deified while other countries were vilified as decadent societies. Hitler and his associates manipulated and exploited the frenzied nationalism they had created and turned the German rank and file into blind and fanatical worshippers of a nearly "divine" leader. Marching abroad to make slaves of the populations of foreign countries—France, Russia, Poland, and others—the Nazis offered one of the most horrible spectacles of nationalism degenerating into contempt and hatred.

The best example of recent constructive nationalism has been the fight of Asian and African peoples against colonialism and for national self-determination. The main goal of national self-determination is the freedom of a nationality to determine its own political fate and to manage its own affairs. A second purpose is to unite all members of this nationality within the borders of their own nation-state.

The triumph of national self-determination does not necessarily mean that the members of the nationality who have won their own state will enjoy democratic freedoms as understood in Western terms. Many of the new African states have one-party legislatures and only thinly veiled dictatorial governments. This is due mainly to the lack of political maturity in countries where societies are still tribal and where political values are not commensurate with the ideals and practices of Western democracy. Moreover, self-determination for one nationality may have unfortunate consequences for people of another nationality, as was the case for Englishmen in East and Central Africa and for Frenchmen in North Africa when the countries of these areas received their independence.

The triumph of self-determination has not been an unmixed blessing for the new Asian and African states. They have found it difficult to replace foreign administrators with their own people because trained native personnel are in short supply. They have had to face expenditures formerly borne by the colonial powers and have been confronted with a variety of economic difficulties. We will return to this problem later.

THE FUTURE OF THE NATION-STATE

The loyalties that citizens attach to their state are based at least in part on the implied assumption that the state will provide certain services in return. Among these services are protection from hostile external forces, military as well as economic, and assurance of the necessary conditions for economic well-being and for steady improvement of living standards. Traditionally, protection from external forces presupposed that the government had full control over the state's territory and could prevent hostile penetration of the territorial boundaries. Economic well-being was closely linked to economic self-sufficiency in terms of supply and markets and to assured lines of transportation for needed raw materials.

The tremendous advances made by technology during the twentieth century and especially since World War II cast doubt on the continuing validity of these assumptions. Consequently, the frontiers of a state have been losing their meaning as lines delineating a territory under the complete sovereignty of its government. The main challenges have come from technological developments in warfare—from bombers, long-range ballistic missiles, and orbiting space platforms possibly linked with nuclear weapons. The interior of states can now be effectively struck from outside; even the superpowers, the United States and the Soviet Union, cannot prevent such intrusions into their territory. Other challenges to the sovereign control of territories have come from psychological warfare and changing economic conditions. Radio is extensively used for propaganda, and even the best jamming devices have not been capable of fully silencing the intruding radio voice, no matter how unwelcome it may be. Industrialization and mass production have greatly increased the economic vulnerability of states because of their dependence on external sources of supplies and markets which can be cut off by military and economic warfare.

In a brilliant analysis, Professor John Herz has examined the elements leading to the decline of the nation-state. Although Herz's cogent observations were made in the late 1950's, they are even more applicable today, since technological developments have increased the capabilities of external forces to intrude into the territories of individual nation-states.

What have been the responses of the nation-states to meet the new challenges? The most prominent device to overcome the military deficiencies and vulnerabilities inherent in the new technology has been the formation of regional units, either in the form of traditional alliances or through the establishment of regional international organizations endowed with a variety of institutions for common decision-making. While alliances between states date back to the beginning of recorded history, regional organizations are of much more recent origin and have become especially conspicuous in the wake of the ideological and strategic struggles between the Communist and anti-Communist blocs since World War II.

Within the Free World, it is the North Atlantic Treaty Organization (NATO) which is the most important defense unit. Concerned with the defense of western Europe, its members include the United States, Canada, Great Britain, and a number of other European allies. NATO has not superseded national controls over defense, and employment of nuclear weapons remains within the authority of those states that possess them. Nevertheless, common defense programs are negotiated by the members of NATO, and a beginning has been made in the coordination of nuclear policies. As a consequence, the independence of the participating governments in the formulation and execution of their military policies becomes somewhat restricted, although final decisions remain within the sphere of their national competence. Other Free World military organizations include the South East Asia Treaty Organization (SEATO), a modified version of NATO with responsibilities mainly in Asia; the Organization of American States (OAS), concerned with inter-American defense problems; and the Central Treaty Organization (CENTO), whose major interests lie in the Middle East and western Asia.

The Communist counterpart of NATO is the Warsaw Pact Organization, which includes the Soviet Union and her East European satellite countries such as Poland, Czechoslovakia, Hungary, Romania, and others. While within NATO the views of the United States, by far the greatest contributor, often prevail, the remaining members are not coerced. The Soviet Union has consistently dominated the Warsaw Pact Organization, as seen in the Czechoslovakian developments of late 1968. It is interesting to note that divergent attitudes are coming increasingly to the fore in both NATO and the Warsaw Pact Organization—France has defected from NATO and Romania shows signs of independence—and for this reason the future of both organizations remains somewhat uncertain.

In order to meet their responsibility for the economic well-being of their citizens, a number of states have also formed regional organizations of an economic nature. The most prominent of these are found in Europe. One is the European Economic Community, better known as the Common Market, composed of France, West Germany, Italy, and the Benelux countries. The other is the European Free Trade Association (EFTA) made up of Britain, the Scandinavian countries, Switzerland, Austria, and Portugal. The main objective of these organizations—the formation of a larger market than is offered by the individual member states—is accomplished through the elimination of all tariffs between the participating countries. Both organizations have been successful in materially raising the levels of economic activity and the standard of living of the citizens in the member states. The goals of the Common Market are more extensive than those of EFTA, and there has been hope that the Common Market would lead eventually to the political unification of all of Western Europe, perhaps in the form of a United States of Europe. This hope was based on the initial restrictions of sovereignty of the member states that were stipulated in the Common Market treaty and on the authorization in certain instances to take decisions by majority vote precluding any veto of a member state.

The success of the two European organizations in the creation of mass markets has been contagious, and attempts have been made in Latin America and Africa to emulate them. For a number of reasons, however, the Latin American Free Trade Area (LAFTA) and the Central American Common Market have not come up to the expectations of their founders. Various endeavors in Africa to create larger trading units have been even less successful.

Despite these extensions of existing nation-states into regional organizations for military and economic reasons, no "region-state" has yet developed. The most promising and advanced unit, the European Common Market, has failed to progress on the path to political unification during the last few years and may in fact have slipped back. General de Gaulle's exaltation of nationalism appears to have killed the fledgling European enthusiasm for a united state. Thus we must recognize that the nation-state persists as the supreme unit in international society and is likely to continue to do so at least within the foreseeable future. The fires of nationalism, which seemed to be banked during the first fifteen years after World War II, have been rekindled in western Europe and continue to burn brightly in other parts of the world as well. Man has not yet accepted a compass of loyalties more extensive than the customary one to his national state, and most governments of nation-states appear to view extensions into regional units more as a buttress of their own sovereignty than as a possible transition into a larger political entity.

THE " THIRD WORLD "

One of the most difficult problems facing international society is the continuing gap between the economically advanced countries and the underdeveloped countries of the world. The plight of the latter, which prefer to call themselves the "developing" rather than the underdeveloped countries, is basically that they cannot find the capital they need for improving their desperate economic position. With approximately 70 per cent of the world's population, their contribution to total world production is only 10 per cent. This imbalance has not only economic, but also serious political implications. Most of the developing countries are located in Asia, Africa, and Latin America, and virtually all of the newly independent countries belong to this group. They are frequently referred to as the "Third World."[1]

Eugene Staley, in our fourth selection for this chapter, succinctly describes the economic, social, and political characteristics of the developing world and identifies the countries that fall into this classification. It is obvious from his description that the countries of the Third World have great difficulties in solving their problems by their own efforts. They must rely on outside food supplies, at least in years of poor harvests, and on outside advice regarding the means of birth control if they wish to curb the population explosion, so much more extensive and much more serious in the developing countries than for the economically advanced areas of the world. They depend on outside financial and technical help for industrialization, which is indispensable to increase their national incomes and make them less susceptible to the fluctuations of the prices for their agricultural and mineral export commodities on which they presently rely for the bulk of their revenues. Finally, they need infusions of modern technology and proper schooling for their inhabitants in order to provide the underpinnings for a stable political order.

Unfortunately, aid to the Third World is often tied up with political considerations emanating from the global struggle between the Free World and Communist forces. Yet aid should be dispensed according to economic need and economic promise and should eventually become a cooperative enterprise in which all economically advanced countries should participate in accordance with their national incomes. Such aid is not a matter of charity, but needs to be regarded as the fulfillment of enlightened economic and political self-interest. Without adequate financial aid and technical

---

1 This is an ambiguous term inasmuch as it implies that the globe can be divided into Free World, Communist, and uncommitted countries. While perhaps most of the developing countries fall in the third category, they also are found in the first two categories. See the listing in our selection by Staley.

assistance, the population explosion in the Third World may well become a political revolution whose dimensions and direction nobody can foresee.

THE QUEST FOR PEACE AND THE
BALANCE OF POWER

In our international society, characterized by competition and conflict of national interests and devoid of an enforceable legal order, war has been a frequent intruder. Yet, since 1648, when nation-states became the principals of international society, there have also been prolonged periods of peace, which often were the result of a precarious balancing of powers between the various states.

Although all sovereign states could theoretically participate in a balance-of-power system, the balance was maintained in fact by only a few larger states in Europe. Whenever one state made a bid for dominant power, other states tended to join in an alliance which opposed the first state's quest for ascendancy and the challenge to the status quo. As a consequence, the major challenges in Europe by Louis XIV, Napoleon, and the German Kaiser ultimately ended in defeat at the hands of opposing coalitions.

The balance-of-power system attained its greatest success between 1815 and 1914 when the stability of Europe was developed from the Congress of Vienna, in which the main participants were Great Britain, Austria, France, Prussia, and Russia. Wars were mostly localized, were of relatively short duration, and did not spread into general conflagrations. Aware of the benefits of the system, the victors refrained from eliminating any of the major opponents, even if they were capable of annexing the territory of the defeated country. On the other hand, smaller countries were occasionally gobbled up, as the division of Poland—in three stages—between Russia, Prussia, and Austria demonstrates.

The main elements making up the power of a state permitting it to play a role in the balance-of-power system are the size and location of its territory, its economic strength, the size and skills of its population, its political traditions, and last, but obviously not least, its military force. During the nineteenth century, the stability of the system was enhanced by the fact that industrialization and colonial expansion could be undertaken with relative ease and great profitability, and the pursuit of these activities was much more promising in enlarging the power of a country than military subjugation of a neighbor. Moreover, no dramatic changes in technology, such as the invention of nuclear weapons, upset the power relationship of the member states. However, some gradual changes in the system did take place, which eventually created difficulties. Foremost among them was the unification of both Germany and Italy and the aspirations of these countries for a greater role in world affairs.

Following the traumatic experiences of World War I, which some observers thought of as having been caused by the imperfections of the balance-of-power system, mankind searched for a new device to maintain the peace of the world. The answer seemed to be a system of collective security, which simply means that an attack on any one state would be regarded as an attack on all states participating in the collective security system and requires repulsion of the attack by the combined forces of these states. The resort to collective security was based on the assumption that it would do for international society what police action does for the domestic community. The early organization for collective security was the League of Nations, founded in 1919, which was to replace the insecurity of fluctuating national alliances.

The failure of the League to develop an effective peace-keeping machinery caused widespread disillusionment with the concept of collective security. Of course, contributing in no small measure to this failure was the unwillingness of the United States to join the League. In the meantime, the United States and Japan, two non-European powers, had begun to play increasingly important roles on the world scene. As a result, balance-of-power considerations were gradually shifting from the European plane to the global level.

The end of World War II saw a new effort to establish a collective security system in the form of the United Nations. Founded basically on the concept of co-sovereign equality among the member states, the United Nations charter nevertheless accords veto rights to the five permanent members of the Security Council, the central organ for collective security. As a consequence, collective security action by the United Nations proved to be impossible unless the great Powers—the United States, the Soviet Union, Great Britain, France, and the Republic of China—could come to an agreement.

Another reason for the difficulties of the United Nations in its efforts for peace was the emergence of two superpowers at the end of World War II—the United States and the Soviet Union. When the Russians mastered the secrets of the atomic bomb in the late 1940's, the world moved in the direction of a bipolar balance of power. The two main protagonists of the struggle sought to maintain this balance by building up two tightly controlled blocs of military alliances in which NATO was the main device for the free world camp and the Warsaw Pact for the Communist camp. What kept the world from sliding into another tragedy of a general conflagration during that time was not the United Nations or collective security, but the "balance of terror." Both parties were fully aware that in a nuclear holocaust nobody would be a victor. Our fifth reading, an article by Albert Wohlstetter, discusses the problems inherent in mutual deterrence and the implications for the maintenance of peace.

Toward the end of the 1950's the tight control of the two superpowers over their blocs began to loosen. Some of the West European states, their economies restored and imbued with a new spirit of independence, became reluctant to follow the demands of American policy. In the Communist camp, an ideological and strategic struggle between the Soviet Union and Communist China broke out that created an increasingly wider rift between the two chief Communist powers. At the same time, the East European satellites began to show signs of independent national aspirations, which slowly began to reduce the tight control that the Soviet Union had initially exercised over these countries. In addition, the two superpowers lost their nuclear monopoly. Britain, France, and Communist China were able to become members of the nuclear club, with other countries also approaching the threshold. Instead of a strictly bipolar world, a number of power centers are beginning to emerge in international society. These centers of power play an increasingly important role in the international arena and include not only blocs, but also single states and the United Nations, which has been adopted by many of the weaker states as their favorite forum. The nature of international society that seems to be developing can thus best be labeled polycentric, but the full implications of this system for the future are still obscure at this time. While deterrence continues to keep nuclear danger at bay, the spread of nuclear weapons to more and more countries portends serious hazards. Although the concept of balance of power may still have some application in the emerging polycentric world, the clear and continually present danger of a nuclear debacle makes it more and more imperative that the United Nations be made into a more effective instrument for achieving the peace and well-being of the world. This may be the urgent task for the 1970's, and it is for this reason that we close the chapter with an address by Dean Rusk which evaluates the first twenty-five years of the United Nations and looks at what the next decade may hold for the organization.

Of the Natural Condition of Mankind as Concerning Their Felicity, and Misery

THOMAS HOBBES

Men by nature equal. Nature hath made men so equal, in the faculties of the body, and mind; as that though there be found one man sometimes manifestly stronger in body, or of quicker mind than another; yet when all is reckoned together, the difference between man, and man, is not so considerable, as that one man can thereupon claim to himself any benefit, to which another may not pretend, as well as he. For as to the strength of body, the weakest has strength enough to kill the strongest, either by secret machination, or by confederacy with others, that are in the same danger with himself.

And as to the faculties of the mind, setting aside the arts grounded upon words, and especially that skill of proceeding upon general, and infallible rules, called science; which very few have, and but in few things; as being not a native faculty, born with us; nor attained, as prudence, while we look after somewhat else, I find yet a greater equality amongst men, than that of strength. For prudence, is but experience; which equal time, equally bestows on all men, in those things they equally apply themselves unto. That which may perhaps make such equality incredible, is but a vain conceit of one's own wisdom, which almost all men think they

Reprinted from Thomas Hobbes, *Leviathan,* ed. Michael Oakeshott (Oxford: Basil Blackwell, Publisher, 1957), pp. 80–84.

have in a greater degree, than the vulgar; that is, than all men but themselves, and a few others, whom by fame, or for concurring with themselves, they approve. For such is the nature of men, that howsoever they may acknowledge many others to be more witty, or more eloquent, or more learned; yet they will hardly believe there be many so wise as themselves; for they see their own wit at hand, and other men's at a distance. But this proveth rather that men are in that point equal, than unequal. For there is not ordinarily a greater sign of the equal distribution of any thing, than that every man is contented with his share.

From equality proceeds diffidence. From this equality of ability, ariseth equality of hope in the attaining of our ends. And therefore if any two men desire the same thing, which nevertheless they cannot both enjoy, they become enemies; and in the way to their end, which is principally their own conservation, and sometimes their delectation only, endeavour to destroy, or subdue one another. And from hence it comes to pass, that where an invader hath no more to fear, than another man's single power; if one plant, sow, build, or possess a convenient seat, others may probably be expected to come prepared with forces united, to dispossess, and deprive him, not only of the fruit of his labour, but also of his life, or liberty. And the invader again is in the like danger of another.

From diffidence war. And from this diffidence of one another, there is no way for any man to secure himself, so reasonable, as anticipation; that is, by force, or wiles, to master the persons of all men he can, so long, till he see no other power great enough to endanger him: and this is no more than his own conservation requireth, and is generally allowed. Also because there be some, that taking pleasure in contemplating their own power in the acts of conquest, which they pursue farther than their security requires; if others, that otherwise would be glad to be at ease within modest bounds, should not by invasion increase their power, they would not be able, long time, by standing only on their defence, to subsist. And by consequence, such augmentation of dominion over men being necessary to a man's conservation, it ought to be allowed him.

Again, men have no pleasure, but on the contrary a great deal of grief, in keeping company, where is no power able to over-awe them all. For every man looketh that his companion should value him, at the same rate he sets upon himself: and upon all signs of contempt, or undervaluing, naturally endeavours, as far as he dares, (which amongst them that have no common power to keep them in quiet, is far enough to make them destroy each other), to extort a greater value from his contemners, by damage; and from others, by the example.

...[In] the nature of man, we find three principal causes of quarrel. First, competition; secondly, diffidence; thirdly, glory.

The first, maketh men invade for gain; the second, for safety; and the third, for reputation. The first use violence, to make themselves masters of other men's persons, wives, children, and cattle; the second, to defend them; the third, for trifles, as a word, a smile, a different opinion, and any other sign of undervalue, either direct in their persons, or by reflection in their kindred, their friends, their nation, their profession, or their name.

Out of civil states, there is always war of every one against every one. Hereby it is manifest, that during the time men live without a common power to keep them all in awe, they are in that condition which is called war; and such a war, as is of every man, against every man. For WAR, consisteth not in battle only, or the act of fighting; but in a tract of time, wherein the will to contend by battle is sufficiently known: and therefore the notion of *time,* is to be considered in the nature of war; as it is in the nature of weather. For as the nature of foul weather, lieth not in a shower or two of rain; but in an inclination thereto of many days together: so the nature of war, consisteth not in actual fighting; but in the known disposition thereto, during all the time there is no assurance to the contrary. All other time is PEACE.

The incommodities of such a war. Whatsoever therefore is consequent to a time of war, where every man is enemy to every man; the same is consequent to the time, wherein men live without other security, than what their own strength, and their own invention shall furnish them withal. In such condition, there is no place for industry; because the fruit thereof is uncertain: and consequently no culture of the earth; no navigation, nor use of the commodities that may be imported by sea; no commodious building; no instruments of moving, and removing, such things as require much force; no knowledge of the face of the earth; no account of time; no arts; no letters; no society; and which is worst of all, continual fear, and danger of violent death; and the life of man, solitary, poor, nasty, brutish, and short.

It may seem strange to some man, that has not well weighed these things; that nature should thus dissociate, and render men apt to invade, and destroy one another: and he may therefore, not trusting to this inference, made from the passions, desire perhaps to have the same confirmed by experience. Let him therefore consider with himself, when taking a journey, he arms himself, and seeks to go well accompanied; when going to sleep, he locks his doors; when even in his house he locks his chests; and this when he knows there be laws, and public officers, armed, to revenge all injuries shall be done him; what opinion he has of his fellow-subjects, when he rides armed; of his fellow citizens, when he locks his doors; and of his children, and servants, when he locks his chests. Does he not there as much accuse mankind by his actions, as I do by my words? But neither of us accuse man's nature in it. The desires, and other passions of man, are in themselves no sin. No more are the actions, that proceed from those passions, till they know a law that forbids them: which till laws be made they cannot know: nor can any law be made, till they have agreed upon the person that shall make it.

It may peradventure be thought, there was never such a time, nor condition of war as this; and I believe it was never generally so, over all the world: but there are many places, where they live so now. For the savage people in many places of America, except the government of small families, the concord whereof dependeth on natural lust, have no government at all; and live at this day in that brutish manner, as I said before. Howsoever, it may be perceived what manner of life there would be, where there were no common power to fear, by the manner of life, which men that have formerly lived under a peaceful government, use to degenerate into, in a civil war.

But though there had never been any time, wherein particular men were in a condition of war one against another; yet in all times, kings, and persons of sovereign authority, because of their independency, are in continual jealousies, and in the state and posture of gladiators; having their weapons pointing, and their eyes fixed on one another; that is, their forts, garrisons, and guns upon the frontiers of their kingdoms; and continual spies upon their neighbours; which is a posture of war. But because they uphold thereby, the industry of their subjects; there does not follow from it, that misery, which accompanies the liberty of particular men.

In such a war nothing is unjust. To this war of every man, against every man, this also is consequent; that nothing can be unjust. The notions of right and wrong, justice and injustice have there no place. Where there is no common power, there is no law: where no law, no injustice. Force, and fraud, are in war the two cardinal virtues. Justice, and injustice are none of the faculties neither of the body, nor mind. If they were, they might be in a man that were alone in the world, as well as his senses, and passions. They are qualities, that relate to men in society, not in solitude. It is consequent also to the same condition, that there be no propriety, no dominion, no *mine* and *thine* distinct; but only that to be every man's, that he can get: and for so long, as he can keep it. And thus much for the ill condition, which man by mere nature is actually placed in; though with a possibility to come out of it, consisting partly in the passions, partly in his reason. . . .

What Nationalism Is

CARLTON J. H. HAYES

BASES OF NATIONALITY:
LANGUAGE AND TRADITIONS

Nationalism is an obvious and impelling movement in the modern and contemporary world. It is so obvious, indeed, and so frequently mentioned in the news, that it is apt to be taken for granted, like the rising and setting of the sun, and its importance overlooked.

Nationalism, as we know it, is a modern development. It has had its origin and rise in Europe, and through European influence and example it has been implanted in America and all other areas of Western civilization. But it is now no longer peculiar to the Christian West.

It has recently become an outstanding feature of states and peoples throughout the vast expanses of Asia and Africa, amid the traditional civilizations of Muslim, Hindu, Confucian, and Buddhist. It is especially evidenced across the whole breadth of the Muslim world: in the Turkey of Ataturk, in the Iran of Riza Pahlevi, in the Egypt of Nasser, in the separation of Pakistan from India, in the successful revolt of Indonesia against the Dutch, in the recently won independence of Libya, the Sudan, Somalia, Tunis, and Morocco, and in the Algerian rebellion. It is basic to the conflict between Arabs and Israelis.

Moreover, to a fully developed nationalism in Japan have now been

Reprinted with permission of The Macmillan Company from *Nationalism: A Religion* by Carlton J. H. Hayes. Copyright 1960 by The Macmillan Company.

added the nascent and militant nationalisms of India, Burma, Ceylon, Malaya, Vietnam, Cambodia, Laos, Thailand, and, most recently of colored peoples almost everywhere in Africa. In its latest stage, nationalism is proving the dissolvent of overseas colonial empires of Britain, France, the Netherlands, and Belgium, and probably too, before long, that of Portugal. And we should not overlook the fact that nationalism, as well as communism, is a mark of contemporary Russia and China.

What actually is this nationalism which is now so universal? It may best be understood, I think, by concentrating attention on Europe, and at first on western Europe. For here is its original home; here, its roots demonstrably reach far back into the past; and here, for at least five centuries, it has been an increasingly important factor in the evolution of our historic civilization.

In simplest terms, nationalism may be defined as a fusion of patriotism with a consciousness of nationality. For proper understanding of the matter, both *nationality* and *patriotism* require some explanation.

For centuries and for millenniums—as far back as we have any historical knowledge—the world has contained a large number of different nationalities. In Europe, the smallest of the five major continents, there has long been a variety of diverse nationalities: Greek, Latin, Celtic, German, Baltic, Slavic, Magyar, and so forth, some thirty-three at least at the present time.

Now what is a *nationality*? The word derives from the Latin *natio,* implying a common racial descent, but few, if any, modern nationalities consist of a distinctive "race" in the biological sense. Frenchmen are a nationality compounded of such different types as Mediterranean, Nordic, and Alpine. Germans include long-headed blonds and round-headed brunets. Italians represent curious mixtures of Etruscans, Phoenicians, and primitive Celts, of Saracens, Goths, and Norsemen. And in the United States Negroes belong, not to any African nationality, but, along with whites and red men, to the American nationality. Every nationality of which I have knowledge has been, or is, biologically and racially, a melting pot.

Nor is nationality determined simply by physical geography. To be sure, certain cultural features of Arctic peoples are bound to differ from those of tropical peoples, and both from life in temperate zones. For geographical reasons Czechs can hardly be expected to become a sea-faring nationality, or the English not to become such. Yet, something other than geography has to explain why Englishmen from their island built up in modern times a great navy and merchant marine, while Irishmen from their adjacent island didn't. Or why similar habitats, climates, and pursuits failed to weld Frenchmen and Germans into a single nationality. Or why the mountainous ruggedness of Scotland and Switzerland is supposed to explain the proverbial thriftiness of their inhabitants, but fails utterly to do so in the case of Dutchmen or of the French peasantry.

No, a nationality receives its impress, its character, its individuality, not, unless very incidentally, from physical geography or biological race, but rather from cultural and historical forces. First and foremost among these I would put *language.*

Language is peculiarly human, and at least ever since the legendary Tower of Babel there has been a wide, fluid, and baffling variety of languages. Anthropologists have shown that primitive tribes are marked off from one another by differences of speech. And alike to scholars and laymen it should be obvious that language is the surest badge of nationality. It is the one thing which all persons of a particular country have in common, whether they be rich or poor, good or bad, intelligent or stupid; and it is the one thing which distinguishes them from all other persons. It is common, for example, to all Germans, whether they be long-headed or round-headed, whether they live on the Alpine heights of the Tyrol or at sea level in Hamburg; and it differentiates them from all Frenchmen, including those who may be just like Germans in race and habitat.

Likewise, language is a tangible tie between the present generation of a nation and preceding generations. The English language ties the subjects of Elizabeth II with those of Elizabeth I, and Americans of the twentieth century with those of the seventeenth and eighteenth. Similarly the German language joins people who heard Martin Luther with those who have more recently listened to Adolf Hitler and [still later heard] Konrad Adenauer. Of every nationality, language bespeaks both the solidarity and the continuity of a people. And national literature, in its many forms of prose and poetry, history, and romance, does much to emphasize what is supposedly peculiar to a nationality rather than what is fundamentally common to mankind.

Along with language, and a close second to it in importance in constituting a nationality and distinguishing it from others, are *historical traditions.* These comprise an accumulation of remembered or imagined experiences of the past, an accumulation differing in content and emphasis from one linguistic group to another.

There are several kinds of historical tradition and background. There is (a) a people's religious past, whether, for instance, it was traditionally Christian, and if so whether Catholic like Italy or Spain, or Protestant like Sweden, or Eastern Orthodox like Greece or Russia, or divided between different forms of religion, like Germany and the United States. Religious traditions, it should be stressed, have been very important in shaping human culture, not merely by providing certain beliefs, but by establishing and maintaining particular social *mores,* observances, and habits, and by influencing literature and law.

There is also (b) a people's territorial past, its ancestral soil, involving a popular, sentimental regard for a homeland where one's forebears lived and are buried, a homeland that, though perhaps now fallen somewhat from a once high estate, still evokes memory and emulation of past greatness and glory. I need only mention, by way of illustration, the appeal of Jerusalem and Palestine to Jews, the "auld sod" to Irish, the Hellenic lands and isles to Greeks.

Then there is (c) a people's political past, whether their nation was detached from a big empire or expanded from a tribal state, whether it dominated other peoples or was long subject to alien rule, what government it has traditionally had—monarchical or republican, absolutist or constitutional, or democratic. There is (d) a people's fighting past, its exploits of valor and prowess, whether chiefly by land or by sea, whether victorious or vanquished.

A people may be more united and nationalistic through grief over defeat than through celebration of triumph. Serbs for centuries have recalled in glowing verse and fireside folk tales their valorous but disastrous defeat by the Turks at Kossovo in 1389. The epic fate of the "Invincible Armada" is 1588 stirred and spurred vanquished Spain scarcely less than victorious England.

There is, besides, (e) a people's industrial and economic past, whether it has been more or less advanced— "progressive" or "backward," to use a contemporary dichotomy—in agriculture, or trade, or manufacturing, or in all three, or has been famous for some specialized industry, and whether, too, it has had greater or less class wealth and distinctions. Lastly we may mention (f) a people's cultural past, what distinctive and distinguished literature and architecture and pictorial arts and music it has produced, and what scholarship and learning and degree of popular literacy.

FLUIDITY AND COMPLEXITY OF NATIONALITY

All the foregoing and similar *historical traditions* are matters of culture, and so is *language.* Together, they constitute the cultural bases of nationality. Hence I would define nationality as "a cultural group of people who speak a common language (or closely related dialects) and who possess a community of historical traditions (religious, territorial, political, military, economic, artistic, and intellectual)." When such a group—such a nationality—cherishes in marked degree, and extols, its common language and traditions, the result is *cultural nationalism.*

Cultural nationalism may exist with or without political nationalism. For nationalities can and do exist for fairly long periods without political unity and independence. A notable example has been the Jewish or Israeli nationality; and scarcely less notable have been the Gaelic or Irish, the Polish, and the several Balkan nationalities. A nationality may be partitioned among two or more states, like the German or the Italian or the Basque, or it may be incorporated with others in a single state, like Switzerland or Belgium. Switzerland includes portions of three nationalities: German, French, and Italian. Belgium contains parts of two: French and Dutch-Flemish. If we are to grasp what a nationality is, we must avoid confusing it with state or nation. There is a Swiss state and nation, but, strictly speaking, no Swiss nationality. In like manner, there is a Belgian state and nation, but not a Belgian nationality.

The tendency has been, of course, for cultural nationalism to lead to political nationalism, and for each nationality to strive to establish an independent national state of its own. Yet, even in Europe, this goal has not yet been completely achieved. Countries which are usually thought of as possessing long-established national states, such as Great Britain, France, and Spain, still harbor national minorities with dissident languages and traditions. Besides Englishmen, Britain has Scots, Welsh, and some Irish. Besides Frenchmen, France has Provençals, Bretons, and Flemings. Besides Castilians, Spain has Catalans, Basques, and Portuguese-Galicians.

We should recognize, moreover, the fluidity of nationalities in the long run of history, and the existence of what may be called "subnationalities" or "secondary nationalities." Nationality has always existed throughout human history, just as there has always been differentiated human culture with variety of languages and customs and traditions. But specific nationalities have appeared and disappeared, risen and fallen. We know that in antiquity there were Hittite and Phoenician and Etruscan nationalities, Elamite and Edomite nationalities, but where are they now? They are gone, quite swallowed up long ago; only their names and some of their monuments remain. On the other hand, when they throve, where then were the French and English nationalities? These were nonexistent; their distinctive languages were not formed in antiquity, but only in the Middle Ages.

Since the sixteenth century, members of European nationalities have migrated overseas, carrying with them their languages and traditional culture. Thus the American continents were partitioned among Spanish, Portuguese, French and English nationalities, and South Africa became the home of a segment of the Dutch nationality. All this developed when America and South Africa—to say nothing of Australasia and the Philippines—were far more remote from Europe than they are today. Then there were only sailing vessels and no cables or radio or airplanes. The remoteness of the overseas settlers from Europe and the novel frontier life they led, coping with strange lands and strange peoples, gradually served to qualify and add to the historical traditions which they had originally brought with them from the mother country.

Eventually, as we know, the widening differences were accentuated by the forceful revolutionary breaking of political ties, so that in the Americas an independent United States of English-speaking people emerged, and likewise a group of independent republics of Spanish-speaking peoples, an independent Portuguese-speaking Brazil, and an independent Haiti and autonomous Quebec of French-speaking peoples, while in South Africa the Dutch acquired practical independence. And political independence, it is hardly necessary to point out, has operated to provide the new nations with special historical traditions at variance not only with one another's but those of parental or primary nationalities in Europe.

Wherefore the nationalities in America—English, Spanish, Portuguese, French—may conveniently be described as secondary, or subnationalities. They have the same languages as their counterparts in Europe, with only dialect differences; but they possess and cherish divergent historical traditions, and a firm will to maintain free and sovereign national states. Special bonds of culture and sympathy survive, of course, between secondary nationalities and their respective primary nationalities. Common language means that Shakespeare, Milton, and Keats are as much a heritage of the people of the United States as of England, and, vice versa, that modern American novels find a large market among Englishmen. It also helps to explain why for almost a century and a half there has been no war between Britain and the United States, why, rather, they have fought side by side in the World Wars of the present century, and are likely to stand together in "cold" or "hot" wars of the future. Likewise, common language, with common literature and customs, contributes to a continuing sympathetic feeling between European Spaniards on the one hand and Spanish Americans and Filipinos on the other, and between Portuguese and Brazilians; and this despite marked racial differences.

The Dominion of Canada contains two secondary nationalities: French Canadian, and English-speaking Canadian; and the latter may conceivably consist of such "tertiary" nationalities as British Canadian and Irish Canadian, for example. Among other self-governing members of the British Commonwealth, Australia and New Zealand have come to comprise a secondary nationality each, while the Union of South Africa includes at least three: Dutch, English, and indigenous Negro.

Further illustrative of the fluidity and complexity of nationality, is the existence of sectionalism, with its tendency to create and preserve separatist variations of dialect and historic tradition and to threaten the unity of a people. In the United States we have had a glaring spectacle of sectionalism and of its issue, a century ago, in a long bloody struggle to break an American "secondary" nationality into two: a Northern States' and a Southern States'; and though political union was preserved and fortified, we all know that a kind of peculiar and "tertiary" American nationality has survived to this day in Dixie.

Furthermore, we should remark here that nationalism as an exalting of nationality is somewhat more artificially stimulated, though no less potent, in a country like the United States than in a European country such as England or France or Sweden or Germany. It is naturally so. In Europe everyone is aware of belonging to a particular nationality with distinguishing language and traditions; and one's nationalism is a relatively normal outgrowth and expression of it. In the United States, on the other hand, where the population consists of descendants of immigrants from a great variety of European nationalities, to say nothing of Negroes and Asiatics and indigenous Indian tribesmen, nationalism is invoked and pressed into service as creator and assurer of a novel and unifying American nationality—a national "melting pot."

PATRIOTISM

Nationality is a fact, and from the dawn of history there has been a multiplicity of nationalities in various stages of development or decline. But until people are conscious of nationality and make it the prime object of their *patriotism,* they do not produce cultural or political nationalism.

What, then, is patriotism? It is "love of country," yes. As "love" it is an emotion, involving fondness, sympathy, fidelity, loyalty. In one form or another, it appears to be instinctive with man, a natural part and essential prop of his gregariousness. It is basic to human life in family, in locality, in society.

Love of country is an aggregate of several kinds of loyalty. It involves a "feline" loyalty to familiar places, a "canine" loyalty to familiar persons, a distinctively human loyalty to familiar ideas and usages. There may be various objects of these combined loyalties—of this patriotism. It may be family or clan or tribe. It may be village or town. It may be a province or an empire or any sort of state. It may be a club or a Masonic lodge or a church. It may be a nationality.

Loyalty to familiar places is relatively natural, but it requires artificial effort—purposeful conscious education and training—to render man loyal to the sum total of places, unfamiliar as well as familiar, in an entire country inhabited by his nationality. In French, distinction is usefully made between *patrie* (one's whole nation or "fatherland") and *pays* (one's immediate homeland). Everybody, besides having

a *patrie,* has a *pays.* My own *pays* is New York, particularly the south central part of Upstate New York. Here I was born and spent my youth. Here five generations of both paternal and maternal ancestors lived and are buried. Here is my true home, along the gently flowing Susquehanna and amid the smiling wooded hills. Hither I resort whenever I can. This *pays* is for me a primary and most natural stimulus of patriotic sentiment and loyalty. Yet I have been taught—and am expected—to extend this sentiment and loyalty to such unfamiliar places as Alaska, North Dakota, Oklahoma and Utah, and at the same time to withhold them from Canada and Mexico.

Similarly, loyalty to familiar persons —to family, friends, and neighbors— is natural and usual. But special civic training is required to make a man loyal to the sum total of persons, familiar and unfamiliar, who constitute his whole nationality. And it takes additional training for a man to learn that he should respect and obey, and be patriotic about, national officials who carry on remote from him.

Furthermore, man being man, it is natural for him to be loyal to some ideas and ideals which occur to him and which he thinks good. But most such ideas do not germinate spontaneously within him. Rather, they are carried to, and seeded in him by his fellows. And it necessitates systematic and repeated efforts to implant in the masses of an extended nationality a community of national thought and ideals to which they will be loyal.

Patriotism, therefore, while instinctive in its origin and root, is much more naturally and readily associated with a small community in a restricted area than with a large nationality in a broad expanse of territory. Only through an intensive and extensive educational process will a local group of people become thoroughly aware of their entire nationality and supremely loyal to it.

The cultural bases of nationality, let me repeat, are a common language and common historical traditions. When these by some process of education become the objects of popular emotional patriotism, the result is nationalism.

There are degrees of nationalism, as of any emotion. Our loyalty to nationality and national state may be conditioned by other loyalties—to family, to church, to humanity, to internationalism—and hence restricted in corresponding degree. On the other hand, nationalism may be a paramount, a supreme loyalty, commanding all others. This usually occurs when national emotion is fused with religious emotion, and nationalism itself becomes a religion or a substitute for religion.

The Decline of the Territorial State

JOHN H. HERZ

In view of the tremendous role nation-states—or at least several of them—play in the world today, talking about the "decline" of states manifestly would be absurd. What is referred to in the title of this chapter is the decline of that specific element of statehood which characterized the units composing the modern state system in its classical period, and which I called their "territoriality" or "impermeability." The "model-type" international system built upon units of this structure was that of a plurality of countries—at first all European—bound together by certain common standards, different but not too different in power, all enjoying a certain minimum of protection in and through that system. They would quarrel, try to diminish each other, but they would hardly ever suffer one of theirs

to be extinguished. In their quarrels, which they called wars, they would attack each other, but their fortress-type shells of defense could be breached only by frontal assault and thus even the smaller powers had a goodly chance to resist and survive. Self-contained, centralized, internally pacified, they could rely on themselves for a high degree of external security.

Beginning with the nineteenth century, certain trends emerged which tended to endanger the functioning of the classical system. Directly or indirectly, all of them had a bearing upon that feature of the territorial state which was the strongest guarantee of its independent coexistence with other states of like nature: its hard shell, that is, its defensibility in case of war.

Naturally, many of these new trends concerned war itself and the way in which war was conducted. But it would be a mistake to identify them with what is often referred to as the shift

Reprinted from John H. Herz, *International Politics in the Atomic Age* (New York: Columbia University Press, 1959), pp. 96–108, by permission of the publisher.

from limited war, the war typical of the duel-type contests of the eighteenth century, to the more or less unlimited wars that developed with conscription, "nations in arms," and the increasing destructiveness of weapons in the nineteenth century. For by themselves these developments were not inconsistent with the "classical" aim of war in the era of territorial states: the attempt by one state to enforce its will on that of the opponent by defeating the latter's armed forces and overcoming its defense installations through frontal attack. Instituting universal military service, putting the state's economy on a war-footing, and similar measures served to enhance a country's capacity to defend itself in the traditional way. Rather than endangering the territorial state they served to bolster it. This kind of "unlimited war" must be regarded simply as a more developed form of traditional warfare.

Total war, as distinguished from both kinds of traditional war, limited and unlimited, is involved with developments in warfare which enable belligerents to overleap or by-pass the traditional hard-shell defense of states. As soon as this happens, the traditional relationship between war, on the one hand, and territorial sovereignty and power, on the other, is altered decisively. Arranged in order of increasing effectiveness, these new factors may be listed under the following headings: (a) possibility of economic blockade; (b) ideological-political penetration; (c) air war; and (d) atomic war. It is true that even outside and in some cases prior to the emergence of these factors, growth in offensive power and increase in range and destructiveness of conventional weapons, such as was witnessed in the second half of the nineteenth century, tended by itself to render the smaller among the tradi-

tional units of territorial power obsolete because they became too easily "breachable." Countries like Holland or Belgium, once defensible through fortresses and a corresponding military setup, became simply minor obstacles, unable to resist with their own defensive strength when attacked by the concentrated offensive power of a "big" one. Thus, for example, in significant contrast to the strategy of the Franco-Prussian War of 1870–71, the famous Schlieffen Plan, developed by the German General Staff in the last decades of the nineteenth century for a future war against France as a matter of course encompassed Belgium as merely one flank in the sweeping move into France. But, as the First World War showed, such countries might still continue as elements in contests which aimed at breaking traditional "fronts" of armed forces, if only as links in, or continuations of, fronts formed chiefly by big powers. They ceased to be even that in an age of *Blitzkrieg*, or mechanized warfare, as illustrated by the Second World War. Overrun with no possibility of offering effective resistance, their only hope lay in eventual "liberation" by their more powerful allies. . . . On the other hand, exceptional geographic location, combined with exceptionally favorable topography, might still enable small countries such as Switzerland to survive, if only because of the deterrent effect of their resistance-readiness.

Turning now to the factors which, more generally, have tended to affect old-style territoriality, let us begin with *economic warfare*. It should be said from the outset that "economic blockade" so far has never enabled a belligerent to force another into surrender through "starvation" alone. In the First World War, Germany and her allies were seriously endangered when the

Western Allies cut them off from overseas supplies, particularly foodstuffs. Countering with the submarine, the Germans posed a similar threat to Britain for a while. But German postwar propaganda efforts to blame defeat solely on *Hungerblockade* (plus alleged enemy-instigated subversion), with its companion slogan "im Felde unbesiegt" (undefeated on the battlefield), ran contrary to the fact that a very real effort had been required to defeat the Central Powers on the military fronts. The same thing applies to the Second World War. But blockade was an important contributing factor in both instances. Its importance for the present analysis lies in its unconventional nature, which permits belligerents to by-pass the hard shell of the enemy. Its use reflects an entirely untraditional approach to warmaking; its effect is due to the changed economic status of industrialized nations.

Prior to the industrial age the territorial state was largely self-contained ("self-sufficient"), economically as otherwise. Although one of the customary means of conducting limited war was to try to starve fortresses into surrender, this applied only to the individual links in the shell, and not to entire nations in order to avoid breaching the shell. . . . The Industrial Revolution changed all this, for it made countries like Britain and Germany increasingly dependent on imports. This meant that in war they could survive only by controlling areas beyond their own territory, which would provide them with the food and raw materials they needed. The Germans managed by overrunning food-surplus and raw material producing areas in the initial stages of both world wars, and the British, of course, by keeping the sea lanes open through superior naval power.

In peacetime, economic dependency became one of the causes of a phenomenon which itself contributed to the transformation of the old state system: imperialism. Anticipating war, with its new danger of blockade, countries strove to become more self-sufficient through enlargement of their areas of control. I do not mean to imply that the complex phenomenon of imperialism was exclusively or even chiefly caused by economic interdependence and its impact on war. Clearly, the earlier stage of capitalist industrialism as such had already supplied various motives for expansion, especially in the form of colonialism. But an economic determinism which sees the cause of imperialist expansion only in the profit motive and the ensuing urge for markets or cheap labor overlooks the additional, and very compelling, motivation that lies in power competition and the urge for security in case of war. To the extent that the industrialized nations lost self-sufficiency, they were driven into expansion in a—futile—effort to regain it. Today, if at all, only the control of entire continents enables major nations to survive economically in major wars. This implies that hard-shell military defense, if it is to make any sense, must be a matter of defending more than one single nation; it must extend half way around the world. This, in turn, affects the status of smaller nations, whether they are included in the larger defense perimeter or not. If they are, they tend to become dependent on the chief power in the area; if they are not, they may become "permeable" precisely because of the possibility of economic blockade.

Psychological warfare. The attempt to undermine the morale of an enemy population, or to subvert its loyalty, shares with economic warfare the effect of by-passing old-style territorial defensibility. Like economic blockade, such "ideological-political" penetration is not entirely new, but it was formerly practiced, and practicable, only under quite exceptional circumstances. Short periods when genuine "world-revolutionary" propaganda was circulated, such as in the early stages of the French Revolution, scarcely affected the general practice under which dynasties, and later governments, fought other dynasties or governments with little "ideological" involvement on the part of larger masses or classes. With conscription for military service, loyalty to the cause of one's country of course became more important, but since this new approach to mobilization for war coincided with nationalism (of which it was one expression), it served to increase, rather than to detract from, national coherence and solidarity. Only in rare cases—for instance, where national groups enclosed in and hostile to multinational empires could be appealed to—was there an opening wedge for what we today call "fifth-column" strategies. Even then, to take advantage of such opportunities was considered "ungentlemanlike" and "not to be done" (as, for instance, in the case of Bismarck's appeal to certain nationality groups in Austria-Hungary during his war of 1866).

With the emergence of political belief systems and ideological creeds in our century, however, nations have become susceptible to undermining from within. Although, as in the case of economic blockades, wars have not yet been won solely by subversion of loyalties, the threat has affected the coherence of the territorial state ever since the rise to power of a regime that claims and proclaims to represent not the cause of one particular nation, but that of all mankind, or at least its exploited or suppressed "masses." Bolshevism from

1917 on has provided the second instance in modern history of world-revolutionary propaganda. Communist penetration tactics were subsequently imitated by Nazi-Fascist regimes, and eventually even by the democracies. To be sure, neither Nazi-Fascist propaganda directed to the democracies nor democratic counterpropaganda directed to populations under totalitarian regimes were by themselves sufficient to defeat an enemy in the Second World War; but individual instances of "softening up" countries and then gaining control with the aid of a subversive group within occurred even then. Such tactics have, of course, became all too familiar during the cold war. It is hardly necessary to point out how a new technological development and a new technique of penetration—radio broadcasting—has added to the effectiveness of political penetration through psychological warfare. The radio has rendered units accessible to propaganda and undermining from abroad, which formerly were impenetrable not only in a political but also in a technical sense. Examples abound, from what was probably one of its first effective uses—Nazi radio broadcasting to the Saar during the plebiscite compaign of 1934–35 and to Austria in the summer of 1934—down to the present Nasserite propaganda throughout the Near East.

Thus, new lines of division, cutting horizontally through state units instead of leaving them separated vertically from each other at their frontiers, have now become possible. Under such political-ideological alignments, "aliens" may turn out to be friends, citizens, more treacherous than "enemy aliens"; "friendly" prisoners of war may have to be distinguished from hostile ones, as, in the Second World War in the case of German or Italian PW's, or, more recently, in Korean prison camps;

"refugees" may be revealed as spies or "agents," while "agents" may deliver themselves up as refugees; the Iron Curtain is crossed westward by those who feel that this is the way to escape "slavery," while others cross it eastward to escape "oppression" or "discrimination." How even in peacetime such a new type of loyalties (or disloyalties) can be utilized to weaken the internal coherence and therewith the "impermeability" of nations is vividly portrayed by the statements of French and Italian Communist leaders calling upon their compatriots to consider the Soviet Union a brother instead of an enemy in case of war. And during actual war, political-ideological fissures can be utilized to counter the effects of newly developed means of attack by rendering it more difficult to "pacify" territory "conquered" in the traditional manner of breaching the outer defense wall. Guerrilla warfare then becomes another means of rendering obsolete the classical way of defeating an enemy through defeating his traditional armed forces. Using planes to establish communication with guerrilla forces behind enemy lines, or to drop them supplies or advisers, illustrates the combined effect which political-ideological strategy and air war may have upon the customary type of classical warfare.

Air war, of all the new developments and techniques prior to the atomic age, is the one that has affected the territoriality of nations most radically. With it, so to say, the roof blew off the territorial state. It is true that even this new kind of warfare, up to and including the Second World War, did not by itself account for the defeat of a belligerent, as some of the more enthusiastic prophets of the air age had predicted it would. Undoubtedly, however, it had a massive contributory

effect. And this effect was due to strategic action in the hinterland, rather than to tactical use at the front. It came at least close to defeating one side "vertically," by direct action against the "soft" interior of the country, by-passing the "fronts" and other outer defenses. By striking against cities, "morale," supplies, industries, etc., it foreshadowed the "end of the frontier," that is, the demise of the traditional impermeability of even the militarily most powerful states. . . .

That air warfare was considered something entirely unconventional is seen from the initial reaction to it in the First World War. As in the case of economic warfare, nations steeped in the tradition of classical war were at a loss to understand and appraise the new factors and what had caused them. "Revolutionary" transition from an old to a new system has usually affected moral standards. Each big change tends at first to outrage traditional standards of "fairness," etc. We have referred before to the case of the "gunpowder revolution" at the end of the Middle Ages; the same effect had been engendered when somewhat earlier the bow and arrow defeated armies of clumsy armored knights on horseback, and with them their knightly standards and rituals, or when, in mythological times of antiquity, the horse-drawn battle wagon prevailed over foot soldiers. In the classical age of the modern state system the "new morality" of shooting at human beings from a distance had finally come to be accepted, but the standards of the age clearly distinguished "lawful combatants," i.e., members of the armed forces at the front or in the fortifications, from the "civilian" remainder of the population. Despite the latter's occasional involvement in direct military action or, more frequently, in such indirect effects of the fighting as requisitions or marauding by armed forces, the king of Prussia could still proclaim in 1870 that he was waging war against the emperor of France, and not against women and children. The distinction became obsolete when long-range artillery in the First World War sent shells into Paris, and bombs started dropping on cities far behind the front (on a small scale, it is true, but still "killing women and children"). At the same time "starvation blockades" had started to take their toll from civilians behind the battle lines.

All this at first shocked feelings. Germans felt that the attempt to starve them into surrender was an "unfair" way to wage war, typical of British "hucksters" (as distinguished from German "heroes"); the heroes overlooked that they, too, had tried—unsuccessfully, it is true—to inflict the same suffering on the hucksters. In so far as war from the air was concerned, reactions differed significantly toward air

fighting at the front and air war carried behind the front. In air fighting at the front a kind of "new chivalry" developed, with its peculiar "honor code" among the flyers on both sides. But city bombing was felt to constitute "illegitimate" warfare, and populations were inclined to treat airmen engaging in it as "war criminals." It is well known that this feeling continued into the Second World War with its large-scale "area bombing." Such sentiments of moral outrage reflected the general feeling of helplessness in the face of a war which threatened to destroy the ancient implication of protection inherent in the concept of territorial power. In fact, in the Second World War certain big powers, *qua* territorial states, were on the way to becoming obsolete.

The process has now been completed with the advent of the atomic weapon. With it, whatever remained of the impermeability of states seems to have gone for good.... Now that power can destroy power from center to center everything is different.

The Viewpoint of Underdeveloped Countries

EUGENE STALEY

The economy of every country is "underdeveloped" in the sense that

more can be done to build up its productive power and to improve the economic well-being of its people. The term has come to be used, however, to refer—more politely than by the old word "backward"—to those countries which stand very low in relative income. The usage is loose, the distinction be-

Reprinted from Eugene Staley, *The Future of Underdeveloped Countries* (New York: Harper & Row, Publishers, for the Council on Foreign Relations, 1961), pp. 13–26, by permission of the Council on Foreign Relations, Inc.

tween more developed and less developed countries is one of degree, and there is no point in trying to be very precise in the matter. For those who like their concepts as clear as possible, however, I offer the following definition of an underdeveloped country: A country characterized (1) by mass poverty which is chronic and not the result of some temporary misfortune, and (2) by obsolete methods of production and social organization, which means that the poverty is not entirely due to poor natural resources and hence could presumably be lessened by methods already proved in other countries.

TWO-THIRDS OF THE WORLD'S POPULATION

Table I classifies the countries of the world as highly developed, intermediate, or underdeveloped, mainly on the basis of the best available indexes of national income per person. The underdeveloped group includes almost all of the countries of Asia and Africa, most of Latin America, and some of Europe. . . . Countries falling in the intermediate range include seven in Europe, five in Latin America, plus Japan, the U.S.S.R., Israel, and the Union of South Africa. . . . The highly developed group consists entirely of countries in northwest Europe plus the United States, Canada, Australia, and New Zealand, all settled by northwest Europeans. . . . Thus, two-thirds of the world's population of 2,400,000,000 live in underdeveloped countries, a little more than one-sixth in countries of the intermediate range, and a little less than one-sixth in highly developed countries. . . .

COUNTRIES GROUPED BY LEVEL OF ECONOMIC DEVELOPMENT

A. HIGHLY DEVELOPED

Americas
Canada
United States
Europe
Belgium
Denmark
France
Germany

Netherlands
Norway
Sweden
Switzerland
United Kingdom
Oceania
Australia
New Zealand

B. INTERMEDIATE

Africa
Union of South
Africa
Americas
Argentina
Chile
Cuba
Puerto Rico
Uruguay
Venezuela
Asia
Israel
Japan

Europe
Austria
Czechoslovakia
Finland
Hungary
Ireland
Italy
Poland
Portugal
Spain
Eurasia
U.S.S.R.

C. UNDERDEVELOPED

Africa
Algeria
Angola
Belgian Congo
Cameroons
Egypt
Ethiopia
French Equatorial
Africa
French West
Africa
Gold Coast
Kenya
Liberia
Libya
Madagascar
Morocco
Mozambique
Nigeria
Northern Rhodesia
Nyasaland
Ruanda-Urundi
Sierra Leone
Southern Rhodesia
Sudan

Tanganyika
Tunisia
Uganda
Americas
Bolivia
Brazil
British West
Indies
Colombia
Costa Rica
Dominican Republic
Ecuador
El Salvador
Guatemala
Haiti
Honduras
Mexico
Nicaragua
Paraguay
Peru

Asia
Afghanistan
Borneo

frequently, in such indirect effects of the fighting as requisitions or marauding by armed forces, the king of Prussia could still proclaim in 1870 that he was waging war against the emperor of France, and not against women and children. The distinction became obsolete when long-range artillery in the First World War sent shells into Paris, and bombs started dropping on cities far behind the front (on a small scale, it is true, but still "killing women and children"). At the same time "starvation blockades" had started to take their toll from civilians behind the battle lines.

All this at first shocked feelings. Germans felt that the attempt to starve them into surrender was an "unfair" way to wage war, typical of British "hucksters" (as distinguished from German "heroes"); the heroes overlooked that they, too, had tried—unsuccessfully, it is true—to inflict the same suffering on the hucksters. In so far as war from the air was concerned, reactions differed significantly toward air

fighting at the front and air war carried behind the front. In air fighting at the front a kind of "new chivalry" developed, with its peculiar "honor code" among the flyers on both sides. But city bombing was felt to constitute "illegitimate" warfare, and populations were inclined to treat airmen engaging in it as "war criminals." It is well known that this feeling continued into the Second World War with its large-scale "area bombing." Such sentiments of moral outrage reflected the general feeling of helplessness in the face of a war which threatened to destroy the ancient implication of protection inherent in the concept of territorial power. In fact, in the Second World War certain big powers, *qua* territorial states, were on the way to becoming obsolete.

The process has now been completed with the advent of the atomic weapon. With it, whatever remained of the impermeability of states seems to have gone for good. . . . Now that power can destroy power from center to center everything is different.

The Viewpoint of Underdeveloped Countries

EUGENE STALEY

The economy of every country is "underdeveloped" in the sense that

Reprinted from Eugene Staley, *The Future of Underdeveloped Countries* (New York: Harper & Row, Publishers, for the Council on Foreign Relations, 1961), pp. 13–26, by permission of the Council on Foreign Relations, Inc.

more can be done to build up its productive power and to improve the economic well-being of its people. The term has come to be used, however, to refer—more politely than by the old word "backward"—to those countries which stand very low in relative income. The usage is loose, the distinction between more developed and less developed countries is one of degree, and there is no point in trying to be very precise in the matter. For those who like their concepts as clear as possible, however, I offer the following definition of an underdeveloped country: A country characterized (1) by mass poverty which is chronic and not the result of some temporary misfortune, and (2) by obsolete methods of production and social organization, which means that the poverty is not entirely due to poor natural resources and hence could presumably be lessened by methods already proved in other countries.

TWO-THIRDS OF THE WORLD'S POPULATION

Table I classifies the countries of the world as highly developed, intermediate, or underdeveloped, mainly on the basis of the best available indexes of national income per person. The underdeveloped group includes almost all of the countries of Asia and Africa, most of Latin America, and some of Europe.... Countries falling in the intermediate range include seven in Europe, five in Latin America, plus Japan, the U.S.S.R., Israel, and the Union of South Africa.... The highly developed group consists entirely of countries in northwest Europe plus the United States, Canada, Australia, and New Zealand, all settled by northwest Europeans.... Thus, two-thirds of the world's population of 2,400,000,000 live in underdeveloped countries, a little more than one-sixth in countries of the intermediate range, and a little less than one-sixth in highly developed countries....

COUNTRIES GROUPED BY LEVEL OF ECONOMIC DEVELOPMENT

A. HIGHLY DEVELOPED

Americas	Netherlands
Canada	Norway
United States	Sweden
Europe	Switzerland
Belgium	United Kingdom
Denmark	*Oceania*
France	Australia
Germany	New Zealand

B. INTERMEDIATE

Africa	*Europe*
Union of South	Austria
Africa	Czechoslovakia
Americas	Finland
Argentina	Hungary
Chile	Ireland
Cuba	Italy
Puerto Rico	Poland
Uruguay	Portugal
Venezuela	Spain
Asia	*Eurasia*
Israel	U.S.S.R.
Japan	

C. UNDERDEVELOPED

Africa	Tanganyika
Algeria	Tunisia
Angola	Uganda
Belgian Congo	*Americas*
Cameroons	Bolivia
Egypt	Brazil
Ethiopia	British West
French Equatorial	Indies
Africa	Colombia
French West	Costa Rica
Africa	Dominican Repub-
Gold Coast	lic
Kenya	Ecuador
Liberia	El Salvador
Libya	Guatemala
Madagascar	Haiti
Morocco	Honduras
Mozambique	Mexico
Nigeria	Nicaragua
Northern Rhodesia	Paraguay
Nyasaland	Peru
Ruanda-Urundi	
Sierra Leone	*Asia*
Southern Rhodesia	Afghanistan
Sudan	Borneo

Asia (cont.)

Burma	New Guinea
Ceylon	Pakistan
China	Philippines
Formosa	Saudi Arabia
India	Syria
Indo-China	Thailand
Indonesia	Turkey
Iran	Yemen
Iraq	*Europe*
Jordan	Albania
Korea	Bulgaria
Lebanon	Greece
Malaya	Rumania
Nepal	Yugoslavia

Sources

For income data: United Nations, *Monthly Bulletin of Statistics,* June, 1952, pp. viii–ix; United Nations, Department of Economic Affairs, *National Income and Its Distribution in Under-Developed Countries* (New York: 1951. XVII.3).

For data on urbanization and occupational distribution: Food and Agriculture Organization, *Yearbook of Food and Agricultural Statistics,* 1950. Also, I wish to express thanks to the Population Division of the Bureau of Applied Social Research, Columbia University, and particularly to Dr. Hilda Hertz of the staff, for information from their comparative world surveys file on urbanization and occupational distribution, including historical data which have been of use in...connection with the table above.

Areas with population less than 3/4 million were not included in this table.

The grouping is based mainly on per capita national income, as of 1950 or thereabouts. In Group A the estimated annual income is $450 per capita or more; in Group B, $150 to $450; in Group C, less than $150. However, degree of urbanization and proportion of the working population engaged in nonagricultural occupations were also taken into account, especially to classify countries for which income data are lacking, but also in a few instances to determine that a country should be in a lower or higher group than the one in which income estimates alone would place it. Germany was placed in Group A, although on the basis of 1950 income alone it would fall in Group B. Japan was placed in Group B, although on the basis of 1950 income alone it would fall in Group C. Venezuela was placed in

Group B, although on the basis of 1950 income alone it would fall in Group A.

Two facts stand out. One is the great disparity in income levels over the world. At one end of the scale are the United States and Canada with national incomes of more than $1,000 per person (in the case of the United States, more than $1,500). At the other end are the underdeveloped countries, comprising two-thirds of the world's population, where incomes average less than $150 per person. According to the United Nations Statistical Office, half the people of the world live in countries that have per capita incomes of less than $100, some of them much less. Countries with more than $600 annual income per person include only one-tenth of the world's population. The United States alone, with slightly more than six percent of the world's population, accounted for forty percent of the world total of national income in 1950. Europe, with twenty-five percent of the population, generated another forty percent. Although Asia, Africa, and Latin America together have more than sixty-five percent of the world's population, they produced only seventeen percent of the world's national income.[1]

The other outstanding fact is political. While population is obviously not the only or even the main factor in world power and in the relative influence of nations on trends in world civilization, the sheer numbers of people in the underdeveloped countries give them a potential influence that cannot be overlooked. Their ability to make themselves heard in world affairs has already grown enormously in the last few decades. As they acquire more

---

[1] All figures are for 1950, based on the United Nations *Monthly Bulletin of Statistics,* June, 1952, pp. vii–xi and Table 54.

of the tools of modern production, higher levels of education, and more experience in modern management and government—as seems inevitable—it is likely that they will exert more and more influence on issues both of peace and of war. Given their numbers and their growing technological competence, the underdeveloped countries may in fact hold the balance of the future as between the political system and the way of life which have been evolving over several centuries in the West and the modern reversion to tyranny represented by Communism and other totalitarian systems. Whether most of these countries take a democratic or a Communist or other totalitarian path in their development is likely to determine the course of civilization on our planet.

THE REVOLUTION OF RISING EXPECTATIONS

The poverty of underdeveloped countries means that their people, on a broad average, have a life expectancy only about half that of the people of the highly developed countries. They suffer much of the time from malaria, dysentery, tuberculosis, trachoma, or other ills. They have the services of less than one-sixth as many doctors in proportion of population. Their food supply is about one-third less, measured in calories, than that of developed countries, and when account is taken of the needs of the human body for the relatively expensive "protective" foods, such as milk and meat, the extent of malnutrition is found to be very great indeed. The opportunity to attend school is limited to a small minority in most underdeveloped countries, even for the lower grades. High school, college, and professional training is even

less available. Only one person in four or five, again on a broad average of underdeveloped countries, knows how to read and write. The supply of cloth for clothing, home furnishing, and other purposes is about one-fourth as great per person in underdeveloped as in highly developed countries. Non-human energy to supplement the labor of human beings in industry, agriculture, transport, and household tasks is less than one-twentieth as plentiful, measured in horsepower-hours per person. Incomes, on the average, are less than one-tenth as high.

These disparities in living levels between underdeveloped and highly developed countries appear to have been growing wider, rather than narrowing, in recent years. According to the statistical services of the United Nations, the developed countries are not only far ahead but are pulling further ahead. Their rates of economic progress, on the whole, continue to be more rapid than those of the underdeveloped countries.

Poverty and the hunger, disease, and lack of opportunity for self-development that it implies have been the lot of the ordinary people in the underdeveloped countries for centuries past. The new thing is that now this poverty has become a source of active political discontent. Of course, no statement can be unqualifiedly true of underdeveloped countries so diverse in culture, history, and present situation as those of Asia and Latin America, Africa and Southeastern Europe. . . . But, speaking broadly, it is one of the most profoundly important political facts of the mid-twentieth century that among the people of the underdeveloped countries a ferment is at work which has already produced in some, and is bound to produce in others, irresistible demands for a stepped-up pace of economic and social change. The evidence is overwhelming.

In 1937 the then director of the International Labour Office, Harold Butler, reported on a trip to southern and eastern Asia that "...a great change is stirring Eastern society to its depths. The consciousness of misery has been created by the growing realisation that it is not the inescapable lot of the poor and that chances of a better life now exist. The immemorial passivity and fatalism of the Orient are beginning to yield to the desire for higher standards and the determination to acquire them." He called this "perhaps the most revolutionary movement of our revolutionary age."[2]

Testimony to the same effect by journalists and university scholars whose business it is to follow political and economic movements in the principal underdeveloped regions is emphatic and impressive. . . . Justice Douglas talked with hundreds of people in the rural areas of the Middle East and found that the complaints of the peasants were specific: The absence of medical care comes first, then absence of schools. Next comes land reform; they have a passion for land ownership. Next is the desire to learn how to farm the modern way. The right to vote, to elect a representative government, to expel and punish corrupt officials are also important claims. Finally, the people of the area have a new sense of nationalism which expresses itself in many ways. "There are professional agitators who stir this brew of discontent; but the rebellious drive comes from the masses. I have not seen a village between the Mediterranean and the Pacific that was not stirring uneasily."

Nearly all of the underdeveloped countries have within the past decade set up official agencies charged with planning and promoting economic development. Many of the plans, especially at first, were little more than dreams on paper, but now there is a noticeable trend toward sober, concrete, feasible projects. All this activity indicates a strong social demand for economic advancement.

The need for economic development, and for international assistance to hasten it, is the constant theme of spokesmen for underdeveloped countries in the economic and social organs of the United Nations and the specialized agencies.

In short, a "revolution of rising expectations," as it has been called, is sweeping the underdeveloped nations of the world. Political leaders who nowadays aspire to popular support in underdeveloped countries (and even modern dictators want popular support) must at least talk in favor of economic modernization. Failure to achieve practical, visible improvement in the lot of the ordinary people is more and more going to provoke unrest and bring political extremists to power.

Why is this happening now, not fifty years ago or fifty years hence? The answer lies chiefly in two factors: (1) the examples set by Western nations, which have proved that general poverty is not inevitable, and (2) the miracles of twentieth-century communication, through movies, the press, radio, and travel, including the travel of armies (for example, the demonstration of the fabulous American living standards by GI's on every continent in World War II). Poverty is old, but the awareness of

---

2 Harold Butler, *Problems of Industry in the East* (Geneva: International Labour Office, 1938, Studies and Reports, Series B, No. 29), pp. 65–66.

poverty and the conviction that something can be done about it are new.

It has sometimes been maintained that happiness can be expressed as an equation:

$$\text{Happiness} = \frac{\text{Possessions}}{\text{Desires}}$$

In the Orient, until recently, the standard way to seek happiness has been to cut down on desires. The West in modern times has sought happiness by increasing possessions. There can be no doubt that the ascetic philosophy of the East is losing ground to the activist philosophy of the West. In many Eastern communities the most respected person formerly was the man who withdrew from society, but abnegation is no longer held in such high esteem. The man who tries to better his community and himself is gaining respect.

It is worth stressing that the social stirrings in underdeveloped countries are basically a reflection of the revolutionary technological and economic progress of the Western world, and in considerable part reflect Western ideals. The Soviet revolution and the work of Communist agitators and organizers, however, are influencing the form which discontent takes. Communists turn the discontent to their own purposes and use it to seize power where they can. But revolutionary economic, social, and political changes would be under way in the underdeveloped countries today had there never been a Moscow or a Communist.

POLITICAL AND PSYCHOLOGICAL MOTIVES

It is my conviction that in the United States discussion of the driving forces behind the new demands for economic development generally pays too exclusive attention to desires for more food, clothing, health, and education and neglects the motives that may be labeled political and psychological. These motives are just as strong as desires for improved economic well-being, and in many underdeveloped countries they are even more decisive in their immediate effects on attitudes and government policies.

Factors in the demand for economic modernization in underdeveloped countries, other than the desire to overcome poverty, include:

1. The desire of new, self-conscious nationalisms to attain or preserve independence, and to be free of foreign political or economic dominance, real or imagined.

2. The desire for the means of national defense and security. In some cases there may be an unavowed or latent desire for expansion at the expense of neighbors.

3. The desire for national and personal respect, status, prestige, and importance in the world, which experience shows not to be readily accorded to "backward," weak countries or their citizens.

The historical decision to modernize Japan and the activity of the Japanese state in promoting that country's extraordinarily rapid development were determined by men much less concerned with popular welfare than with military power. At first they sought military power in order to resist foreign encroachment, later to realize Japan's own ambitions for expansion.

Turkey under Mustapha Kemal Ataturk turned to modern methods, but not in order that the ordinary citizen could have more food and health services. The main impulse was to make Turkey strong.

Of course, state policy in most countries is more concerned today than formerly with economic well-being for the citizens. Even so, considerations like national power for defense or offense and psychological imponderables, such as a respected and important position in the world, have by no means lost their compelling force. An Indian economist, after describing traditional social obstacles which impede economic development, writes that the "most important" factor at work to break through barriers is "the wave of national feeling that is sweeping the backward areas of the world. Nationalism is everywhere associated with a twofold objective. Firstly, to be able to order one's own affairs, and secondly, to attain a position of dignity and importance in the community of nations."

The lesson that a country with backward technology and a poor economy is militarily weak and politically uninfluential has not been lost upon the leaders of today's underdeveloped countries. Many have only recently gained political independence or still aspire to attain it, and one of the strongest compulsions for economic development is the desire to build up economic power as a foundation for independence.

Ambition for a respected status in the world must not be underrated among the driving forces behind economic development programs. Many, perhaps most, of the present-day leaders of underdeveloped countries have known in bitter personal experience the humiliation of "colored" peoples exposed to the arrogance of some members of the white race. In some areas there are resentful memories of the social discrimination that characterized the old colonialism—clubs for the white rulers only, no "natives" allowed—and of other tokens of inferiority and exploitation. These things, which Westerners tend to forget, combine with conditions of appalling human need and the passions of new nationalisms to produce attitudes and demands which would hardly be human if they were always sweetly reasonable. As a Pakistani put it, "We want freedom from contempt."

Prestige is involved in development, as well as living levels, independence, and security. The experience of an international agency in one of the Latin American countries is not uncommon: when the organization's engineers were asked to advise on construction of a steel mill they showed how to design one that would cost about 12 million dollars, but the country's representatives wanted a much larger and more complex one to cost about 80 millions. Prestige, not economic calculation, was the ruling factor. There is a strong feeling, not entirely rational but powerful none the less, which associates export of raw materials and import of manufactured goods with "colonial" status. Sensitive national pride rebels against the thought that raw materials producers are "hewers of wood and drawers of water" for the industrially advanced countries. Here is one of the roots of the demand for industrialization, as distinct from the improvements in the efficiency of agriculture and commerce which in some circumstances may be more immediately helpful in a country's economic development.

The Communists, who are supposed to be economic determinists, have played most adeptly on these "noneconomic" motives in their practical work as agitators in underdeveloped countries. . . . Much of Western policy, on the other hand, even of the enlightened sort which concerns itself with technical and economic assistance, shows too little appreciation of the psychological and political realities, tending to assume that all realities must be economic. A sort of third-hand Marxism makes us suppose that if people are discontented it must be because they are hungry. Hunger is certainly a factor in underdeveloped countries, but other desires also motivate human beings and act very powerfully on politics in these countries, as elsewhere. A crude economic interpretation of political attitudes is almost always wrong.

Where political-psychological motivations come into conflict with desires for better economic well-being, the priority of the political is generally rather clear. Does Iran want more to get maximum income from its oil industry or to satisfy nationalistic emotions by ending foreign management? Could one imagine an Indonesian patriot agreeing that it would be better to go back to Dutch rule, supposing it could be proved that this would surely advance living levels for the people (which no patriot would be willing to suppose in the first place)? Debates on economic development in the United Nations are marked by reiterated assertions from spokesmen of underdeveloped countries that, while they need financial help for their projects on a much larger scale than has been forthcoming, they are determined that no loans or investments or grants shall be a means of infringing on their national freedom. Burma has refused on political grounds proffered American aid which it badly needs.

SOCIETIES IN MOTION

The new nationalisms of the underdeveloped countries and their passion for equality, respect, and status, like their new awareness of poverty, have some of their roots in the West's own cultural contributions. The ideas and ideals which produced the struggles for parliamentary rule in Britain, the American Declaration of Independence, the liberty, equality, fraternity, and the rights of man of the French Revolution, and the national unifications of Germany and Italy are now at work in new places. Not only mechanical inventions like radio, the airplane, and improved roads are having their impact on underdeveloped countries; so are social inventions like the free public school, universal suffrage, business corporations, trade unions, and social insurance. In lands with different cultural settings and historical backgrounds, where recent relations with the West have been tinged with inferiority and resentment, the effects of these cultural borrowings are not readily predictable.

Also available and being borrowed in some places are social inventions of the Communists, such as new strategy and tactics in revolution, comprehensive five-year plans, and methods of rule by police and propaganda. What the end results will be no one can tell, though we may be sure they will be important not only for the people of these countries but also for us.

The underdeveloped countries are in motion, and economic modernization of some kind, accompanied by drastic social and political changes as well, is on the way in practically all of them, though at different speeds and in a variety of directions. This does not mean that the resistance to change, which has kept some of these countries static for centuries, has entirely disappeared. The inertia of long-established habits and institutions is still a very important fact. So is the open or secret opposition of powerful individuals and groups that fear to lose their present privileged positions. In countries experiencing a strong cultural impact from outside there is always a struggle between the two kinds of response distinguished by Arnold Toynbee: (1) flexible adaptation, in which portions of the outside culture are taken over, and (2) "zealotism," a defense against change by resort to rigid and fanatical orthodoxy. Zealotism still plays a role in some areas, for example in Arab countries and among certain African peoples. But the impact of the industrial revolution has now become so overwhelming that few of the underdeveloped countries are likely to delay for long their switch to the more feasible response of adaptation.

As a measure of the changed climate of opinion in most underdeveloped countries we may recall that in China only about a century ago the first rail-way had to be torn up because of popular opposition; people threw their bodies in front of the engine. Conservatives of that day opposed the establishment of schools to teach the youth of China science and technology. Still further back, Emperor Ch'ien Lung had sent the famous message to Britain's King George III: "Our Celestial Empire possesses all things in prolific abundance, and lacks no product within its own borders; there is no need to import the manufactures of outside barbarians." The technical assistance officials of the United States or the United Nations would be much surprised to receive a communication in this tenor from any government today!

The Delicate Balance of Terror

ALBERT WOHLSTETTER

The first shock administered by the Soviet launching of sputnik has almost dissipated. The flurry of statements and investigations and improvised responses has died down, leaving a small residue: a slight increase in the schedule of bomber and ballistic missile production, with a resulting small increment in our defense expenditures for the current fiscal year; a considerable enthusiasm for space travel; and some stirrings of interest in the teaching of mathematics and physics in the secondary schools. Western defense policy has almost re-

Reprinted by special permission from *Foreign Affairs*, January 1959 issue. Copyright © by the Council on Foreign Relations, Inc., New York.

turned to the level of activity and the emphasis suited to the basic assumptions which were controlling before sputnik.

One of the most important of these assumptions—that a general thermonuclear war is extremely unlikely—is held in common by most of the critics of our defense policy as well as by its proponents. Because of its crucial rôle in the Western strategy of defense, I should like to examine the stability of the thermonuclear balance which, it is generally supposed, would make aggression irrational or even insane. The balance, I believe, is in fact precarious, and this fact has critical implications for policy. Deterrence in the 1960s is neither assured nor impossible but will be the product of sustained intelligent effort and hard choices, responsibly made. As a major illustration important both for defense and foreign policy, I shall treat the particularly stringent conditions for deterrence which affect forces based close to the enemy, whether they are U.S. forces or those of our allies, under single or joint control. I shall comment also on the inadequacy as well as the necessity of deterrence, on the problem of accidental outbreak of war, and on disarmament.[1]

THE PRESUMED AUTOMATIC BALANCE

I emphasize that requirements for deterrence are stringent. We have heard so much about the 'atomic stalemate and the receding probability of war which it has produced that this may strike the reader as something of an exaggeration. Is deterrence a necessary consequence of both sides having a nuclear delivery capability, and is all-out war nearly obsolete? Is mutual extinction the only outcome of a general war? This belief, frequently expressed by references to Mr. Oppenheimer's simile of the two scorpions in a bottle, is perhaps the prevalent one. It is held by a very eminent and diverse group of people—in England by Sir Winston Churchill, P. M. S. Blackett, Sir John Slessor, Admiral Buzzard and many others; in France by such figures as Raymond Aron, General Gallois and General Gazin; in this country by the titular heads of both parties as well as almost all writers on military and for-

eign affairs, by both Henry Kissinger and his critic, James E. King, Jr., and by George Kennan as well as Dean Acheson. Mr. Kennan refers to American concern about surprise attack as simply obsessive;[2] and many people have drawn the consequence of the stalemate as has Blackett, who states: "If it is in fact true, as most current opinion holds, that strategic air power has abolished global war, then an urgent problem for the West is to assess how little effort must be put into it to keep global war abolished."[3] If peace were founded firmly on mutual terror, and mutual terror on symmetrical nuclear capabilities, this would be, as Churchill has said, "a melancholy paradox"; none the less a most comforting one.

Deterrence, however, is not automatic. While feasible, it will be much harder to achieve in the 1960s than is generally believed. One of the most disturbing features of current opinion is the underestimation of this difficulty. This is due partly to a misconstruction of the technological race as a problem in matching striking forces, partly to a wishful analysis of the Soviet ability to strike first.

Since sputnik, the United States has made several moves to assure the world (that is, the enemy, but more especially our allies and ourselves) that we will match or overmatch Soviet technology and, specifically, Soviet offense technology. We have, for example, accelerated the bomber and ballistic missile programs, in particular the intermediate-range ballistic missiles. The problem

---

1 I want to thank C. J. Hitch, M. W. Hoag, W. W. Kaufman, A. W. Marshall, H. S. Rowen and W. W. Taylor for suggestions in preparation of this article.

2 George F. Kennan, "A Chance to Withdraw Our Troops in Europe," *Harper's Magazine,* February 1958, p. 41.
3 P. M. S. Blackett, *Atomic Weapons and East-West Relations* (New York: Cambridge University Press, 1956), p. 32.

has been conceived as more or better bombers—or rockets; or sputniks; or engineers. This has meant confusing deterrence with matching or exceeding the enemy's ability to strike first. Matching weapons, however, misconstrues the nature of the technological race. Not, as is frequently said, because only a few bombs owned by the defender can make aggression fruitless, but because even many might not. One outmoded A-bomb dropped from an obsolete bomber might destroy a great many supersonic jets and ballistic missiles. To deter an attack means being able to strike back in spite of it. It means, in other words, a capability to strike second. In the last year or two there has been a growing awareness of the importance of the distinction between a "strike-first" and a "strike-second" capability, but little, if any, recognition of the implications of this distinction for the balance of terror theory.

Where the published writings have not simply underestimated Soviet capabilities and the advantages of a first strike, they have in general placed artificial constraints on the Soviet use of the capabilities attributed to them. They assume, for example, that the enemy will attack in mass over the Arctic through our Distant Early Warning line, with bombers refueled over Canada—all resulting in plenty of warning. Most hopefully, it is sometimes assumed that such attacks will be preceded by days of visible preparations for moving ground troops. Such assumptions suggest that the Soviet leaders will be rather bumbling or, better, coöperative. However attractive it may be for us to narrow Soviet alternatives to these, they would be low in the order of preference of any reasonable Russians planning war.

THE QUANTITATIVE NATURE OF THE PROBLEM AND THE UNCERTAINTIES

In treating Soviet strategies it is important to consider Soviet rather than Western advantage and to consider the strategy of both sides quantitatively. The effectiveness of our own choices will depend on a most complex numerical interaction of Soviet and Western plans. Unfortunately, both the privileged and unprivileged information on these matters is precarious. As a result, competent people have been led into critical error in evaluating the prospects for deterrence. Western journalists have greatly overestimated the difficulties of a Soviet surprise attack with thermonuclear weapons and vastly underestimated the complexity of the Western problem of retaliation.

One intelligent commentator, Richard Rovere, recently expressed the common view: "If the Russians had ten thousand warheads and a missile for each, and we had ten hydrogen bombs and ten obsolete bombers, . . . aggression would still be a folly that would appeal only to an insane adventurer." Mr. Rovere's example is plausible because it assumes implicitly that the defender's hydrogen bombs will with certainty be visited on the aggressor; then the damage done by the ten bombs seems terrible enough for deterrence, and any more would be simply redundant. This is the basis for the common view. The example raises questions, even assuming the delivery of the ten weapons. For instance, the targets aimed at in retaliation might be sheltered and a quite modest civil defense could hold within tolerable limits the damage done to such city targets by ten delivered bombs. But the essential point is that the weapons would not be very likely to reach their targets. Even if the bombers were dispersed at ten different points, and protected by shelters so blast resistant as to stand up anywhere outside the lip of the bomb crater—even inside the fire ball itself—the chance of one of these bombers surviving the huge attack directed at it would be on the order of one in a million. (This calculation takes account of the unreliability and inaccuracy of the missile.) And the damage done by the small minority of these ten planes that might be in the air at the time of the attack, armed and ready to run the gauntlet of an alert air defense system, if not zero, would be very small indeed compared to damage that Russia has suffered in the past. For Mr. Rovere, like many other writers on this subject, numerical superiority is not important at all.

For Joseph Alsop, on the other hand, it is important, but the superiority is on our side. Mr. Alsop recently enunciated as one of the four rules of nuclear war: "The aggressor's problem is astronomically difficult; and the aggressor requires an overwhelming superiority of force."[4] There are, he believes, no fewer than 400 SAC bases in the NATO nations alone and many more elsewhere, all of which would have to be attacked in a very short space of time. The "thousands of coördinated air sorties and/or missile firings," he concludes, are not feasible. Mr. Alsop's argument is numerical and has the virtue of demonstrating that at least the relative numbers are important. But the numbers he uses are very wide of the mark. He overestimates the number of such bases by a factor of more than ten,[5] and in any case, missile firings on the scale of a thousand or more

involve costs that are by no means out of proportion, given the strategic budgets of the great powers. Whether or not thousands are needed depends on the yield and the accuracy of the enemy missiles, something about which it would be a great mistake for us to display confidence.

Perhaps the first step in dispelling the nearly universal optimism about the stability of deterrence would be to recognize the difficulties in analyzing the uncertainties and interactions between our own wide range of choices and the moves open to the Soviets. On our side we must consider an enormous variety of strategic weapons which might compose our force, and for each of these several alternative methods of basing and operation. These are the choices that determine whether a weapons system will have any genuine capability in the realistic circumstances of a war. Besides the B-47E and the B-52 bombers which are in the United States strategic force now, alternatives will include the B-52G (a longer-range version of the B-52); the Mach 2 B-58A bomber and a "growth" version of it; the Mach 3 B-70 bomber; a nuclear-powered bomber possibly carrying long-range air-to-surface missiles; the Dynasoar, a manned glide-rocket; the Thor and the Jupiter, liquid-fueled intermediate-range ballistic missiles; the Snark intercontinental cruise missile; the Atlas and the Titan intercontinental ballistic missiles; the submarine-launched Polaris and Atlantis rockets; and Minuteman, one potential solid-fueled successor to the Thor and Titan; possibly unmanned bombardment satellites; and many others which are not yet gleams in anyone's eye and some that are just that.

The difficulty of describing in a brief article the best mixture of weapons for the long-term future beginning in 1960, their base requirements, their potential-

---

[4] Joseph Alsop, "The New Balance of Power," *Encounter*, May 1958, p. 4. It should be added that, since these lines were written, Mr. Alsop's views have altered.

[5] *The New York Times*, September 6, 1958, p. 2.

ity for stabilizing or upsetting the balance among the great powers, and their implications for the alliance, is not just a matter of space or the constraint of security. The difficulty in fact stems from some rather basic insecurities. These matters are wildly uncertain; we are talking about weapons and vehicles that are some time off and, even if the precise performances currently hoped for and claimed by contractors were in the public domain, it would be a good idea to doubt them.

Recently some of my colleagues picked their way through the graveyard of early claims about various missiles and aircraft: their dates of availability, costs and performance. These claims are seldom revisited or talked about: *de mortuis nil nisi bonum*. The errors were large and almost always in one direction. And the less we knew, the more hopeful we were. Accordingly the missiles benefited in particular. For example, the estimated cost of one missile increased by a factor of over 50— from about $35,000 in 1949 to some $2 million in 1957. This uncertainty is critical. Some but not all of the systems listed can be chosen and the problem of choice is essentially quantitative. The complexities of the problem, if they were more widely understood, would discourage the oracular confidence of writers on the subject of deterrence.

Some of the complexities can be suggested by referring to the successive obstacles to be hurdled by any system providing a capability to strike second, that is, to strike back. Such deterrent systems must have (a) a stable, "steady-state" peacetime operation within feasible budgets (besides the logistic and operational costs there are, for example, problems of false alarms and accidents). They must have also the ability (b) to survive enemy attacks, (c) to make and communicate the decision to retaliate, (d) to reach

enemy territory with fuel enough to complete their mission, (e) to penetrate enemy active defenses, that is, fighters and surface-to-air missiles, and (f) to destroy the target in spite of any "passive" civil defense in the form of dispersal or protective construction or evacuation of the target itself.

Within limits the enemy is free to use his offensive and defensive forces so as to exploit the weaknesses of each of our systems. He will also be free, within limits, in the 1960s to choose that composition of forces which will make life as difficult as possible for the various systems we might select. It would be quite wrong to assume that we have the same degree of flexibility or that the uncertainties I have described affect a totalitarian aggressor and the party attacked equally. A totalitarian country can preserve secrecy about the capabilities and disposition of his forces very much better than a Western democracy. And the aggressor has, among other enormous advantages of the first strike, the ability to weigh continually our performance at each of the six barriers and to choose that precise time and circumstance for attack which will reduce uncertainty. It is important not to confuse our uncertainty with his. Strangely enough, some military commentators have not made this distinction and have founded their certainty of deterrence on the fact simply that there are uncertainties.

Unwarranted optimism is displayed not only in the writings of journalists but in the more analytic writings of professionals. The recent writings of General Gallois[6] parallel rather closely Mr. Alsop's faulty numerical proof that surprise attack is astronomically diffi-

6 General Pierre M. Gallois, "A French General Analyzes Nuclear-Age Strategy," *Réalités*, Nov. 1958, p. 19; "Nuclear Aggression and National Suicide," *The Reporter*, Sept. 18, 1958, p. 23.

cult—except that Gallois' "simple arith-metic," to borrow his own phrase, turns essentially on some assumptions which are at once inexplicit and extremely optimistic with respect to the blast resistance of dispersed missile sites sub-jected to attack from relatively close range.[7] Mr. Blackett's recent book, *Atomic Weapons and East-West Rela-tions,* illustrates the hazards confront-ing a most able analyst in dealing with the piecemeal information available to the general public. Mr. Blackett, a Nobel prize-winning physicist with war-time experience in military operations research, lucidly summarized the public information available when he was writing in 1956 on weapons for all-out war. But much of his analysis was based on the assumption that H-bombs could not be made small enough to be carried in an intercontinental missile. It is now widely known that intercontinental bal-listic missiles will have hydrogen war-heads, and this fact, a secret at the time, invalidates Mr. Blackett's calcu-lations and, I might say, much of his optimism on the stability of the balance of terror. In sum, one of the serious obstacles to any widespread rational judgment on these matters of high policy is that critical elements of the problem *have* to be protected by secrecy. However, some of the principal conclusions about deterrence in the early 1960s can be fairly firmly based, and based on public information.

THE DELICACY OF THE BALANCE OF TERROR

The most important conclusion is that we must expect a vast increase in the weight of attack which the Soviets can deliver with little warning, and the

[7] See footnote 9.

growth of a significant Russian capa-bility for an essentially warningless at-tack. As a result, strategic deterrence, while feasible, will be extremely diffi-cult to achieve, and at critical junctures in the 1960s, we may not have the power to deter attack. Whether we have it or not will depend on some difficult strategic choices as to the future composition of the deterrent forces as well as hard choices on its basing, operations and defense.

Manned bombers will continue to make up the predominant part of our striking force in the early 1960s. None of the popular remedies for their defense will suffice—not, for example, mere increase of alertness (which will be offset by the Soviet's increasing capability for attack without significant warning), nor simple dispersal or sheltering alone or mobility taken by itself, nor a mere piling up of inter-ceptors and defense missiles around SAC bases. Especially extravagant ex-pectations have been placed on the air-borne alert—an extreme form of defense by mobility. The impression is rather widespread that one-third of the SAC bombers are in the air and ready for combat at all times.[8] This belief is belied by the public record. According to the Symington Committee Hearings in 1956, our bombers averaged 31 hours of flying per month, which is about 4 percent of the average 732-hour month. An Air Force representative expressed the hope that within a couple of years, with an increase in the ratio of crews to aircraft, the bombers would reach 45

[8] See, for example, "NATO, A Critical Appraisal," by Gardner Patterson and Edgar S. Furniss, Jr., Princeton University Con-ference on NATO, Princeton, June 1957, p. 32: "Although no one pretended to know, the hypothesis that one-third of the striking force of the United States Strategic Air Command was in the air at all times was regarded by most as reasonable."

hours of flight per month—which is 6 percent. This 4 to 6 percent of the force includes bombers partially fueled and without bombs. It is, moreover, only an average, admitting variance down as well as up. Some increase in the number of armed bombers aloft is to be expected. However, for the current generation of bombers, which have been designed for speed and range rather than endurance, a continuous air patrol for one-third of the force would be extremely expensive.

On the other hand, it would be unwise to look for miracles in the new weapons systems, which by the mid-1960s may constitute a considerable portion of the United States force. After the Thor, Atlas and Titan there are a number of promising developments. The solid-fueled rockets, Minuteman and Polaris, promise in particular to be extremely significant components of the deterrent force. Today they are being touted as making the problem of deterrence easy to solve and, in fact, guaranteeing its solution. But none of the new developments in vehicles is likely to do that. For the complex job of deterrence, they all have limitations. The unvaryingly immoderate claims for each new weapons system should make us wary of the latest "technological breakthroughs." Only a very short time ago the ballistic missile itself was supposed to be intrinsically invulnerable on the ground. It is now more generally understood that its survival is likely to depend on a variety of choices in its defense.

It is hard to talk with confidence about the mid- and late-1960s. A systematic study of an optimal or a good deterrent force which considered all the major factors affecting choice and dealt adequately with the uncertainties would be a formidable task. In lieu of this, I shall mention briefly why none

of the many systems available or projected dominates the others in any obvious way. My comments will take the form of a swift run-through of the characteristic advantages and disadvantages of various strategic systems at each of the six successive hurdles mentioned earlier.

The first hurdle to be surmounted is the attainment of a stable, steady-state peacetime operation. Systems which depend for their survival on extreme decentralization of controls, as may be the case with large-scale dispersal and some of the mobile weapons, raise problems of accidents and over a long period of peacetime operation this leads in turn to serious political problems. Systems relying on extensive movement by land, perhaps by truck caravan, are an obvious example; the introduction of these on European roads, as is sometimes suggested, would raise grave questions for the governments of some of our allies. Any extensive increase in the armed air alert will increase the hazard of accident and intensify the concern already expressed among our allies. Some of the proposals for bombardment satellites may involve such hazards of unintended bomb release as to make them out of the question.

The cost to buy and operate various weapons systems must be seriously considered. Some systems buy their ability to negotiate a given hurdle—say, surviving the enemy attack—only at prohibitive cost. Then the number that can be bought out of a given budget will be small and this will affect the relative performance of competing systems at various other hurdles, for example penetrating enemy defenses. Some of the relevant cost comparisons, then, are between competing systems; others concern the extra costs to the enemy of canceling an additional expenditure of our own. For example, some dispersal is essential, though usually it is expensive; if the dispersed bases are within a warning net, dispersal can help to provide warning against some sorts of attack, since it forces the attacker to increase the size of his raid and so makes it more liable to detection as well as somewhat harder to coördinate. But as the sole or principal defense of our offensive force, dispersal has only a brief useful life and can be justified financially only up to a point. For against our costs of construction, maintenance and operation of an additional base must be set the enemy's much lower costs of delivering one extra weapon. And, in general, any feasible degree of dispersal leaves a considerable concentration of value at a single target point. For example, a squadron of heavy bombers costing, with their associated tankers and penetration aids, perhaps \$500,000,000 over five years, might be eliminated, if it were otherwise unprotected, by an enemy intercontinental ballistic missile costing perhaps \$16,000,000. After making allowance for the unreliability and inaccuracy of the missile, this means a ratio of some ten for one or better. To achieve safety by *brute* numbers in so unfavorable a competition is not likely to be viable economically or politically. However, a viable peacetime operation is only the first hurdle to be surmounted.

At the second hurdle—surviving the enemy offense—ground alert systems placed deep within a warning net look good against a manned bomber attack, much less good against intercontinental ballistic missiles, and not good at all against ballistic missiles launched from the sea. In the last case, systems such as the Minuteman, which may be sheltered and dispersed as well as alert, would do well. Systems involving launching platforms which are mobile and concealed, such as Polaris submarines, have particular advantage for surviving an enemy offense.

However, there is a third hurdle to be surmounted—namely that of making the decision to retaliate and communicating it. Here, Polaris, the combat air patrol of B-52s, and in fact all of the mobile platforms—under water, on the surface, in the air and above the air—have severe problems. Long distance communication may be jammed and, most important, communication centers may be destroyed.

At the fourth hurdle—ability to reach enemy territory with fuel enough to complete the mission—several of our short-legged systems have operational problems such as coördination with tankers and using bases close to the enemy. For a good many years to come, up to the mid-1960s in fact, this will be a formidable hurdle for the greater part of our deterrent force. The next section of this article deals with this problem at some length.

The fifth hurdle is the aggressor's long-range interceptors and close-in missile defenses. To get past these might require large numbers of planes and missiles. (If the high cost of overcoming an earlier obstacle—using extreme dispersal or airborne alert or the like—limits the number of planes or missiles bought, our capability is likely to be penalized disproportionately here.) Or getting through may involve carrying heavy loads of radar decoys, electronic jammers and other aids to defense penetration. For example, vehicles like Minuteman and Polaris, which were made small to facilitate dispersal or mobility, may suffer here because they can carry fewer penetration aids.

At the final hurdle—destroying the target in spite of the passive defenses that may protect it—low-payload and low-accuracy systems, such as Minuteman and Polaris, may be frustrated by blast-resistant shelters. For example, five half-megaton weapons with an average inaccuracy of two miles might be expected to destroy half the population of a city of 900,000, spread over 40 square miles, provided the inhabitants are without shelters. But if they are provided with shelters capable of resisting over-pressures of 100 pounds per square inch, approximately 60 such weapons would be required; and deep rock shelters might force the total up to over a thousand.

Prizes for a retaliatory capability are not distributed for getting over one of these jumps. A system must get over all six. I hope these illustrations will suggest that assuring ourselves the power to strike back after a massive thermonuclear surprise attack is by no means as automatic as is widely believed.

In counteracting the general optimism as to the ease and, in fact, the inevitability of deterrence, I should like to avoid creating the extreme opposite impression. Deterrence demands hard, continuing, intelligent work, but it can be achieved. The job of deterring rational attack by guaranteeing great damage to an aggressor is, for example, very much less difficult than erecting a nearly airtight defense of cities in the face of full-scale thermonuclear surprise attack. Protecting manned bombers and missiles is much easier because they may be dispersed, sheltered or kept mobile, and they can respond to warning with greater speed. Mixtures of these and other defenses with complementary strengths can preserve a powerful remainder after attack. Obviously not all our bombers and missiles need to survive in order to fulfill their mission. To preserve the majority of our cities intact in the face of surprise attack is immensely more difficult, if not impossible. (This does not mean

that the aggressor has the same problem in preserving his cities from retaliation by a poorly-protected, badly-damaged force. And it does not mean that *we* should not do more to limit the extent of the catastrophe to our cities in case deterrence fails. I believe we should.) Deterrence, however, provided we work at it, is feasible, and, what is more, it is a crucial objective of national policy.

What can be said, then, as to whether general war is unlikely? Would not a general thermonuclear war mean "extinction" for the aggressor as well as the defender? "Extinction" is a state that badly needs analysis. Russian casualties in World War II were more than 20,000,000. Yet Russia recovered extremely well from this catastrophe. There are several quite plausible circumstances in the future when the Russians might be quite confident of being able to limit damage to considerably less than this number—if they make sensible strategic choices and we do not. On the other hand, the risks of not striking might at some juncture appear very great to the Soviets, involving, for example, disastrous defeat in peripheral war, loss of key satellites with danger of revolt spreading—possibly to Russia itself—or fear of an attack by ourselves. Then, striking first, by surprise, would be the sensible choice for them, and from their point of view the smaller risk.

It should be clear that it is not fruitful to talk about the likelihood of general war without specifying the range of alternatives that are pressing on the aggressor and the strategic postures of both the Soviet bloc and the West. Deterrence is a matter of comparative risks. The balance is not automatic. First, since thermonuclear weapons give an enormous advantage to the aggressor, it takes great ingenuity and realism at any given level of nuclear technology to devise a stable equilibrium. And second, this technology itself is changing with fantastic speed. Deterrence will require an urgent and continuing effort.

THE USES AND RISKS OF BASES CLOSE TO THE SOVIETS

It may now be useful to focus attention on the special problems of deterrent forces close to the Soviet Union. First, overseas areas have played an important rôle in the past and have a continuing though less certain rôle today. Second, the recent acceleration of production of intermediate-range ballistic missiles and the negotiation of agreements with various NATO powers for their basing and operation have given our overseas bases a renewed importance in deterring attack on the United States—or so it would appear at first blush. Third, an analysis can throw some light on the problems faced by our allies in developing an independent ability to deter all-out attack on themselves, and in this way it can clarify the much agitated question of nuclear sharing. Finally, overseas bases affect in many critical ways, political and economic as well as military, the status of the alliance.

At the end of the last decade, overseas bases appeared to be an advantageous means of achieving the radius extension needed by our short-legged bombers, of permitting them to use several axes of attack, and of increasing the number of sorties possible in the course of an extended campaign. With the growth of our own thermonuclear stockpile, it became apparent that a long campaign involving many re-uses of a large proportion of our bombers was not likely to be necessary. With

the growth of a Russian nuclear-delivery capability, it became clear that this was most unlikely to be feasible.

Our overseas bases now have the disadvantage of high vulnerability. Because they are closer than the United States to the Soviet Union, they are subject to a vastly greater attack by a larger variety as well as number of vehicles. With given resources, the Soviets might deliver on nearby bases a freight of bombs with something like 50 to 100 times the yield that they could muster at intercontinental range. Missile accuracy would more than double. Because there is not much space for obtaining warning—in any case, there are no deep-warning radar nets —and, since most of our overseas bases are close to deep water from which submarines might launch missiles, the warning problem is very much more severe than for bases in the interior of the United States.

As a result, early in the 1950s the U.S. Air Force decided to recall many of our bombers to the continental United States and to use the overseas bases chiefly for refueling, particularly poststrike ground refueling. This reduced drastically the vulnerability of U.S. bombers and at the same time retained many of the advantages of overseas operation. For some years now SAC has been reducing the number of aircraft usually deployed overseas. The purpose is to reduce vulnerability and has little to do with any increasing radius of SAC aircraft. The early B-52 radius is roughly that of the B-36; the B-47, roughly that of the B-50 or B-29. In fact the radius limitation and therefore the basing requirements we have discussed will not change substantially for some time to come. We can talk with comparative confidence here, because the U.S. strategic force is itself largely determined for this period. Such a force changes more slowly than is generally realized. The vast majority of the force will consist of manned bombers, and most of these will be of medium range. *Some* U.S. bombers will be able to reach *some* targets from *some* U.S. bases within the 48 states without landing on the way back. On the other hand, some bomber-target combinations are not feasible without pre-target landing (and are therefore doubtful). The Atlas, Titan and Polaris rockets, when available, can of course do without overseas bases (though the proportion of Polaris submarines kept at sea can be made larger by the use of submarine tenders based overseas). But even with the projected force of aerial tankers, the greater part of our force, which will be manned bombers, cannot be used at all in attacks on the Soviet Union without at least some use of overseas areas.

What of the bases for Thor and Jupiter, our first intermediate-range ballistic missiles? These have to be close to the enemy, and they must of course be operating bases, not merely refueling stations. The Thors and Jupiters will be continuously in range of an enormous Soviet potential for surprise attack. These installations therefore reopen, in a most acute form, some of the serious questions of ground vulnerability that were raised about six years ago in connection with our overseas bomber bases. The decision to station the Thor and Jupiter missiles overseas has been our principal public response to the Russian advances in rocketry, and perhaps our most plausible response. Because it involves our ballistic missiles it appears directly to answer the Russian rockets. Because it involves using European bases, it appears to make up for the range superiority of the Russian intercontinental missile. And most important, it directly involves the NATO powers and gives them an element of control.

There is no question that it was genuinely urgent not only to meet the Russian threat but to do so visibly, in order to save the loosening NATO alliance. Our allies were fearful that the Soviet ballistic missiles might mean that we were no longer able or willing to retaliate against the Soviet Union in case of an attack on them. We hastened to make public a reaction which would restore their confidence. This move surely appears to increase our own power to strike back, and also to give our allies a deterrent of their own, independent of our decision. It has also been argued that in this respect it merely advances the inevitable date at which our allies will acquire "modern" weapons of their own, and that it widens the range of Soviet challenges which Europe can meet. But we must face seriously the question whether this move will in fact assure either the ability to retaliate or the decision to attempt it, on the part of our allies or ourselves. And we should ask at the very least whether further expansion of this policy will buy as much retaliatory power as other ways of spending the considerable sums involved. Finally, it is important to be clear whether the Thor and Jupiter actually increase the flexibility or range of response available to our allies.

One justification for this move is that it disperses retaliatory weapons and that this is the most effective sanction against the thermonuclear aggressor. The limitations of dispersal have already been discussed, but it remains to examine the argument that overseas bases provide *widespread* dispersal, which imposes on the aggressor insoluble problems of coördination.

There is of course something in the notion that forcing the enemy to attack

258

THE INTERNATIONAL SOCIETY

many political entities increases the seriousness of his decision, but there is very little in the notion that dispersal in several countries makes the problem of destruction more difficult in the military sense. Dispersal does not require separation by the distance of oceans— just by the lethal diameters of enemy bombs. And the task of coördinating bomber attacks on Europe and the eastern coast of the United States, say, is not appreciably more difficult than coördinating attacks on our east and west coasts. In the case of ballistic missiles, the elapsed time from firing to impact on the target can be calculated with high accuracy. Although there will be some failures and delays, times of firing can be arranged so that impact on many dispersed points is almost simultaneous—on Okinawa and the United Kingdom, for instance, as well as on California and Ohio. Moreover, it is important to keep in mind that these far-flung bases, while distant from each other and from the United States, are on the whole close to the enemy. To eliminate them, therefore, requires a smaller expenditure of resources on his part than targets at intercontinental range. For close-in targets he can use a wider variety of weapons carrying larger payloads and with higher accuracy.

The seeming appositeness of an overseas-based Thor and Jupiter as an answer to a Russian intercontinental ballistic missile stems not so much from any careful analysis of their retaliatory power under attack as from the directness of the comparison they suggest: a rocket equals a rocket, an intercontinental missile equals an intermediate-range missile based at closer range to the target. But this again mistakes the nature of the technological race. It conceives the problem of deterrence as that of simply matching or exceeding

the aggressor's capability to strike first. A surprising proportion of the debate on defense policy has betrayed this confusion. Matching technological developments are useful for prestige, and such demonstrations have a vital function in preserving the alliance and in reassuring the neutral powers. But propaganda is not enough. The only reasonably certain way of maintaining a reputation for strength is to display an actual power to our friends as well as our enemies. We should ask, then, whether further expansion of the current programs for basing Thor and Jupiter is an efficient way to increase American retaliatory power. If overseas bases are considered too vulnerable for manned bombers, will not the same be true for missiles?

The basis for the hopeful impression that they will not is rather vague, including a mixture of hypothetical properties of ballistic missiles in which perhaps the dominant element is their supposedly much more rapid, "push-button" response. What needs to be considered here are the response time of such missiles (including decision, preparation and launch times), and how they are to be defended.

The decision to fire a missile with a thermonuclear warhead is much harder to make than a decision simply to start a manned aircraft on its way, with orders to return to base unless instructed to continue to its assigned target. This is the "fail-safe" procedure practised by the U.S. Air Force. In contrast, once a missile is launched, there is no method of recall or deflection which is not subject to risks of electronic or mechanical failure. Therefore such a decision must wait for much more unambiguous evidence of enemy intentions. It must and will take a longer time to make and is less likely to be made at all. Where more than one country is involved, the joint decision is harder still, since there is opportunity to disagree about the ambiguity of the evidence, as well as to reach quite different interpretations of national interest. On much less momentous matters the process of making decisions in NATO is complicated, and it should be recognized that such complexity has much to do with the genuine concern of the various NATO powers about the danger of accidentally starting World War III. Such fears will not be diminished with the advent of I.R.B.M.s. In fact, widespread dispersion of nuclear armed missiles raises measurably the possibility of accidental war.

Second, it is quite erroneous to suppose that by contrast with manned bombers the first I.R.B.M.s can be launched almost as simply as pressing a button. Count-down procedures for early missiles are liable to interruption, and the characteristics of the liquid oxygen fuel limits the readiness of their response. Unlike JP-4, the fuel used in jet bombers, liquid oxygen cannot be held for long periods of time in these vehicles. In this respect such missiles will be *less* ready than alert bombers. Third, the smaller warning time available overseas makes more difficult any response. This includes, in particular, any active defense, not only against ballistic missile attacks but, for example, against low altitude or various circuitous attacks by manned aircraft.

Finally, passive defense by means of shelter is more difficult, given the larger bomb yields, better accuracies and larger forces available to the Russians at such close range. And if the press reports are correct, the plans for I.R.B.M. installations do not call for bomb-resistant shelters. If this is so, it should be taken into account in measuring the actual contribution of these installations to the West's retaliatory

power. Viewed as a contribution to deterring all-out attack on the United States, the Thor and Jupiter bases seem unlikely to compare favorably with other alternatives. If newspaper references to hard bargaining by some of our future hosts are to be believed, it would seem that such negotiations have been conducted under misapprehensions on both sides as to the benefits to the United States.

But many proponents of the distribution of Thor and Jupiter—and possibly some of our allies—have in mind not an increase in U.S. deterrence but the development of an independent capability in several of the NATO countries to deter all-out attack against themselves. This would be a useful thing if it can be managed at supportable cost and if it does not entail the sacrifice of even more critical measures of protection. But aside from the special problems of joint control, which would affect the certainty of response adversely, precisely who their legal owner is will not affect the retaliatory power of the Thors and Jupiters one way or the other. They would not be able to deter an attack which they could not survive. It is curious that many who question the utility of American overseas bases (for example, our bomber bases in the United Kingdom) simply assume that, for our allies, possession of strategic nuclear weapons is one with deterrence.

There remains the view that the provision of these weapons will broaden the range of response open to our allies. In so far as this view rests on the belief that the intermediate-range ballistic missile is adapted to limited war, it is wide of the mark. The inaccuracy of an I.R.B.M. requires high-yield warheads, and such a combination of inaccuracy and high yield, while quite appropriate and adequate against unprotected targets in a general war, would scarcely come within even the most lax, in fact reckless, definition of limited war. Such a weapon is inappropriate for even the nuclear variety of limited war, and it is totally useless for meeting the wide variety of provocation that is well below the threshold of nuclear response. In so far as these missiles will be costly for our allies to install, operate and support, they are likely to displace a conventional capability that might be genuinely useful in limited engagements. More important, they are likely to be used as an excuse for budget cutting. In this way they will accelerate the general trend toward dependence on all-out response and so will have the opposite effect to the one claimed.

Nevertheless, if the Thor and Jupiter have these defects, might not some future weapon be free of them? Some of these defects, of course, will be overcome in time. Solid fuels or storable liquids will eventually replace liquid oxygen, reliabilities will increase, various forms of mobility or portability will become feasible, accuracies may even be so improved that such weapons can be used in limited wars. But these developments are all years away. In consequence, the discussion will be advanced if a little more precision is given such terms as "missiles" or "modern" or "advanced weapons." We are not distributing a generic "modern" weapon with all the virtues of flexibility in varying circumstances and of invulnerability in all-out war. But even with advances in the state of the art on our side, it will remain difficult to maintain a deterrent, especially close in under the enemy's guns.

It follows that, though a wider distribution of nuclear weapons may be inevitable, or at any rate likely, and though some countries in addition to the Soviet Union and the United States

may even develop an independent deterrent, it is by no means inevitable or even very likely that the power to deter all-out thermonuclear attack will be widespread. This is true even though a minor power would not need to guarantee as large a retaliation as we in order to deter attack on itself. Unfortunately, the minor powers have smaller resources as well as poorer strategic locations.[9] Mere membership

9 General Gallois argues that, while alliances will offer no guarantee, "a small number of bombs and a small number of carriers suffice for a threatened power to protect itself against atomic destruction." (*Réalités, op. cit.,* p. 71.) His numerical illustrations give the defender some 400 underground launching sites (*ibid.,* p. 22, and *The Reporter, op. cit.,* p. 25) and suggest that their elimination would require between 5,000 and 25,000 missiles—which is "more or less impossible"—and that in any case the aggressor would not survive the fallout from his own weapons. Whether these are large numbers of targets from the standpoint of the aggressor will depend on the accuracy, yield and reliability of offense weapons as well as the resistance of the defender's shelters and a number of other matters not specified in the argument. General Gallois is aware that the expectation of survival depends on distance even in the ballistic missile age and that our allies are not so fortunate in this respect. Close-in missiles have better bomb yields and accuracies. Moreover, manned aircraft—with still better yields and accuracies—can be used by an aggressor here since warning of their approach is very short. Suffice it to say that the numerical advantage General Gallois cites is greatly exaggerated. Furthermore, he exaggerates the destructiveness of the retaliatory blow against the aggressor's cities by the remnants of the defender's missile force—even assuming the aggressor would take no special measures to protect his cities. But particularly for the aggressor—who does not lack warning—a civil defense program can moderate the damage done by a poorly organized attack. Finally, the suggestion that the aggressor would not survive the fall-out from his own weapons is simply in error. The rapid-decay fission products which are the major lethal

in the nuclear club might carry with it prestige, as the applicants and nominees expect, but it will be rather expensive, and in time it will be clear that it does not necessarily confer any of the expected privileges enjoyed by the two charter members. The burden of deterring a general war as distinct from limited wars is still likely to be on the United States and therefore, so far as our allies are concerned, on the military alliance.

There is one final consideration. Missiles placed near the enemy, even if they could not retaliate, would have a potent capability for striking first by surprise. And it might not be easy for the enemy to discern their purpose. The existence of such a force might be a considerable provocation and in fact a dangerous one in the sense that it would place a great burden on our deterrent force which more than ever would have to guarantee extreme risks to the attacker—worse than the risks of waiting in the face of this danger. When not coupled with the ability to strike in retaliation, such a capability might suggest—erroneously, to be sure, in the case of the democracies—an intention to strike first. If so, it would

---

problem in the locality of a surface burst are not a serious difficulty for the aggressor. The amount of the slow-decay products, strontium-90 and cesium-137, in the atmosphere would rise considerably. If nothing were done to counter it, this might, for example, increase by many times the incidence of such relatively rare diseases as bone cancer and leukemia. However, such a calamity, implying an increase of, say, 20,000 deaths per year for a nation of 200,000,000, is of an entirely different order from the catastrophe involving tens of millions of deaths, which General Gallois contemplates elsewhere. And there are measures that might reduce even this effect drastically. (See the RAND Corporation Report R-322-RC, *Report on a Study of Non-Military Defense*, July 1, 1958.)

tend to provoke rather than to deter general war.

I have dealt here with only one of the functions of overseas bases: their use as a support for the strategic deterrent force. They have a variety of important military, political and economic rôles which are beyond the scope of this paper. Expenditures in connection with the construction or operation of our bases, for example, are a form of economic aid and, moreover, a form that is rather palatable to the Congress. There are other functions in a central war where their importance may be very considerable and their usefulness in a limited war might be substantial.

Indeed nothing said here should suggest that deterrence is in itself an adequate strategy. The complementary requirements of a sufficient military policy cannot be discussed in detail here. Certainly they include a more serious development of power to meet limited aggression, especially with more advanced conventional weapons than those now available. They also include more energetic provision for active and passive defenses to limit the dimensions of the catastrophe in case deterrence should fail. For example, an economically feasible shelter program might make the difference between 50,000,000 survivors and 120,000,000 survivors.

But it would be a fatal mistake to suppose that because strategic deterrence is inadequate by itself it can be dispensed with. Deterrence is not dispensable. If the picture of the world I have drawn is rather bleak, it could none the less be cataclysmically worse. Suppose both the United States and the Soviet Union had the power to destroy each others' retaliatory forces and society, given the opportunity to administer the opening blow. The situation would then be something like the old-fashioned Western gun duel. It would be extraordinarily risky for one side *not* to attempt to destroy the other, or to delay doing so, since it not only can emerge unscathed by striking first but this is the sole way it can reasonably hope to emerge at all. Evidently such a situation is extremely unstable. On the other hand, if it is clear that the aggressor too will suffer catastrophic damage in the event of his aggression, he then has strong reason not to attack, even though he can administer great damage. A protected retaliatory capability has a stabilizing influence not only in deterring rational attack, but also in offering every inducement to both powers to reduce the chance of accidental war.

The critics who feel that deterrence is "bankrupt" sometimes say that we stress deterrence too much. I believe this is quite wrong if it means that we are devoting too much effort to protect our power to retaliate; but I think it is quite right if it means that we have talked too much of a strategic threat as a substitute for many things it cannot replace.

DETERRENCE, ACCIDENTS AND DISARMAMENT

Up to now I have talked mainly about the problem of deterring general war, of making it improbable that an act of war will be undertaken deliberately, with a clear understanding of the consequences, that is, rationally. That such deterrence will not be easy to maintain in the 1960s simply expresses the proposition that a surprise thermonuclear attack might *not* be an irrational or insane act on the part of the aggressor. A deterrent strategy is aimed at a rational enemy. Without a deterrent, general war is likely. With it, however, war might still occur.

In order to reduce the risk of a rational act of aggression, we are being forced to undertake measures (increased alertness, dispersal, mobility) which, to a significant extent, increase the risk of an irrational or unintentional act of war. The accident problem is serious, and it would be a great mistake to dismiss the recent Soviet charges on this subject as simply part of the war of nerves. In a clear sense the great multiplication and spread of nuclear arms throughout the world, the drastic increase in the degree of readiness of these weapons, and the decrease in the time available for the decision on their use must inevitably raise the risk of accident. The B-47 accidents this year at Sidi Slimane and at Florence, S. C., and the recent Nike explosion are just a beginning. Though incidents of this sort are not themselves likely to trigger misunderstanding, they suggest the nature of the problem.

There are many sorts of accidents that could happen. There can be electronic or mechanical failures of the sort illustrated by the B-47 and Nike mishaps; there can be aberrations of individuals, perhaps quite low in the echelon of command; there can be miscalculations on the part of governments as to enemy intent and the meaning of ambiguous signals. Not all deterrent strategies will involve the risk of accident equally. One of the principles of selecting a strategy should be to reduce the chance of accident, wherever we can, without a corresponding increase in vulnerability to a rational surprise attack. This is the purpose of the "fail-safe" procedures for launching SAC.

These problems are also relevant to the disarmament question. The Russians, exploiting an inaccurate United Press report which suggested that SAC started en masse toward Russia in response to frequent radar "ghosts," cried out against these supposed Arctic flights. The United States response, and its sequels, stated correctly that such flights had never been undertaken except in planned exercises and would not be undertaken in response to such unreliable warning. We pointed out the importance of quick response and a high degree of readiness in the protection of the deterrent force. The nature of the fail-safe precaution was also described.

We added, however, to cap the argument, that if the Russians were really worried about surprise attack they would accept the President's "open skies" proposal. This addition, however, conceals an absurdity. Aerial photography would have its uses in a disarmament plan—for example, to check an exchange of information on the location of ground bases. However, so far as surprise is concerned, an "open skies" plan would have direct use only to discover attacks requiring much more lengthy, visible and unambiguous preparations than are likely today.[10] The very readiness of our own strategic force suggests a state of technology which outmodes the "open skies" plan as a counter to surprise attack. Not even the most advanced reconnaissance equipment can disclose an intention from 40,000 feet. Who can say what the men in the blockhouse of an I.C.B.M. base have in mind? Or, for that matter, what is the final destination of training flights or fail-safe flights starting over the Pacific or North Atlantic from staging areas?

The actions that need to be taken on our own to deter attack might use-

---

10 Aerial reconnaissance, of course, could have an *indirect* utility here for surveying large areas to determine the number and location of observation posts needed to provide more timely warning.

fully be complemented by bilateral agreements for inspection and reporting and, possibly, limitation of arms and of methods of operating strategic and naval air forces. But the protection of our retaliatory power remains essential; and the better the protection, the smaller the burden placed on the agreement to limit arms and modes of operation and to make them subject to inspection. Reliance on "open skies" alone to prevent surprise would invite catastrophe and the loss of power to retaliate. Such a plan is worthless for discovering a well prepared attack with I.C.B.M.s or submarine-launched missiles or a routine mass training flight whose destination could be kept ambiguous. A tremendous weight of weapons could be delivered in spite of it.

Although it is quite hopeless to look for an inspection scheme which would permit abandonment of the deterrent, this does not mean that some partial agreement on inspection and limitation might not help to reduce the chance of any sizable surprise attack. We should explore the possibilities of agreements involving limitation and inspection. But how we go about this will be conditioned by our appreciation of the problem of deterrence itself.

The critics of current policy who perceive the inadequacy of the strategy of deterrence are prominent among those urging disarmament negotiations, an end to the arms race and a reduction of tension. This is a paramount interest of some of our allies. The balance of terror theory is the basis for some of the more light-hearted suggestions: if deterrence is automatic, strategic weapons on one side cancel those of the other, and it should be easy for both sides to give them up. So James E. King, Jr., one of the most sensible writers on the subject of limited war, suggests that weapons needed for "un-limited" war are those which both sides can most easily agree to abolish, simply because "neither side can antici-pate anything but disaster" from their use. "Isn't there enough stability in the 'balance of terror,'" he asks, "to justify our believing that the Russians can be trusted—within acceptable limits—to abandon the weapons whose 'utility is confined to the threat or conduct of a war of annihilation'?"[11]

Indeed, if there were no real danger of a rational attack, then accidents and the "nth" country problem would be the only problems. As I have indicated, they are serious problems and some sorts of limitation and inspection agree-ment might diminish them. But if there is to be any prospect of realistic and useful agreement, we must reject the theory of automatic deterrence. And we must bear in mind that the more exten-sive a disarmament agreement is, the smaller the force that a violator would have to hide in order to achieve com-plete domination. Most obviously, *"the abolition* of the weapons necessary in a general or 'unlimited' war" would offer the most insuperable obstacles to an inspection plan, since the violator could gain an overwhelming advantage from the concealment of even a few weapons. The need for a deterrent, in this connection too, is ineradicable.

SUMMARY

Almost everyone seems concerned with the need to relax tension. However, relaxation of tension, which everyone thinks is good, is not easily distin-guished from relaxing one's guard, which almost everyone thinks is bad. Relaxation, like Miltown, is not an end

---

11 James E. King, Jr., "Arms and Man in the Nuclear-Rocket Era," *The New Repub-lic,* September 1, 1958.

in itself. Not all danger comes from tension. To be tense where there is danger is only rational.

What can we say then, in sum, on the balance of terror theory of auto-matic deterrence? It is a contribution to the rhetoric rather than the logic of war in the thermonuclear age. The notion that a carefully planned surprise attack can be checkmated almost effort-lessly, that, in short, we may resume our deep pre-sputnik sleep, is wrong and its nearly universal acceptance is terribly dangerous. Though deterrence is not enough in itself, it is vital. There are two principal points.

First, deterring general war in both the early and late 1960s will be hard at best, and hardest both for ourselves and our allies wherever we use forces based near the enemy.

Second, even if we can deter general war by a strenuous and continuing ef-fort, this will by no means be the whole of a military, much less a foreign policy. Such a policy would not of itself re-move the danger of accidental outbreak or limit the damage in case deterrence failed; nor would it be at all adequate for crises on the periphery.

A generally useful way of concluding a grim argument of this kind would be to affirm that we have the resources, intelligence and courage to make the correct decisions. That is, of course, the case. And there is a good chance that we will do so. But perhaps, as a small aid toward making such decisions more likely, we should contemplate the pos-sibility that they may *not* be made. They *are* hard, *do* involve sacrifice, *are* affected by great uncertainties and con-cern matters in which much is alto-gether unknown and much else must be hedged by secrecy; and, above all, they entail a new image of ourselves in a world of persistent danger. It is by no means *certain* that we shall meet the test.

The First Twenty-Five Years
of the United Nations—
From San Francisco to the 1970's

DEAN RUSK

My assignment—to talk about the first 25 years of the United Nations—is unusual punishment for a Secretary of State. It is difficult enough to be a reasonably accurate historian of world affairs years later, after all the evidence is in. It is nothing short of foolhardy to foretell the future—especially when you are trying to tinker with the future to make it come out the way you think it should.

...I decided to try to look ahead as well as to look back. For, if we are to act wisely in world affairs, we must have some sense of direction, some conviction about the way human events are moving, some expectations about the forces and counterforces just over the horizon. I do have some expectations for the United Nations over the next five or ten years, and I might as well state them straightaway.

I believe that the influence of the United Nations will be even greater in the 1970's than it is today.

I believe also that the executive capacity of the United Nations to act in support of the purposes of the charter will be greater in the 1970's than it is today.

Department of State Bulletin, Vol. L, No. 1283, Jan. 27, 1964. (The Dag Hammarskjold Memorial Lecture, prepared for delivery by Secretary of State Dean Rusk and read by Harlan Cleveland, Assistant Secretary for International Organization Affairs, at Columbia University, New York, N.Y., on Jan. 10.

I hold these convictions despite valid cause for concern and some necessary reservations. I shall try to explain why.

THE U. N.: A NECESSITY FOR OUR TIMES

Let me begin by observing that it means little to study the performance of an institution against abstract standards without reference to the realities —and even the illusions—of the total environment in which it must operate. In that context the first thing that strikes one about the United Nations is that international organization is a plain necessity of our times. This is so for both technical and political reasons.

The technical reasons stem, of course, from the headlong rush of scientific discovery and technological advance. That process has overrun the hypothetical question as to whether there is to be an international community that requires organization. It has left us with the practical question of *what kind* of international community we have the wit to organize around the scientific and technical imperatives of our time. In the words of Ogden Nash:

When geniuses all in every nation
Hasten us towards obliteration,
Perhaps it will take the dolts and geese
To drag us backward into peace.

World community is a fact
—because instantaneous international communication is a fact;

—because fast international transport is a fact;

—because matters ranging from the control of communicable disease to weather reporting and forecasting demand international organization;

—because the transfer of technology essential to the spread of industrialization and the modernization of agriculture can be assisted by international organizations;

—because modern economics engage nations in a web of commercial, financial, and technical arrangements at the international level.

The advance of science, and the technology that follows, creates an insistent demand to build international technical and regulatory institutions which lend substance to world community. Few people seem to realize just how far this movement has gone. The United States is now a member of 53 international organizations. We contribute to 22 international operating programs, mostly sponsored by these same organizations. And last year we attended 547 international intergovernmental conferences, mostly on technical subjects. We do these things because they are always helpful and often downright essential to the conduct of our national and international affairs.

It is obvious that in the 1970's we shall require more effective international organization—making for a more substantial world community—than we have today. We already know that in the next decade we shall become accustomed to international communication, including television, via satellites in outer space. We shall travel in aircraft that fly at speeds above a thousand, and perhaps above two thousand, miles per hour. Industrialization will pursue its relentless course. Cities and their suburbs will keep on growing. The world economy will become increasingly inter-

dependent. And science will rush ahead, leaving to us the task of fashioning institutions—increasingly on the international level—to administer its benefits and circumscribe its dangers.

So, while nations may cling to national values and ideas and ambitions and prerogatives, science has created a functional international society, whether we like it or not. And that society, like any other, must be organized.

Anyone who questions the *need* for international technical organizations like the United Nations agencies dealing with maritime matters, civil aviation, telecommunications, atomic energy, and meteorology simply does not recognize the times in which we live.

In a world caught up in an urgent drive to modernize areas containing two-thirds of the human race, there is need also for the United Nations specialized agencies dealing with health, agriculture, labor standards, education, and other subjects related to national development and human welfare. A massive effort to transfer and adapt modern technology from the more to the less advanced areas is a part of the great drama of our age. This sometimes can be done best through, or with the help of, the institutions of the international community.

And the international organizations concerned with trade and monetary and financial affairs are important to the expanding prosperity of the world economy.

ADJUSTMENT TO REALITY OF POLITICAL WORLD

The need for political organs at the international level is just as plain as the need for technical agencies.

You will recall that the decision to try to form a new international organization to preserve peace grew out of the agonies of the Second World War. The United States took the lead in this enterprise. President Franklin D. Roosevelt and Secretary of State Cordell Hull sought to avoid repeating what many believed to have been mistakes in political tactics which kept the United States from joining the League of Nations. They consulted at every stage the leaders of both political parties in both Houses of Congress. They insisted that the formation of this organization should be accomplished, if possible, *before* the end of the war.

Most of our allies readily endorsed this objective and cooperated in achieving it. You will recall that the charter conference at San Francisco convened before the end of the war against Hitler and that the United States Senate consented to ratification of the charter in July 1945, before the end of the war in the Pacific. The vote in the Senate was 89 to 2, reflecting a national consensus bordering on unanimity. The significance of that solemn action was especially appreciated by those of us who were in uniform.

The commitment of the United States to the United Nations was wholehearted. We threw our best efforts and some of our best men into getting it organized and moving. We set about binding the wounds of war. We demobilized our armed forces and drastically reduced our military budget. We proposed—not only proposed but worked hard to obtain agreement—that atomic energy should be put under control of an agency of the United Nations, that it should be devoted solely to peaceful purposes, that nuclear weapons should be abolished and forever forbidden.

What happened? Stalin refused to cooperate. Even before the guns were silent, he set in motion a program of imperialistic expansion, in violation of his pledges to the Western Allies and in contravention of the principles of the United Nations.

You will recall that the United Nations was designed on the assumption that the great powers in the alliance destined to be victors in the Second World War would remain united to maintain the future peace of the world. The United Nations would be the instrument through which these powers, in cooperation with others, of course, would give effect to their mutual determination to keep the peace against any threats that might arise from some future Mussolini or Hitler. World peace was to be enforced by international forces carrying the flag of the United Nations but called into action and directed by agreement among the major powers. Action without big-power agreement was not ruled out by the charter, but such agreement was assumed to be the prior condition of an effective peace organization. Indeed, it was stated repeatedly by early supporters of the United Nations that the organization could not possibly work unless the wartime Allies joined in collective action within the United Nations to exert their combined power to make it work.

That view of the postwar world rapidly turned out to be an illusory hope. One might well have expected— as many good people did—that when the conceptual basis for the United Nations fell to the ground, the organization would fall down beside it.

But all great institutions are flexible. The United Nations adjusted gradually to the political and power realities of the quite different world that came into being. In the absence of major-power agreement in the Security Council, it drew on the charter's authority to balance that weakness with a greater reliance upon the General Assembly.

By adapting to political reality the United Nations lived and grew in effectiveness, in prestige, and in relevance. It could not act in some of the ways the founding fathers intended it to act, but it went on to do many things that the founding fathers never envisaged as being necessary. The most dramatic reversal of its intended role is seen in the fact that, while the United Nations could not bring the great powers together, it could on occasion keep them apart by getting between them—by becoming the "man in the middle"—as it did in differing ways in the Middle East and in the Congo.

In short, the political organs of the United Nations survived and did effective work under the shadow of a nuclear arms race of awesome proportions, despite the so-called cold war between the major powers whose unity was once presumed to be its foundation.

This was not bound to happen. It is evident that in the political environment of the second half of the twentieth century both technical and political reasons dictate the need for large-scale and diversified international organizations. But it does not necessarily follow that the United Nations was destined to work in practice—or even to survive. Indeed, its very survival may be more of an achievement than it seems at first blush. That it has steadily grown in its capacity to act is even more remarkable.

It has survived and grown in effectiveness because a great majority of the nations of the world have been determined to make it work. They have repulsed those who sought to wreck or paralyze it. They have remained determined not only to keep it alive but to improve and strengthen it. To this we owe in part the peace of the world.

PRESERVER AND REPAIRER OF WORLD PEACE

Indeed, it is difficult to avoid the conclusion that the existence of the General Assembly and the Security Council these past 18 years was a plain necessity for the preservation and repair of world peace. The failures would still have been failures, but without the U. N. some of the successes might not have been possible.

In the world of today any breach of the peace could lead to the destruction of civilization. In the thermonuclear age any instrumentality with a potential for deterring war can hardly be described as less than indispensable to mankind. In 18 brief years the United Nations has helped to deter or to terminate warfare in Iran and Greece, in Kashmir and Korea, in the Congo and the Caribbean, and twice in the Middle East and twice in the Western Pacific. It is not fanciful to speculate that any or all of us may owe our lives to the fact that these dangers were contained, with the active and persistent help of the processes of the United Nations.

With half a dozen international disputes chronically or repeatedly at the flash point, with forces of change bordering on violence loose in the world, our very instinct to survival informs us that we must keep building the peacekeeping machinery of the United Nations—and keep it lubricated with funds and logistical support.

And if we are to entertain rational hopes for general disarmament, we know that the U. N. must develop a reliable system for reconciling international conflict without resort to force. For peace in the world community—like peace in smaller communities—means not an end of conflict but an accepted system of dealing with conflict and with change through nonviolent means.

" SWITCHBOARD FOR BILATERAL DIPLOMACY "

Traditional bilateral diplomacy—of the quiet kind—has a heavier task today than at any time in history. But with the annual agenda of urgent international business growing apace, with the birth of more than half a hundred new nations in less than two decades, an institution that can serve as an annual diplomatic conference becomes almost a necessity. As a general manager of our own nation's diplomatic establishment, I cannot imagine how we could conduct or coordinate our foreign affairs if we were limited to dealing directly through bilateral channels with the 114 nations with which we have diplomatic relations tonight.

At the last General Assembly representatives of 111 countries met for more than 3 months to discuss, negotiate, and debate. Two more countries became U. N. members, to make it 113.* When the tumult and the shouting had died, the General Assembly had adopted, curiously enough, 113 resolutions. This is what we have come to call parliamentary diplomacy.

But outside the formal agenda the General Assembly also has become the world's greatest switchboard for bilateral diplomacy. For many of the young and small nations, lacking a fully developed diplomatic service, the United Nations is the main, sometimes the only, general mechanism available for the conduct of their diplomacy.

Without formal decision the opening of each new Assembly has turned into

---

* At present the United Nations has more than 120 members.

something like an informal conference of the foreign ministers of the world community. In New York last fall, in a period of 11 days, I conferred with the foreign ministers or heads of government of 54 nations.

I believe that too many items are placed on the agenda of the General Assembly. Too many issues are debated and not enough are negotiated. I feel strongly that members should take more seriously article 33 of the charter which pledges them to seek solutions to their disputes "first of all...by negotiation, enquiry, mediation, conciliation, arbitration, judicial settlement, resort to regional agencies or arrangements, or other peaceful means of their own choice" before bringing disputes to the U. N. at all.

But the point here is that it is hard to imagine the conduct of diplomacy throughout the year without a meeting of the General Assembly to deal in one forum and, in a more or less systematic manner, with subjects which demand widespread diplomatic attention among the members of the world community.

The need for an annual diplomatic conference, the need for a peacekeeping deterrent to wars large and small, and the need for an international monitor of peaceful change are plain enough. They seem to me to warrant the conclusion that the political organs as well as the technical organs of the United Nations have been very useful to the world at large for the past decade and a half. Common sense informs us that they can be even more useful in the years ahead.

RECOGNIZING THE PEACEKEEPING CAPACITY OF U. N.

I suspect that the near future will witness another period of adjustment for the United Nations. Some adjustments are, indeed, required—because the political environment is changing and so is the structure of the U. N. itself.

For one thing the cobweb syndrome, the illusion that one nation or bloc of nations could, by coercion, weave the world into a single pattern directed from a single center of power, is fading into limbo. That other illusion, the bipolar theory, of a world divided permanently between two overwhelming centers of power with most other nations clustered about them, is fading too. The reality of a world of great diversity with many centers of power and influence is coming into better focus.

Meanwhile, a first brake has been placed on the nuclear arms race, and the major powers are searching for other agreements in areas of common interest. One is entitled to hope that the major power conflicts which so often have characterized U. N. proceedings in the past will yield more and more to great-power cooperation; indeed, there was some evidence to sustain such a hope in the actions of the 18th General Assembly.

As long as a member possessing great power was intent on promoting conflict and upheaval—the better to coerce the world into its own image—that member might well regard the United Nations as a threat to its own ambitions. But suppose it is agreed that all members, despite their deep differences, share a common interest in survival and therefore a common interest in preventing resort to force anywhere in the world. Then the peacekeeping capacity of the United Nations can be seen realistically for what it is: an indispensable service potentially in the national interest of all members—in the common interest of even rival states.

If this reality is grasped by the responsible leaders of all the large powers, then the peacekeeping capacity of the United Nations will find some degree of support from all sides, not as a rival system of order but as contributor to, and sometimes guarantor of, the common interest in survival.

It would be a great service to peace if there could develop common recognition of a common interest in the peacekeeping capacity of the United Nations. That recognition is far from common now. My belief that it will dawn is based on the fact that it would serve the national interests of all nations, large and small, and because sooner or later nations can be expected to act in line with their national interests.

Peace will not be achieved by repeating worn-out propaganda themes or resetting rusty old traps. But if our Soviet friends are prepared to act on what Chairman Khrushchev says in part of his New Year's message—that war over territorial questions is unacceptable, that nations should not be the targets of direct or indirect aggression, that we should use the United Nations and every other means of peaceful settlement—then let us together build up the peacekeeping machinery of the United Nations to prevent even small wars in our flammable world.

For small wars could too easily, too quickly, lead to nuclear war, and nuclear war can too easily, too quickly, prove fatal to friend and foe alike.

PROBLEMS AFFECTED BY GROWTH

Meanwhile the internal structure of the United Nations has been changing radically over the past several years. The United Nations began life with 51 members. When its headquarters building was designed United Nations officials believed they were foresighted in planning for an eventual membership of 75. This year major alterations will be undertaken to make room for the present 113 members and more. It is a fair guess that membership of the U. N. will level off during the next decade at 125 to 130 members.

This more than doubling of the U. N.'s membership is proud testament to the tidal sweep through the old colonial areas of the doctrine of self-determination of peoples. It is a triumph of largely peaceful change. It is a tribute to those advanced countries which have helped bring dependent areas to self-government and independence and made possible their free choice of their own destiny. It is a striking and welcome result of the greatest wave of national liberation in all time. It also has important implications for all U. N. members—the new members and the older members too—and for the U. N. itself.

The most prosaic—but nonetheless important—implication is for methods of work in the General Assembly. With more than twice as many voices to be heard, views to be reconciled, and votes to be cast and counted, on a swelling agenda of business, there is obvious danger that the General Assembly will be swamped.

I already have suggested that the agenda may be unnecessarily bloated, that in many cases private discourse and real progress are preferable to public debate and symbolic resolution and that the U.N. might well be used more as a court of last resort and less as a forum of original jurisdiction.

But I think still more needs to be done. If the expanded Assembly is to work with reasonable proficiency, it must find ways of delegating some of its work to units less cumbersome than

committees of 113 members. The General Assembly is the only parliamentary body in the world that tries to do most of its business in committees-of-the-whole. The Assembly has, in fact, moved to establish several subcommittees, including one to consider financing peacekeeping operations, and perhaps more thought should now be given to the future role of such committees in the work of the organization.

The radical expansion of the membership raises problems for the newer and smaller nations. They rightly feel that they are underrepresented on some organs—notably the Security Council and the Economic and Social Council—whose membership was based on the U.N.'s original size and composition.

The growth of membership also raises problems for the middle-range powers, who were early members and have reason to feel that they are next in line for a larger voice.

And it raises problems—or potential problems—for the larger powers too.

The rapid and radical expansion of the General Assembly may require some adaptation of procedures if the U.N. is to remain relevant to the real world and therefore effective in that world.

Theoretically, a two-thirds majority of the General Assembly could now be formed by nations with only 10 percent of the world's population, or who contribute, altogether, 5 percent of the assessed budget. In practice, of course, this does not happen, and I do not share the dread expressed by some that the General Assembly will be taken over by its "swirling majorities."

But even the theoretical possibility that a two-thirds majority, made up primarily of smaller states, could recommend a course of action for which other nations would bear the primary responsibility and burden is one that requires thoughtful attention.

There are two extreme views of how national influence should be expressed in the work of the United Nations. At one extreme is the contention that no action at all should be taken by the United Nations without the unanimous approval of the permanent members of the Security Council. This is a prescription for chronic paralysis. The United Nations was never intended to be kept in such a box. The rights and duties of the General Assembly are inherent in the charter. The United Nations has been able to develop its capacity to act precisely because those rights were not blocked by the requirement of big-power unanimity.

At the other extreme are those few who feel that nothing should matter except the number of votes that can be mustered—that what a majority wants done must be done regardless of what states make up the majority. This notion flies in the face of common sense. The plain fact of the matter is that the United Nations simply cannot take significant action without the support of the members who supply it with resources and have the capacity to act.

Some have suggested that all General Assembly votes should be weighed to reflect population, or wealth, or level of contributions, or some combination of these or other factors. I do not believe that so far-reaching an answer would be realistic or practical. The equal vote in the General Assembly for each member—however unequal in size, wealth, experience, technology, or other criterion—is rooted in the idea of "sovereign equality." And that idea is not one which any nation, large or small, is eager to abandon.

I do not pretend to have the final answer, nor is it timely or appropriate for any member to formulate the answer without wide and careful consultations with others in the world community. However, extended discussions lie ahead on such questions as expanding the councils, scales of payment for peacekeeping, and procedures for authorizing peacekeeping operations.

I shall not discuss U.N. finances in detail tonight. But let me say that the first principle of a healthy organization is that all its members take part in its work and contribute their proper shares to its financial support. Two years ago more than half the U.N. members were behind in their dues—some because of political objections but many simply because they were not paying. I am glad to see that most members are now beginning to act on the principle of collective financial responsibility. But there remains a serious problem of large nations that have not been willing to pay for peacekeeping operations.

I would hope that the discussions which lie ahead will not only strengthen the financial underpinnings of the U.N. but, among other things, develop an acceptable way for the General Assembly to take account of capacity to act, of responsibility for the consequences, and of actual contributions to the work of the U.N. Such a way must be found if the United Nations machinery is to be relevant to the tasks that lie ahead—in peacekeeping, in nation building, and in the expansion of human rights.

All adjustment is difficult. Adaptation of the U.N. to recent changes in the environment may take time. It will require a shift away from some hardened ideas and some rigid patterns of action and reaction—perhaps on all sides. It will require—to come back to Hammarskjold's words—"perseverance and patience, a firm grip on realities, careful but imaginative planning, a clear awareness of the dangers. . . ."

To ask all this may seem to be asking a great deal. But I am inclined toward confidence because the U.N. already